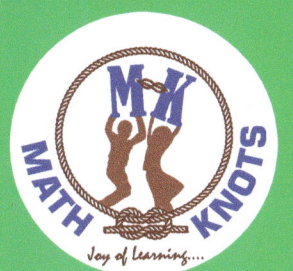

My Book

This book belongs to

Name:_____

www.math-knots.com

Cover Design by :
MATH-KNOTS LLC

First Edition :
December, 2018

Author:
Gowri Vemuri

Questions: mathknots.help@gmail.com

* CogAT® and Cognitive Abilities Test ® are registered trademarks of Riverside Publishing company

(A Houghton Mifflin Harcourt company) is neither affiliated, nor sponsors or endorses this product.

This book is dedicated to:

My Mom, who is my best critic, guide and supporter.

To what I am today, and what I am going to become tomorrow,

is all because of your blessings, unconditional affection and support.

This book is dedicated to the

strongest women of my life ,

my dearest mom

and

to all those moms in this universe.

G.V.

www.math-knots.com

www.math-knots.com

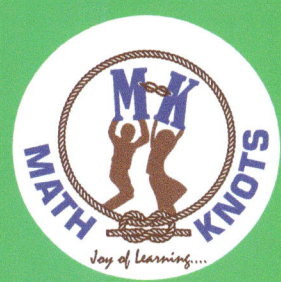

What is CoGAT ?

The Cognitive Ability Test® (CoGAT) test measures skills in young children from K-12, in various sections of Verbal, Quantitative and Non-Verbal, Thinking and Analytical. Many counties and states conduct this test to identify kids for CoGAT serves as one of the basic measures to identify the gifted and Talented pool for accelerated educational programs in many counties and states.

Cognitive skills are the skills the brain uses to think, learn, read, remember, pay attention, and solve problems. Kids develop these skills as part of their growing up. Our book helps kids, in channelizing their skills.

As Einstein said Education is not the learning of facts, but the training of minds to think. We want to bring joy of learning while channelizing the young minds thinking to reach their optimum potential. Students get familiarized with various strategies, tips and techniques thus improving their thinking abilities. All our tests are created in a multi-color, kid friendly format. For each test is based on theme for the students to have a little fun as they learn. As the students get familiarize with testing format, their vocabulary also builds up.

Our tests give an edge and simulate the testing pattern, in such a way that child feels very comfortable when they take the test in their schools.

Various counties and states apply multiple criteria for selecting kids for gifted or Advanced Academic programs and CogAT is one of the basic criteria. CogAT comprises of the following three main categories

- Verbal Section
- Quantitative Aptitude
- Non-Verbal Section.

Our Practice tests are based on the following:

Verbal Section:

Students are tested in the areas of vocabulary, comprehension of ideas, and the relation between various words. The test comprises of the below three sub sections/tests.

1. **Verbal Classification**

Three words that are alike in some way and form a group are given to the students, along with four choices to choose. One of the four choices don't belong to the group. Student has to identify the odd man and bubbles the correct option in the bubble sheet.

2. Sentence Completion

A sentence is given to the student with four picture options. Student uses the vocabulary and comprehension skills and choses the right picture that makes the best sense in the sentence. StudentBubbles the correct option in the bubble sheet.

3. Verbal Analogies

The student is given three words. The first two words go together. The third word goes with one of the answer choices. The student is asked to choose the word that goes with the third word the same way that the second word goes with the first. Student Bubbles the correct option in the bubble sheet.

Quantitative Aptitude Section:

The Quantitative Aptitude sub sections tests the student's abstract reasoning, quantitative reasoning, analytical and problem-solving skills. The test comprises of the below three sub sections/tests.

1. Quantitative Relations/Number Analogies

Figures in the first row belong to each other in a certain way. Student is expected to identify the number analogy in the first row. The figures in the second row follow the same analogy as the first row. Student analyzes and thinks through to find the right choice from the given four options. Student Bubbles the correct option in the bubble sheet.

2. Number Series

Series of beads are given on various strings /rods. Student identifies the number series and figures out the beads on missing rod/string. Student Bubbles the correct option in the bubble sheet.

3. Equation Building /Number Puzzles

A number equation is given in a kid friendly format. Student solves for the number that goes in the place of the question mark. Student Bubbles the correct option in the bubble sheet.

Non-Verbal Section (Spatial Reasoning):

The Nonverbal Battery comprises of the most unique problems to students. The questions on these tests are based on geometric shapes and figures. The tests require visualization, thinking and analytical abilities. The test comprises of the below three sub tests.

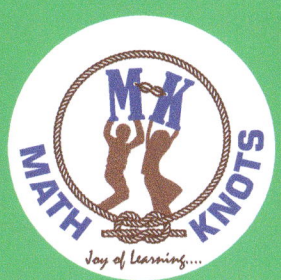

What is CoGAT ?

1. Figure Classification

The student is given three figures that are a like in some way. Four answer choices are given to choose from and one of the choices belong to the given group in a certain way. Students analyzes the figures to choose the right option and bubbles the correct option in the bubble sheet.

2. Figure Analogies/ Figure Matrices

Figures in the first row belong to each other in a certain way. Student is expected to identify the figure analogy between figures in the first row. The figures in the second row follow the same analogy as the first row. Student analyzes and thinks through to find the right choice from the given four options and bubbles the correct option in the bubble sheet.

3. Figure Analysis/Paper Folding

A Square, Rectangle or any shape figure is folded once or more as shown in the figure. Holes are punched to the folded figure and opened completely. Students are expected to think through on how the figure will look like after opening it up and bubbles the correct option in the bubble sheet.

Book Includes, detailed solutions and tips, that will help kids do well in the **CoGAT test.**

Do Visit our website www.math-knots.com for more products and also for our online subscription.

Math-Knots ------- Joy of Learning

INDEX

www.math-knots.com

INDEX

Start from the middle of right choice and fully fill the bubble completely.

Wrong

A    B ◯   C ◯   D ◯

Wrong

A ◯   B ◯   C   D ◯

Wrong

A ◯   B ◯   C   D ◯

Partial Filled Bubble is not correct.

Correct

A ◯   B ◯   C ⬤   D ◯

www.math-knots.com

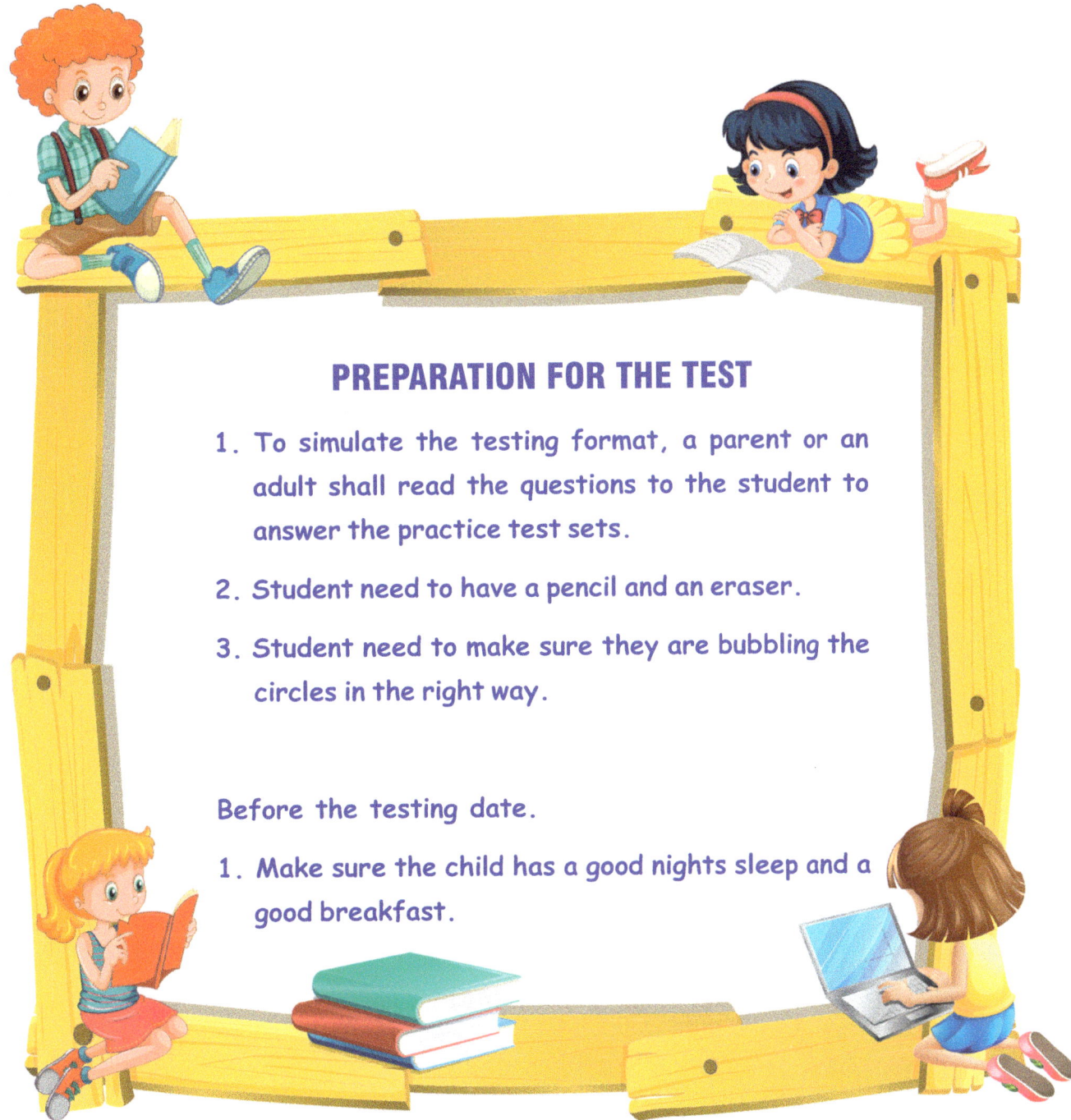

PREPARATION FOR THE TEST

1. To simulate the testing format, a parent or an adult shall read the questions to the student to answer the practice test sets.

2. Student need to have a pencil and an eraser.

3. Student need to make sure they are bubbling the circles in the right way.

Before the testing date.

1. Make sure the child has a good nights sleep and a good breakfast.

www.math-knots.com

TEST - 1

VERBAL SECTION

VERBAL CLASSIFICATION

Lets Start the Test...

www.math-knots.com

www.math-knots.com

Sample Three words are related in a certain way. Four options are given. Identify the choice that does not belong to the group?

One   **Two**   **Three**

Six   Eight   Five   Gate

A ◯   B ◯   C ◯   D ◯

Solution : D

Three words in the question belong to one group. One of the four choices doesn't belong to the same group. Identify and bubble the correct choice. In the given question all three in first row are words as well as numbers in words. Lets take a look at the answers. All choices are words but three are numbers in words and one other word gate, which is incorrect.

All the questions in verbal classification test 1 are to be answered following the below question (instruction).

Three words are related in a certain way. Four options are given. Identify the choice that <u>does not belong</u> to the group ?

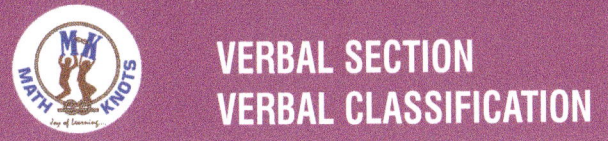
1. **Australia**   **Africa**   **Asia**

    North America   London   Europe   Antarctica

    A ○   B ○   C ○   D ○

2. **Cottage**   **Bungalow**   **Farm House**

    Palace   Manor   Villa   Portico

    A ○   B ○   C ○   D ○

3. **Ear**   **Hand**   **Leg**

    Heart   Lower Limb   Nail   Cheek

    A ○   B ○   C ○   D ○

4. **Arithmetic**   **Fractions**   **Decimals**

    Geometry   Algebra   Mathematics   Calculus

    A ○   B ○   C ○   D ○

5. **Dollar**   **Pound**   **Dinar**

    Peso   Rupee   Money   Euro

    A ○   B ○   C ○   D ○

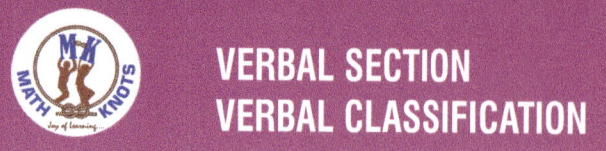

6. **Adorned**   **Ornate**   **Elaborate**

   Showy   Fancy   Beautify   Dull

   A◯   B◯   C◯   D◯

7. **Honey**   **Amber**   **Gold**

   Mustard   Teal   Banana   Lemon

   A◯   B◯   C◯   D◯

8. **Boar**   **Bull**   **Dog**

   Duck   Buck   Rooster   Tiger

   A◯   B◯   C◯   D◯

9. **Prism**   **Cube**   **Cylinder**

   Cone   Sphere   Pyramid   Pentagon

   A◯   B◯   C◯   D◯

10. **Look**   **Scan**   **Glimpse**

   View   See   Wink   Gaze

   A◯   B◯   C◯   D◯

20   www.math-knots.com

11. **Friendship** **Affection** **Harmony**

Closeness   Intimacy   Fondness   Animosity

A◯   B◯   C◯   D◯

12. **Ring** **Watch** **Bangle**

Armlet   Tiara   Wristband   Charm

A◯   B◯   C◯   D◯

13. **Actress** **Hero** **Actor**

Performer   Artist   Heroine   Producer

A◯   B◯   C◯   D◯

14. **Earth** **Venus** **Moon**

Milky way   Sun   Neptune   Jupitar

A◯   B◯   C◯   D◯

15. **Apple** **Mango** **Cherry**

Orange   Potato   Plum   Grapes

A◯   B◯   C◯   D◯

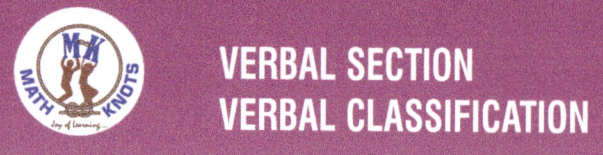

16. **Cricket**   **Flea**   **Beetle**

Scorpion   Bug   Hopper   Insect

A ◯   B ◯   C ◯   D ◯

17. **Perfect**   **Present**   **Future**

Past Future   Progressive   Interrogative   Future Simple

A ◯   B ◯   C ◯   D ◯

18. **Chlorine**   **Neon**   **Sulphur**

Nitrogen   Iodine   Radon   Lead

A ◯   B ◯   C ◯   D ◯

TEST - 1

VERBAL SECTION

SENTENCE COMPLETION

Lets Start the Test...

www.math-knots.com

Sample

Look at the question with the Tennis Ball. Maya is trying to solve the below brain teaser. "Rik has more stamps then Ryan. Ryan has more stamps than Luke. Who has more stamps?" Bubble the correct option.

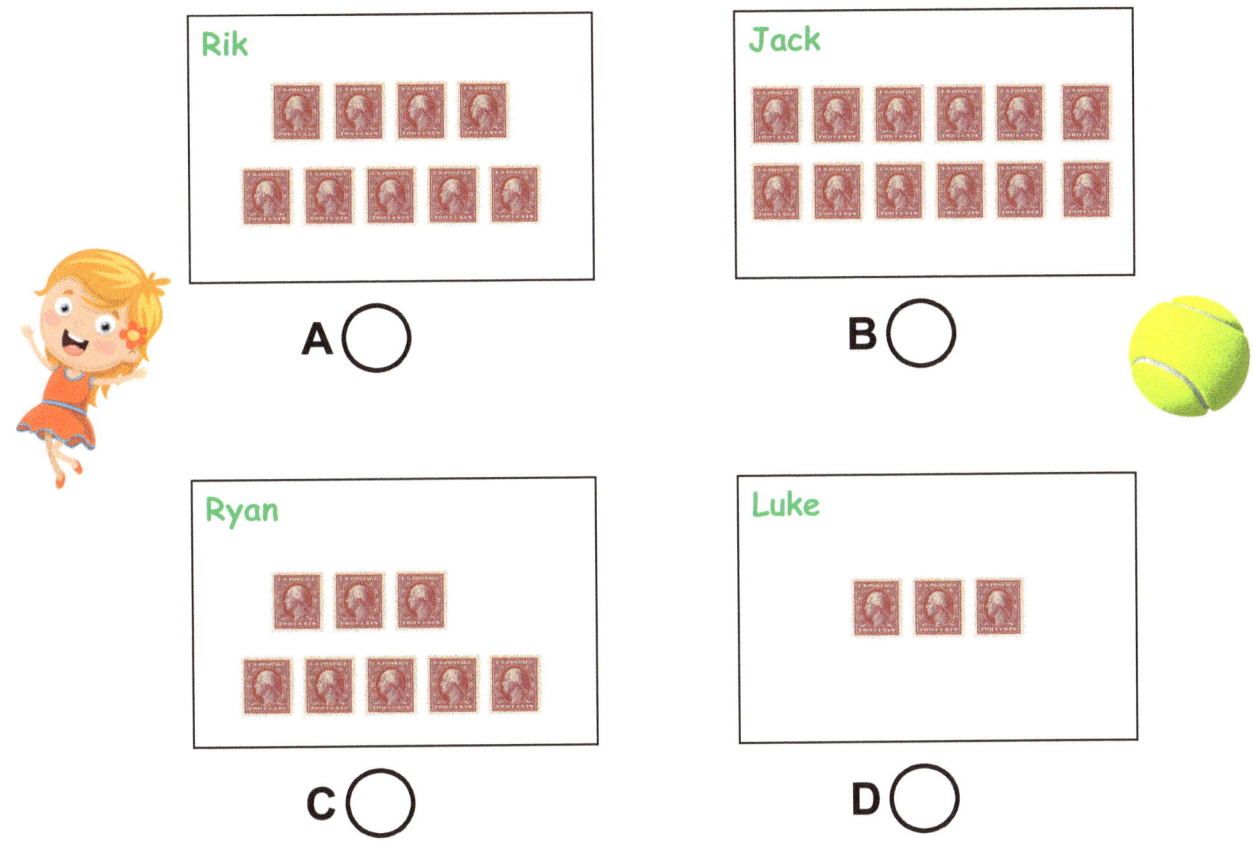

Solution : A

The Correct choice is A. The question doesn't compare with what Jack has.

Rik has the most stamps.

Rik > Ryan > Luke

www.math-knots.com

VERBAL SECTION
SENTENCE COMPLETION

Q-1 Look at the question with the Square. Help Anne to find out which of the below options do not belong to the same group. Identify the correct picture and help her to bubble the right choice.

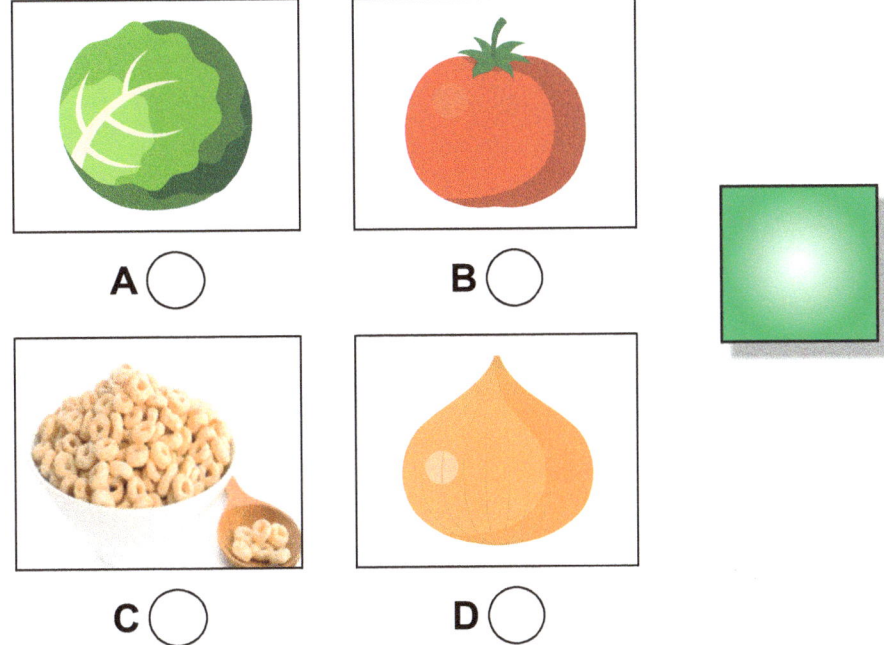

A ◯ B ◯

C ◯ D ◯

Q-2 Look at the question with the Diamond. Jack is trying to solve the below brain teaser. Can you please help him to solve? "Sam weighs less than Tom and Tom weighs less than Tim. Who weighs most?" Identify the correct solution and help him to bubble the right choice.

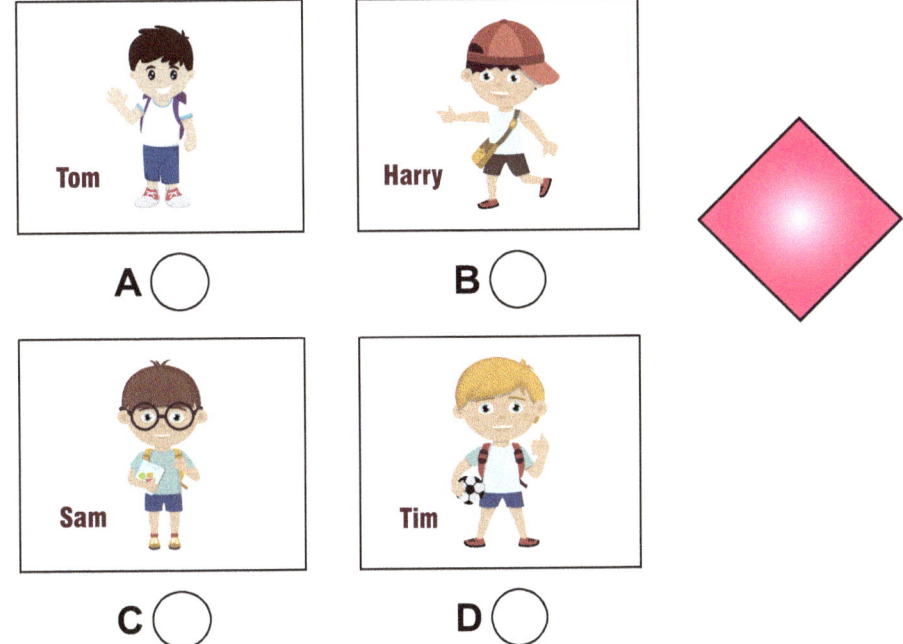

A ◯ B ◯

C ◯ D ◯

27

Q-3 Look at the question with the Pentagon. Help Lola to find out which of the below can fly. Identify the correct picture and help her to bubble the right choice.

A ◯   B ◯

C ◯   D ◯

Q-4 Look at the question with the Triangle. Kyla's daughter Beth comes home with fever from school. Which of the below do you think Kyla needs to find out the temperature. Identify the correct picture and help her to bubble the right choice.

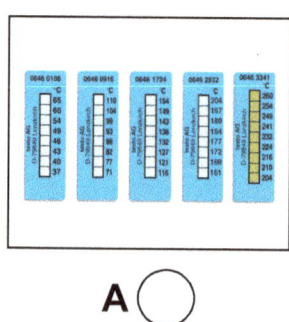 

A ◯   B ◯

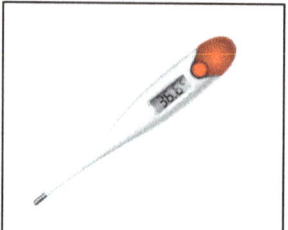 

C ◯   D ◯

www.math-knots.com

Q-5 Look at the question with the Septagon. Ricky's friend Sam's favorite Sport uses a bat which has a mesh. Help Ricky to find his friends favorite sport. Identify the correct picture and help him to bubble the right choice.

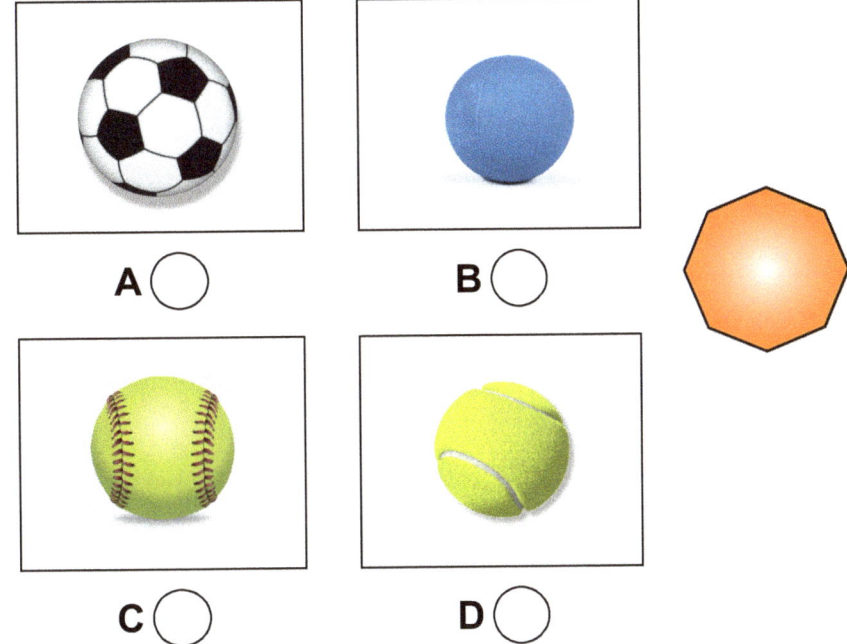

Q-6 Look at the question with the Hexagon Mia is standing facing west and then she makes a right turn and then again, a right turn. Which direction is Mia facing now? Identify the correct picture and help her to bubble the right choice.

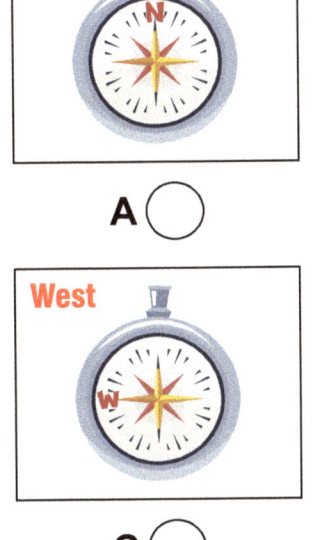

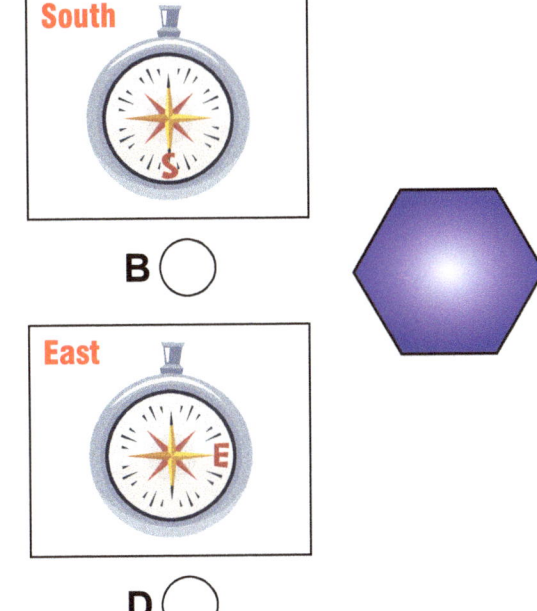

29

Q-7 Look at the question with the Octagon. Mary is working on her science project. Topic give to the class is Fruits and Vegetables. She wanted to know which vegetables grow under the ground. Which of the below vegetable grows under the ground? Identify the correct picture and help her to bubble the right choice.

Q-8 Look at the question with the Trapezoid. Raksha bakes a lot of cookies for her school bake sale. She wants to sell them by pounds. Which of the below does she need to take with her for the bake sale. Identify the correct picture and help her to bubble the right choice.

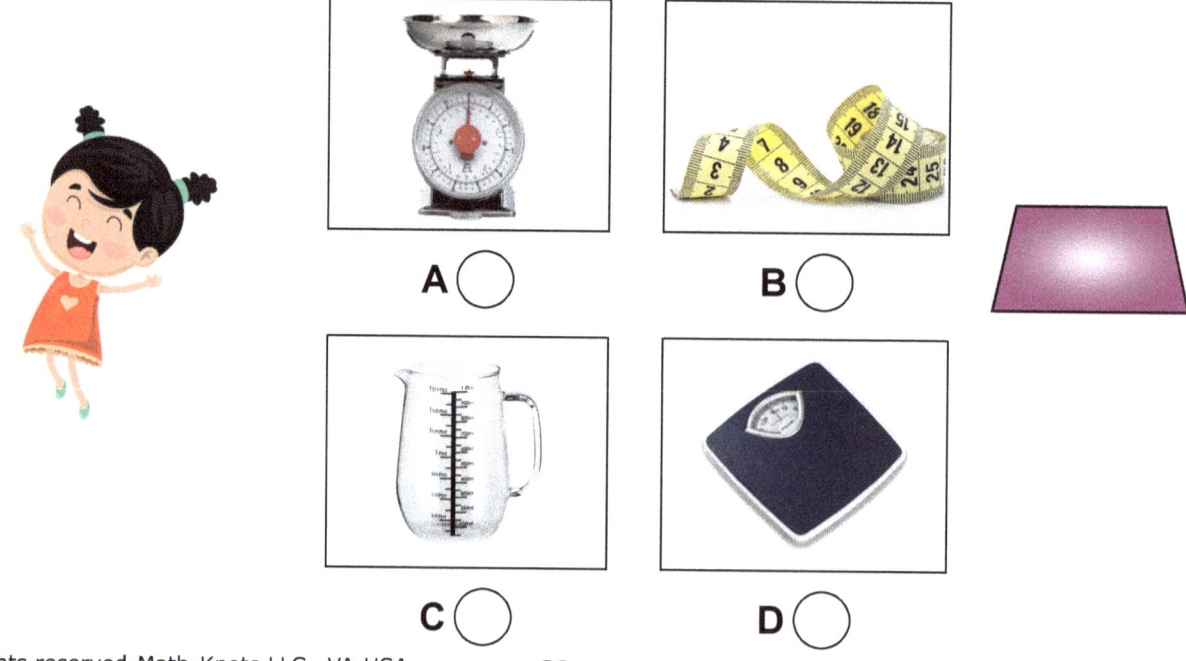

www.math-knots.com

Q-9

Look at the question with the Parallelogram. Lisa goes to the store to buy her school supplies. She is looking for something with which she can't write or draw with it. Which of the below options is she looking to buy? Identify the correct picture and help her to bubble the right choice.

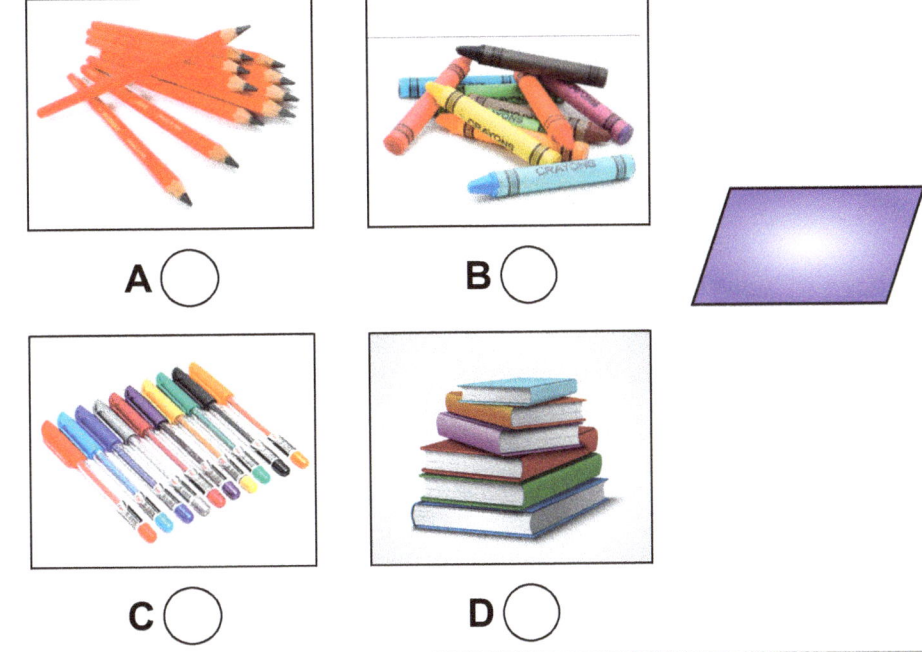

A ◯   B ◯

C ◯   D ◯

Q-10

Look at the question with the Oval. Ben went to the Zoo with his class today. He is looking to connect the color of Zebra to the given four choices as below. Identify the correct picture that resembles the same. Help him to bubble the right choice.

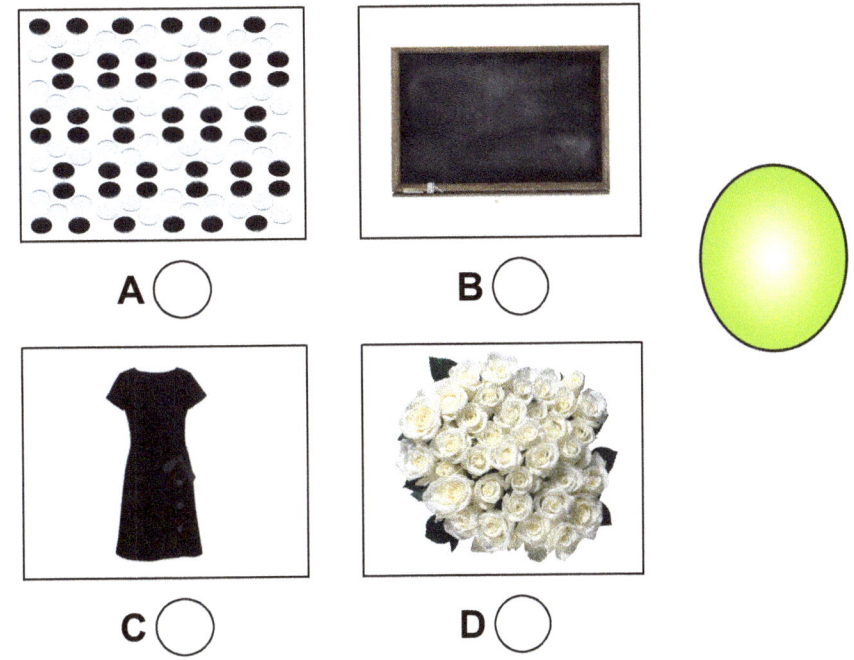

A ◯   B ◯

C ◯   D ◯

www.math-knots.com

Q-11 Look at the question with the Heart. Ryan is learning about various sounds in his science class. Which of the following rings? Help him to identify the correct picture and to bubble the right choice.

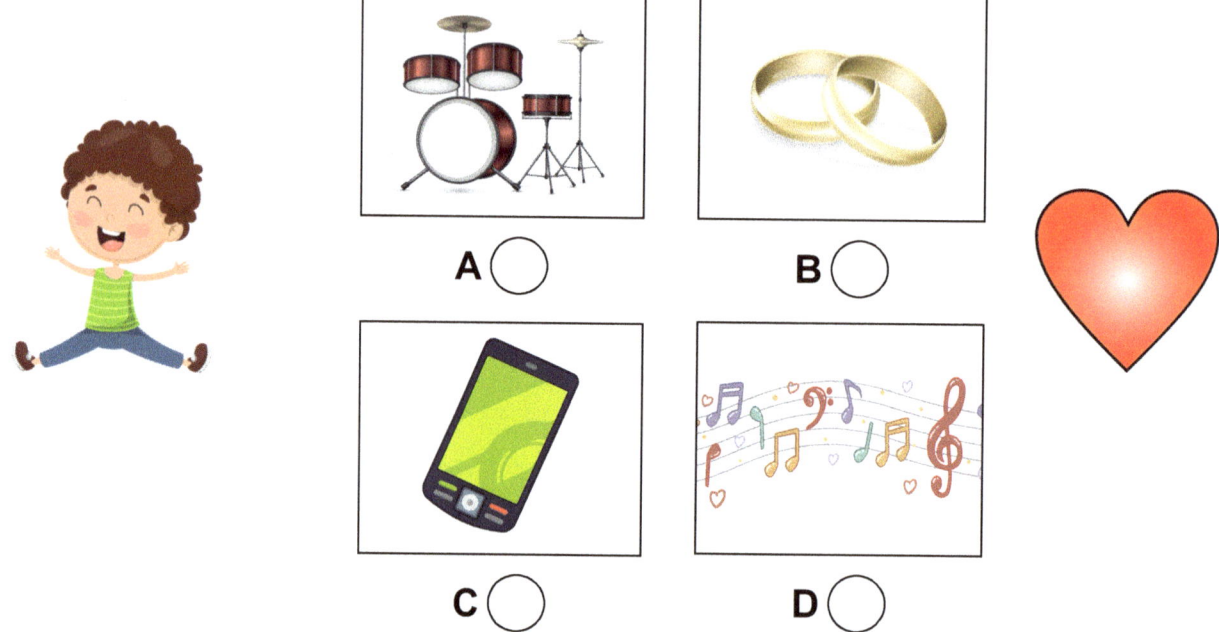

A ◯ B ◯

C ◯ D ◯

Q-12 Look at the question with the Snow Flake. David is trying to solve the below brain teaser. "Octagon has more sides than Pentagon. Pentagon has more sides than Square. Which figure has most sides? " Identify the correct solution and help him to bubble the right choice.

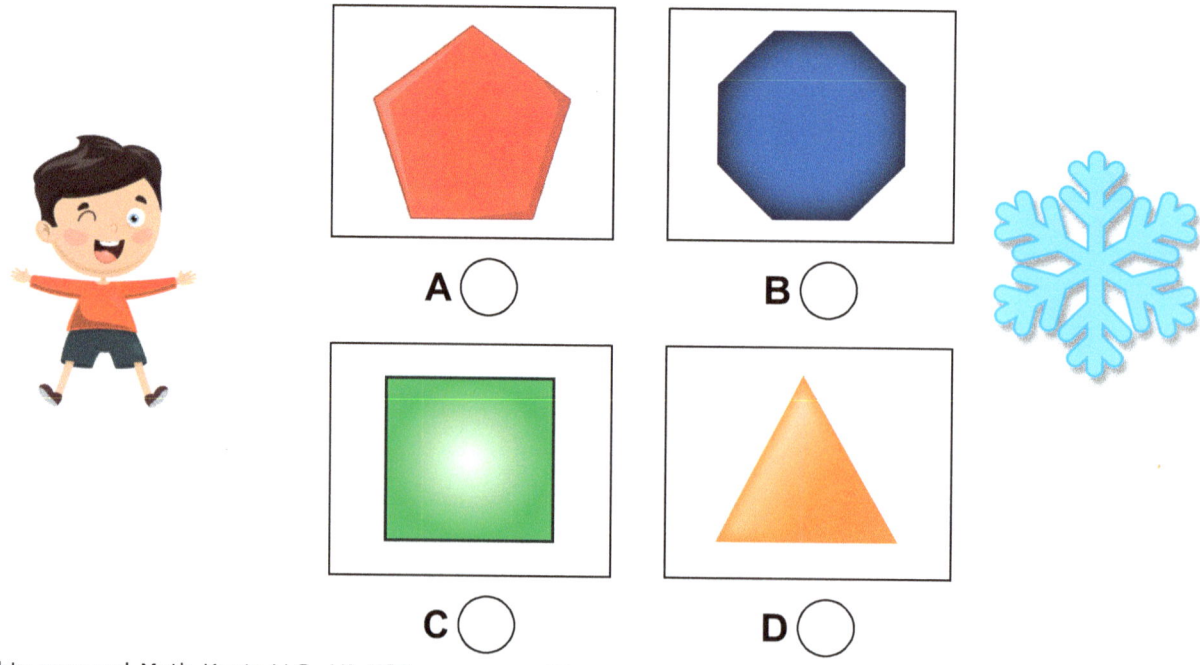

A ◯ B ◯

C ◯ D ◯

www.math-knots.com

Q-13 Look at the question with the Plus Sign. Oded is learning about electricity in his science class. Which of the following choices does not need electricity to operate? Help him to identify the correct picture and to bubble the right choice.

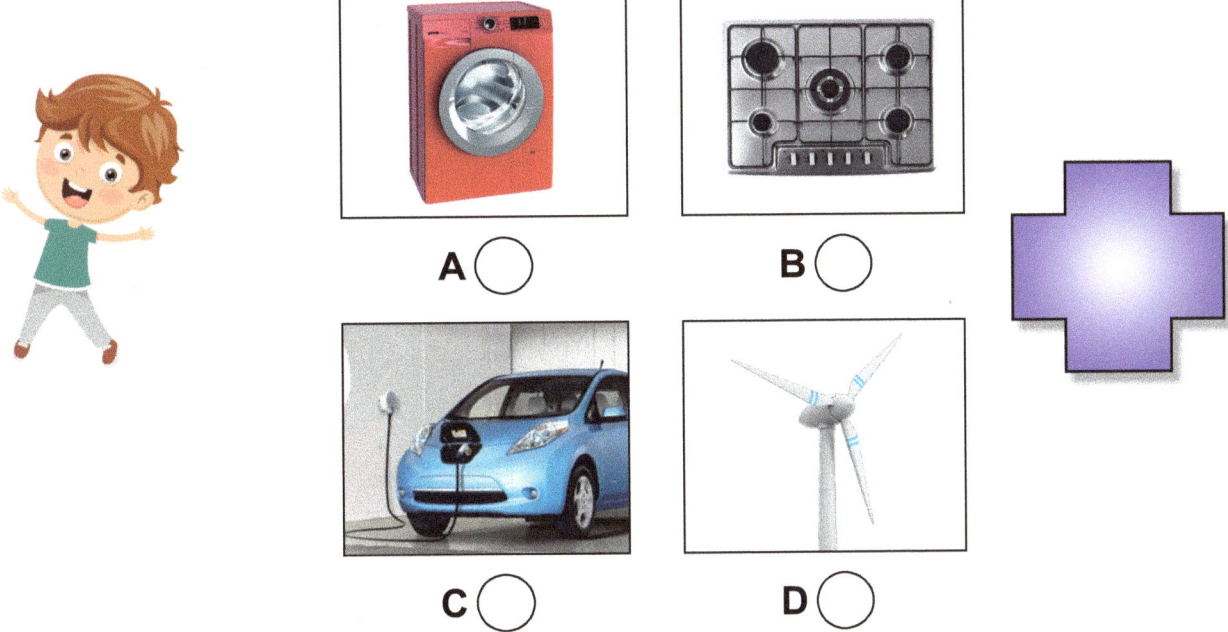

Q-14 Look at the question with the Smiley. Urmi wakes up from sleep and feels her mouth is smelling badly. So, what do you think she needs now? Help her to identify the correct picture and to bubble the right choice.

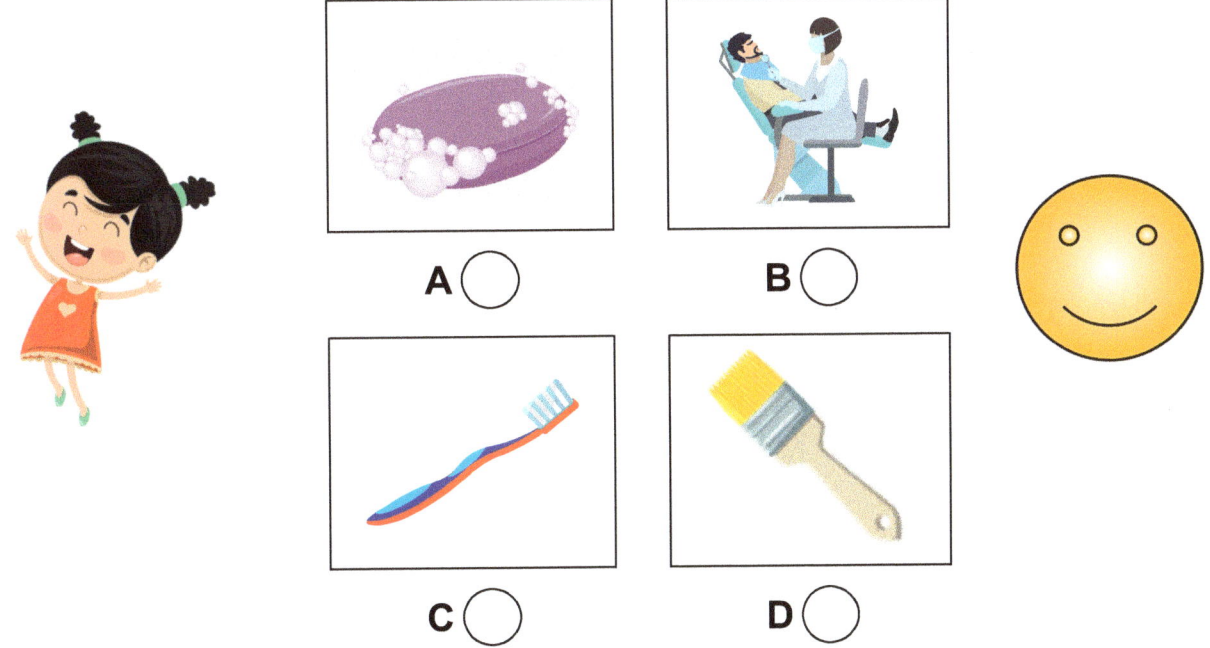

www.math-knots.com

Q-15 Look at the question with the Moon. Ken wants to build a writing table for his 5-year-old daughter. He goes to the store to buy the necessary tools. what do you think he shall buy from the below options? Help him to identify the correct picture and to bubble the right choice.

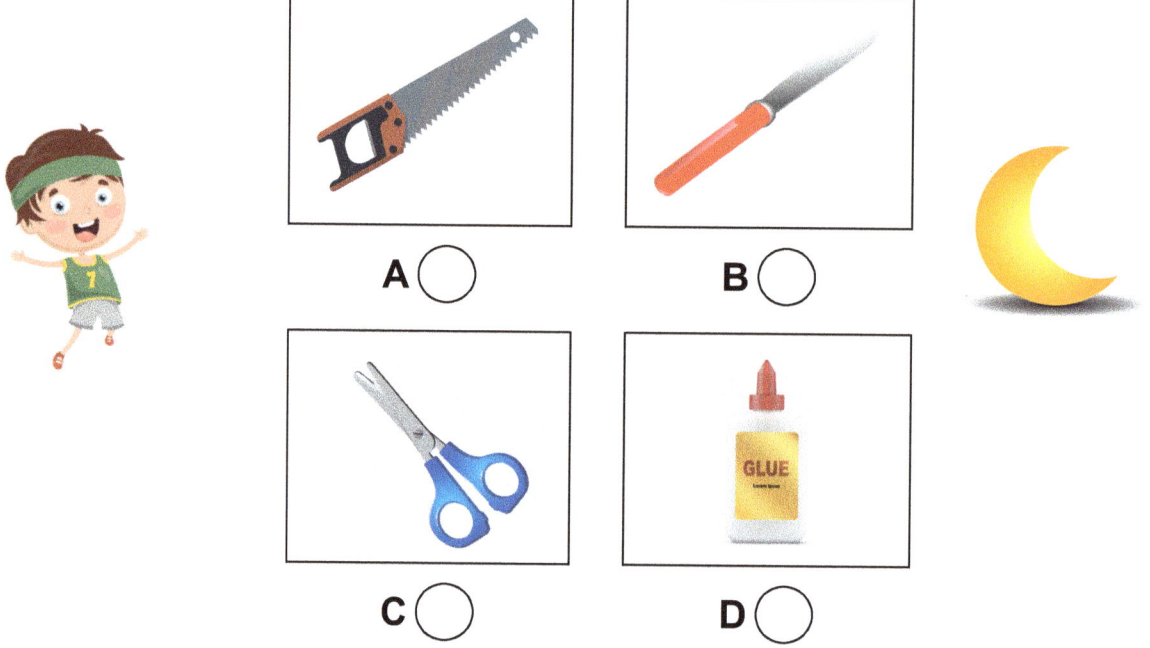

A ◯   B ◯

C ◯   D ◯

Q-16 Look at the question with the Stars. Jia loves to play her music by modulating air flow. Help her to choose the right instrument from the below. Help her to identify the correct picture and to bubble the right choice.

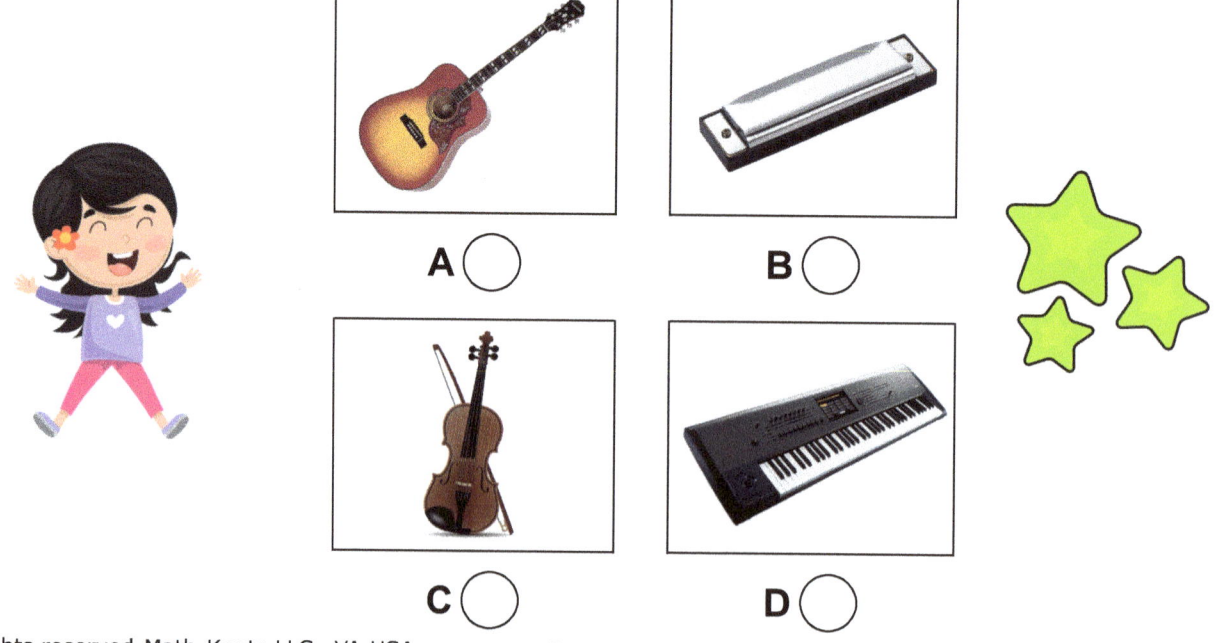

A ◯   B ◯

C ◯   D ◯

Q-17 Look at the question with the Clouds. Jane loves Berries and she uses lots of berries in her cereal every day morning. Which of the below fruits do you think Jane doesn't eat in her cereal? Help her to identify the correct picture and to bubble the right choice.

Q-18 Look at the question with the Cylinder. Lara is learning about various holidays. Help her to find which of the below does not represent St. Patricks day. Identify the correct picture and help her to bubble the right choice.

TEST - 1

VERBAL SECTION

VERBAL ANALOGIES

Lets Start the Test...

37   www.math-knots.com

www.math-knots.com

Sample The first two words are related in a certain way as the next two words. Identify the missing word.

Clouds : White :: Sky : ?

Bold   Blue   Silver   Yellow

A ◯   B ◯   C ◯   D ◯

Solution : B

First analogy is color of the clouds which is white. Color of sky is blue.

Right choice is B.

Student needs to think through how the first two are related and then relate it to next analogy in the same way. Bubble the correct option.

All the questions in verbal analogies test 1 are to be answered following the below question (instruction).

The first two words are related in a certain way as the next two words. <u>Identify the missing word.</u>

1.   Sunglasses : Summer :: Gloves :   ?

Winter   Fall   Autumn   Spring

A◯   B◯   C◯   D◯

2.   Donkey : Stable :: Goat :   ?

Kennel   Burrow   Pen   Coop

A◯   B◯   C◯   D◯

3.   10 : Number :: A :   ?

Consonenent   Writing   Language   Alphabet

A◯   B◯   C◯   D◯

4.   Pentagon : 5 :: Quadrilateral :   ?

7   4   5   3

A◯   B◯   C◯   D◯

5.   Gold : Yellow :: Tree :   ?

Green   Orange   Red   White

A◯   B◯   C◯   D◯

www.math-knots.com

6.   Thermometer : Temperature :: Rain Gauge :   ?

Humidity   Wind   Precipitation   Sky

A◯   B◯   C◯   D◯

7.   Wings : Birds :: Fins : ?

Birds   Sparrow   Ladybug   Fish

A◯   B◯   C◯   D◯

8.   Thankgiving : November :: Memorial Day :   ?

May   December   April   February

A◯   B◯   C◯   D◯

9.   Up : Down :: Right :   ?

Corner   Below   Above   Left

A◯   B◯   C◯   D◯

10.   Cow : Calf :: Cat : ?

Spider ling   Kitten   Foal   Ducklet

A◯   B◯   C◯   D◯

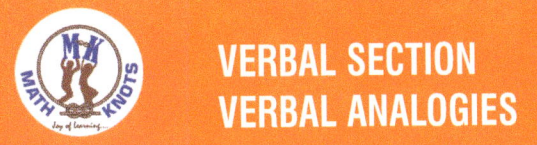
11. **Insects : 6 legs :: Octopus :   ?**

8 legs   5 legs   10 legs   12 legs

A ◯   B ◯   C ◯   D ◯

12. **Medicines : Pharmacy :: Food :   ?**

Book Store   School   Restaurant   Office

A ◯   B ◯   C ◯   D ◯

13. **Ship : Water :: Train :   ?**

Road   Sky   Sub Way   Track

A ◯   B ◯   C ◯   D ◯

14. **Telescope : Magnification :: Accelerometer :   ?**

Acceleration   Voltage   Survey   Magnetic Field

A ◯   B ◯   C ◯   D ◯

15. **Christmas : Christmas Tree :: July Fourth :   ?**

Turkey   Green   Labor Day   Fire Crackers

A ◯   B ◯   C ◯   D ◯

16.   **Green : Spinach :: Orange :   ?**

Tomato   Carrot   Peppers   Banana

A◯   B◯   C◯   D◯

17.   **Zebra : Stripes ::   Lady Bug :   ?**

Dots   Solid color   Zig Zag   Lines

A◯   B◯   C◯   D◯

18.   **Hurricanes : Ocean :: Tornado :   ?**

Storm   Waves   Land   Sky

A◯   B◯   C◯   D◯

www.math-knots.com

TEST - 1

QUANTITATIVE APTITUDE
NUMBER ANALOGIES

Lets Start the Test...

www.math-knots.com

Sample

Look at the question with the Parrot. Two boxes in the first row are related in a certain way which is similar to two boxes in the second row. Ken is trying to fill the bubble under the correct option. Help him to select from options A, B, C, and D.

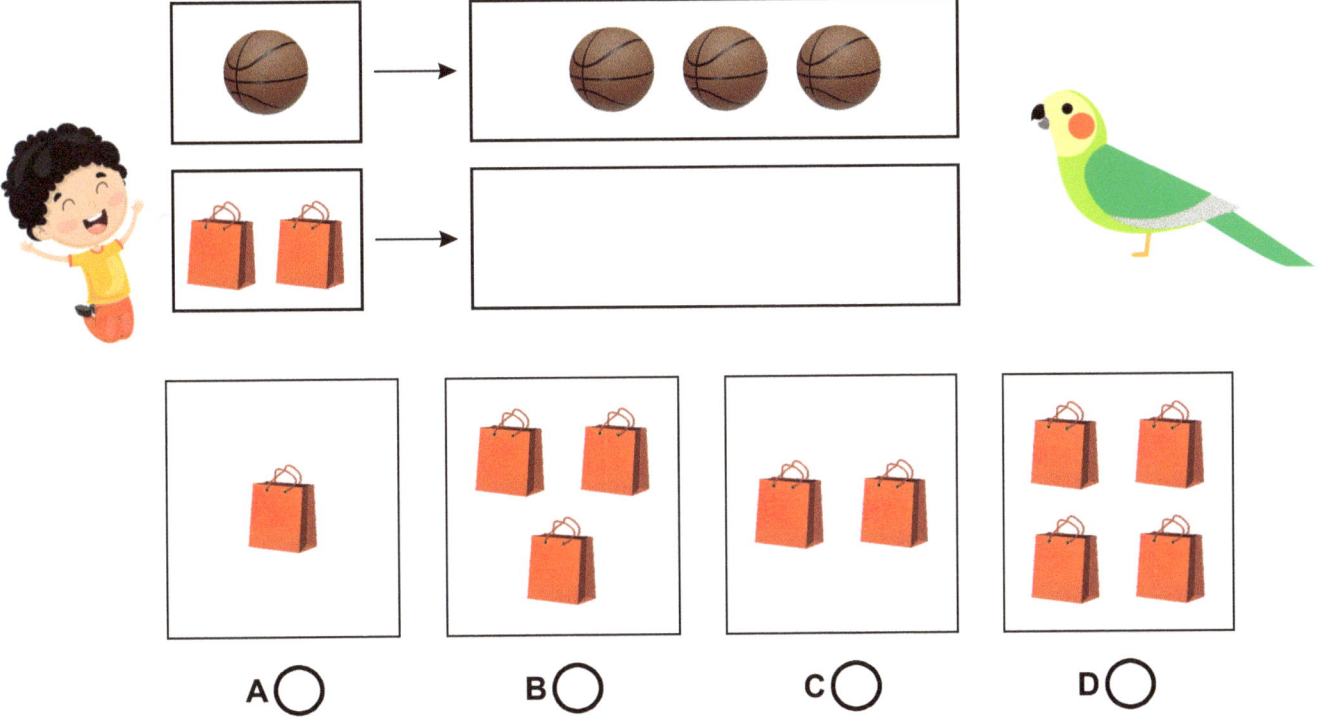

A ◯   B ◯   C ◯   D ◯

Solution : D

In first row, one ball to three balls [(1+2) adding two more]

In second row, two bags by adding two more will become four bags.

The analogies can be formed by adding or subtracting a certain number meaning increasing or decreasing by a certain quantity. Students needs to understand the right analogy and bubble the correct option.

www.math-knots.com

Q-1 Look at the question with the Game Console. Two boxes in the first row are related in a certain way which is similar to two boxes in the second row. Sam is trying to fill the bubble under the correct option. Help him to select from options A, B, C, and D.

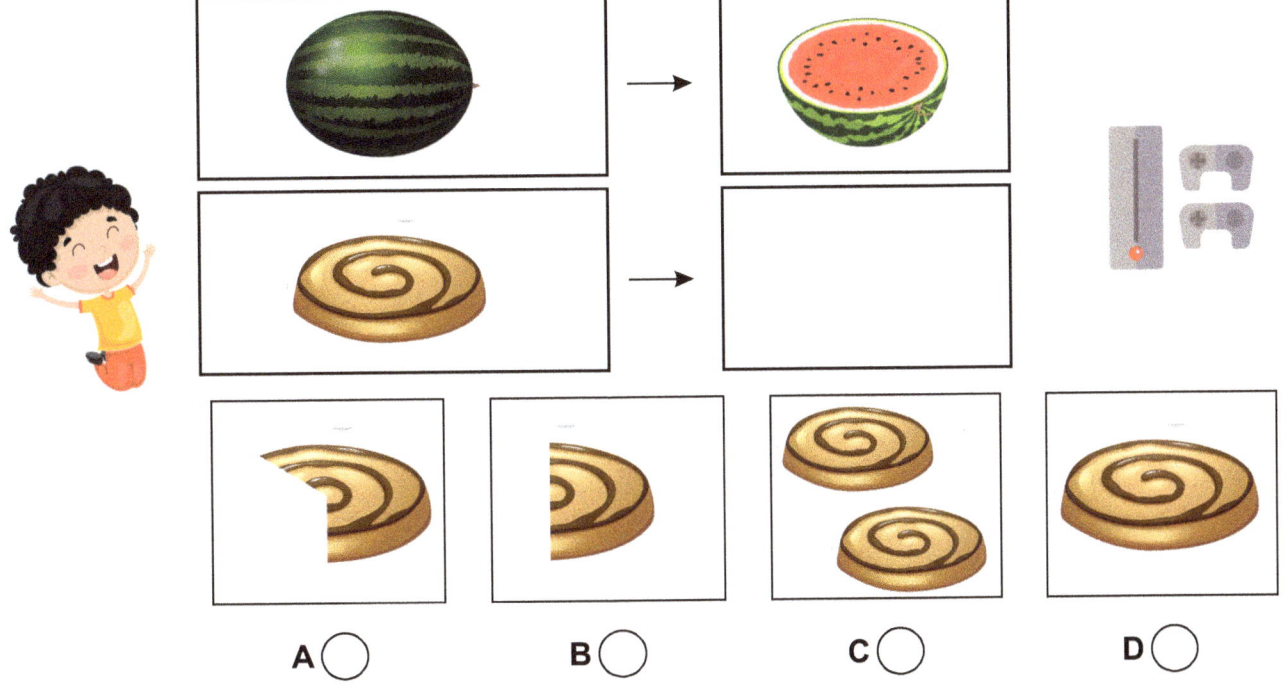

A ◯   B ◯   C ◯   D ◯

Q-2 Look at the question with the Smart Watch. Two boxes in the first row are related in a certain way which is similar to two boxes in the second row. Mary is trying to fill the bubble under the correct option. Help her to select from options A, B, C, and D.

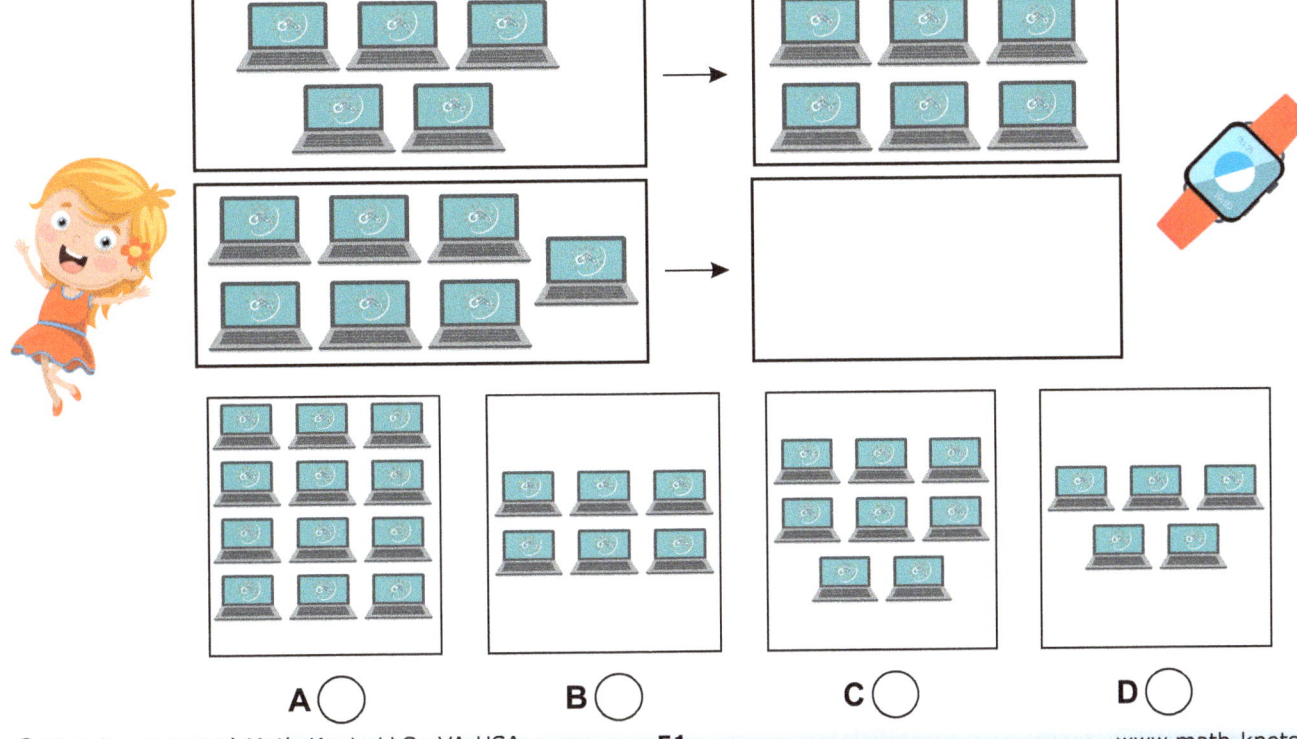

A ◯   B ◯   C ◯   D ◯

www.math-knots.com

Q-3

Look at the question with the Head Set. Two boxes in the first row are related in a certain way which is similar to two boxes in the second row. Feona is trying to fill the bubble under the correct option. Help her to select from options A, B, C, and D.

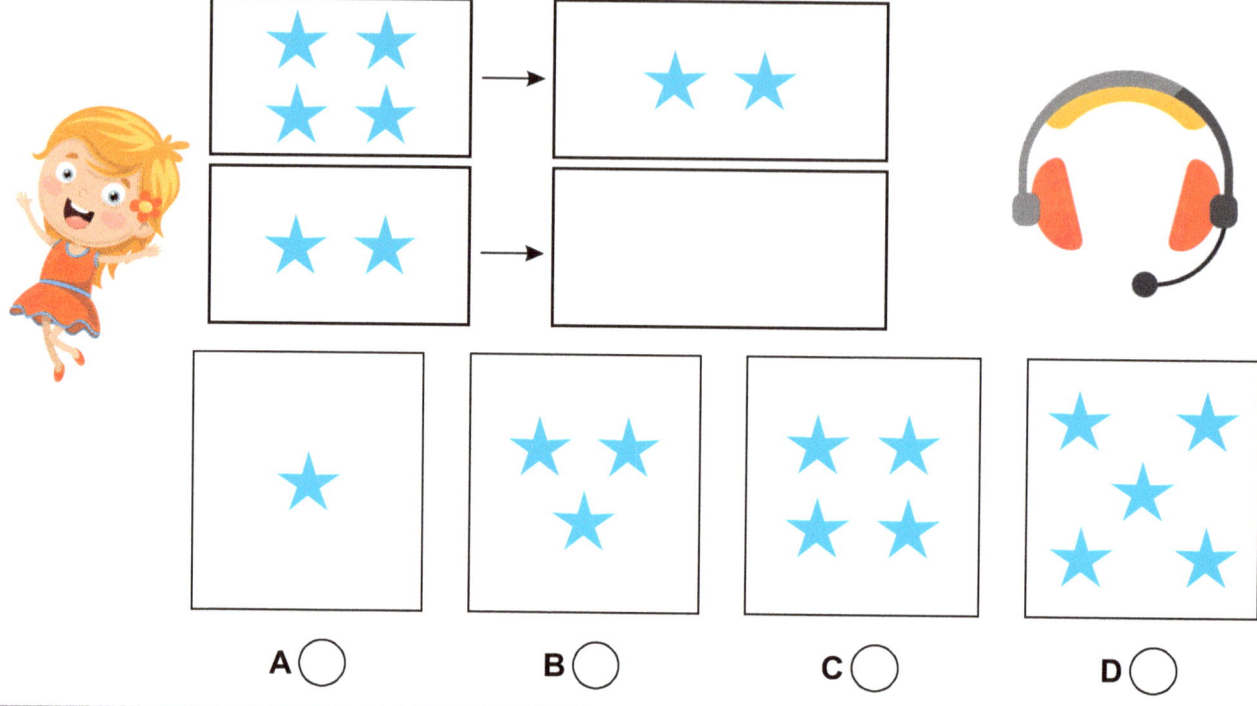

A ◯　　B ◯　　C ◯　　D ◯

Q-4

Look at the question with the UPS. Two boxes in the first row are related in a certain way which is similar to two boxes in the second row. Robert is trying to fill the bubble under the correct option. Help him to select from options A, B, C, and D.

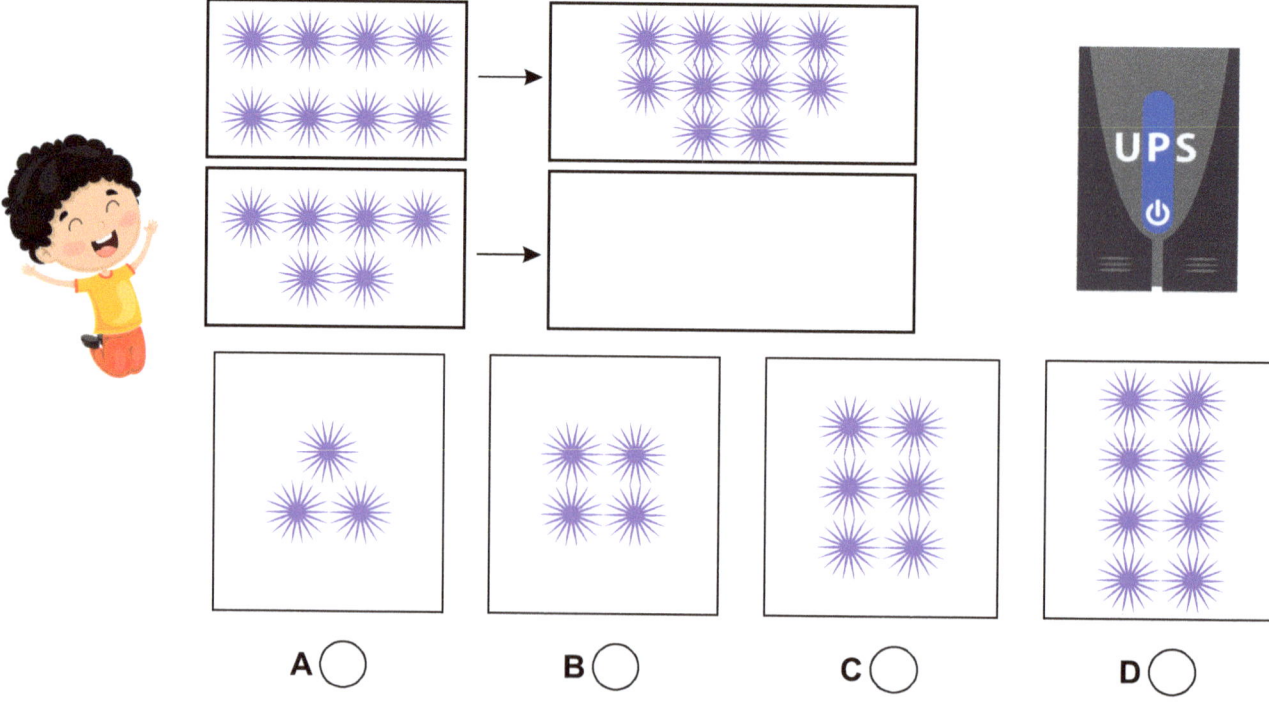

A ◯　　B ◯　　C ◯　　D ◯

www.math-knots.com

Q-5 Look at the question with the Kindle. Two boxes in the first row are related in a certain way which is similar to two boxes in the second row. David is trying to fill the bubble under the correct option. Help him to select from options A, B, C, and D.

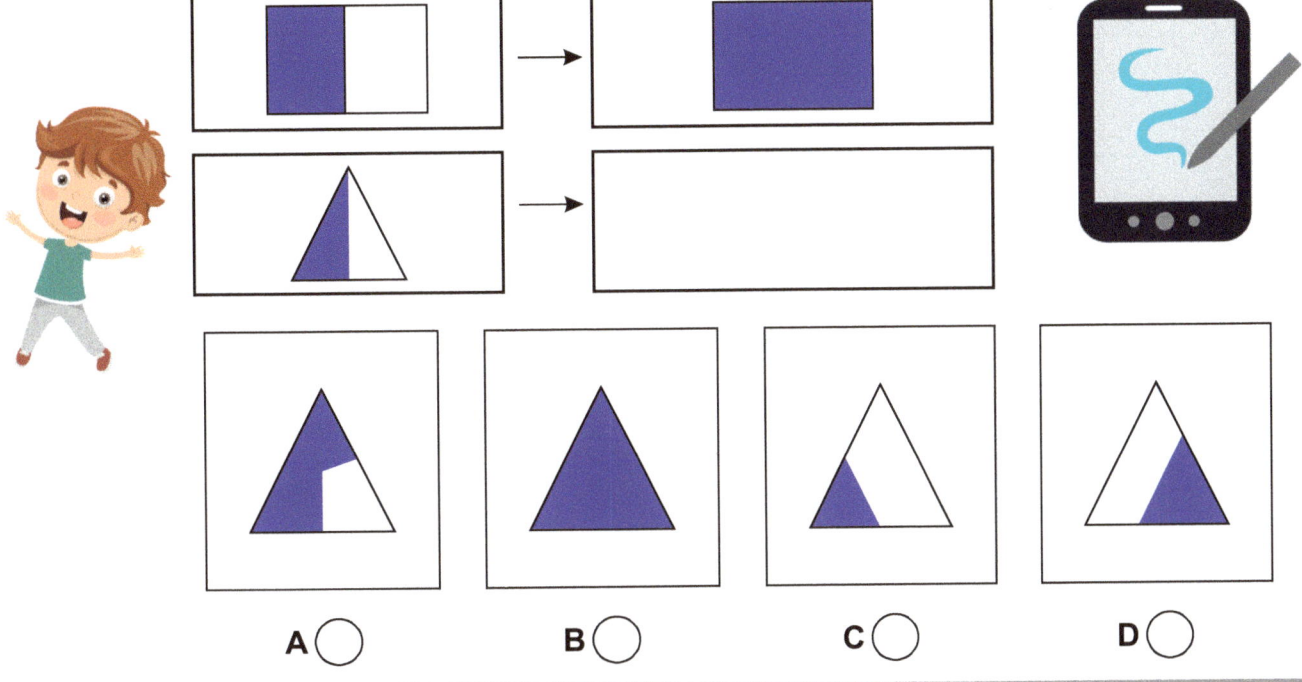

A ○   B ○   C ○   D ○

Q-6 Look at the question with the Mouse. Two boxes in the first row are related in a certain way which is similar to two boxes in the second row. Sofia is trying to fill the bubble under the correct option. Help her to select from options A, B, C, and D.

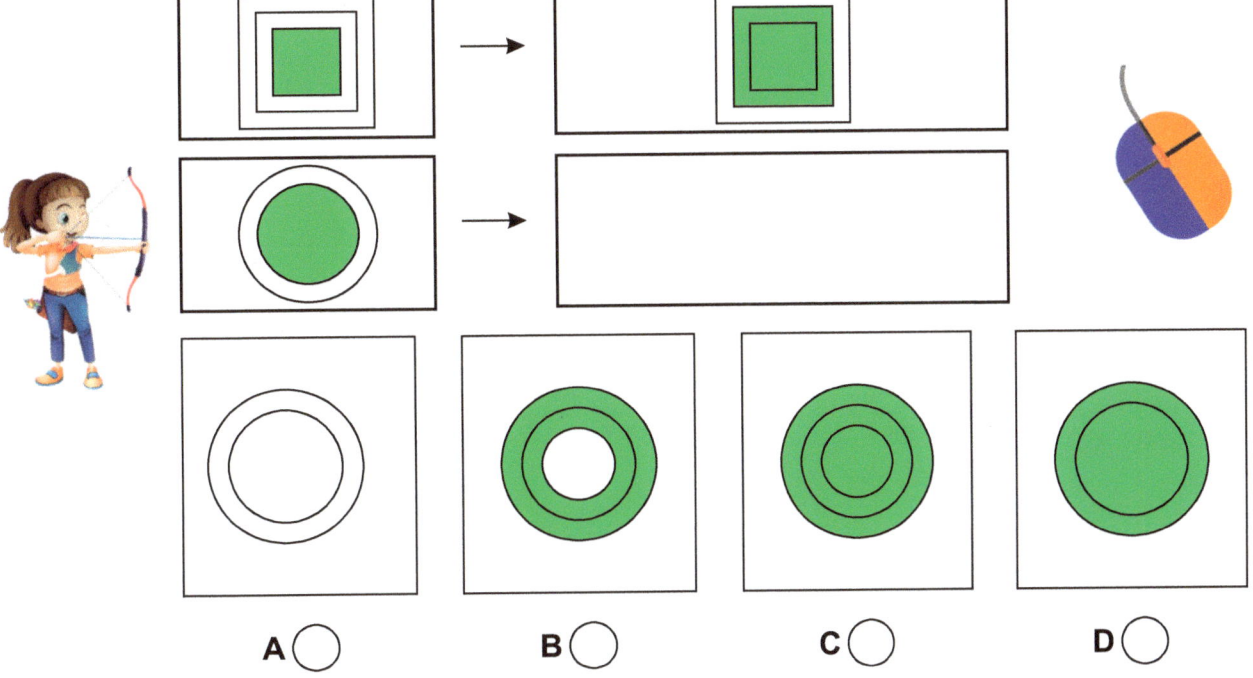

A ○   B ○   C ○   D ○

www.math-knots.com

Q-7 Look at the question with the Scanner. Two boxes in the first row are related in a certain way which is similar to two boxes in the second row. Ava is trying to fill the bubble under the correct option. Help her to select from options A, B, C, and D.

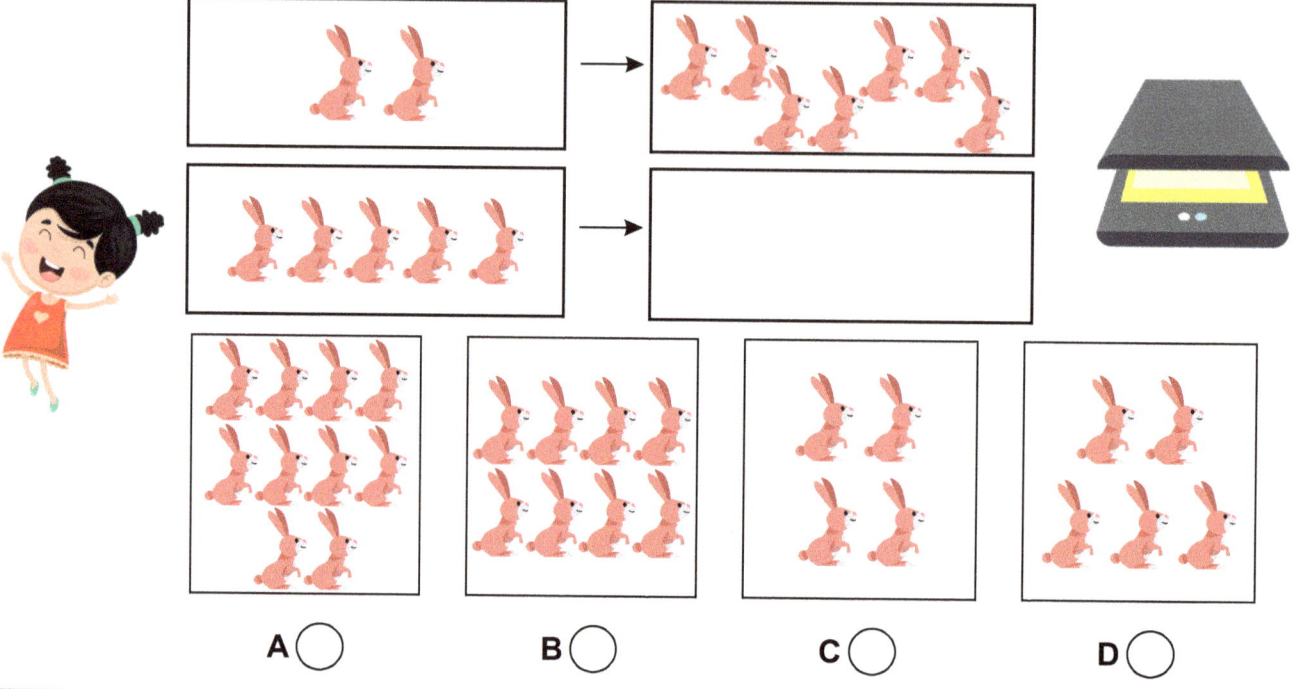

A ◯   B ◯   C ◯   D ◯

Q-8 Look at the question with the Printer. Two boxes in the first row are related in a certain way which is similar to two boxes in the second row. Johnson is trying to fill the bubble under the correct option. Help him to select from options A, B, C, and D.

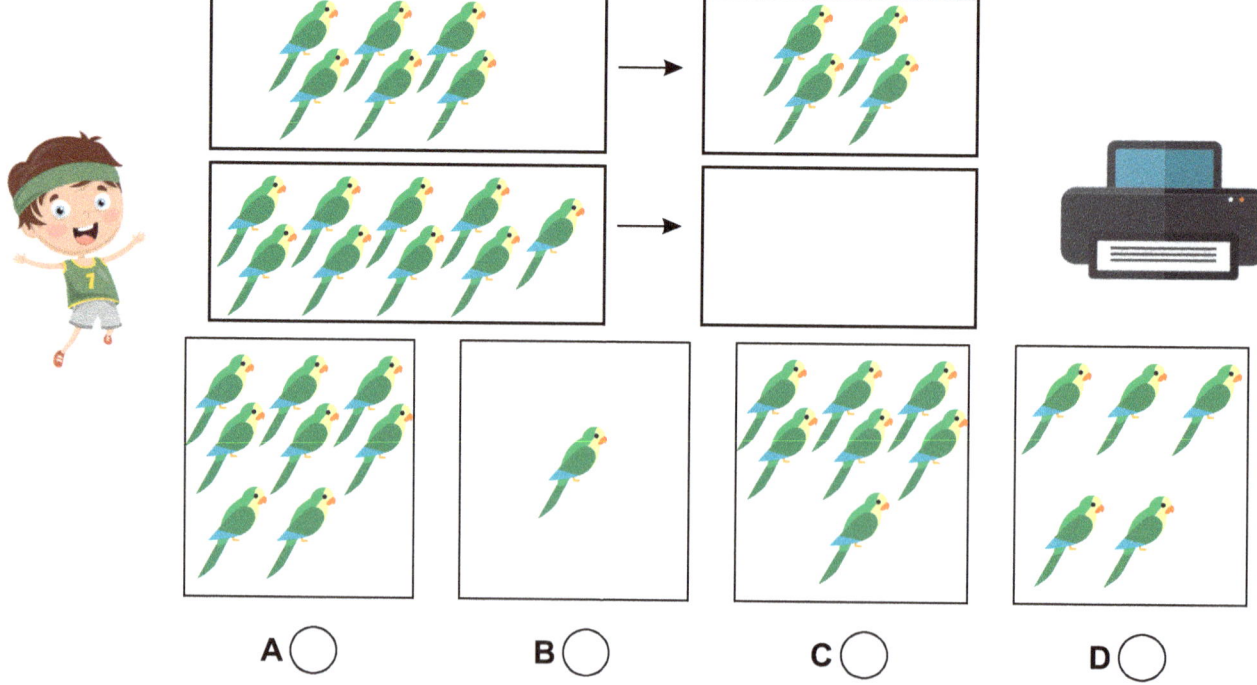

A ◯   B ◯   C ◯   D ◯

www.math-knots.com

Q-9

Look at the question with the CD Player. Two boxes in the first row are related in a certain way which is similar to two boxes in the second row. Alice is trying to fill the bubble under the correct option. Help her to select from options A, B, C, and D.

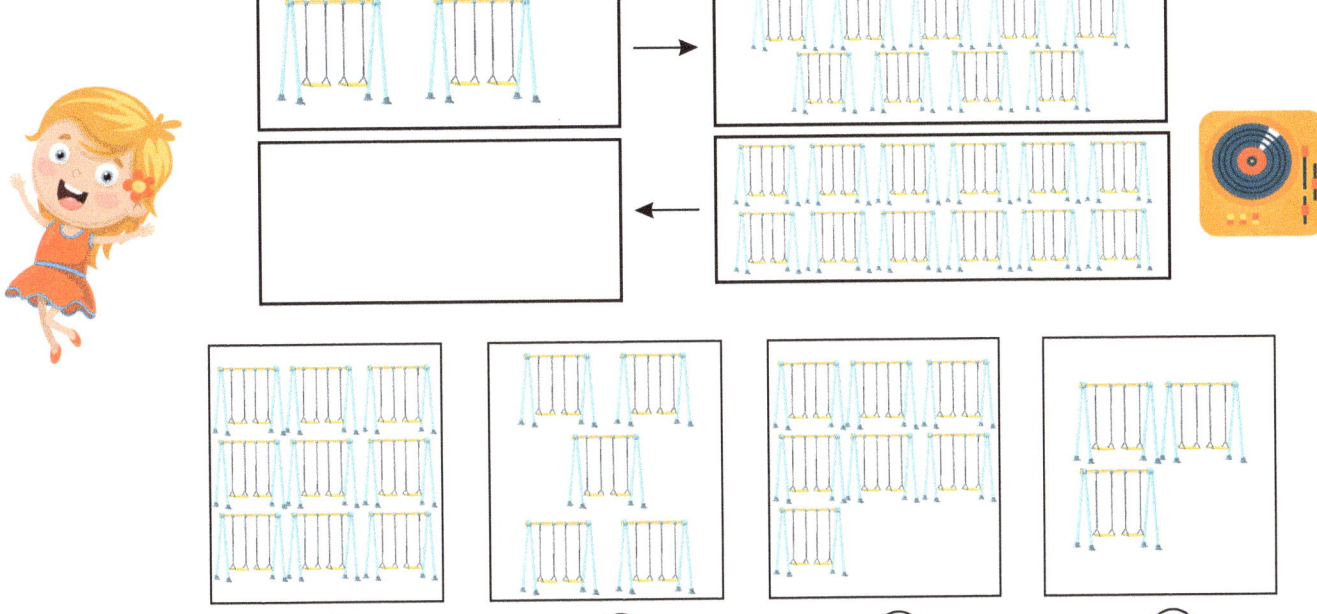

A ◯   B ◯   C ◯   D ◯

Q-10

Look at the question with the Blue Tooth. Two boxes in the first row are related in a certain way which is similar to two boxes in the second row. Lucas is trying to fill the bubble under the correct option. Help him to select from options A, B, C, and D.

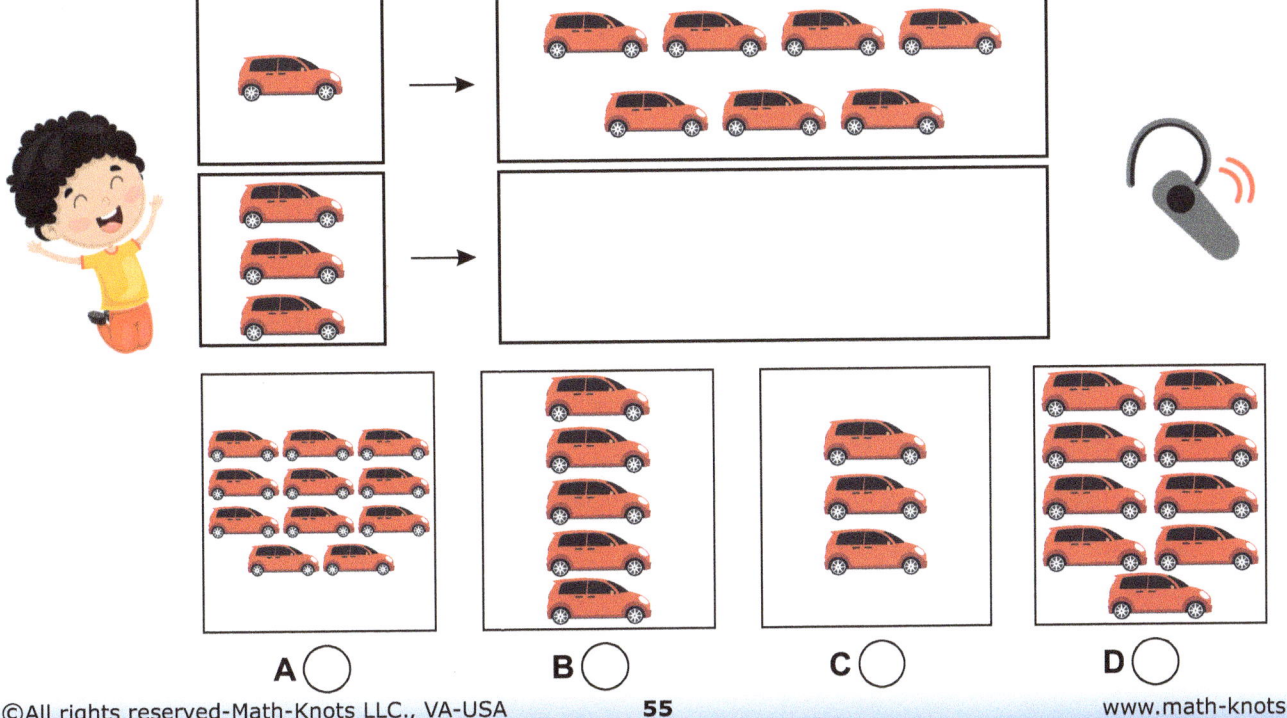

A ◯   B ◯   C ◯   D ◯

www.math-knots.com

Q-11 Look at the question with the Floppy Disk. Two boxes in the first row are related in a certain way which is similar to two boxes in the second row. Ella is trying to fill the bubble under the correct option. Help her to select from options A, B, C, and D.

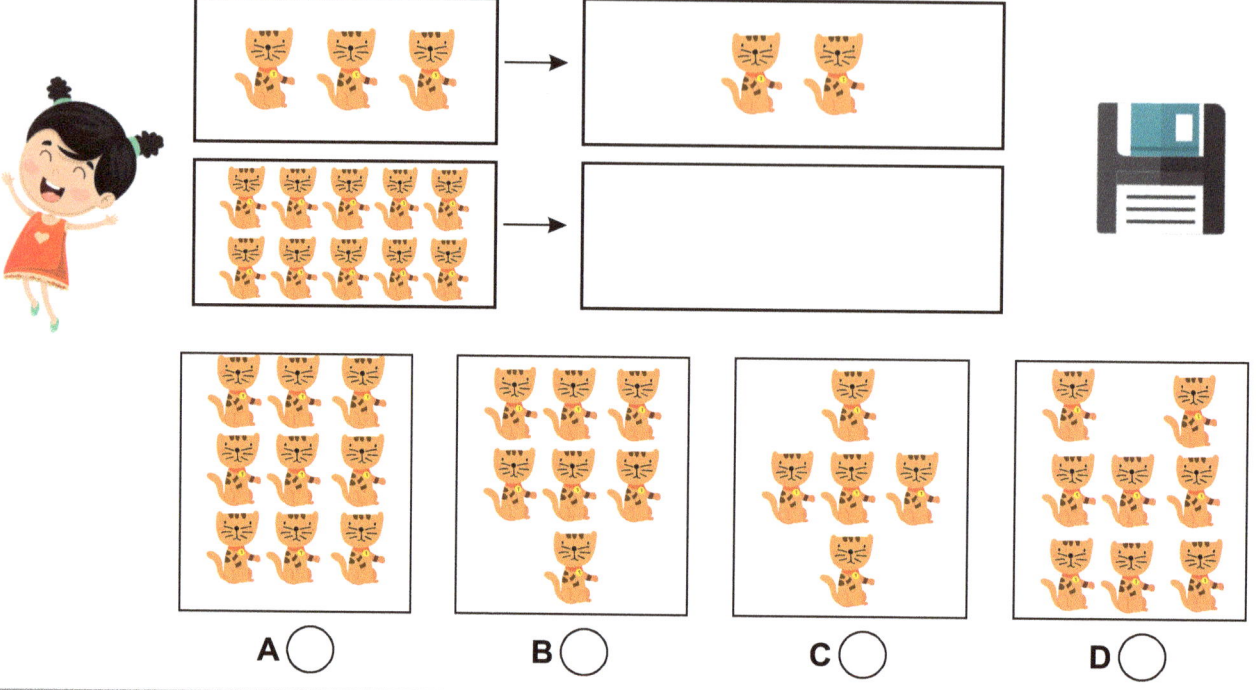

Q-12 Look at the question with the Microchip. Two boxes in the first row are related in a certain way which is similar to two boxes in the second row. Samuel is trying to fill the bubble under the correct option. Help him to select from options A, B, C, and D.

www.math-knots.com

Q-13

Look at the question with the Web Camera. Two boxes in the first row are related in a certain way which is similar to two boxes in the second row. Bella is trying to fill the bubble under the correct option. Help her to select from options A, B, C, and D.

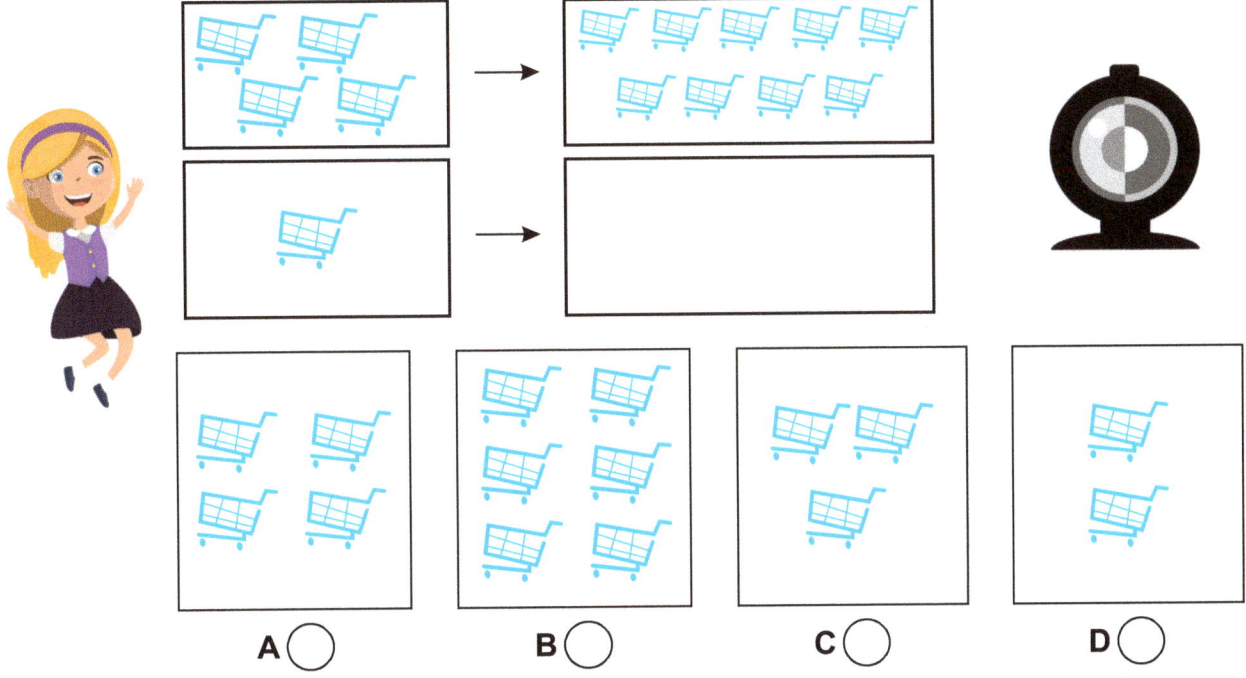

A ◯ B ◯ C ◯ D ◯

Q-14

Look at the question with the Jack Connector. Two boxes in the first row are related in a certain way which is similar to two boxes in the second row. Skylar is trying to fill the bubble under the correct option. Help her to select from options A, B, C, and D.

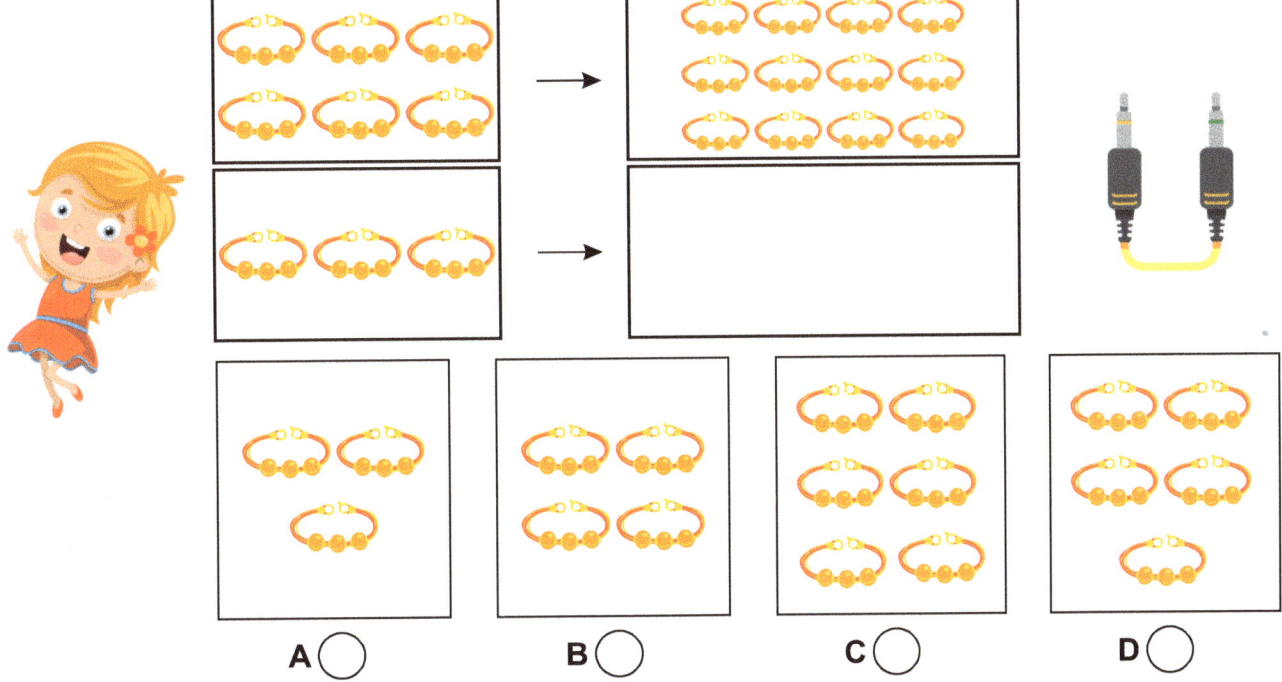

A ◯ B ◯ C ◯ D ◯

Q-15

Look at the question with the tablet HDMI Cable. Two boxes in the first row are related in a certain way which is similar to two boxes in the second row. Hannah is trying to fill the bubble under the correct option. Help her to select from options A, B, C, and D.

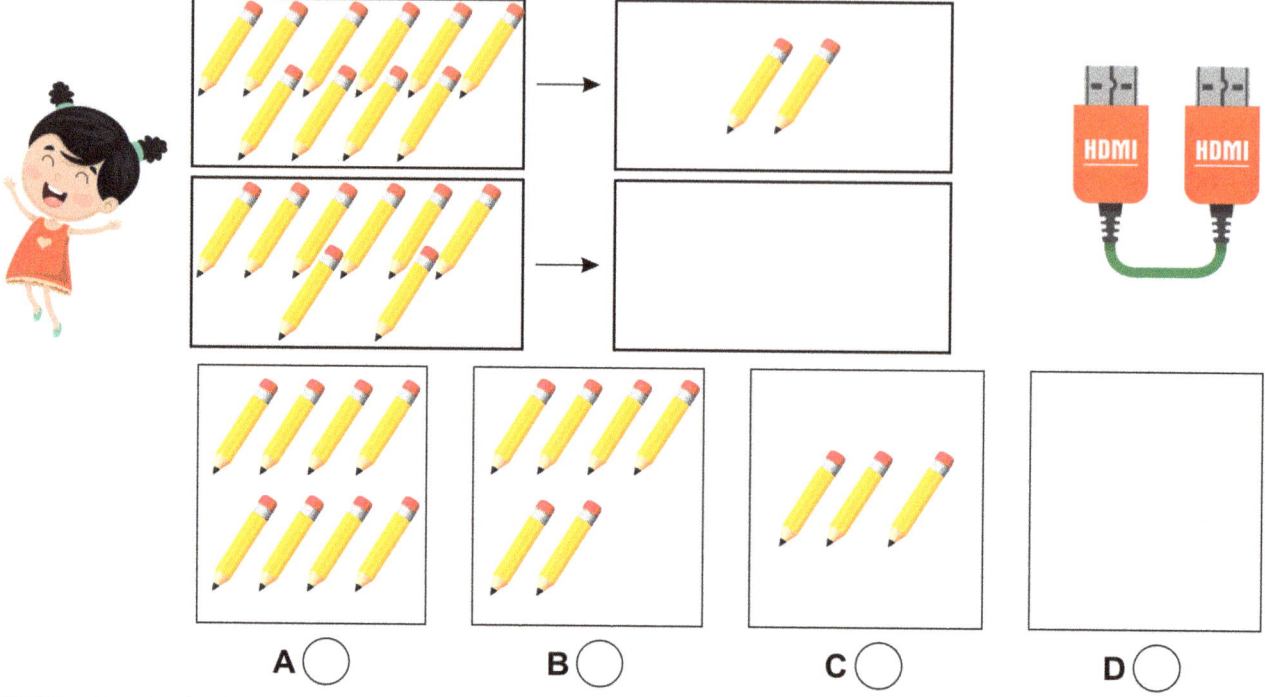

A ◯   B ◯   C ◯   D ◯

Q-16

Look at the question with the usb Flashdrive. Two boxes in the first row are related in a certain way which is similar to two boxes in the second row. Mathew is trying to fill the bubble under the correct option. Help him to select from options A, B, C, and D.

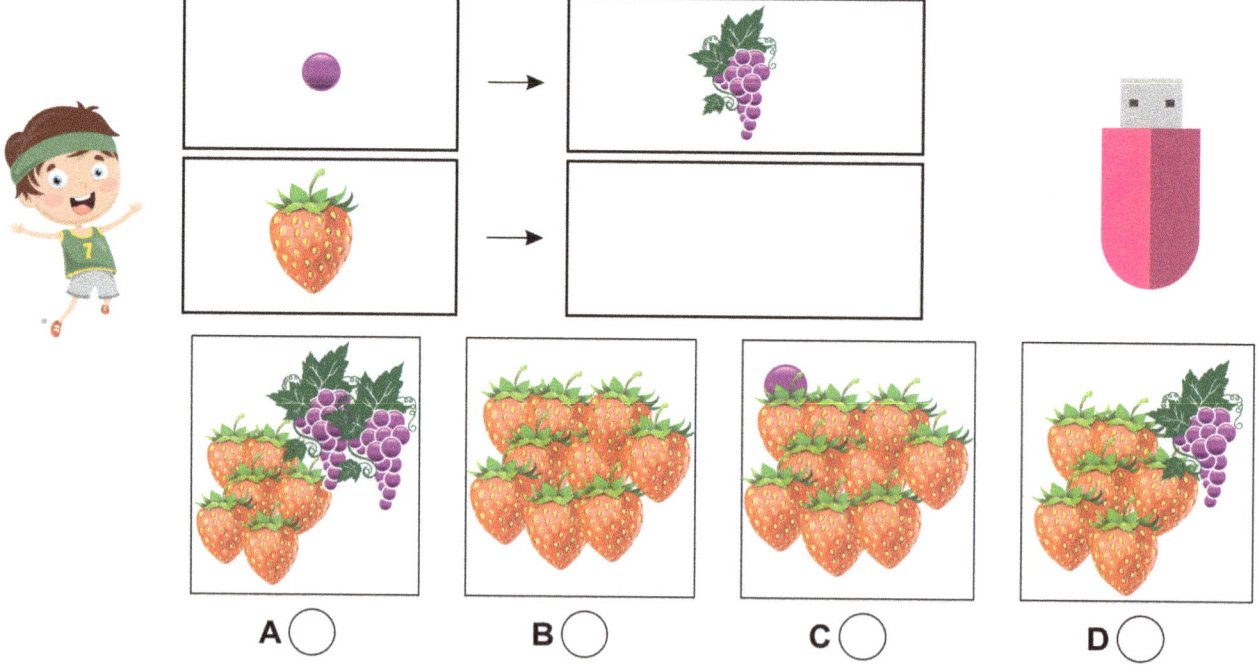

A ◯   B ◯   C ◯   D ◯

www.math-knots.com

Q-17 Look at the question with the Tablet PC. Two boxes in the first row are related in a certain way which is similar to two boxes in the second row. Joseph is trying to fill the bubble under the correct option. Help him to select from options A, B, C, and D.

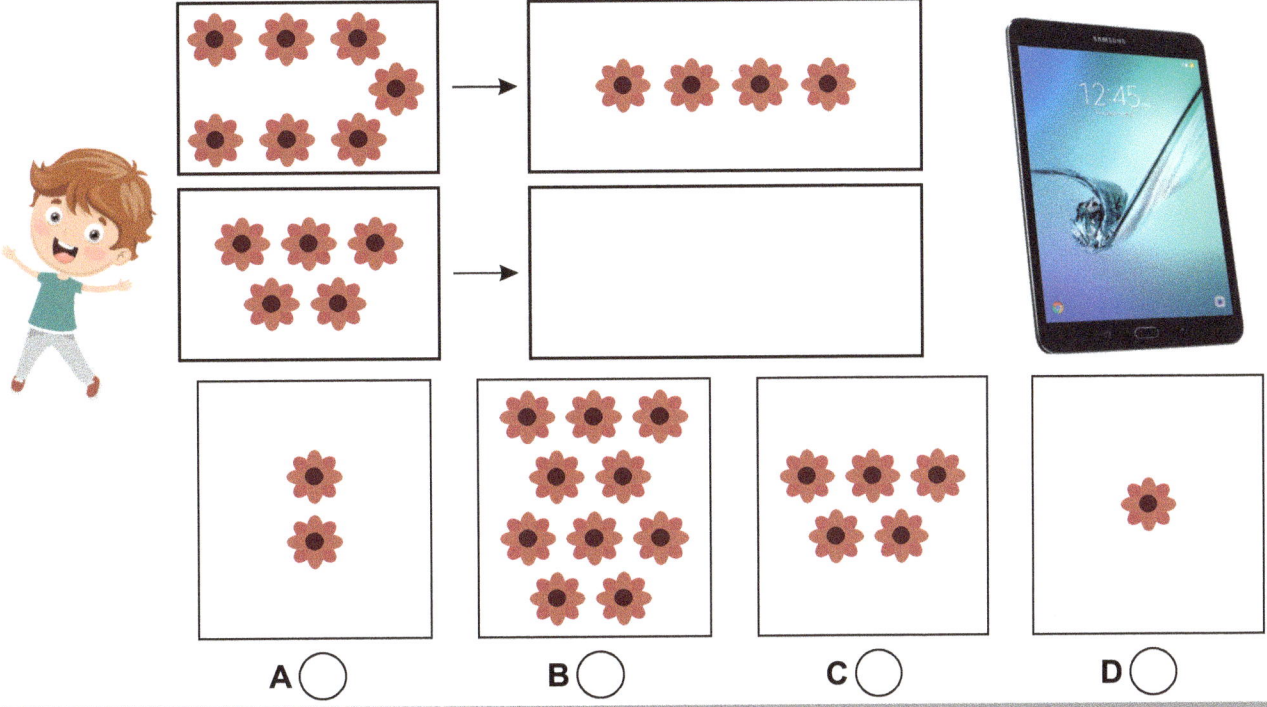

A ◯   B ◯   C ◯   D ◯

Q-18 Look at the question with the Mp3 Player. Two boxes in the first row are related in a certain way which is similar to two boxes in the second row. Chloe is trying to fill thebubble under the correct option. Help her to select from options A, B, C, and D.

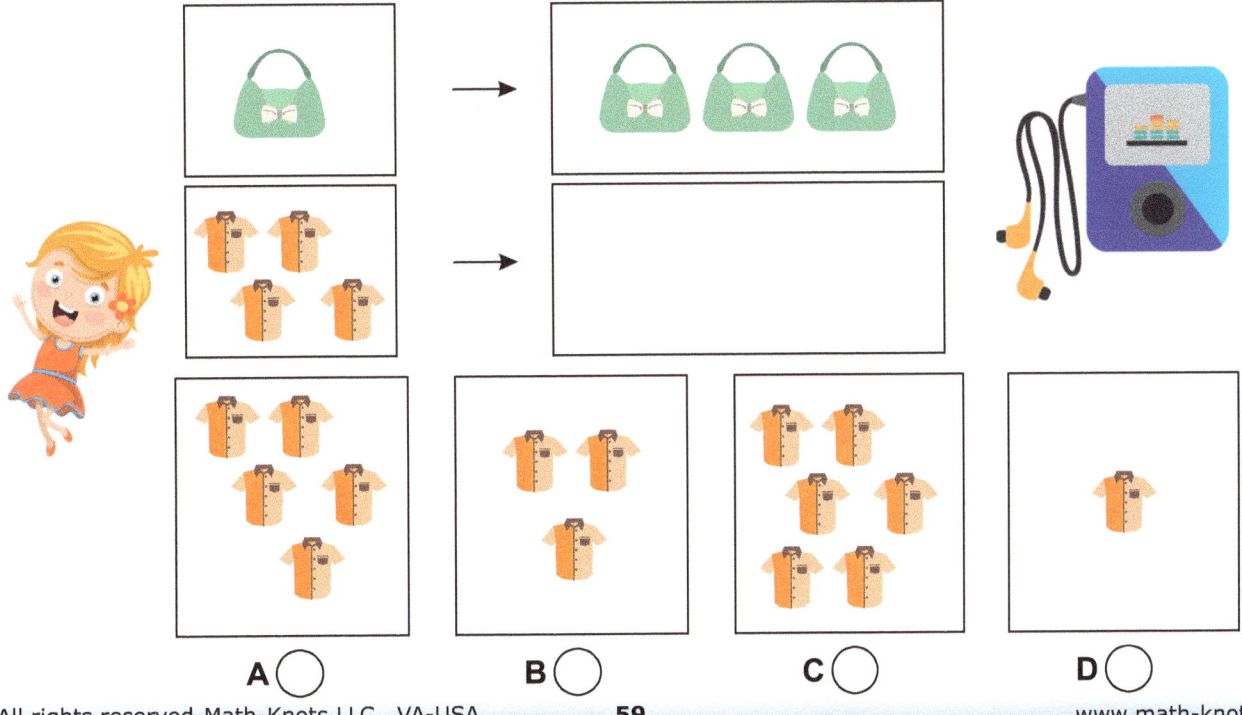

A ◯   B ◯   C ◯   D ◯

www.math-knots.com

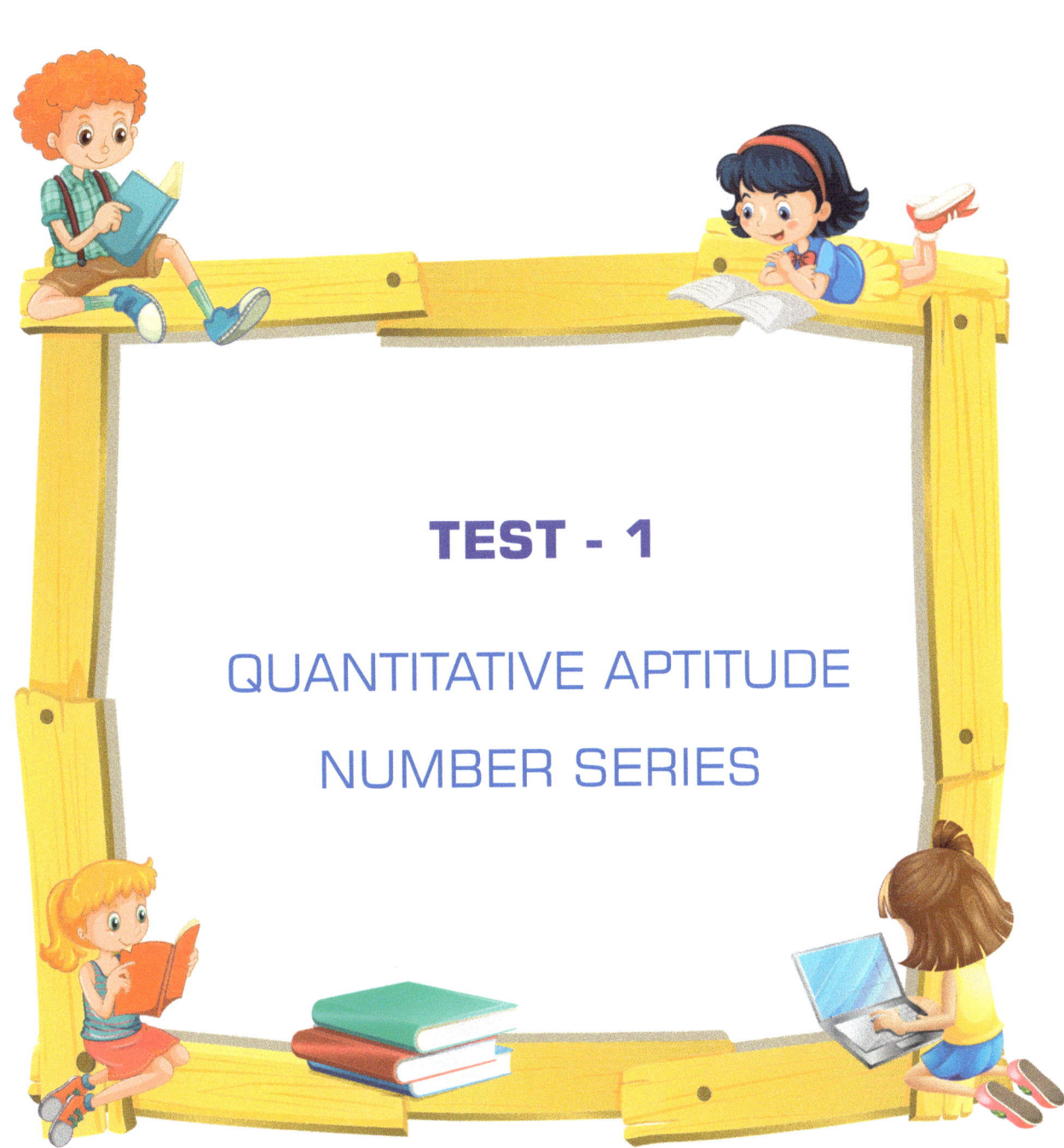

TEST - 1

QUANTITATIVE APTITUDE

NUMBER SERIES

Lets Start the Test...

www.math-knots.com

Sample Look at the question with the Triangle. Cathy is making a pattern with her hexagon shaped beads. Can you help her to identify what goes in the empty string from the given four options A, B, C, and D.

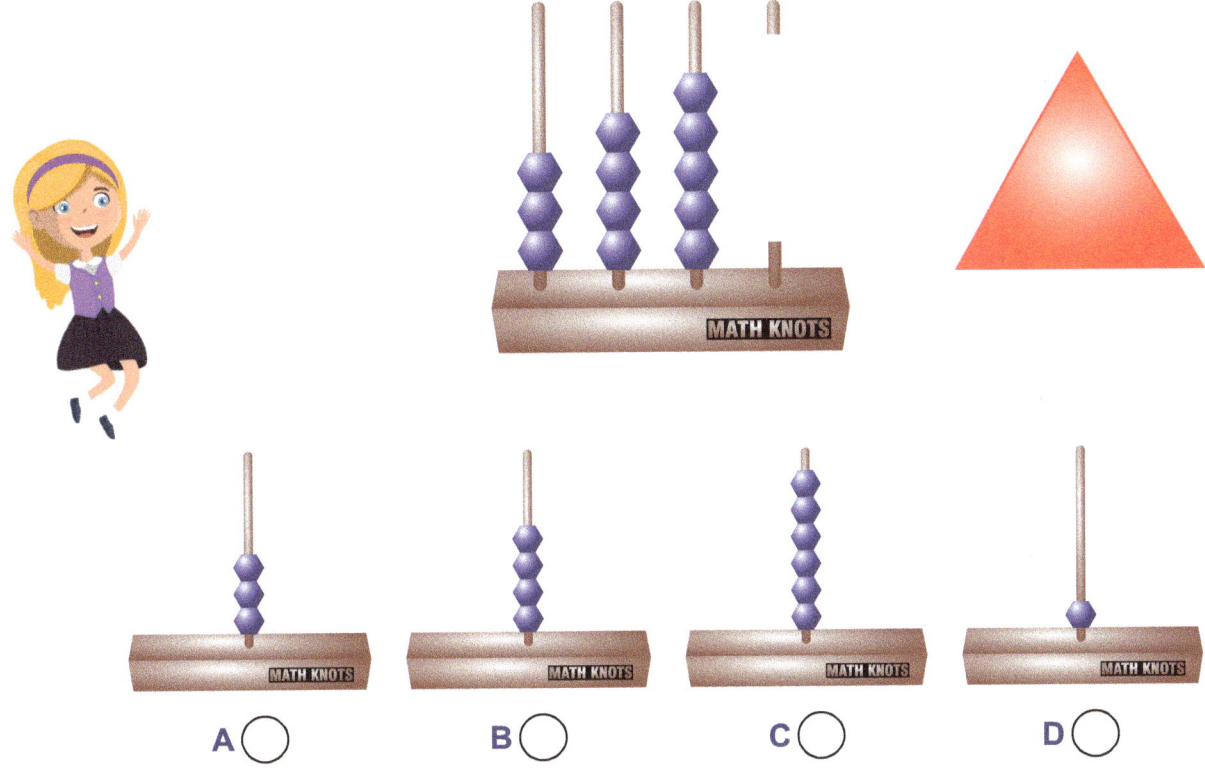

Solution : C

3, 4, 5.....

The beads are increasing by 1. So next string should have six beads. Option C is the correct choice. The patterns can increase or decrease by a certain number of beads. Students are supposed to identify the correct pattern and answer the correct choice.

www.math-knots.com

Q-1 Look at the question with the Truck. Joseph is making a pattern with his hexagon shaped beads. Can you help him to identify what goes in the empty string from the given four options A, B, C, and D.

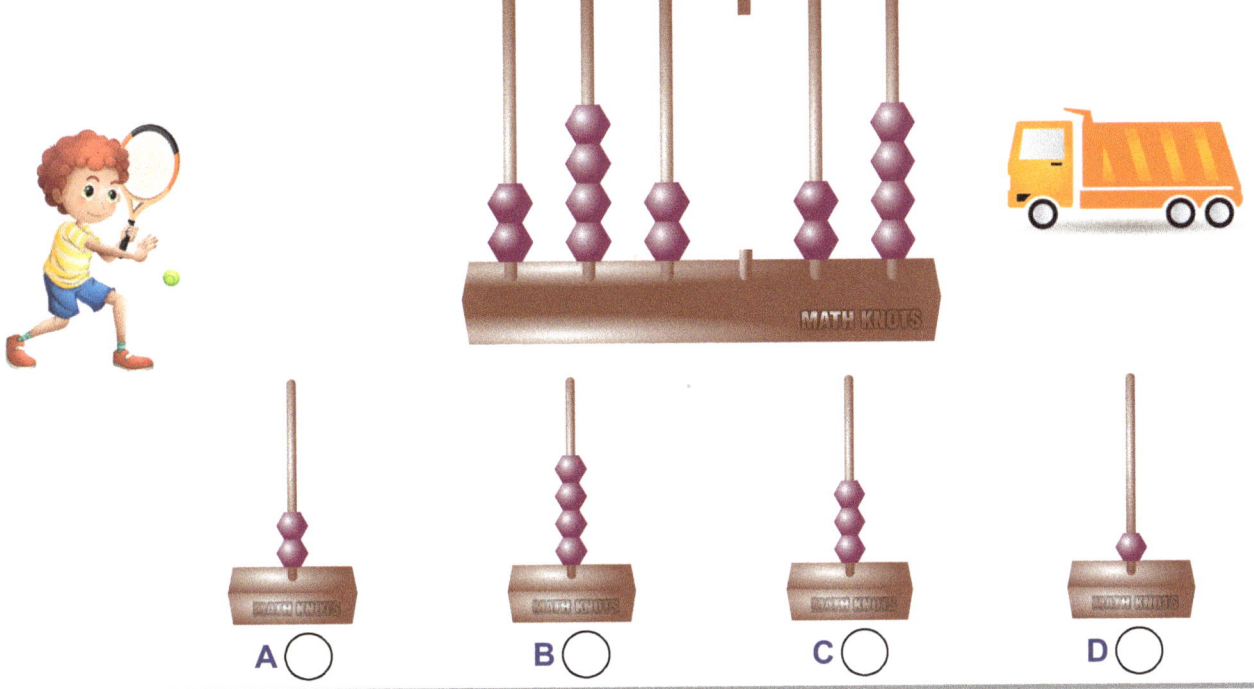

A ◯ B ◯ C ◯ D ◯

Q-2 Look at the question with the look at Bike, Jane is making a pattern with her hexagon shaped beads. Can you help her to identify what goes in the empty string from the given four options A, B, C, and D.

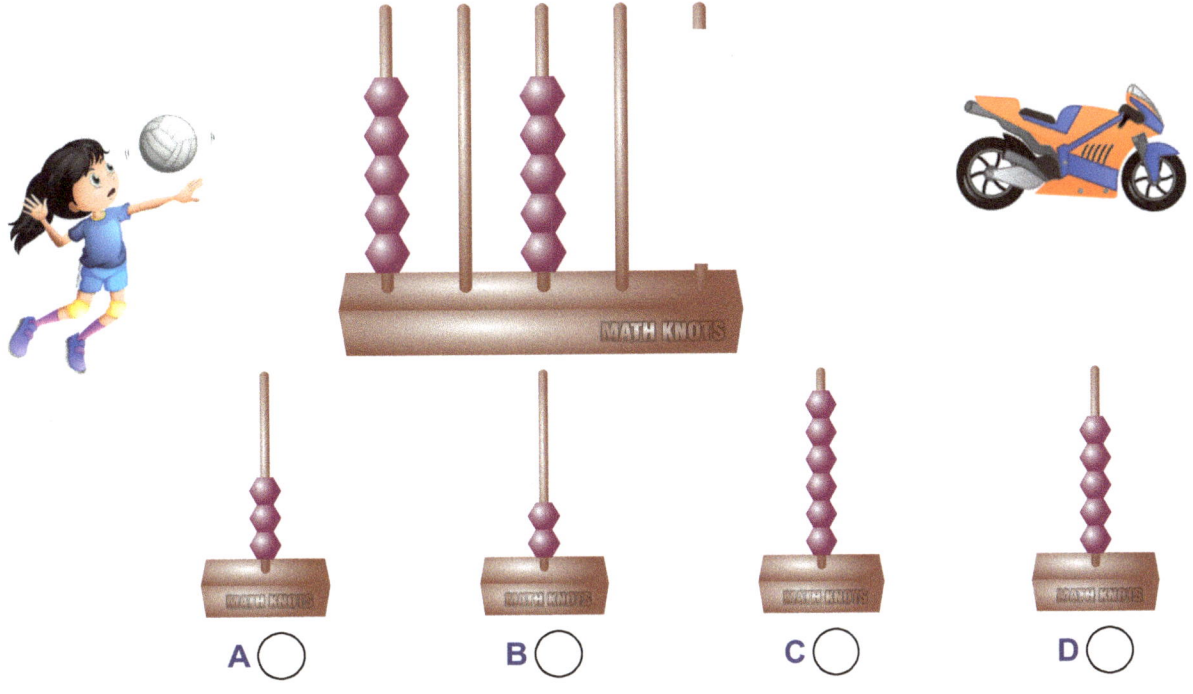

A ◯ B ◯ C ◯ D ◯

www.math-knots.com

Q-3 Look at the question with the Tanker. Logan is making a pattern with his hexagon shaped beads. Can you help him to identify what goes in the empty string from the given four options A, B, C, and D.

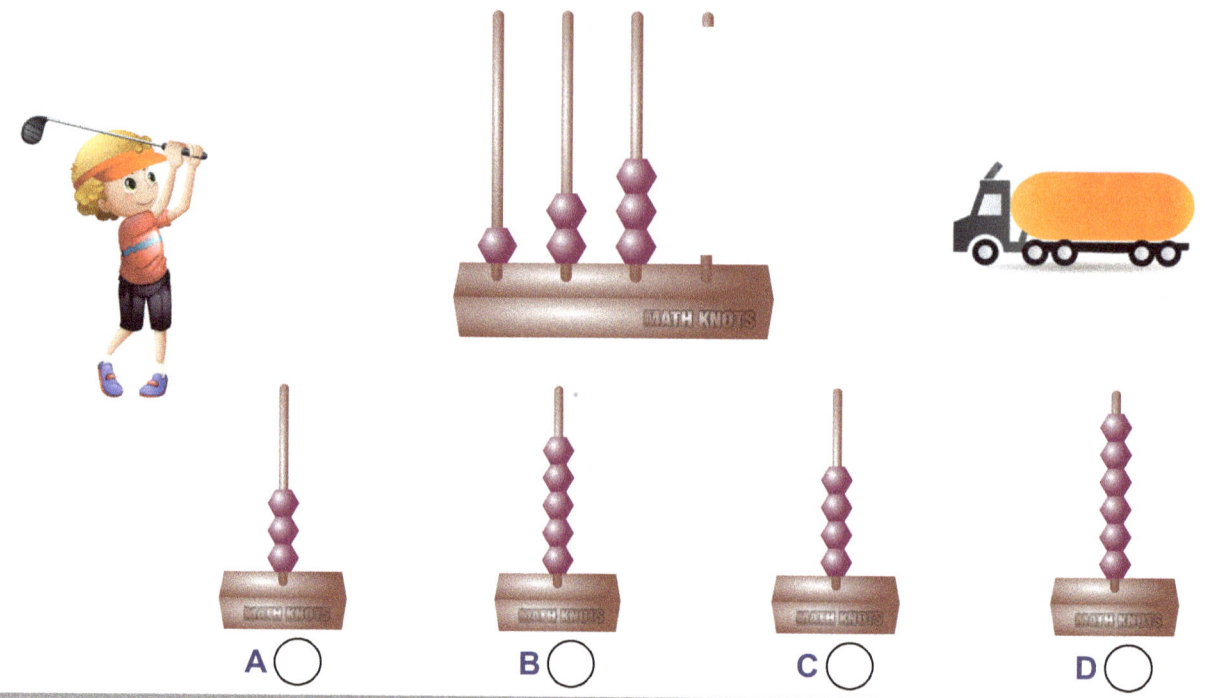

A ◯   B ◯   C ◯   D ◯

Q-4 Look at the question with the Crane, Ava is making a pattern with her hexagon shaped beads. Can you help her to identify what goes in the empty string from the given four options A, B, C, and D.

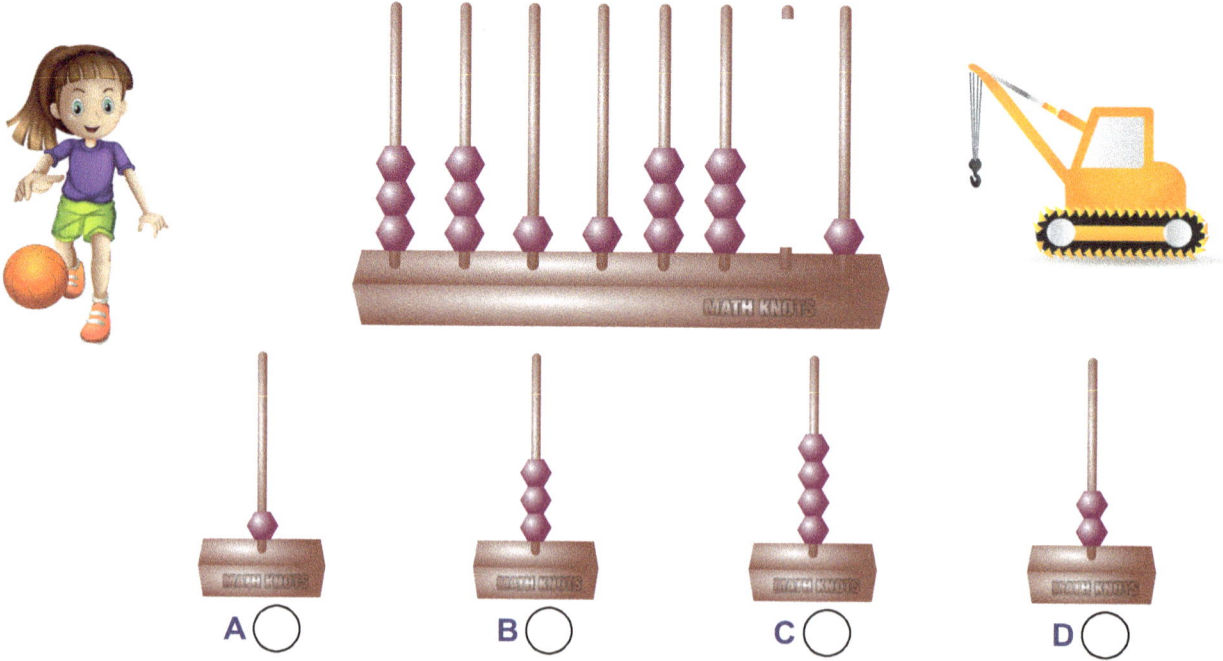

A ◯   B ◯   C ◯   D ◯

Q-5 Look at the question with the Van. Robert is making a pattern with his hexagon shaped beads. Can you help him to identify what goes in the empty string from the given four options A,B,C, and D.

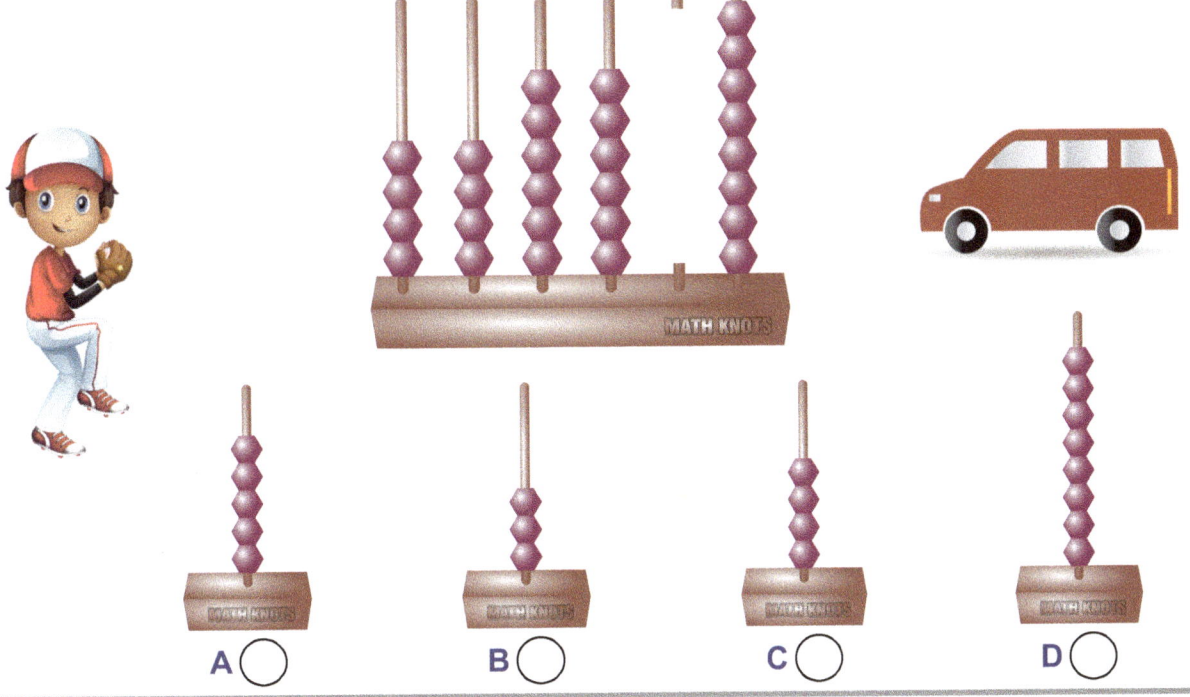

A ◯ B ◯ C ◯ D ◯

Q-6 Look at the question with the Helicopter, Emma is making a pattern with her hexagon shaped beads. Can you help her to identify what goes in the empty string from the given four options A,B,C, and D.

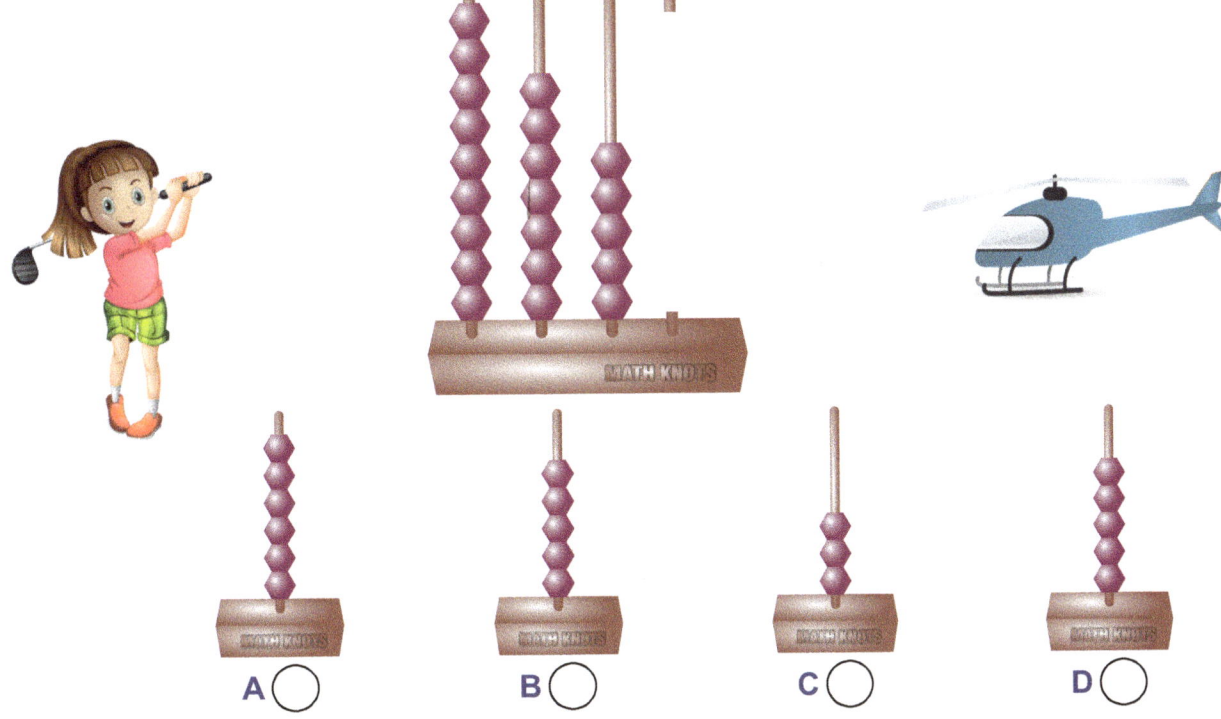

A ◯ B ◯ C ◯ D ◯

www.math-knots.com

Q-7 Look at the question with the Flight. Harry is making a pattern with his hexagon shaped beads. Can you help him to identify what goes in the empty string from the given four options A, B, C, and D.

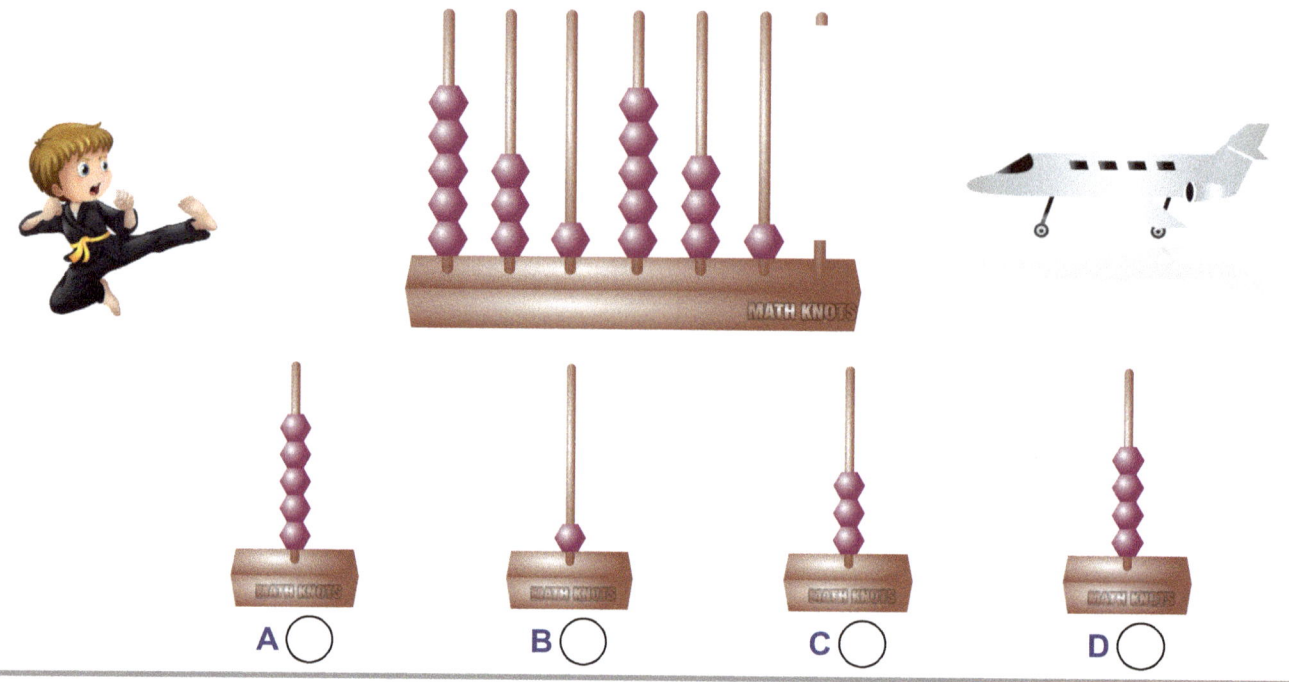

A ◯   B ◯   C ◯   D ◯

Q-8 Look at the question with the Ship, Margaret is making a pattern with her hexagon shaped beads. Can you help her to identify what goes in the empty string from the given four options A, B, C, and D.

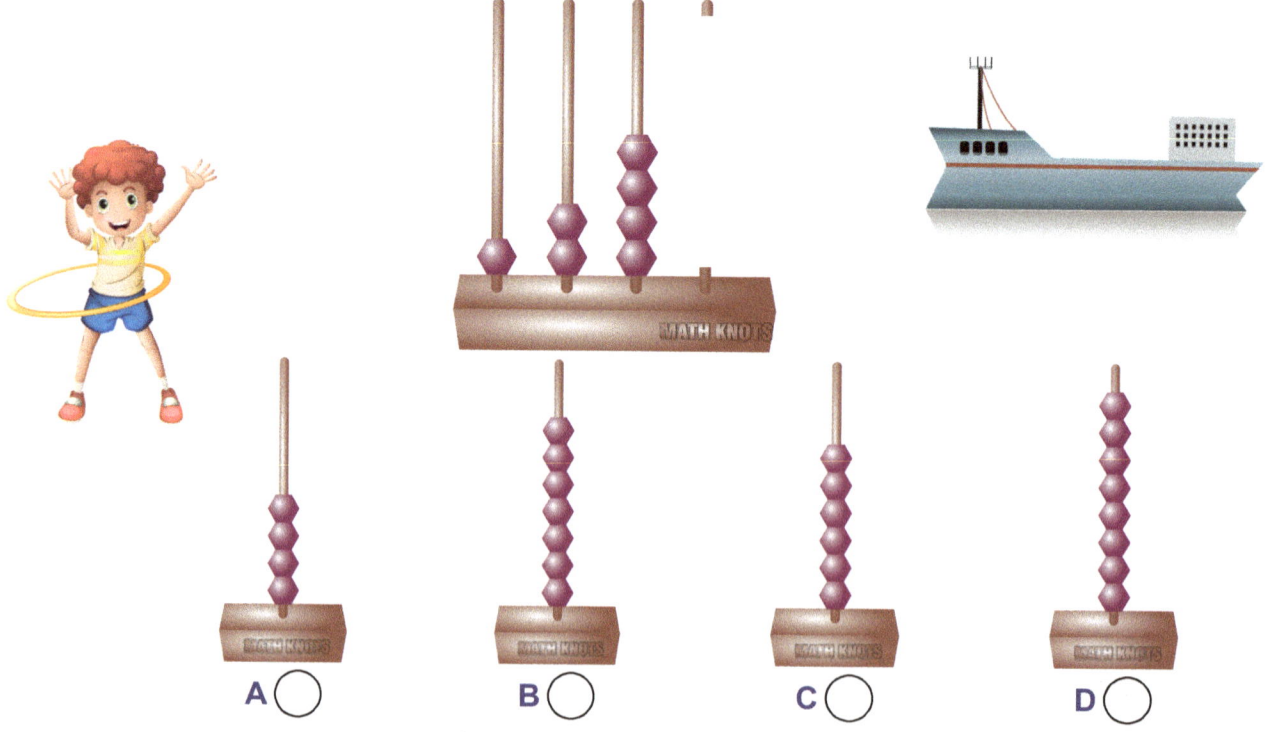

A ◯   B ◯   C ◯   D ◯

www.math-knots.com

Q-9 Look at the question with the Bullet Train. Elizabeth is making a pattern with her hexagon shaped beads. Can you help her to identify what goes in the empty string from the given four options A,B,C, and D.

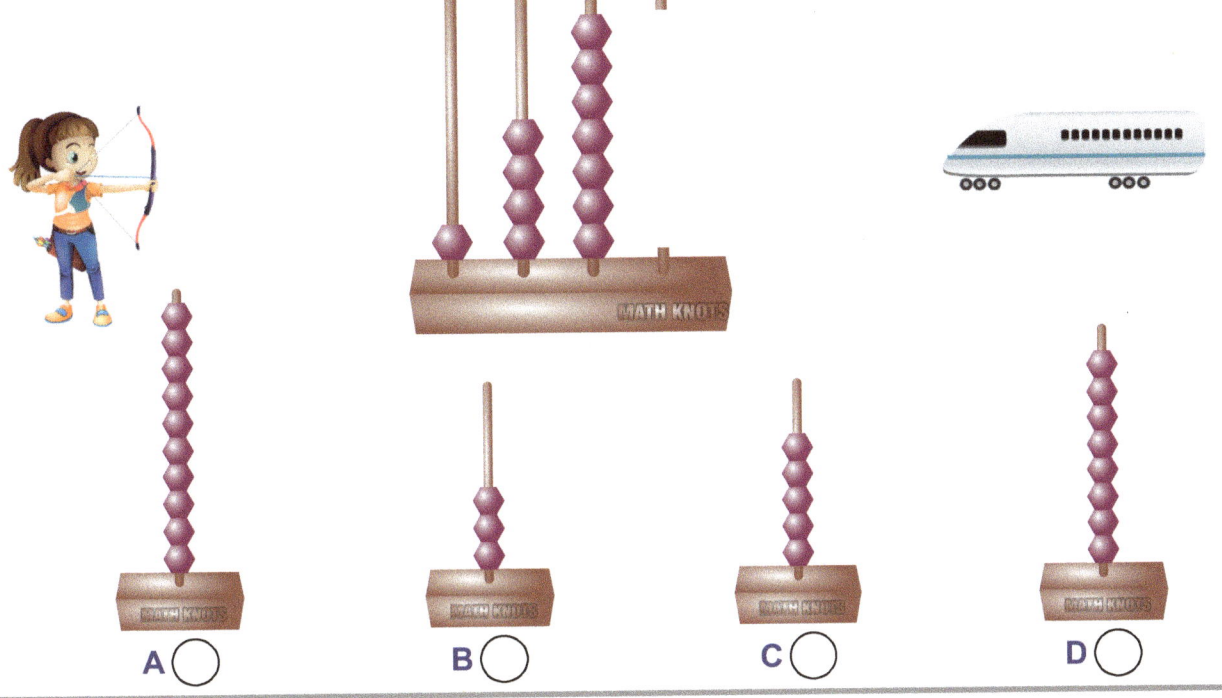

A ◯   B ◯   C ◯   D ◯

Q-10 Look at the question with the Truck. Skylar is making a pattern with her hexagon shaped beads. Can you help her to identify what goes in the empty string from the given four options A,B,C, and D.

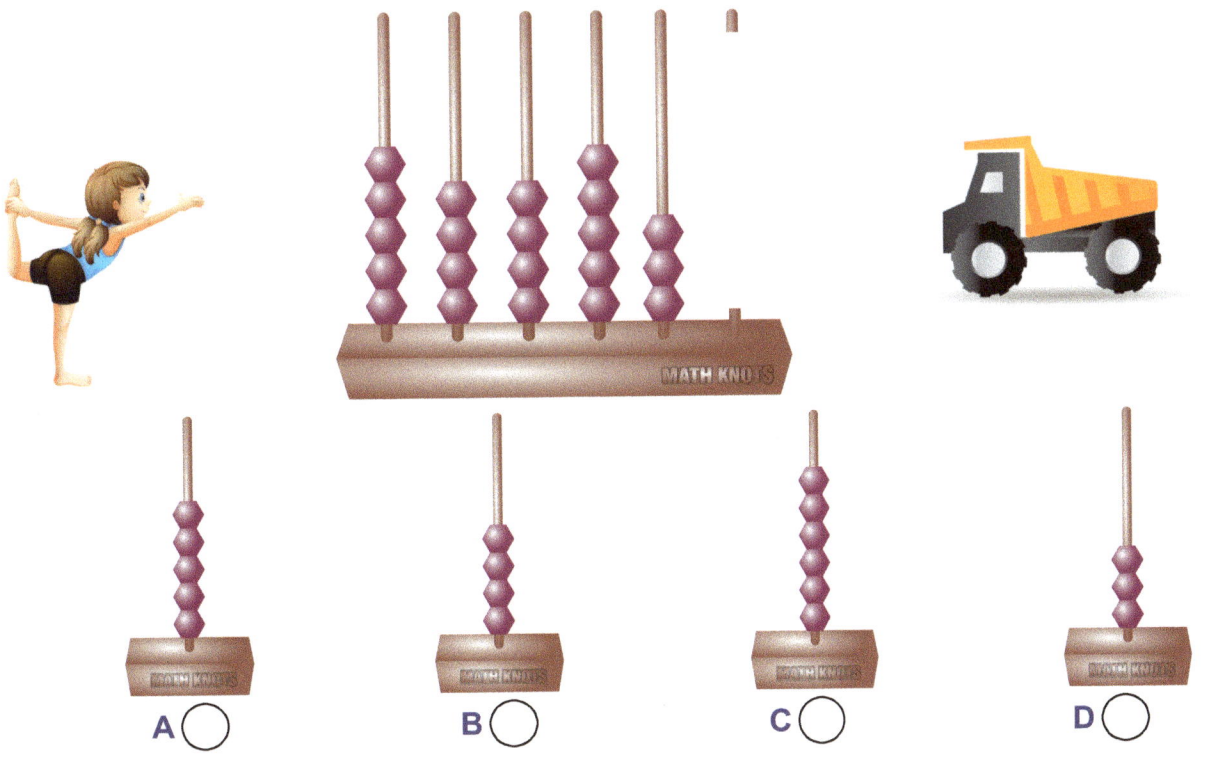

A ◯   B ◯   C ◯   D ◯

www.math-knots.com

Q-11 Look at the question with the Scooter. Brooklyn is making a pattern with his hexagon shaped beads. Can you help him to identify what goes in the empty string from the given four options A,B,C, and D.

A ◯   B ◯   C ◯   D ◯

Q-12 Look at the question with the Van. Caroline is making a pattern with her hexagon shaped beads. Can you help her to identify what goes in the empty string from the given four options A,B,C, and D.

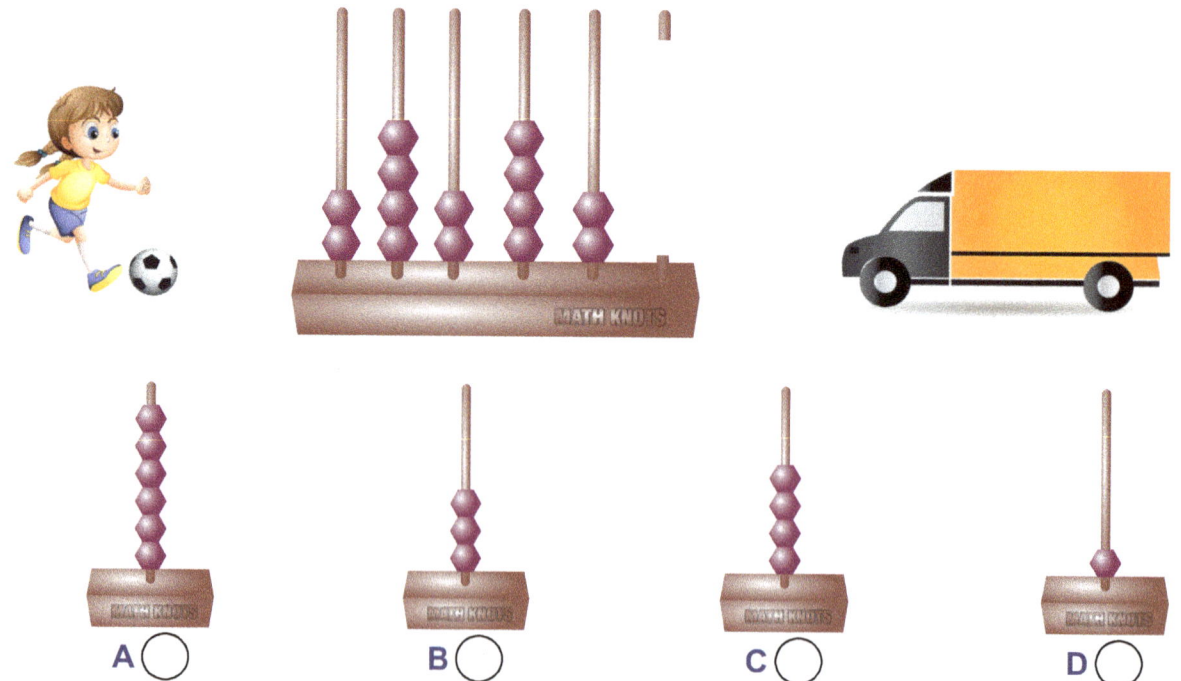

A ◯   B ◯   C ◯   D ◯

www.math-knots.com

Q-13 Look at the question with the Concrete Mixing Truck. Amy is making a pattern with her hexagon shaped beads. Can you help her to identify what goes in the empty string from the given four options A,B,C, and D.

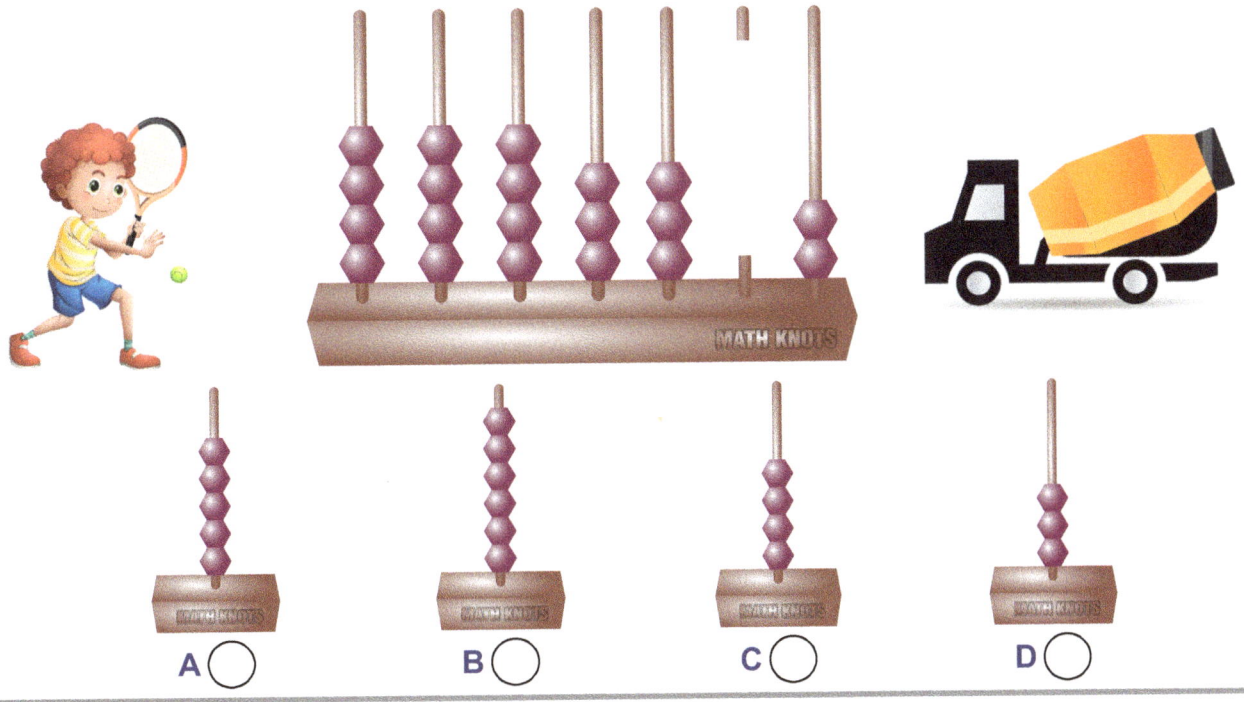

A ◯   B ◯   C ◯   D ◯

Q-14 Look at the question with the Loader Truck. Andy is making a pattern with his hexagon shaped beads. Can you help him to identify what goes in the empty string from the given four options A,B,C, and D.

A ◯   B ◯   C ◯   D ◯

www.math-knots.com

Q-15

Look at the question with the Car. Chloe is making a pattern with her hexagon shaped beads. Can you help her to identify what goes in the empty string from the given four options A,B,C, and D.

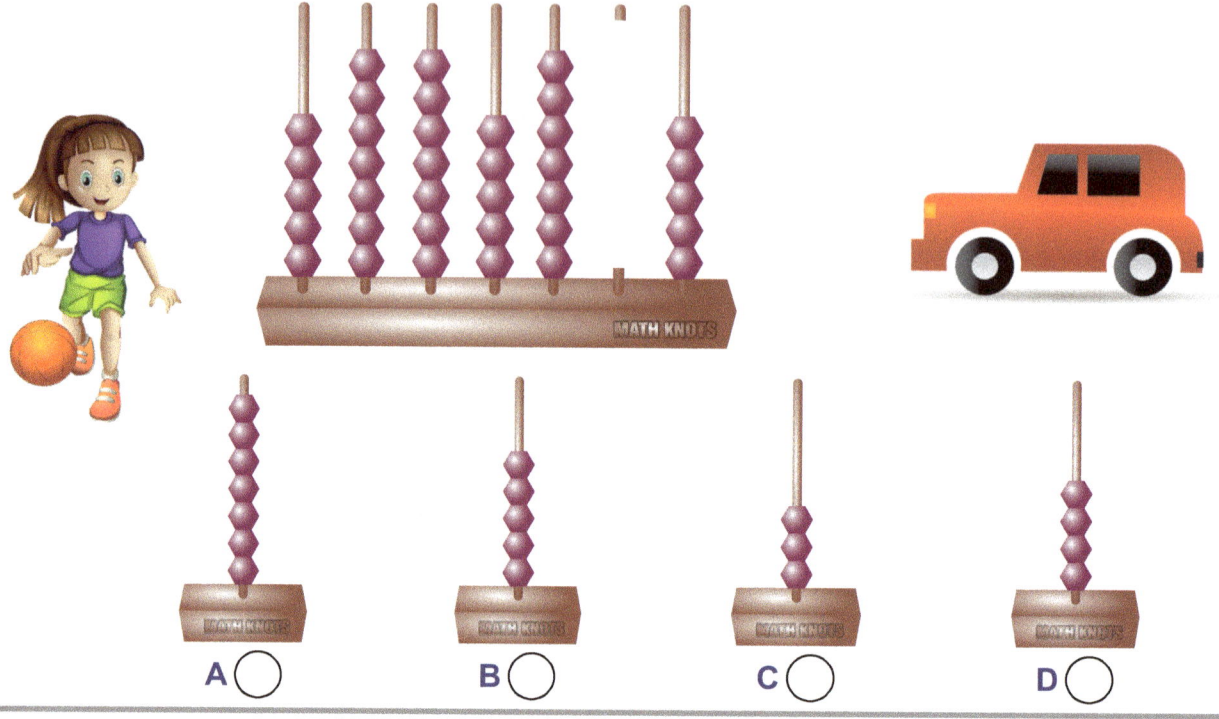

A ◯   B ◯   C ◯   D ◯

Q-16

Look at the question with the Bicycle. Mary is making a pattern with her hexagon shaped beads. Can you help her to identify what goes in the empty string from the given four options A,B,C, and D.

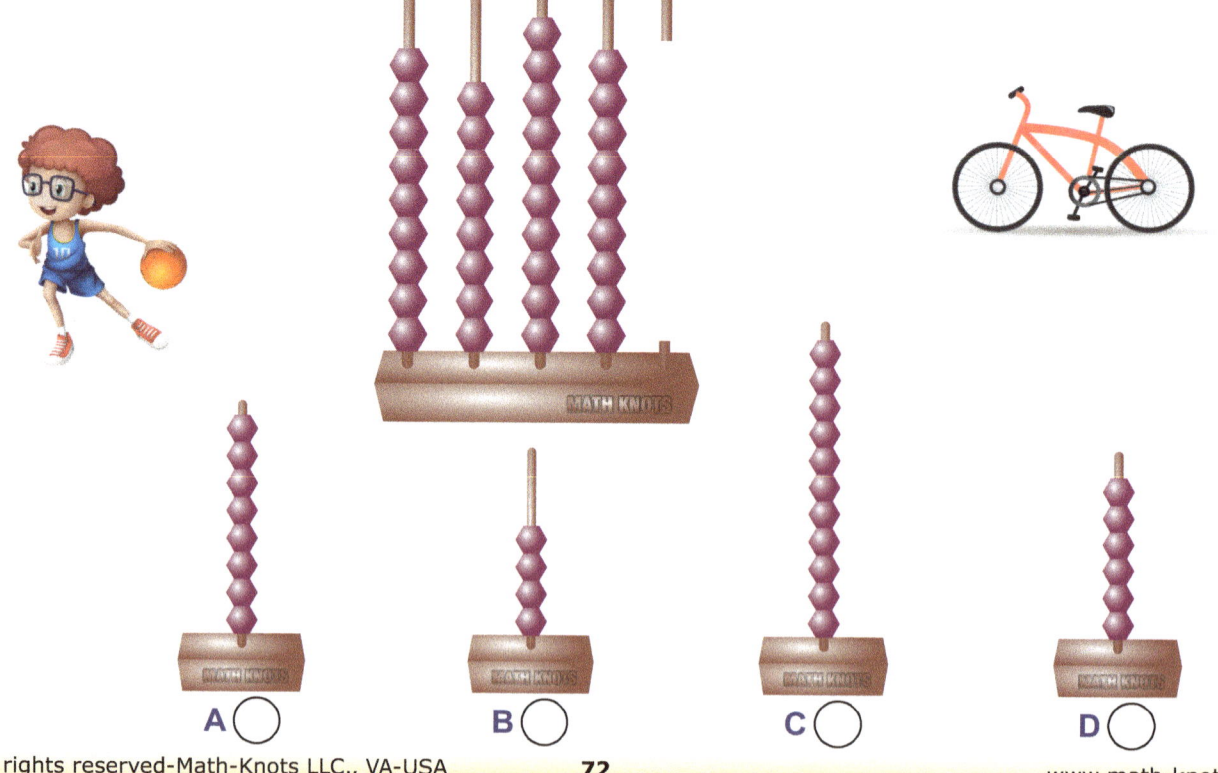

A ◯   B ◯   C ◯   D ◯

www.math-knots.com

Q-17 Look at the question with the Flight. Pamela is making a pattern with her hexagon shaped beads. Can you help her to identify what goes in the empty string from the given four options A, B, C, and D.

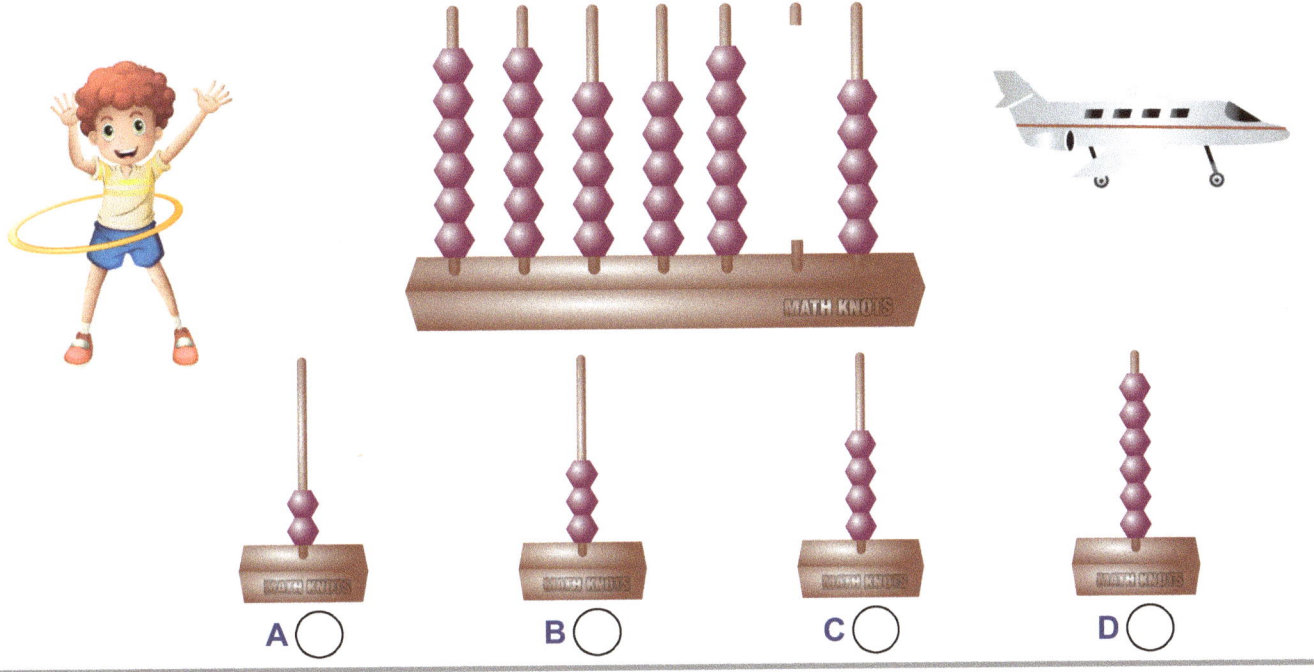

A ○   B ○   C ○   D ○

Q-18 Look at the question with the Bike. Ethan is making a pattern with her hexagon shaped beads. Can you help him to identify what goes in the empty string from the given four options A, B, C, and D.

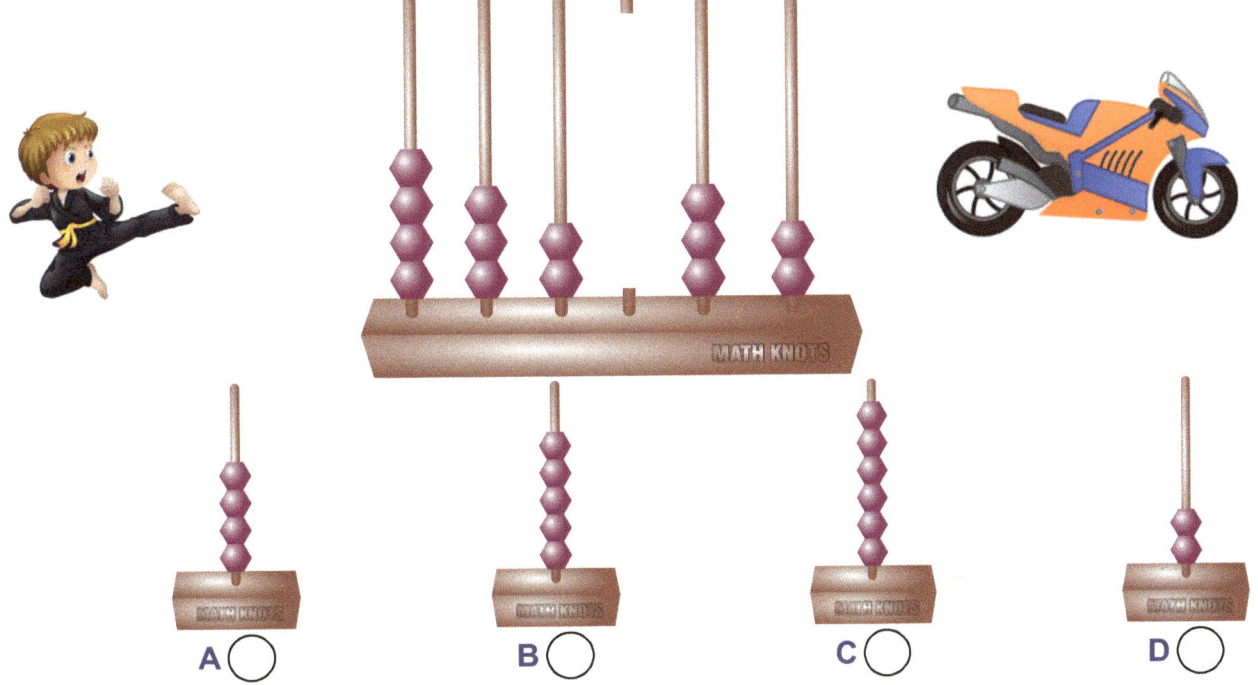

A ○   B ○   C ○   D ○

www.math-knots.com

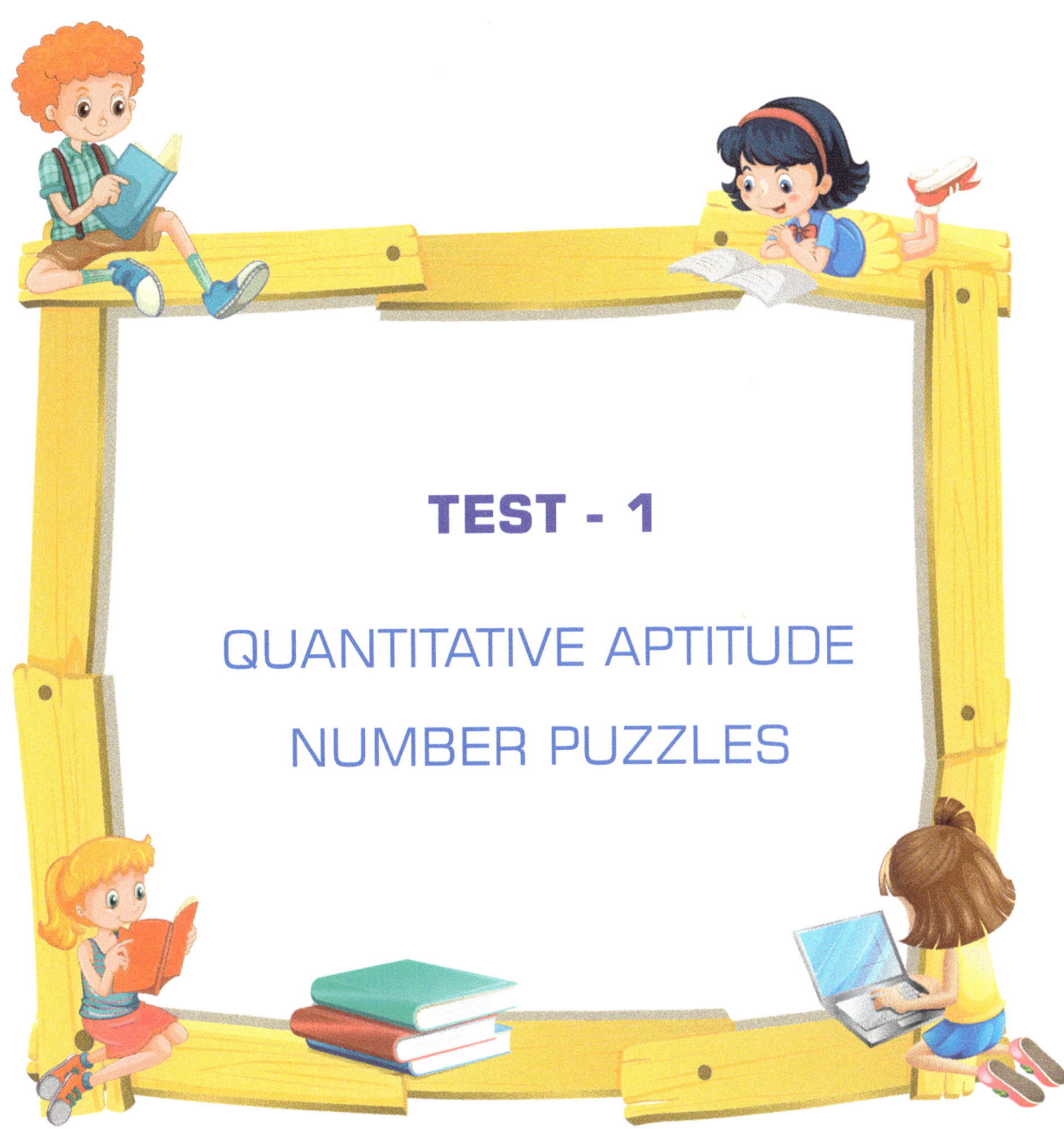

TEST - 1

QUANTITATIVE APTITUDE

NUMBER PUZZLES

Lets Start the Test...

Sample

Look at the question and put your finger on the Guitar. Ryan is wondering what is the missing number under the question mark ? Help him to find the missing number under the question mark and fill in the bubble.

2 + ? = 3

| 1 | 0 | 5 | 2 |
| A○ | B○ | C○ | D○ |

Solution : A

How much should be added to 2 to make it 3

3 - 2 = 1

Meaning if we add 1 to 2 we get a total of three

Q-1 Look at the question and put your finger on the Sheep. Kevin is wondering what is the missing number under the question mark ? Help him to find the missing number under the question mark and fill in the bubble.

$$4 + ? = 8$$

4	0	2	8
A◯	B◯	C◯	D◯

Q-2 Look at the question and put your finger on the Turtle. Lilly is wondering what is the missing number under the question mark ? Help her to find the missing number under the question mark and fill in the bubble.

$$16 + ? = 22$$

5	7	0	6
A◯	B◯	C◯	D◯

Q-3 Look at the question and put your finger on the Parrot. Riky is wondering what is the missing number under the question mark ? Help him to find the missing number under the question mark and fill in the bubble.

A ◯ 18 B ◯ 19 C ◯ 17 D ◯ 32

Q-4 Look at the question and put your finger on the Vampires Bat. Luke is wondering what is the missing number under the question mark ? Help him to find the missing number under the question mark and fill in the bubble.

A ◯ 15 B ◯ 11 C ◯ 8 D ◯ 7

www.math-knots.com

Q-5 Look at the question and put your finger on the Walrus. Bella is wondering what is the missing number under the question mark ? Help her to find the missing number under the question mark and fill in the bubble.

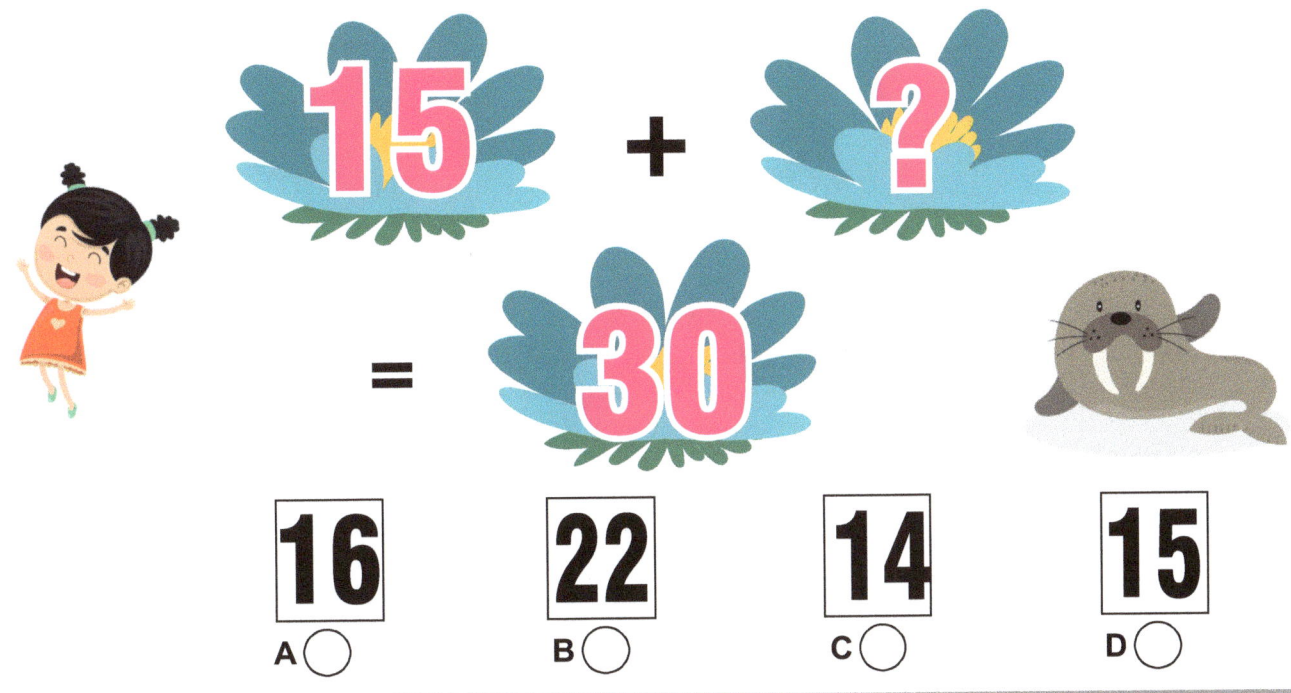

A ◯ 16   B ◯ 22   C ◯ 14   D ◯ 15

Q-6 Look at the question and put your finger on the Fish. Emma is wondering what is the missing number under the question mark ? Help her to find the missing number under the question mark and fill in the bubble.

A ◯ 18   B ◯ 0   C ◯ 1   D ◯ 8

www.math-knots.com

Q-7 Look at the question and put your finger on the Yak. Sarah is wondering what is the missing number under the question mark ? Help her to find the missing number under the question mark and fill in the bubble.

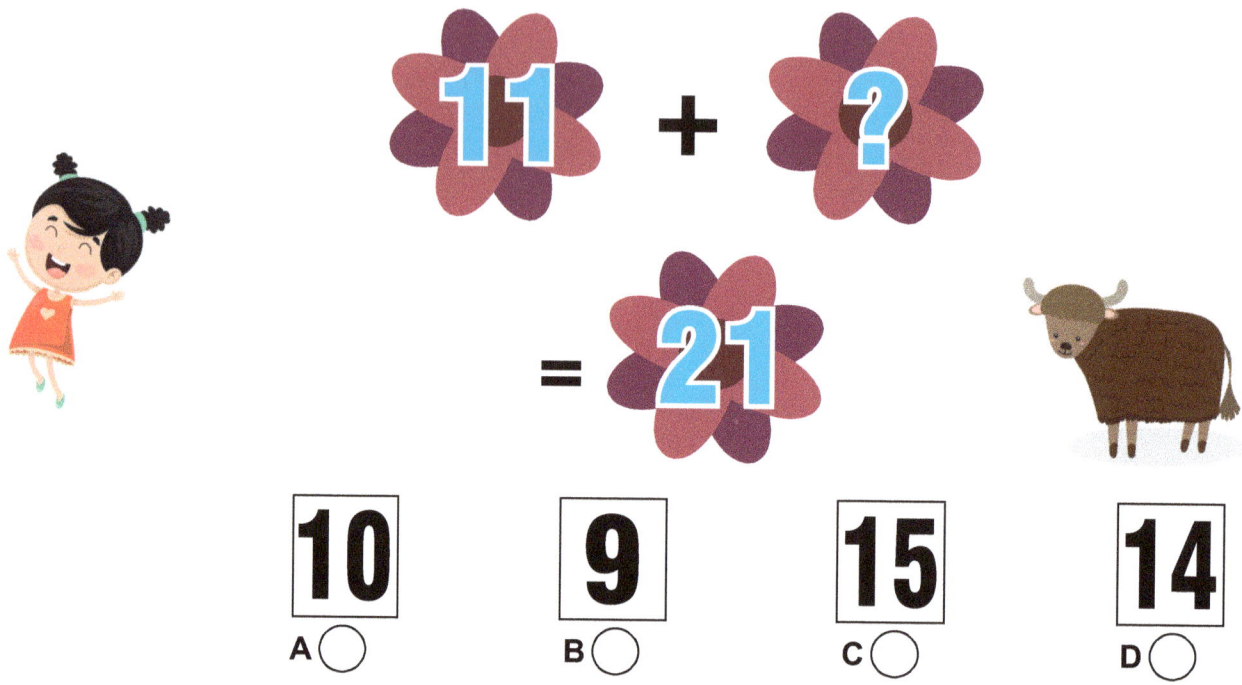

10	9	15	14
A◯	B◯	C◯	D◯

Q-8 Look at the question and put your finger on the Zebra. Carter is wondering what is the missing number under the question mark ? Help him to find the missing number under the question mark and fill in the bubble.

0	3	9	6
A◯	B◯	C◯	D◯

Q-9

Look at the question and put your finger on the Peacock. Zoe is wondering what is the missing number under the question mark ? Help her to find the missing number under the question mark and fill in the bubble.

 +

=

1	9	6	2
A ◯	B ◯	C ◯	D ◯

Q-10

Look at the question and put your finger on the Bird. Joshua is wondering what is the missing number under the question mark ? Help him to find the missing number under the question mark and fill in the bubble.

 +

=

4	6	5	7
A ◯	B ◯	C ◯	D ◯

www.math-knots.com

Q-11 Look at the question and put your finger on the Cow. Julia is wondering what is the missing number under the question mark ? Help her to find the missing number under the question mark and fill in the bubble.

$$12 + ? + 12 = 36$$

14	12	10	11
A○	B○	C○	D○

Q-12 Look at the question and put your finger on the Dolphin. Aaron is wondering what is the missing number under the question mark ? Help him to find the missing number under the question mark and fill in the bubble.

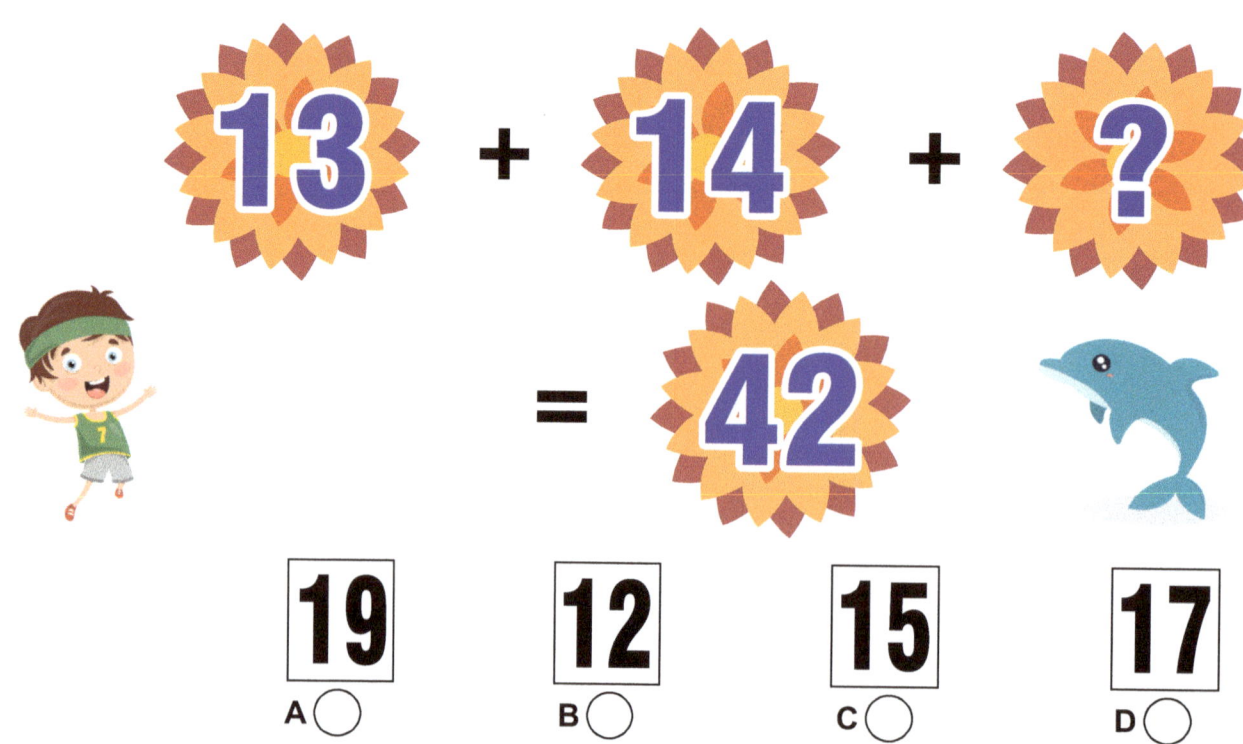

$$13 + 14 + ? = 42$$

19	12	15	17
A○	B○	C○	D○

www.math-knots.com

Q-13 Look at the question and put your finger on the Elephant. Henry is wondering what is the missing number under the question mark ? Help him to find the missing number under the question mark and fill in the bubble.

$25 + ? + 25 = 50$

A ◯ **0** B ◯ **10** C ◯ **25** D ◯ **20**

Q-14 Look at the question and put your finger on the Fox. Stella is wondering what is the missing number under the question mark ? Help her to find the missing number under the question mark and fill in the bubble.

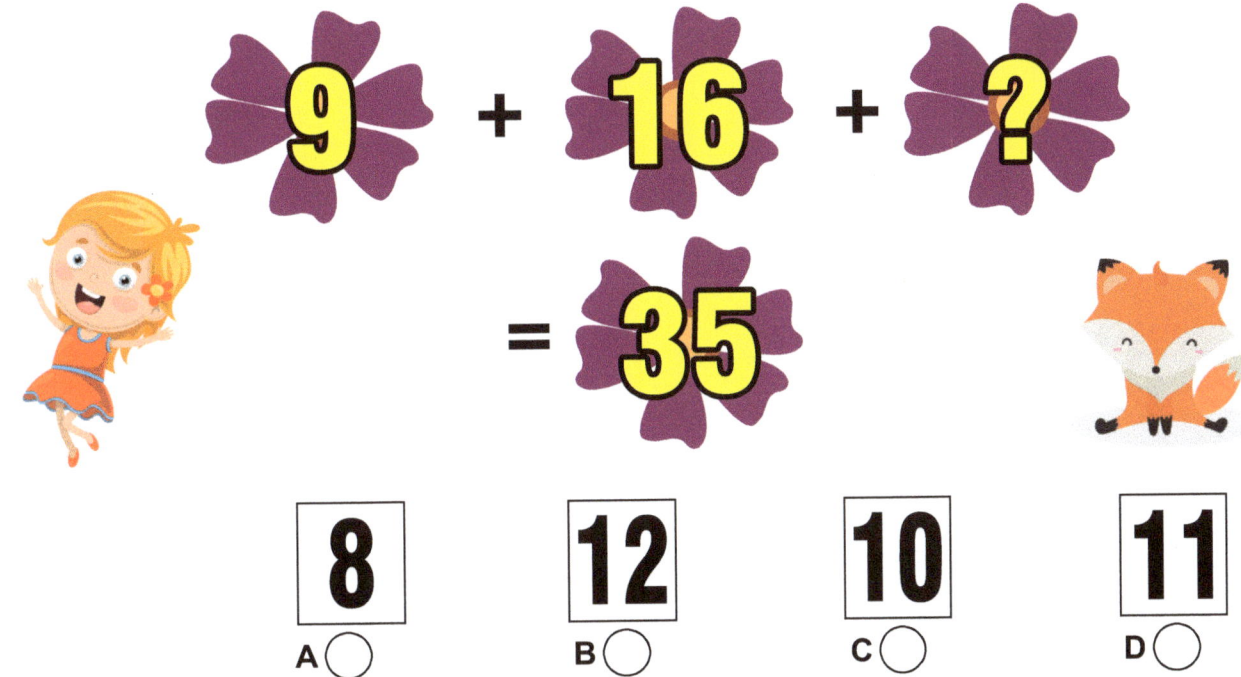

$9 + 16 + ? = 35$

A ◯ **8** B ◯ **12** C ◯ **10** D ◯ **11**

www.math-knots.com

Q-15 Look at the question and put your finger on the Giraffe. Ruby is wondering what is the missing number under the question mark ? Help her to find the missing number under the question mark and fill in the bubble.

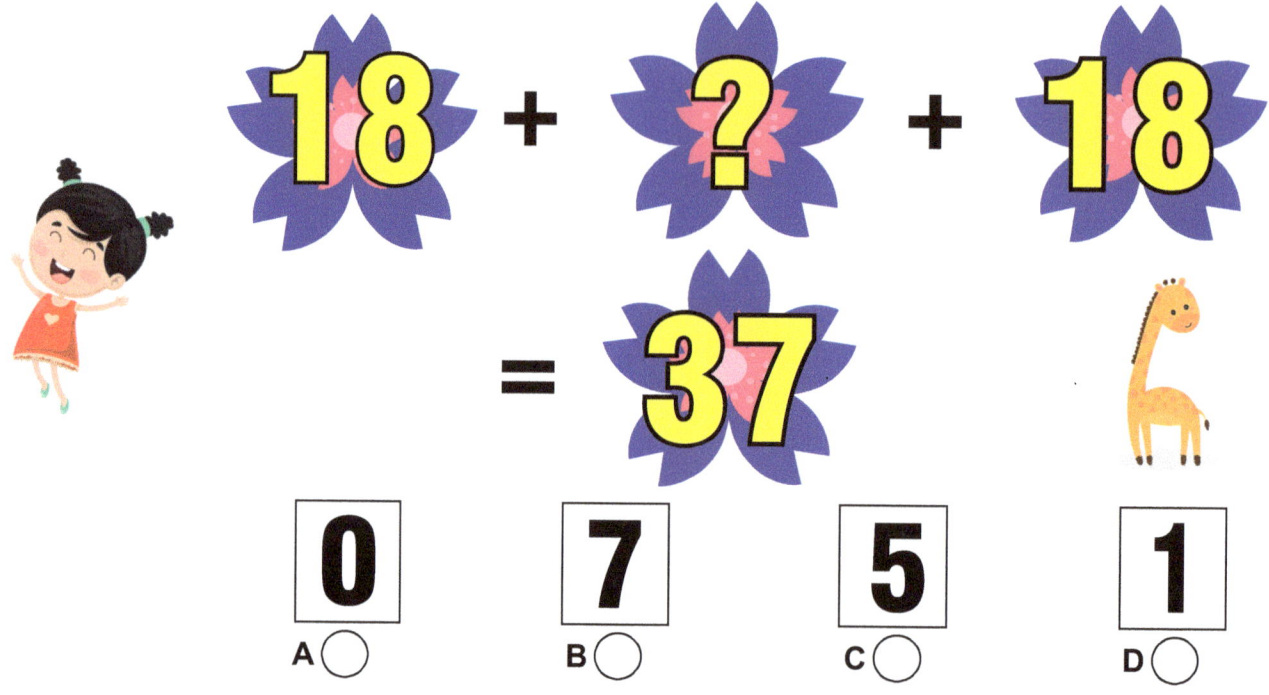

18 + ? + 18
= 37

A	B	C	D
0	7	5	1

Q-16 Look at the question and put your finger on the Hegehog. Diana is wondering what is the missing number under the question mark ? Help her to find the missing number under the question mark and fill in the bubble.

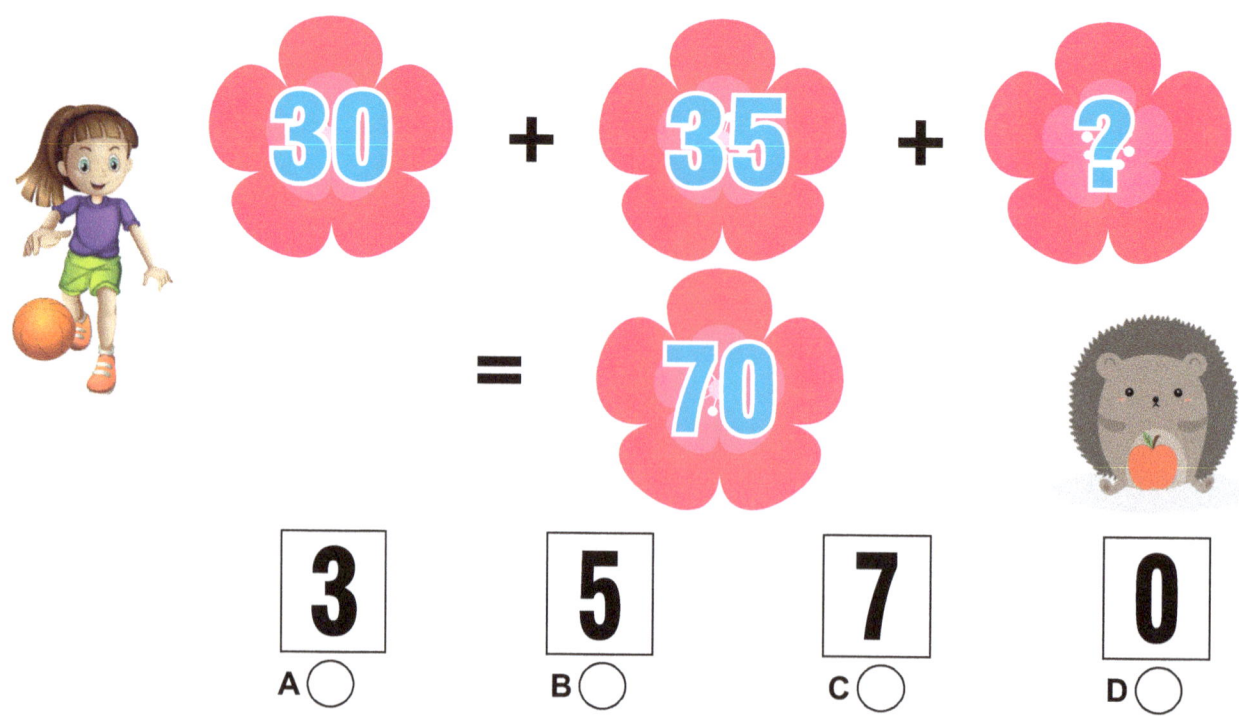

30 + 35 + ?
= 70

A	B	C	D
3	5	7	0

www.math-knots.com

Q-17 Look at the question and put your finger on the Iguana. Nina is wondering what is the missing number under the question mark ? Help her to find the missing number under the question mark and fill in the bubble.

$$40 + 41 + ? = 88$$

A ◯ 5   B ◯ 6   C ◯ 0   D ◯ 7

Q-18 Look at the question and put your finger on the Jelly Fish. Lola is wondering what is the missing number under the question mark ? Help her to find the missing number under the question mark and fill in the bubble.

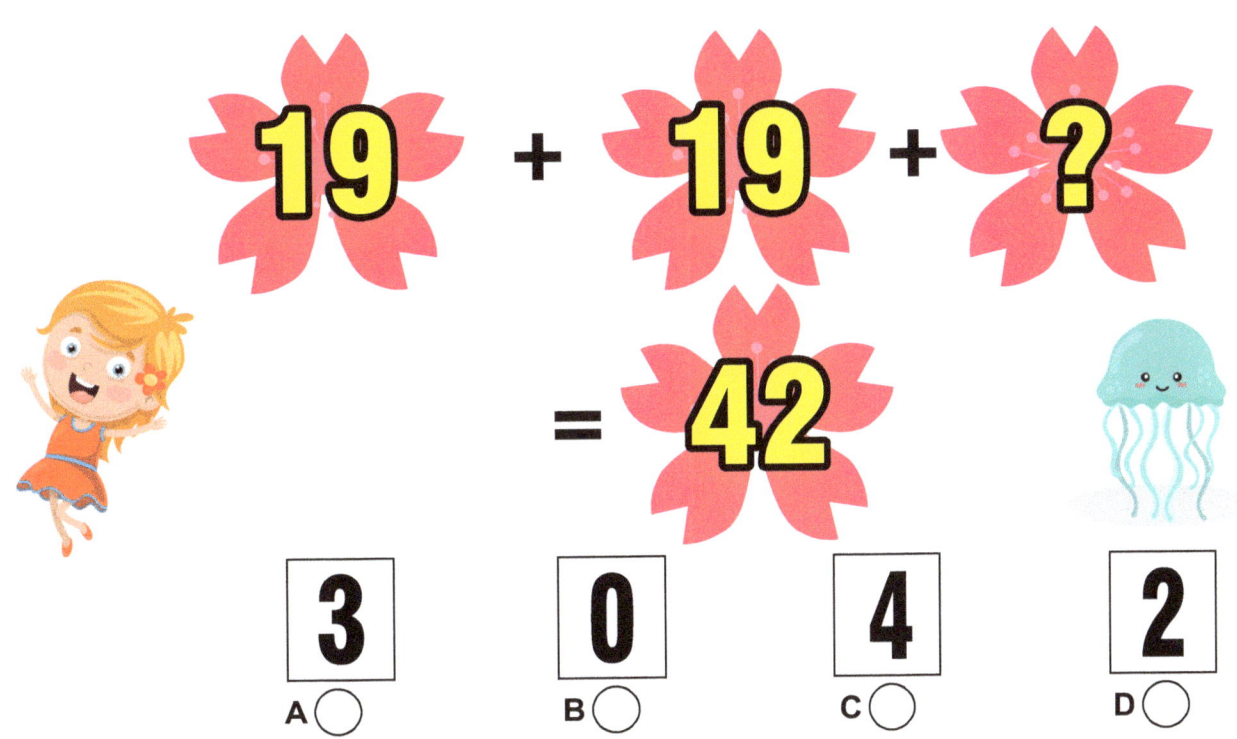

$$19 + 19 + ? = 42$$

A ◯ 3   B ◯ 0   C ◯ 4   D ◯ 2

www.math-knots.com

Q-19 Look at the question and put your finger on the Koala Bear. Erick is wondering what is the missing number under the question mark ? Help him to find the missing number under the question mark and fill in the bubble.

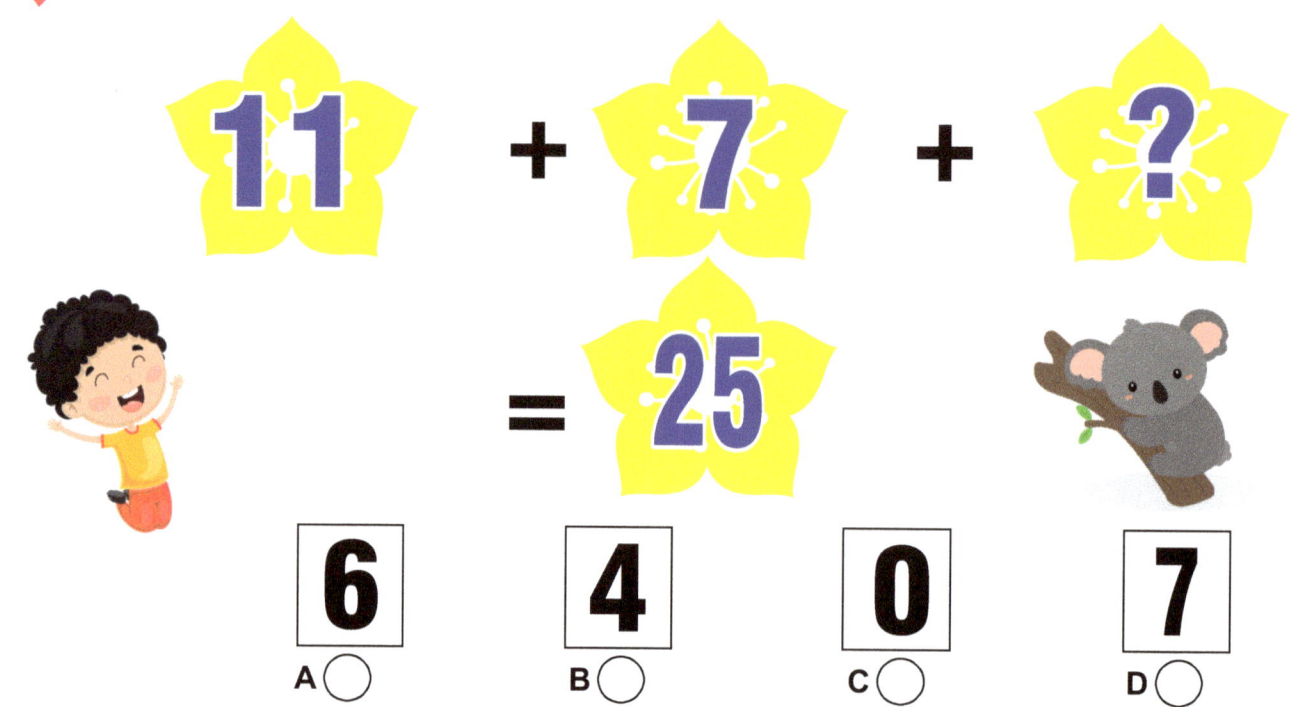

6	4	0	7
A◯	B◯	C◯	D◯

Q-20 Look at the question and put your finger on the Lion. Amber is wondering what is the missing number under the question mark ? Help her to find the missing number under the question mark and fill in the bubble.

50	25	10	20
A◯	B◯	C◯	D◯

www.math-knots.com

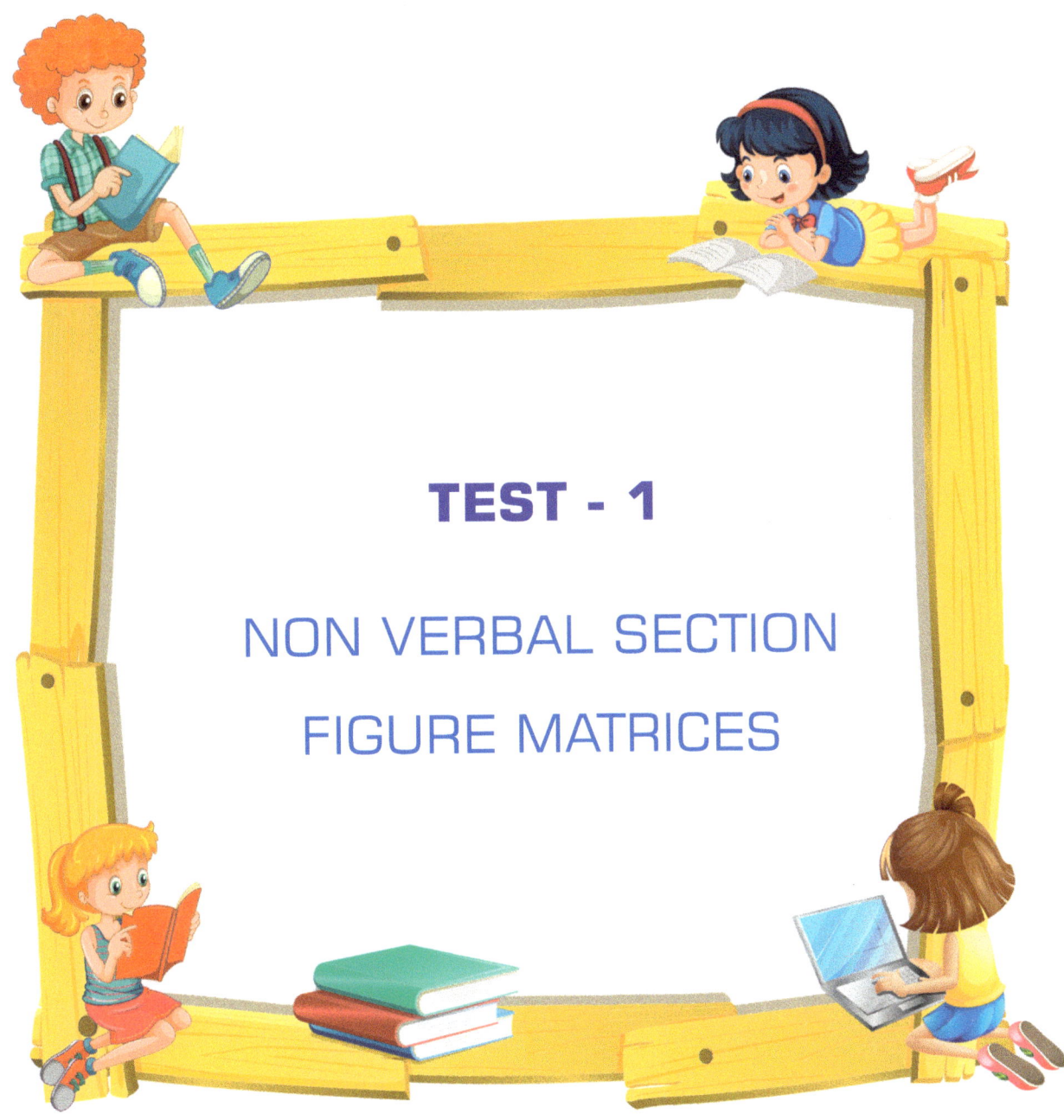

TEST - 1

NON VERBAL SECTION

FIGURE MATRICES

Lets Start the Test...

www.math-knots.com

Sample Look at the question with the Tree. The first three pictures belong to one group in a common way. Help Bob to find out which of the below options belong to the same group. Identify the correct picture and help him to bubble the right choice.

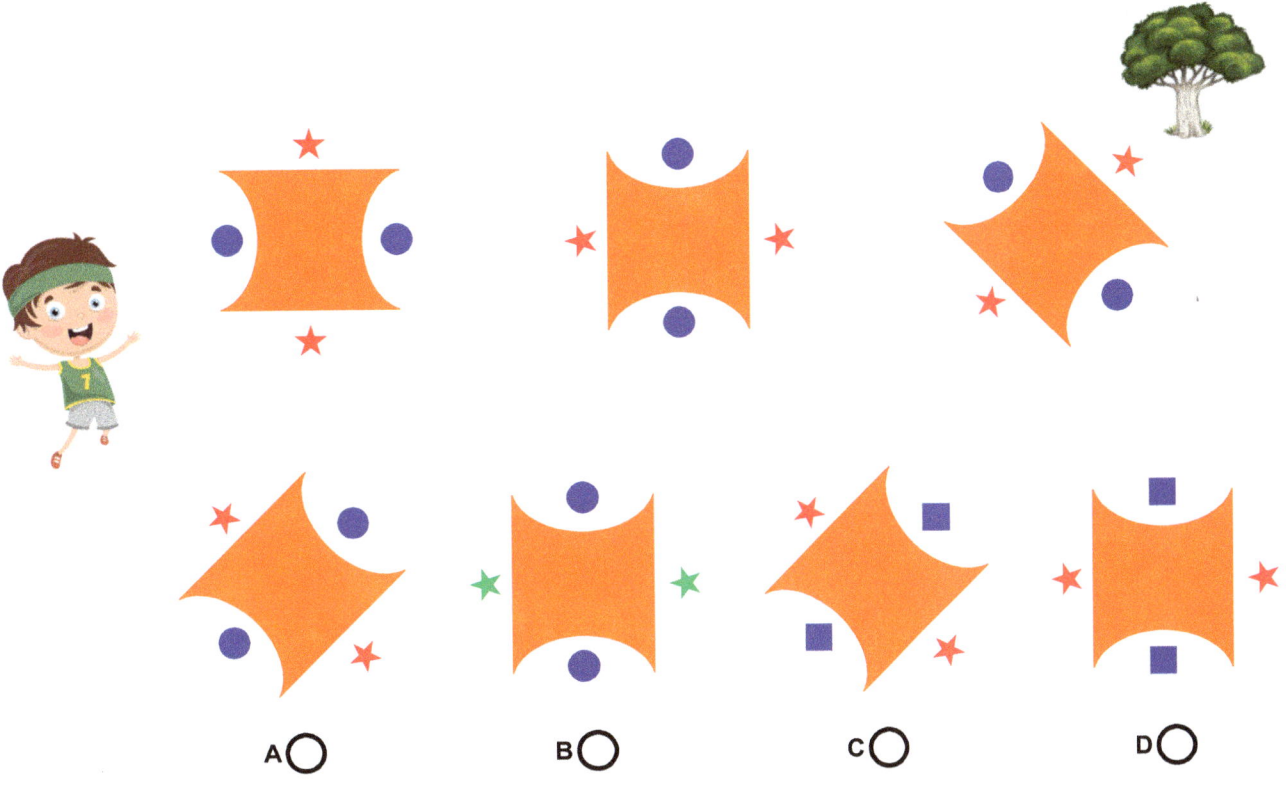

Solution : A

Option A is the only right choice. Option A matches the rest of the figure group in the same way. The other option vary in some way. Pay attention to all options before answering the right choice.

Q-1

Look at the question with the Coconut. The first three pictures belong to one group in a common way. Help Jacob to find out which of the below options belong to the same group. Identify the correct picture and help him to bubble the right choice.

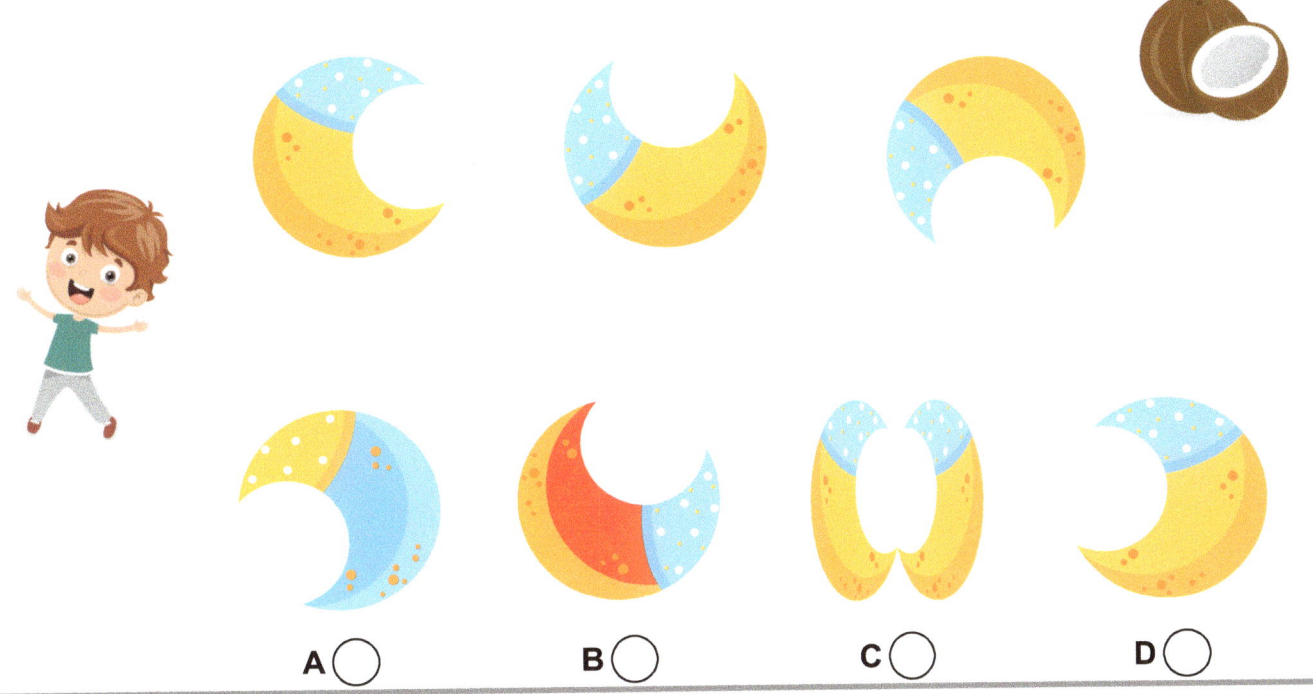

A ◯ B ◯ C ◯ D ◯

Q-2

Look at the question with the Banana. The first three pictures belong to one group in a common way. Help Emma to find out which of the below options belong to the same group. Identify the correct picture and help her to bubble the right choice.

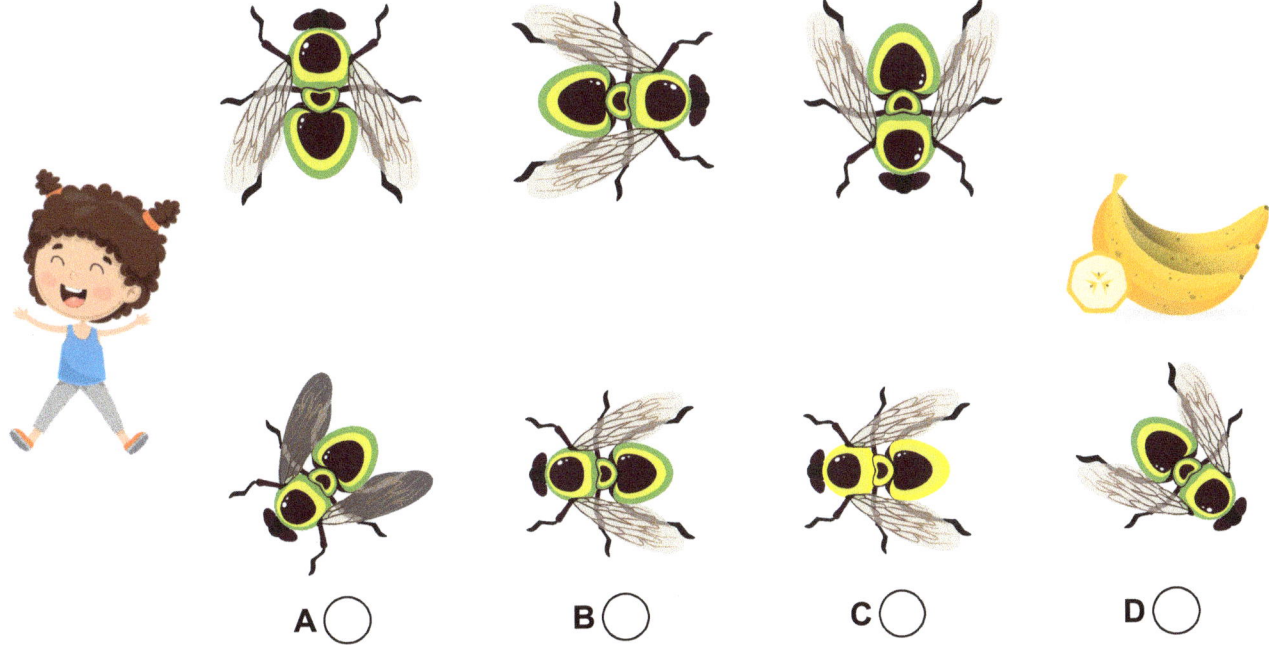

A ◯ B ◯ C ◯ D ◯

www.math-knots.com

Q-3 Look at the question with the Mangosteen. The first three pictures belong to one group in a common way. Help Michael to find out which of the below options belong to the same group. Identify the correct picture and help him to bubble the right choice.

A ◯   B ◯   C ◯   D ◯

Q-4 Look at the question with the Apple. The first three pictures belong to one group in a common way. Help Olivia to find out which of the below options belong to the same group. Identify the correct picture and help her to bubble the right choice.

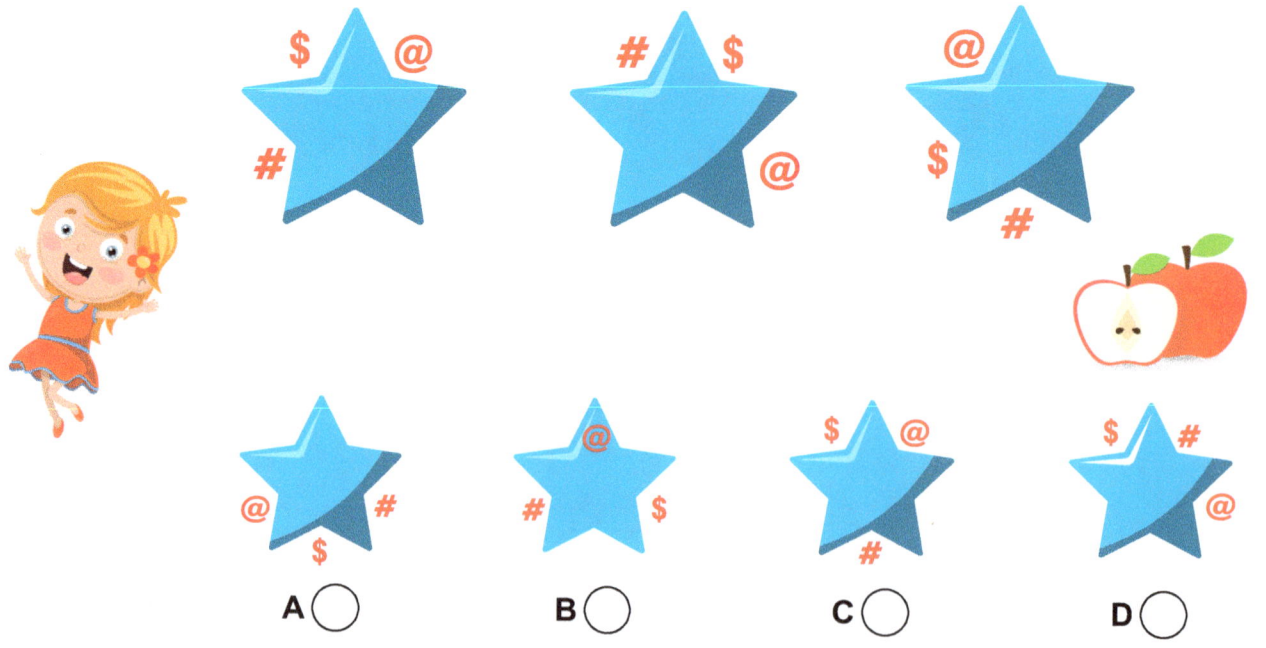

A ◯   B ◯   C ◯   D ◯

www.math-knots.com

Q-5

Look at the question with the Pear. The first three pictures belong to one group in a common way. Help Matthew to find out which of the below options belong to the same group. Identify the correct picture and help him to bubble the right choice.

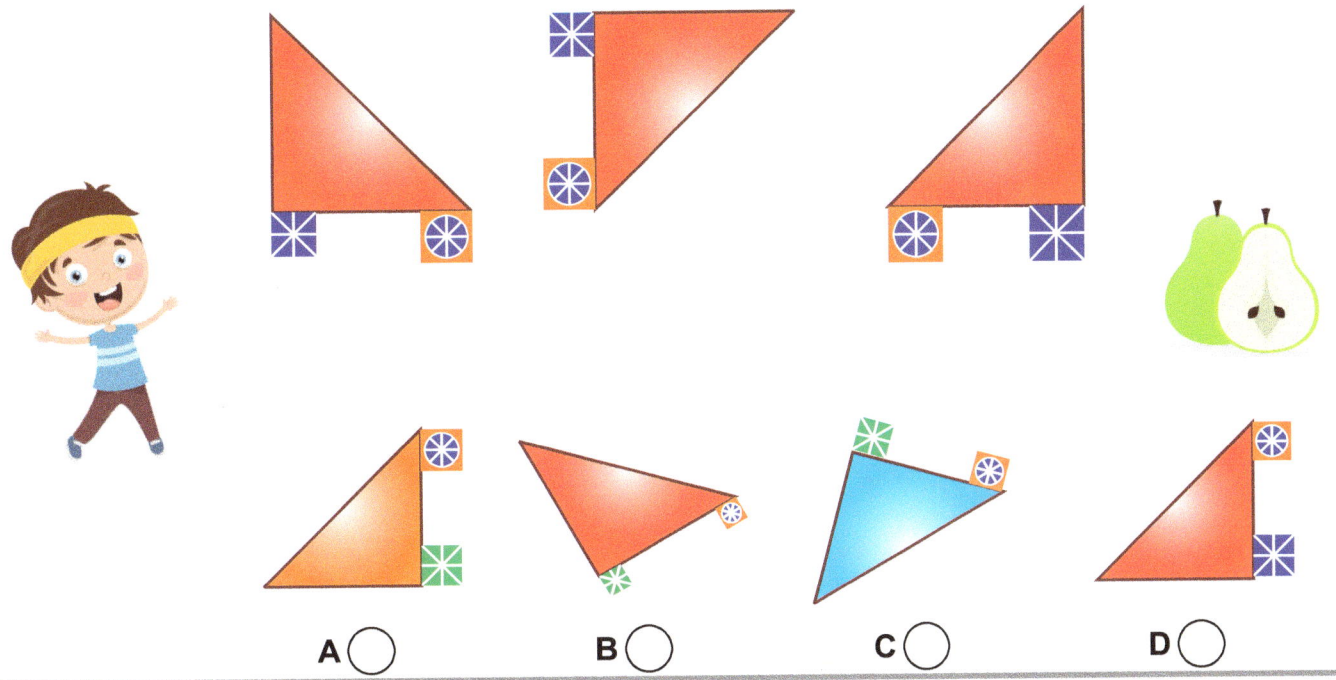

A ◯   B ◯   C ◯   D ◯

Q-6

Look at the question with the Durian. The first three pictures belong to one group in a common way. Help Sophia to find out which of the below options belong to the same group. Identify the correct picture and help her to bubble the right choice.

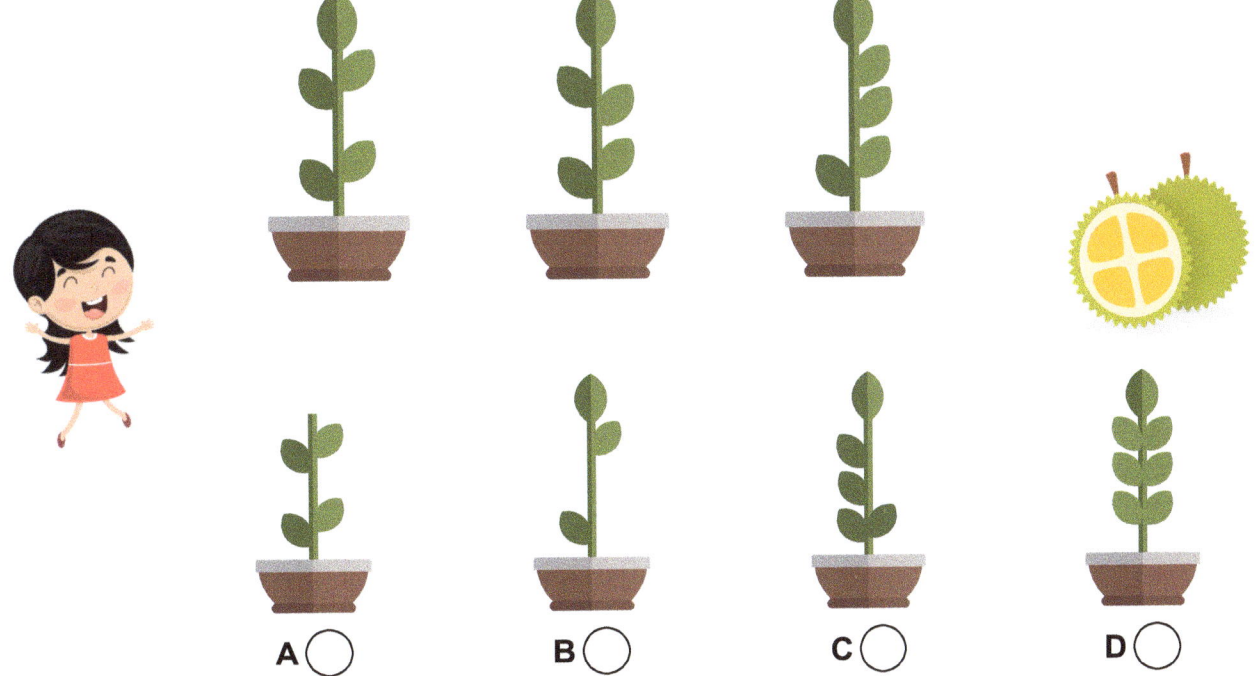

A ◯   B ◯   C ◯   D ◯

Q-7

Look at the question with the Peach. The first three pictures belong to one group in a common way. Help Ethan to find out which of the below options belong to the same group. Identify the correct picture and help him to bubble the right choice.

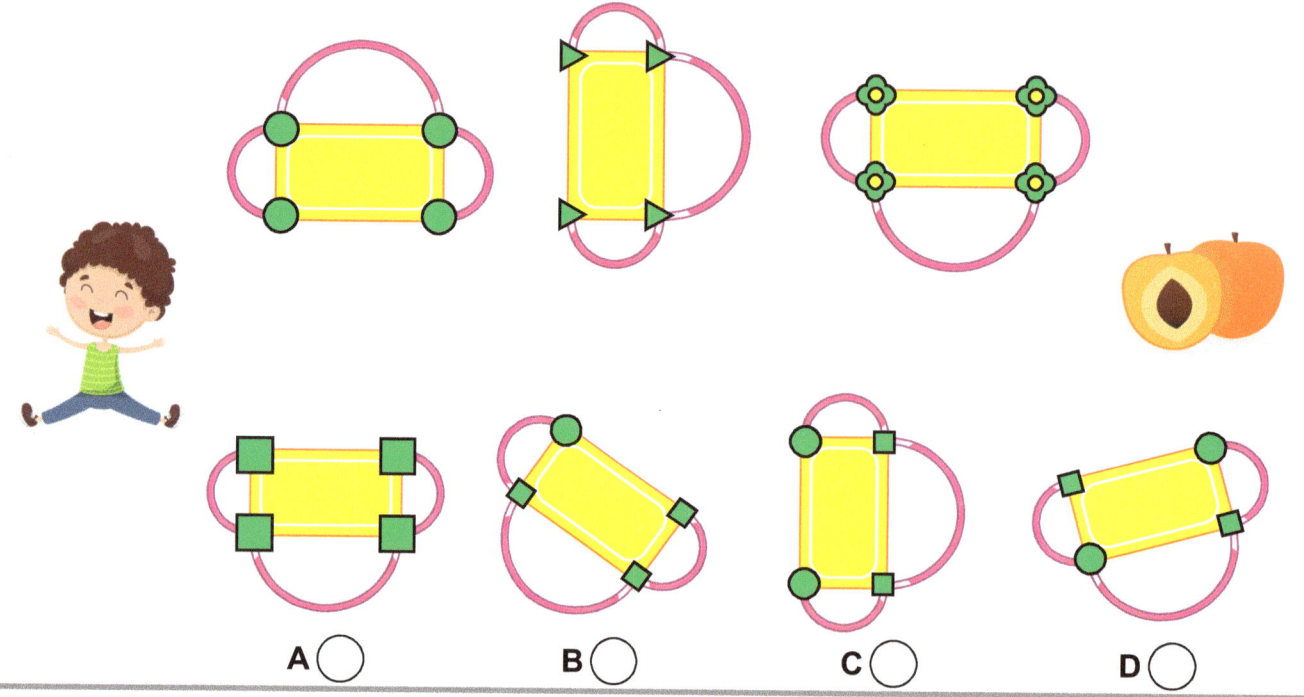

A ⃝   B ⃝   C ⃝   D ⃝

Q-8

Look at the question with the Dragon Fruit. The first three pictures belong to one group in a common way. Help Elizabeth to find out which of the below options belong to the same group. Identify the correct picture and help her to bubble the right choice.

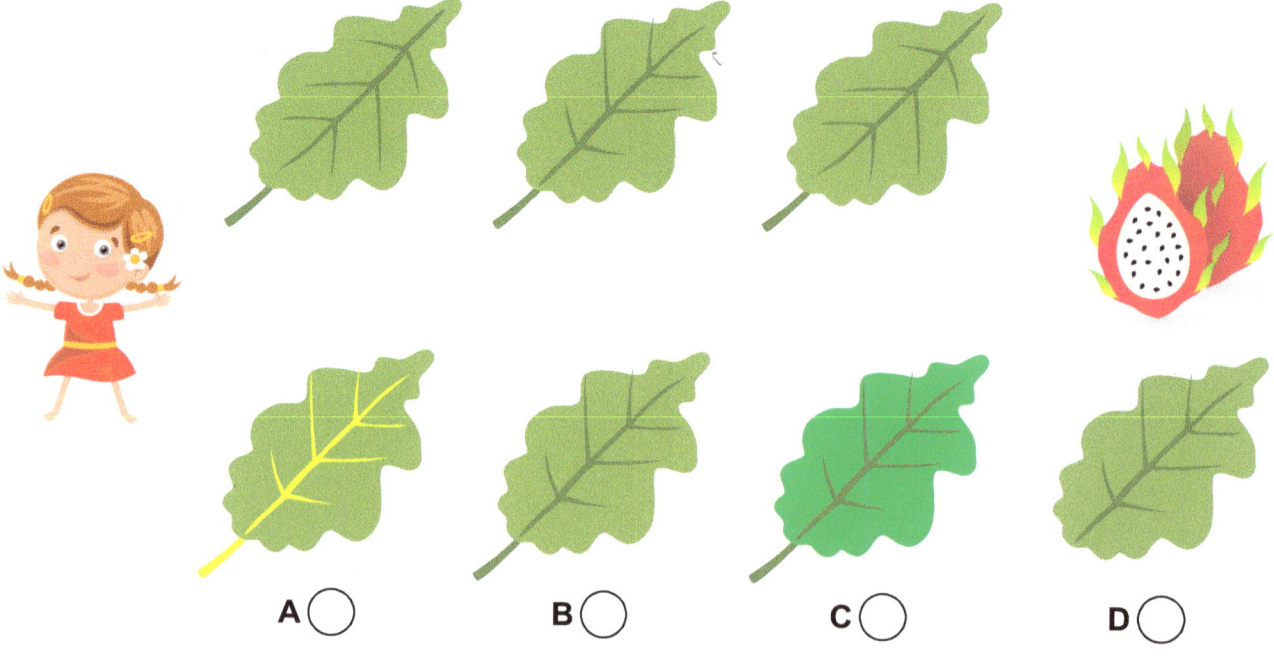

A ⃝   B ⃝   C ⃝   D ⃝

www.math-knots.com

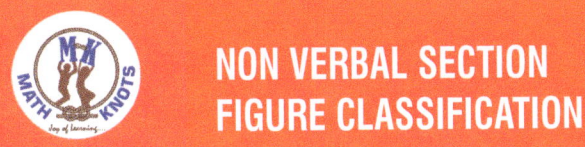
Q-9

Look at the question with the Plum. The first three pictures belong to one group in a common way. Help Andrew to find out which of the below options belong to the same group. Identify the correct picture and help him to bubble the right choice.

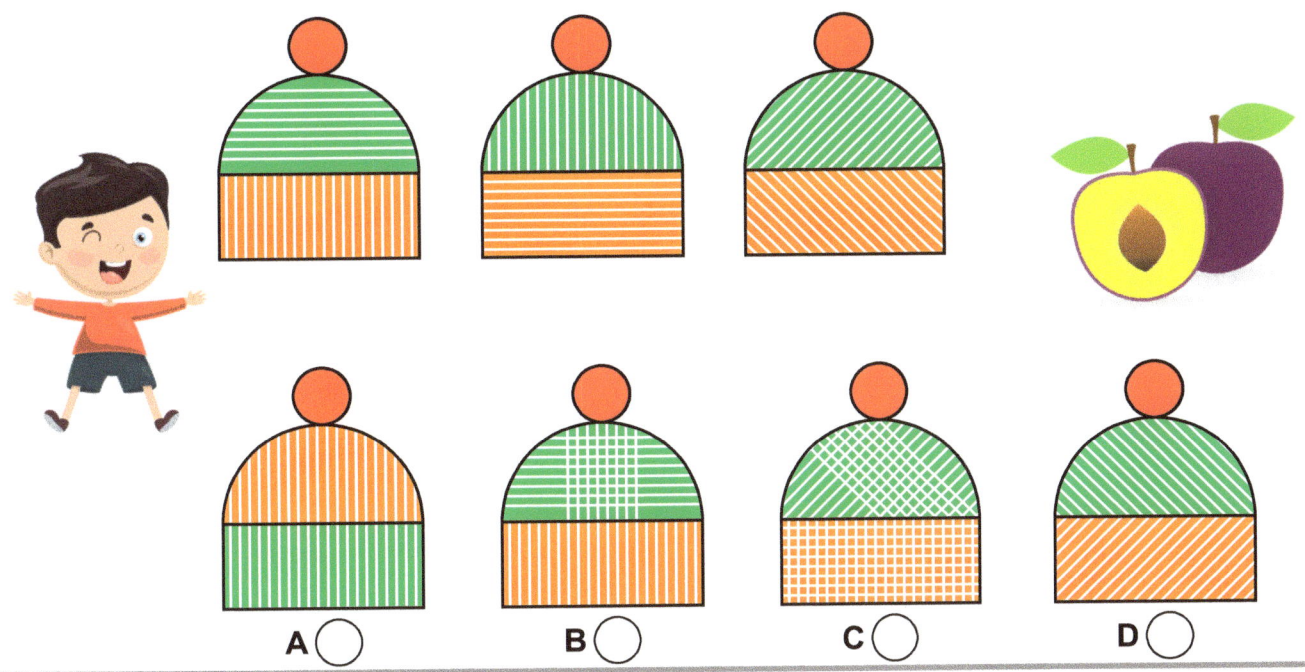

A◯ B◯ C◯ D◯

Q-10

Look at the question with the Papaya. The first three pictures belong to one group in a common way. Help Jessica to find out which of the below options belong to the same group. Identify the correct picture and help her to bubble the right choice.

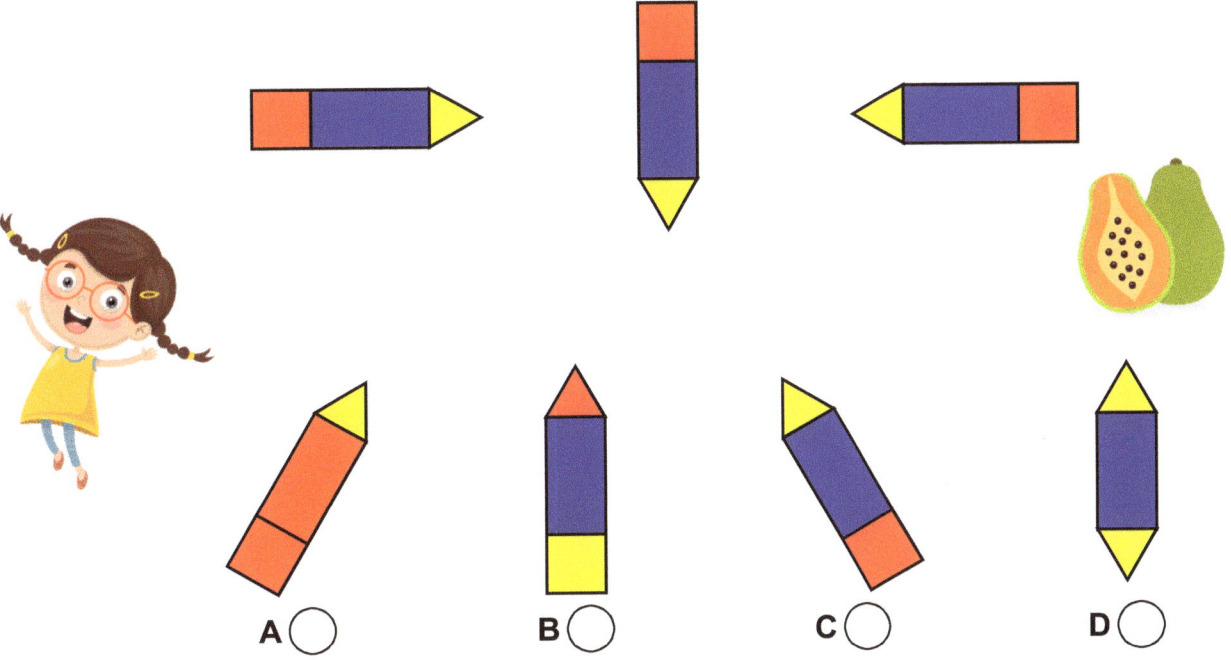

A◯ B◯ C◯ D◯

www.math-knots.com

Q-11

Look at the question with the Watermelon. The first three pictures belong to one group in a common way. Help Daniel to find out which of the below options belong to the same group. Identify the correct picture and help him to bubble the right choice.

 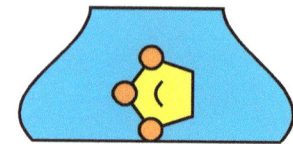 

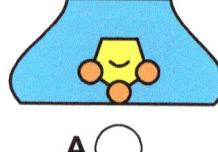 A ○ 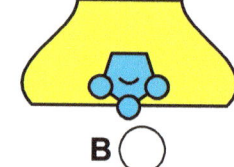 B ○ 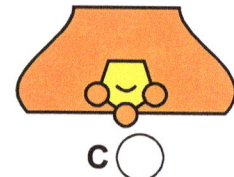 C ○  D ○

Q-12

Look at the question with the Orange. The first three pictures belong to one group in a common way. Help Julia to find out which of the below options belong to the same group. Identify the correct picture and help her to bubble the right choice.

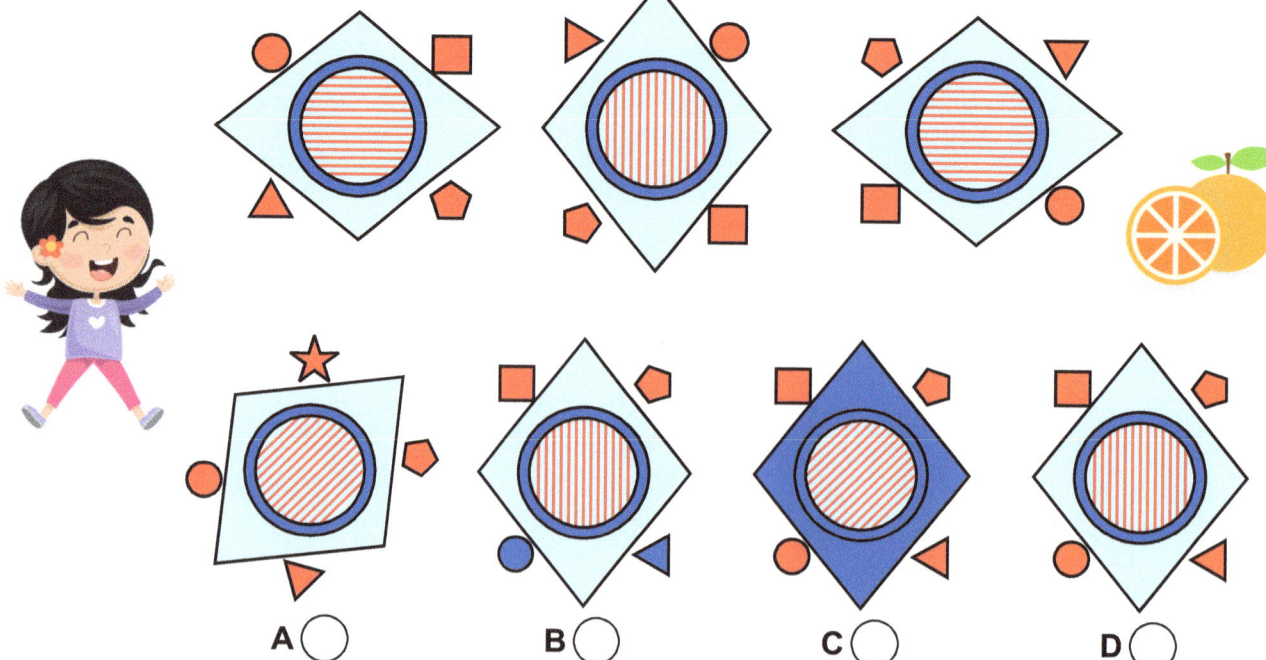

A ○   B ○   C ○   D ○

www.math-knots.com

Q-13 Look at the question with the Kiwi. The first three pictures belong to one group in a common way. Help Anthony to find out which of the below options belong to the same group. Identify the correct picture and help him to bubble the right choice.

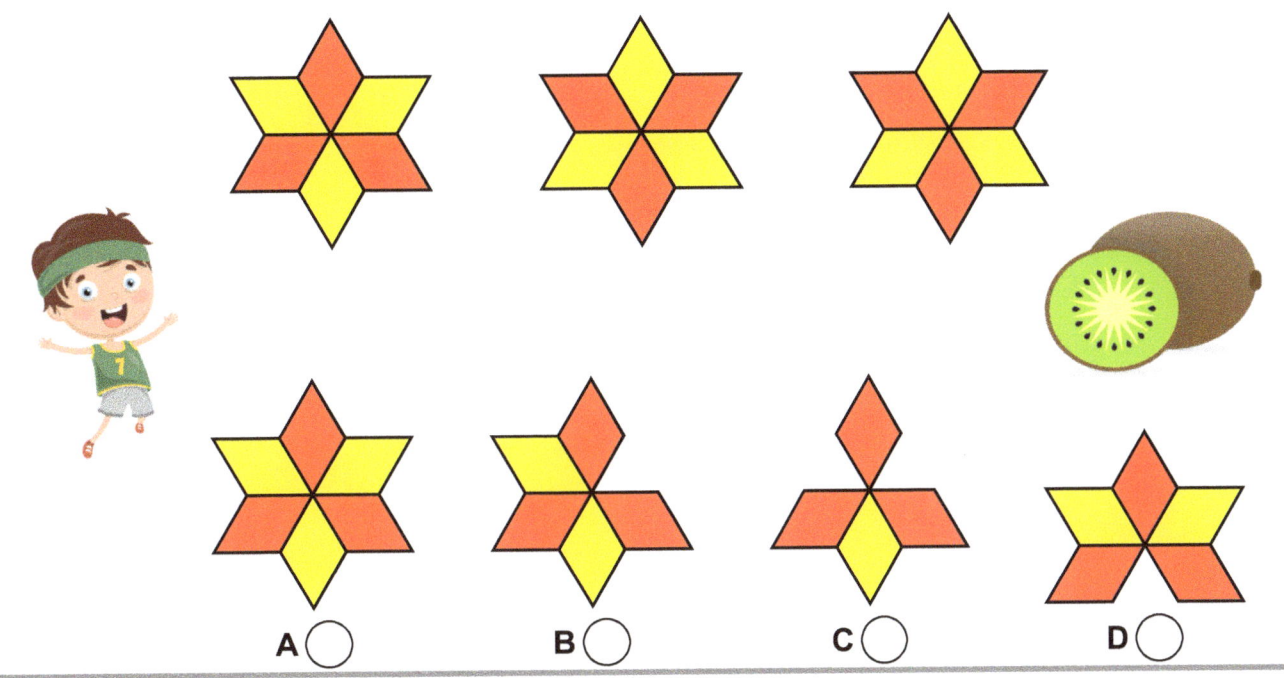

A◯ B◯ C◯ D◯

Q-14 Look at the question with the Lemon. The first three pictures belong to one group in a common way. Help Jenna to find out which of the below options belong to the same group. Identify the correct picture and help her to bubble the right choice.

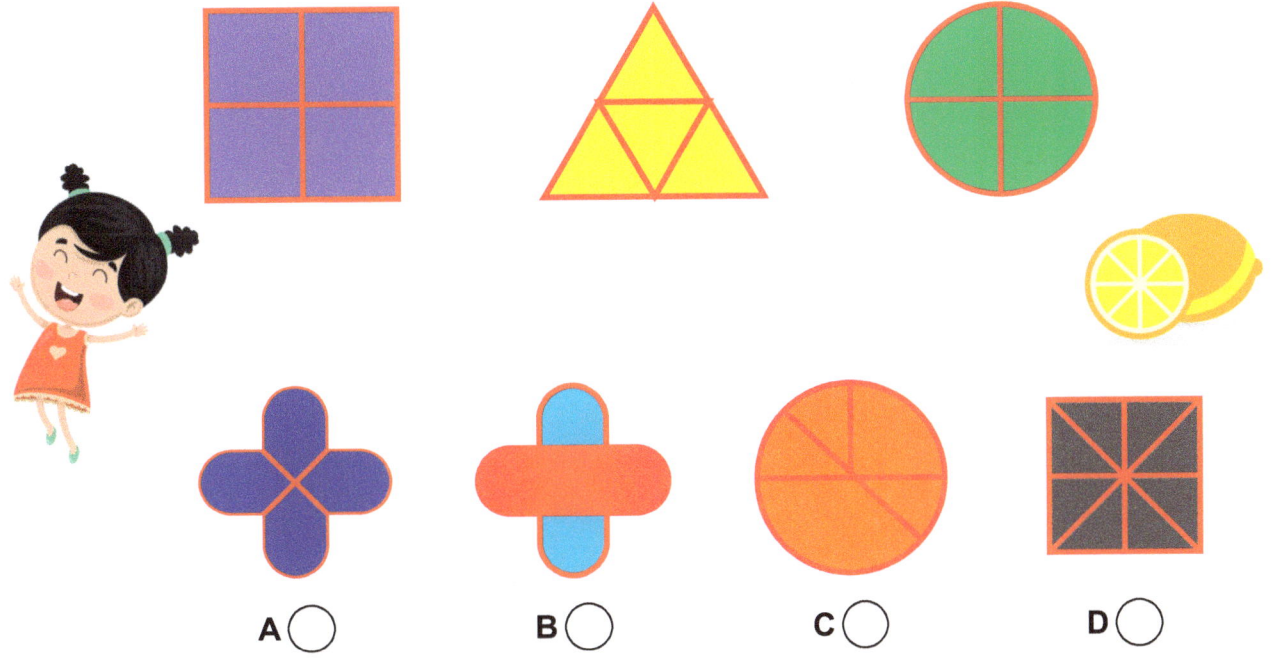

A◯ B◯ C◯ D◯

www.math-knots.com

Q-15 Look at the question with the Avocado. The first three pictures belong to one group in a common way. Help William to find out which of the below options belong to the same group. Identify the correct picture and help him to bubble the right choice.

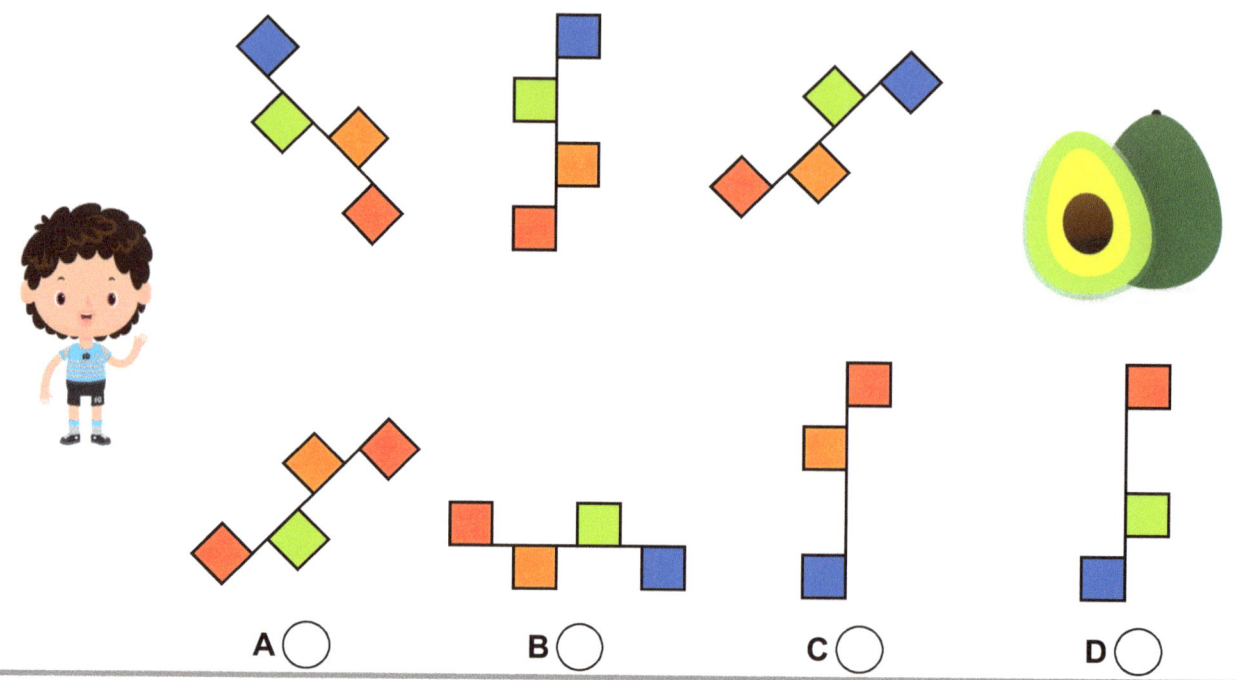

A ◯   B ◯   C ◯   D ◯

Q-16 Look at the question with the Grapes. The first three pictures belong to one group in a common way. Help Mary to find out which of the below options belong to the same group. Identify the correct picture and help her to bubble the right choice.

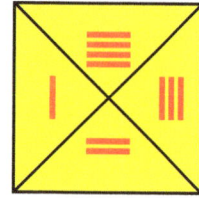

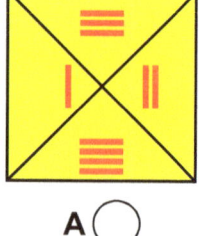
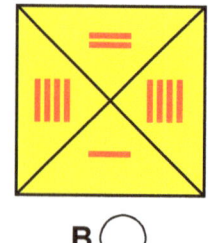
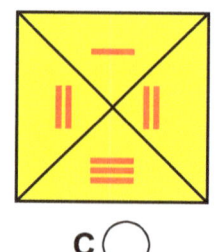
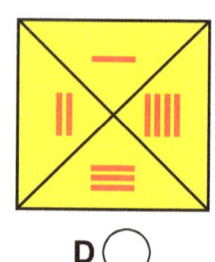

A ◯   B ◯   C ◯   D ◯

www.math-knots.com

Q-17 Look at the question with the Capsicum. The first three pictures belong to one group in a common way. Help David to find out which of the below options belong to the same group. Identify the correct picture and help him to bubble the right choice.

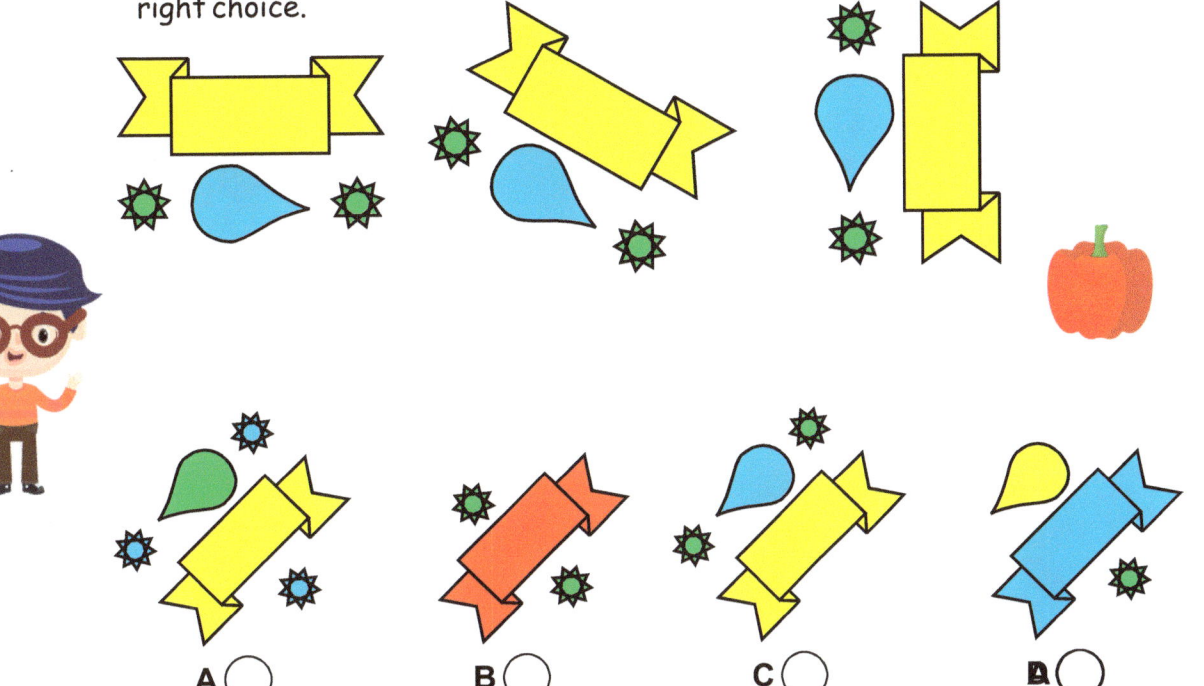

A ◯   B ◯   C ◯   D ◯

Q-18 Look at the question with the Cucumber. The first three pictures belong to one group in a common way. Help Amy to find out which of the below options belong to the same group. Identify the correct picture and help her to bubble the right choice.

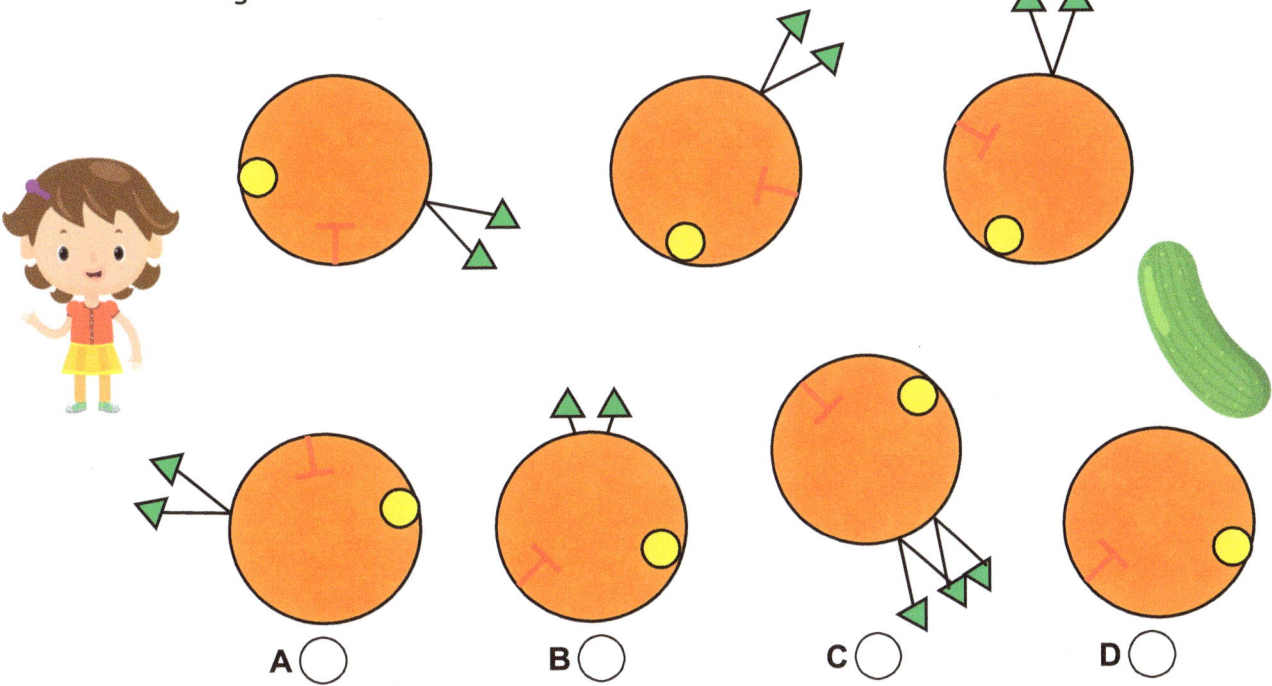

A ◯   B ◯   C ◯   D ◯

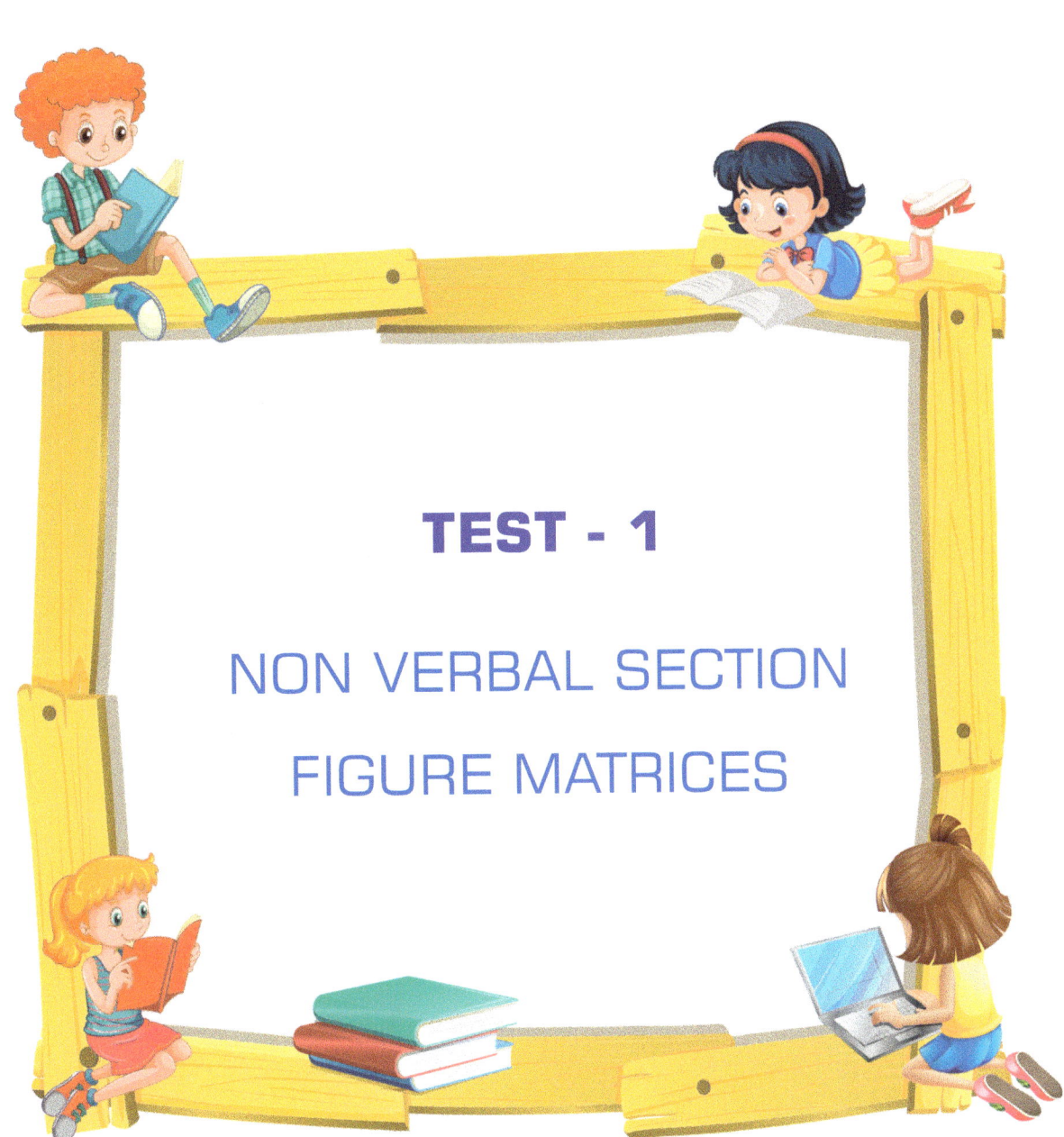

TEST - 1

NON VERBAL SECTION

FIGURE MATRICES

Lets Start the Test...

www.math-knots.com

Sample Look at the question with the Grapes. The first row has some thing in common as the second row. Can you help Mary to identify what goes in the space of the question mark from the four given options A, B, C, and D. Choose the correct option.

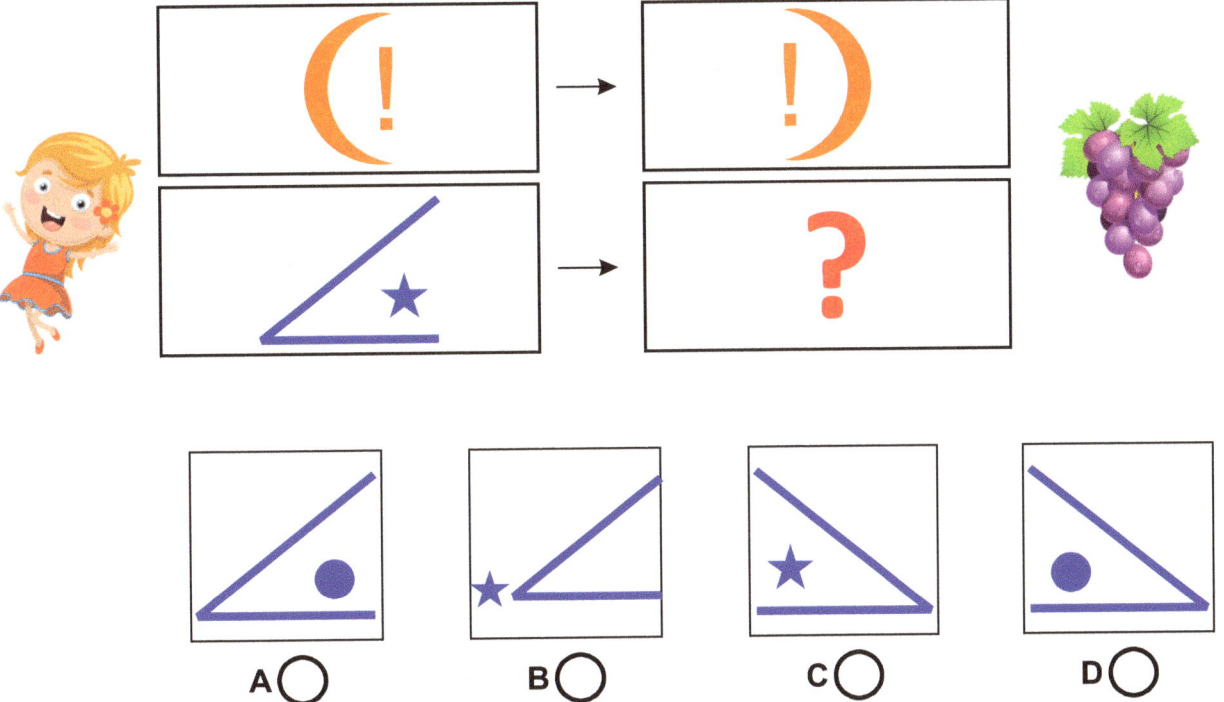

Solution : C

Option C is the right choice.

Two pictures in the first row are related in a certain way and the figures and flipped.

When the picture in the second row is flipped it will be match to option C. Students need to pay attention. Figures can be turning clock wise into anti clock wise, and other possibilities.

www.math-knots.com

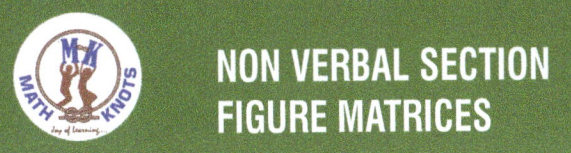
Q-1

Look at the question with the Lion Fish. The first row has some thing in common as the second row. Can you help Sophia to identify what goes in the space of the question mark from the four given options A, B, C, and D. Choose the correct option.

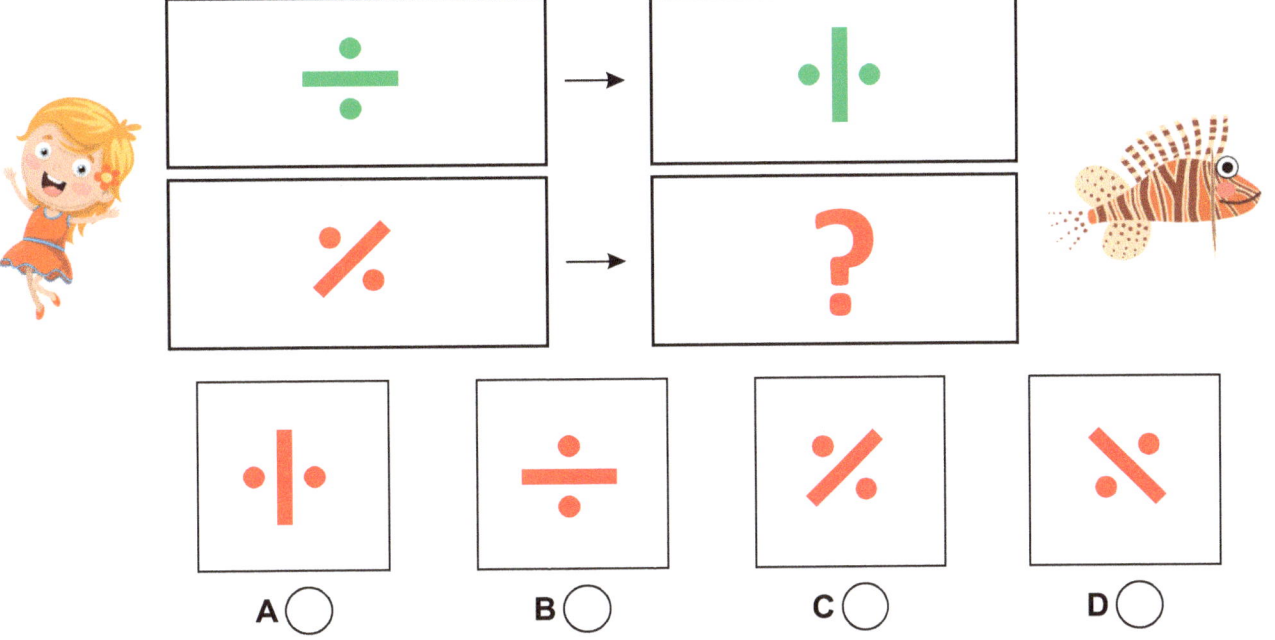

Q-2

Look at the question with the Blow Fish. The first row has some thing in common as the second row. Can you help George to identify what goes in the space of the question mark from the four given options A, B, C, and D. Choose the correct option.

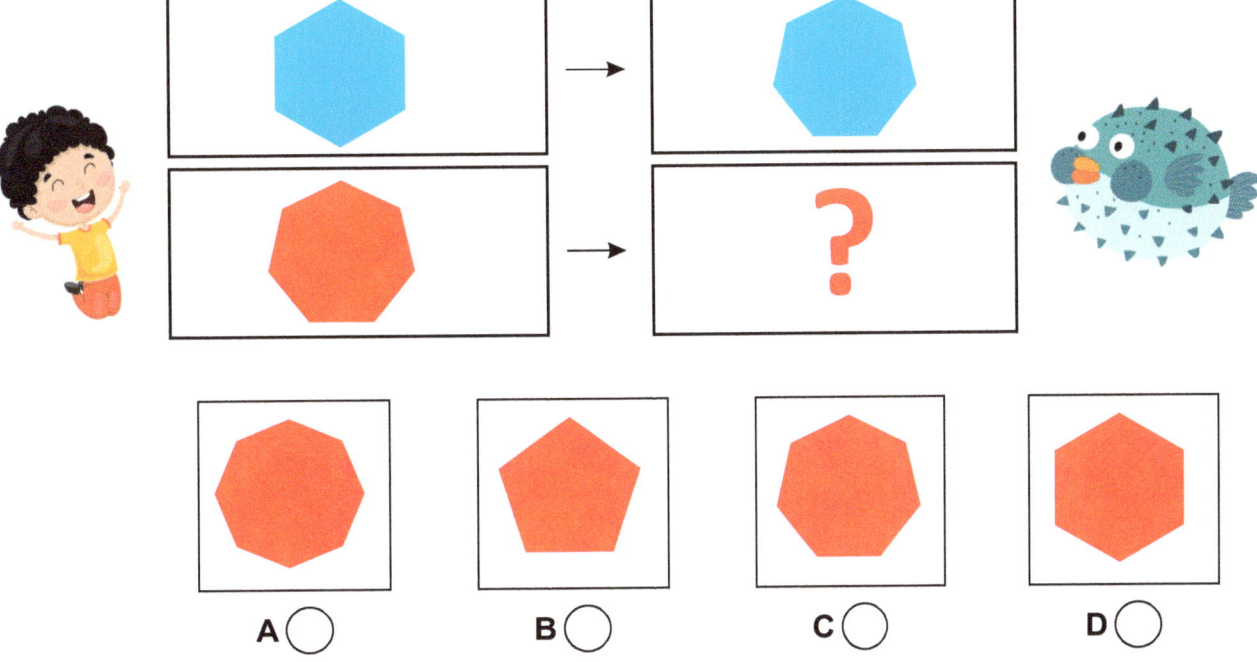

Q-3 Look at the question with the Jackknife Fish. The first row has some thing in common as the second row. Can you help Harry to identify what goes in the space of the question mark from the four given options A, B, C, and D. Choose the correct option.

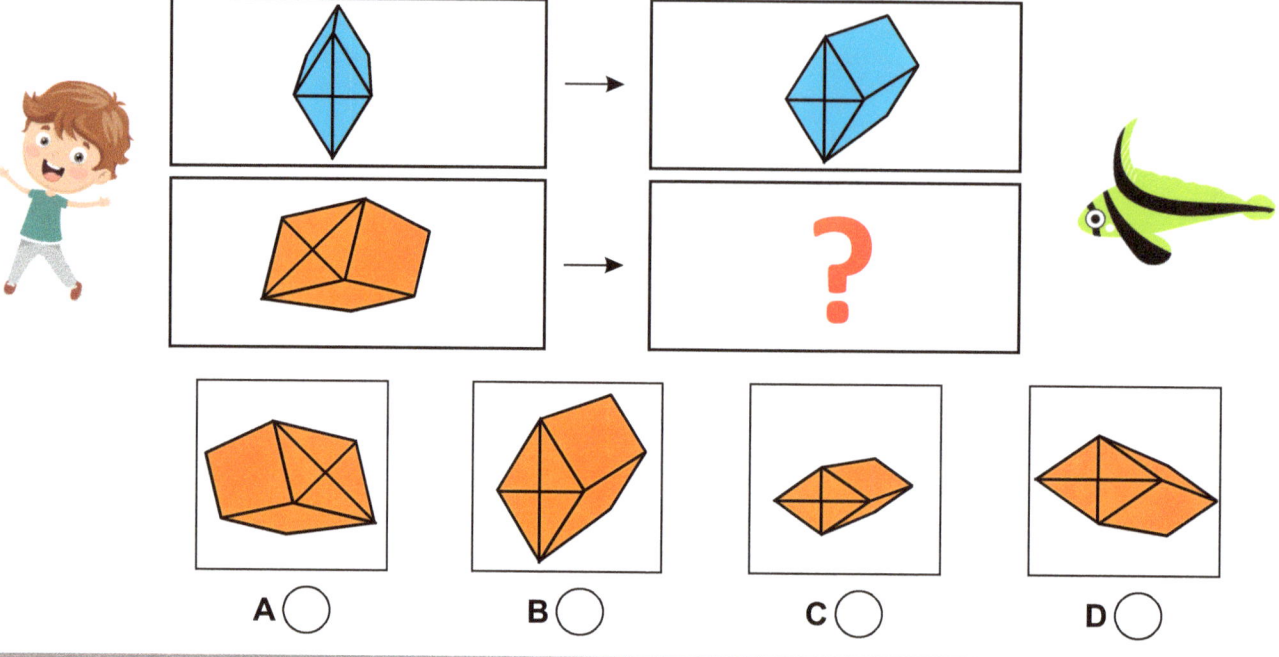

A ○ B ○ C ○ D ○

Q-4 Look at the question with the Sponge Fish. The first row has some thing in common as the second row. Can you help Jack to identify what goes in the space of the question mark from the four given options A, B, C, and D. Choose the correct option.

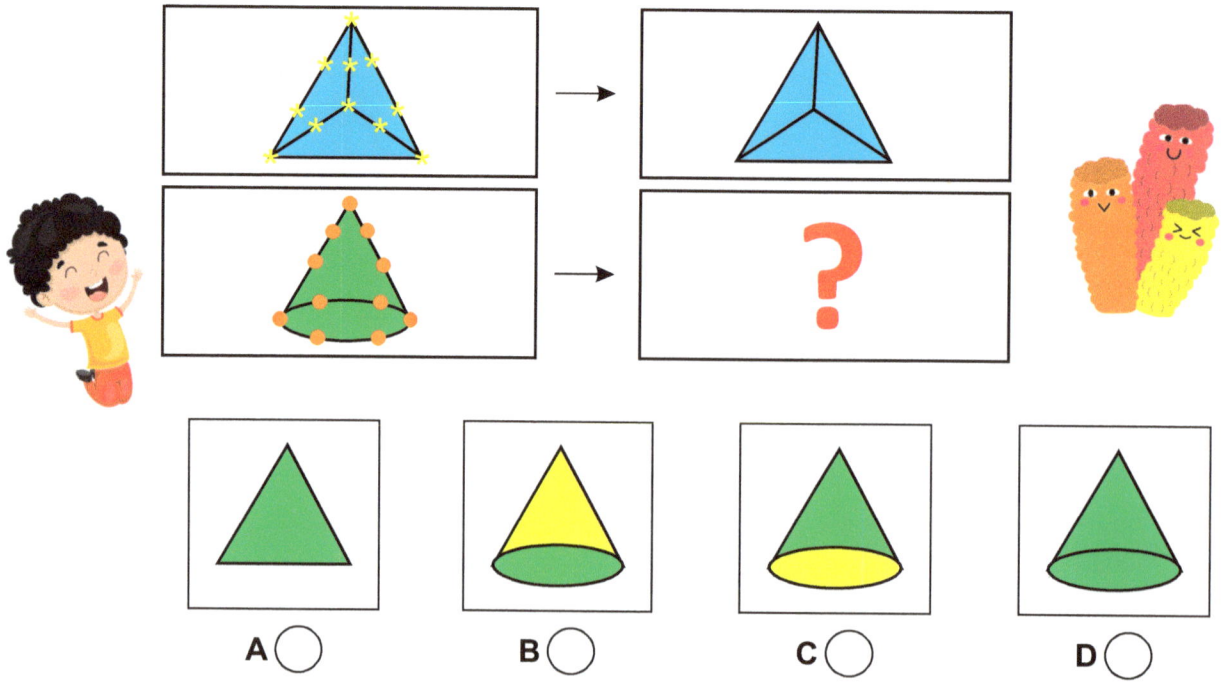

A ○ B ○ C ○ D ○

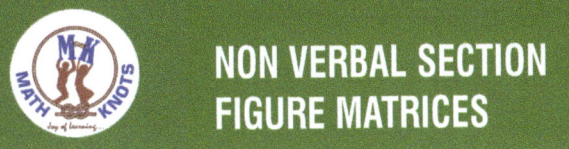
Q-5 Look at the question with the Blob Fish. The first row has some thing in common as the second row. Can you help Emily to identify what goes in the space of the question mark from the four given options A, B, C, and D. Choose the correct option.

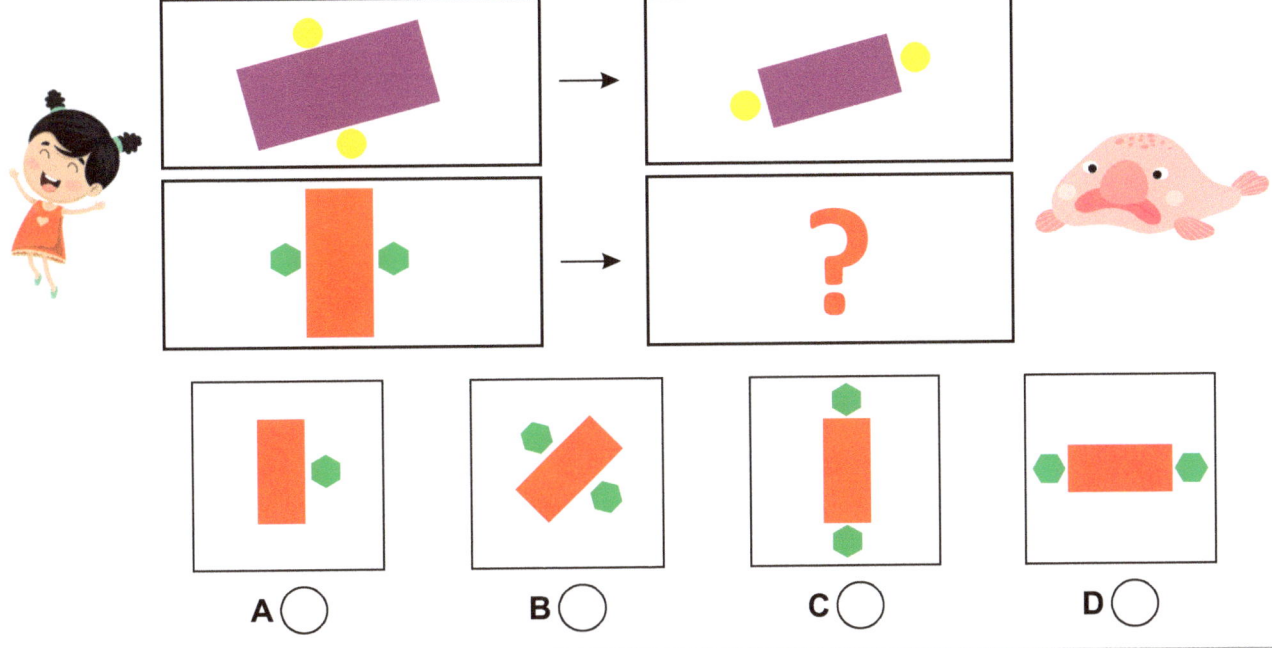

Q-6 Look at the question with the Hammerhead Shark. The first row has some thing in common as the second row. Can you help Isabella to identify what goes in the space of the question mark from the four given options A, B, C, and D. Choose the correct option.

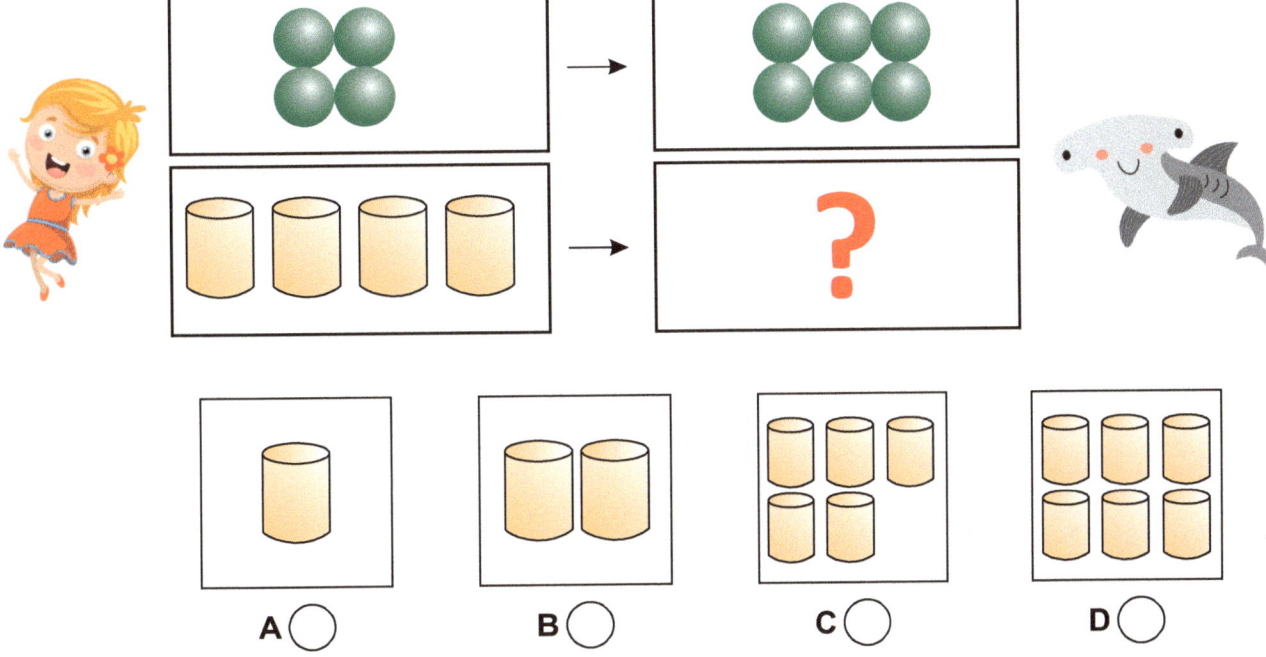

Q-7 Look at the question with the Angel Fish. The first row has some thing in common as the second row. Can you help Leo to identify what goes in the space of the question mark from the four given options A, B, C, and D. Choose the correct option.

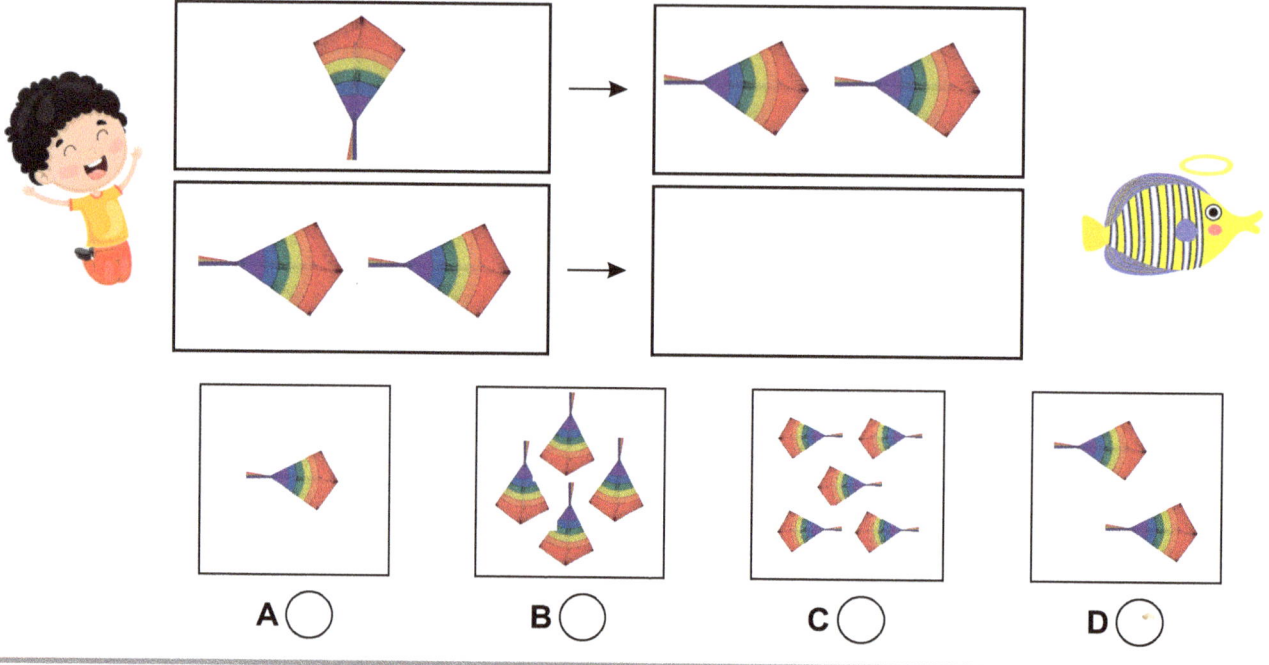

A◯ B◯ C◯ D◯

Q-8 Look at the question with the Red Waratah Anemone Fish. The first row has some thing in common as the second row. Can you help Alice to identify what goes in the space of the question mark from the four given options A, B, C, and D. Choose the correct option.

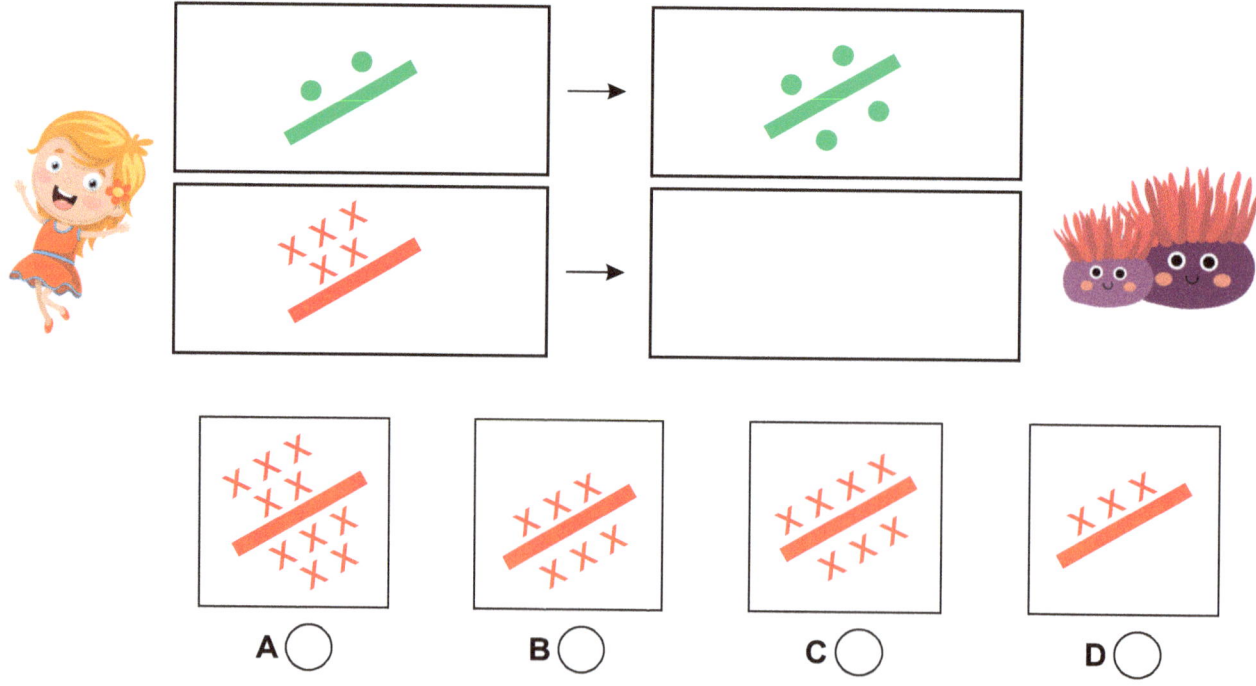

A◯ B◯ C◯ D◯

www.math-knots.com

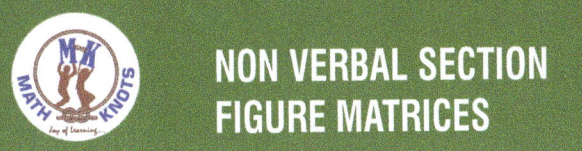

Q-9

Look at the question with the Hermit Crab. The first row has some thing in common as the second row. Can you help James to identify what goes in the space of the question mark from the four given options A, B, C, and D. Choose the correct option.

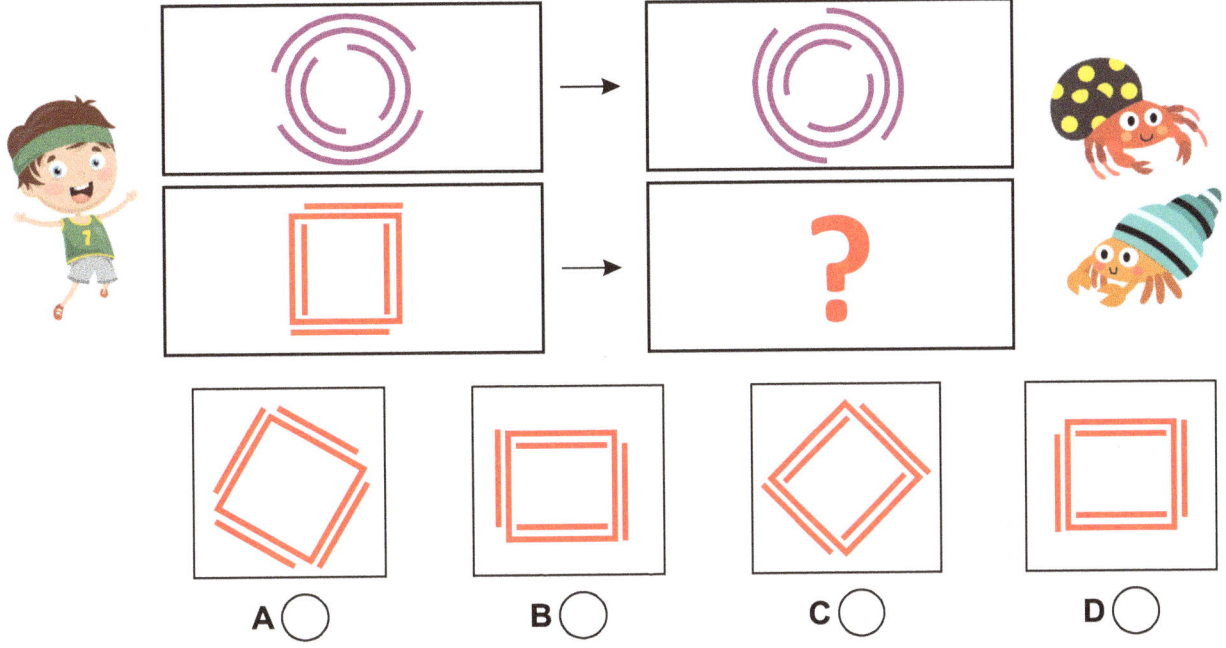

A ◯   B ◯   C ◯   D ◯

Q-10

Look at the question with the Manta Ray. The first row has some thing in common as the second row. Can you help Isha to identify what goes in the space of the question mark from the four given options A, B, C, and D. Choose the correct option.

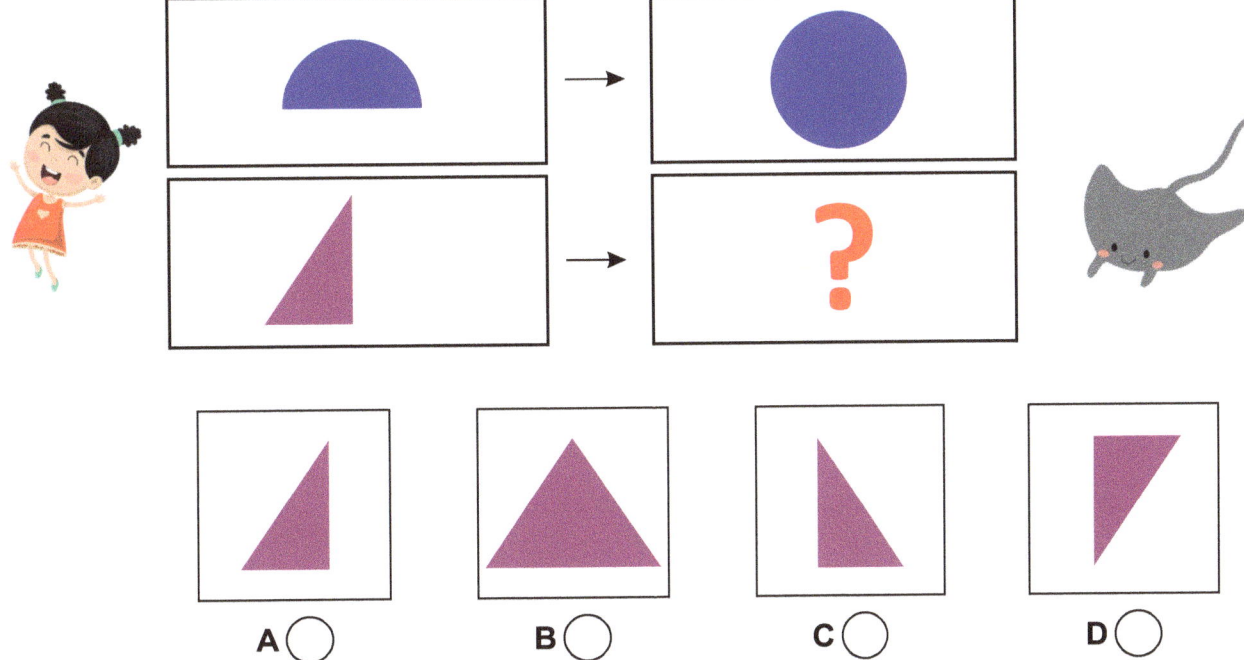

A ◯   B ◯   C ◯   D ◯

Q-11 Look at the question with the Mussel. The first row has some thing in common as the second row. Can you help Ava to identify what goes in the space of the question mark from the four given options A, B, C, and D. Choose the correct option.

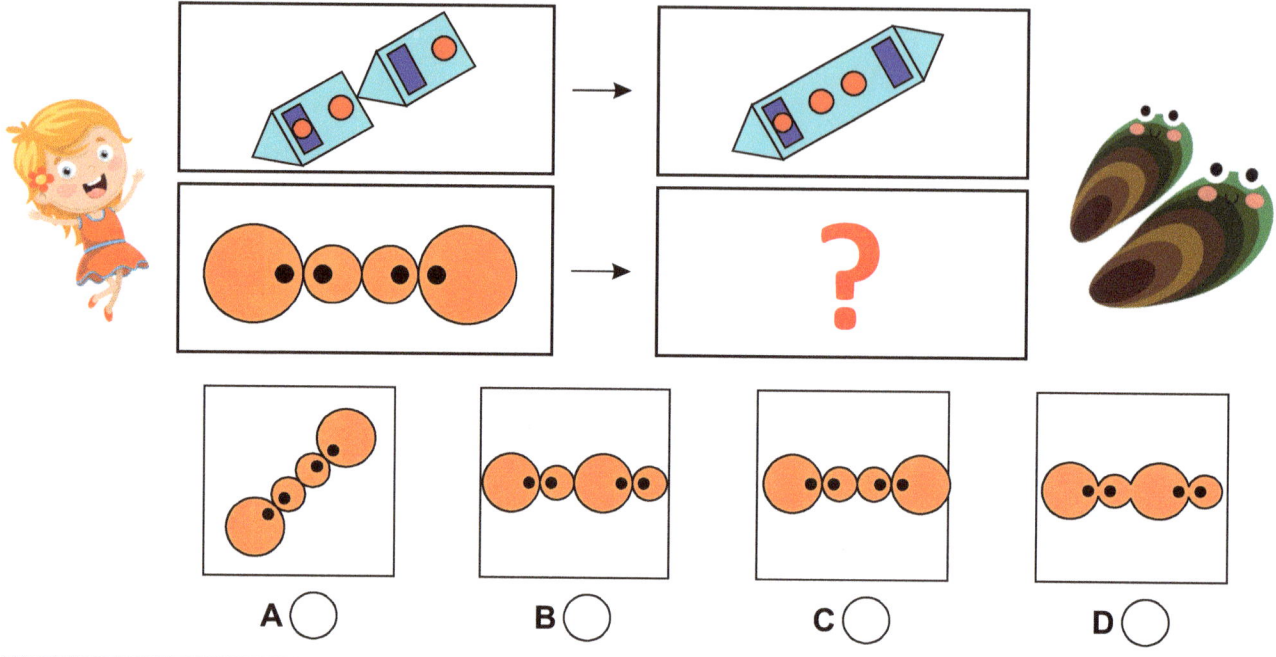

A ○   B ○   C ○   D ○

Q-12 Look at the question with the Zooplankton. The first row has some thing in common as the second row. Can you help William to identify what goes in the space of the question mark from the four given options A, B, C, and D. Choose the correct option.

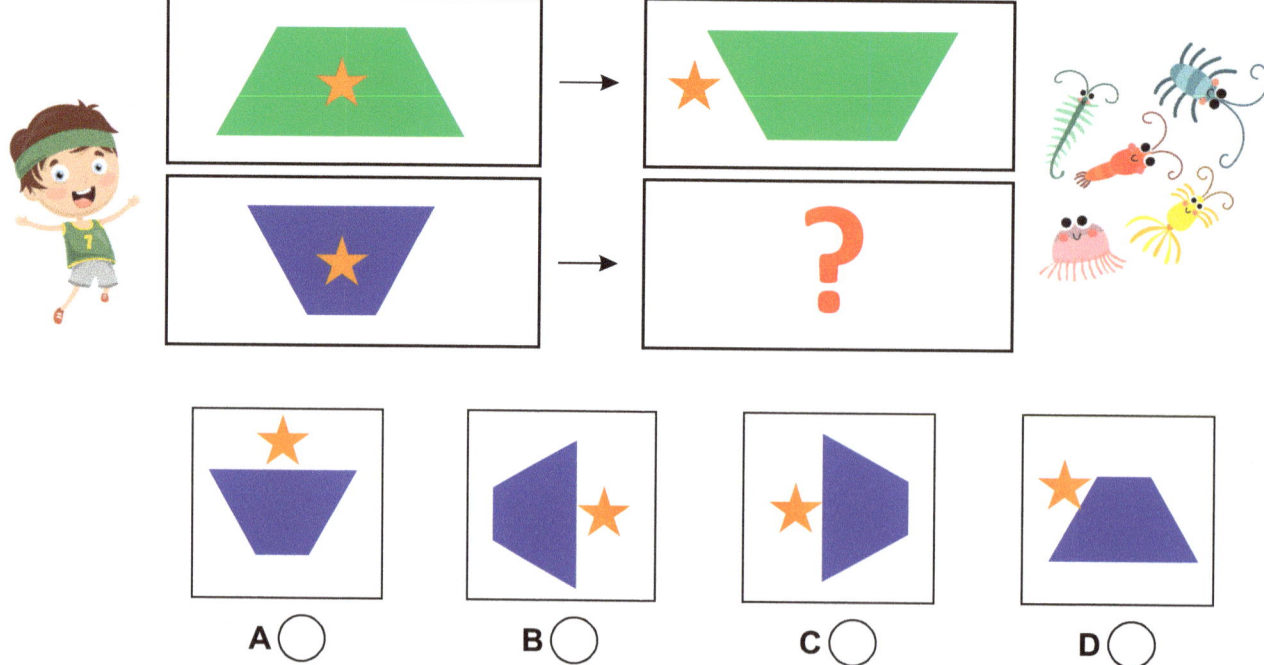

A ○   B ○   C ○   D ○

Q-13 Look at the question with the Sea horse. The first row has some thing in common as the second row. Can you help Thomas to identify what goes in the space of the question mark from the four given options A, B, C, and D. Choose the correct option.

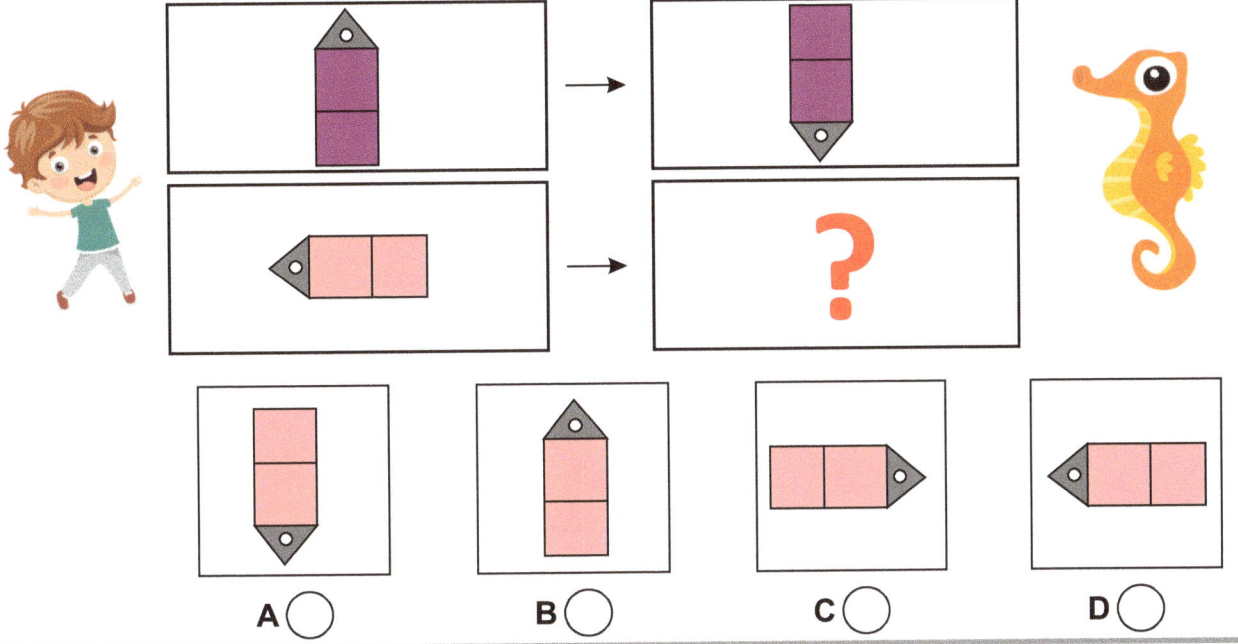

A◯   B◯   C◯   D◯

Q-14 Look at the question with the Tortoise. The first row has some thing in common as the second row. Can you help Olivia to identify what goes in the space of the question mark from the four given options A, B, C, and D. Choose the correct option.

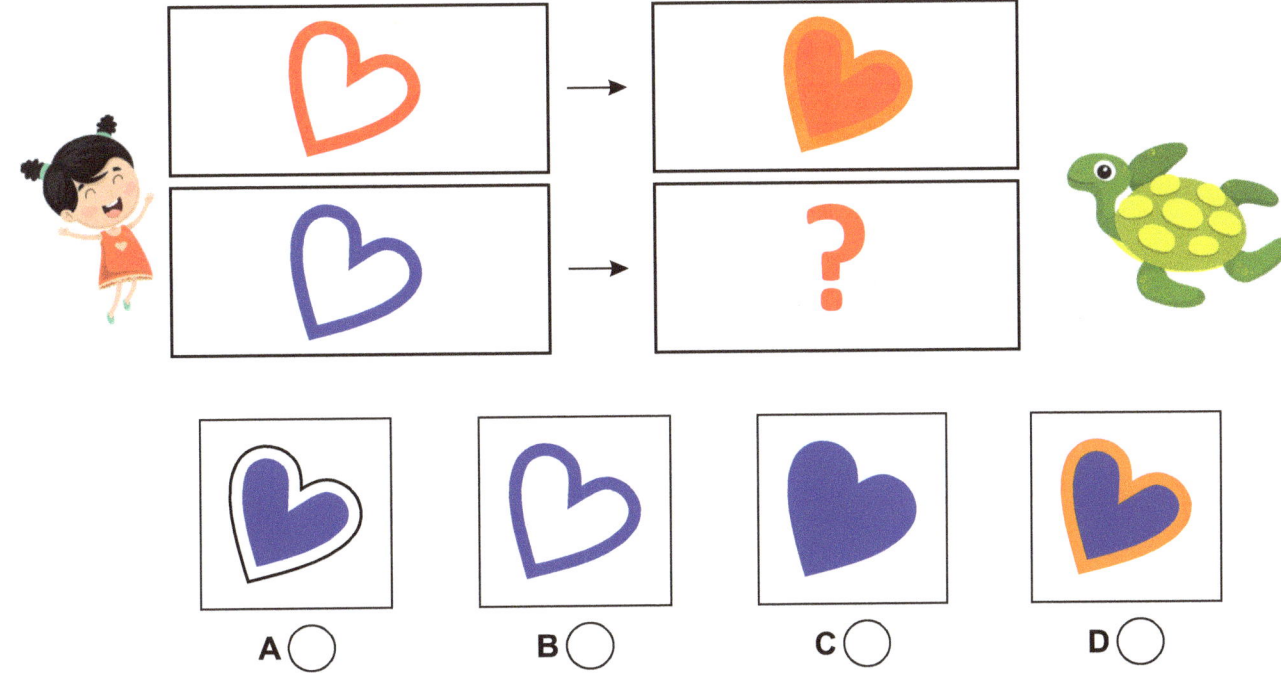

A◯   B◯   C◯   D◯

www.math-knots.com

Q-15

Look at the question with the Star Fish. The first row has some thing in common as the second row. Can you help Emily to identify what goes in the space of the question mark from the four given options A, B, C, and D. Choose the correct option.

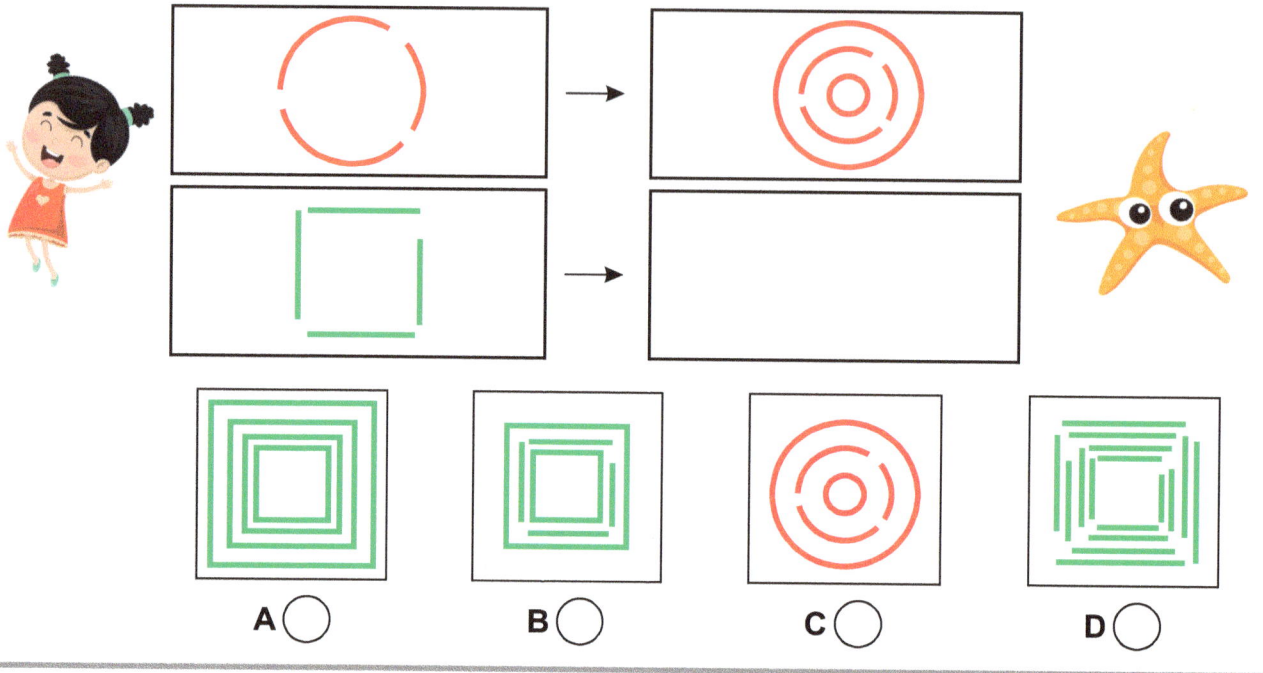

A ◯   B ◯   C ◯   D ◯

Q-16

Look at the question with the Gold Fish. The first row has some thing in common as the second row. Can you help Lily to identify what goes in the space of the question mark from the four given options A, B, C, and D. Choose the correct option.

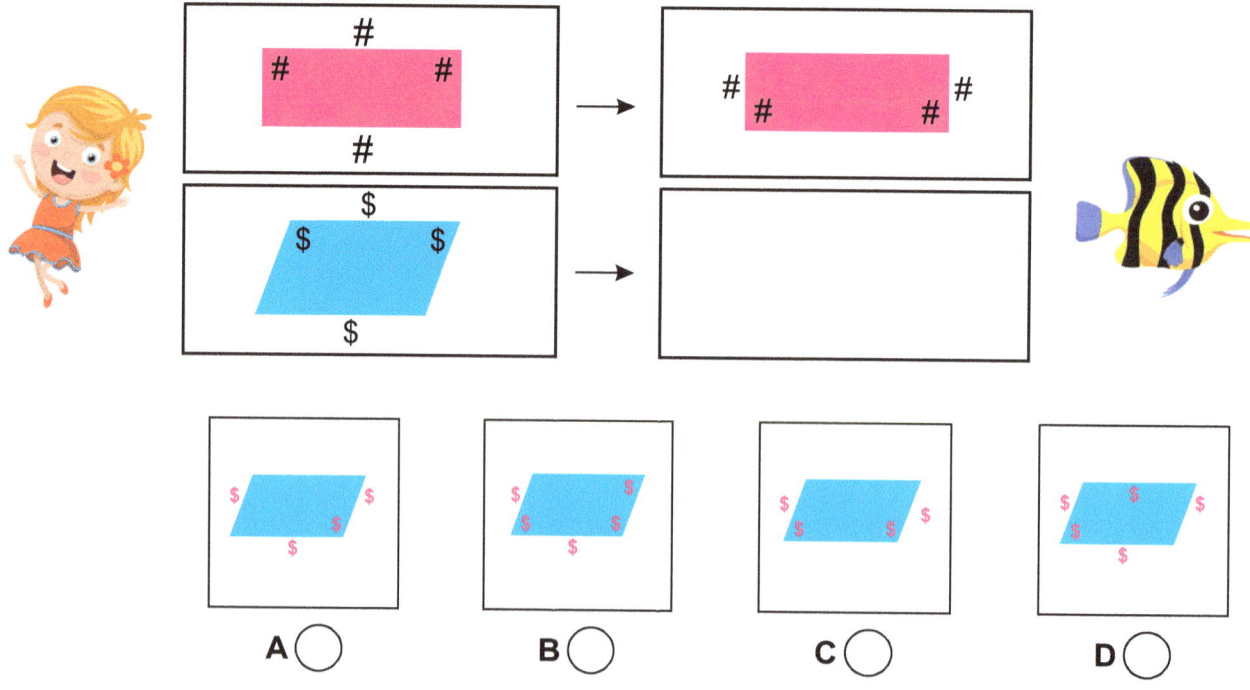

A ◯   B ◯   C ◯   D ◯

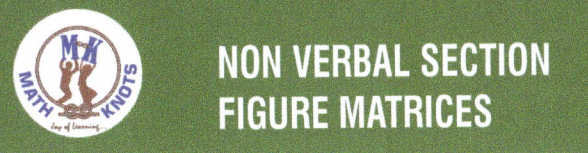

Q-17

Look at the question with the Crab. The first row has some thing in common as the second row. Can you help Jacob to identify what goes in the space of the question mark from the four given options A, B, C, and D. Choose the correct option.

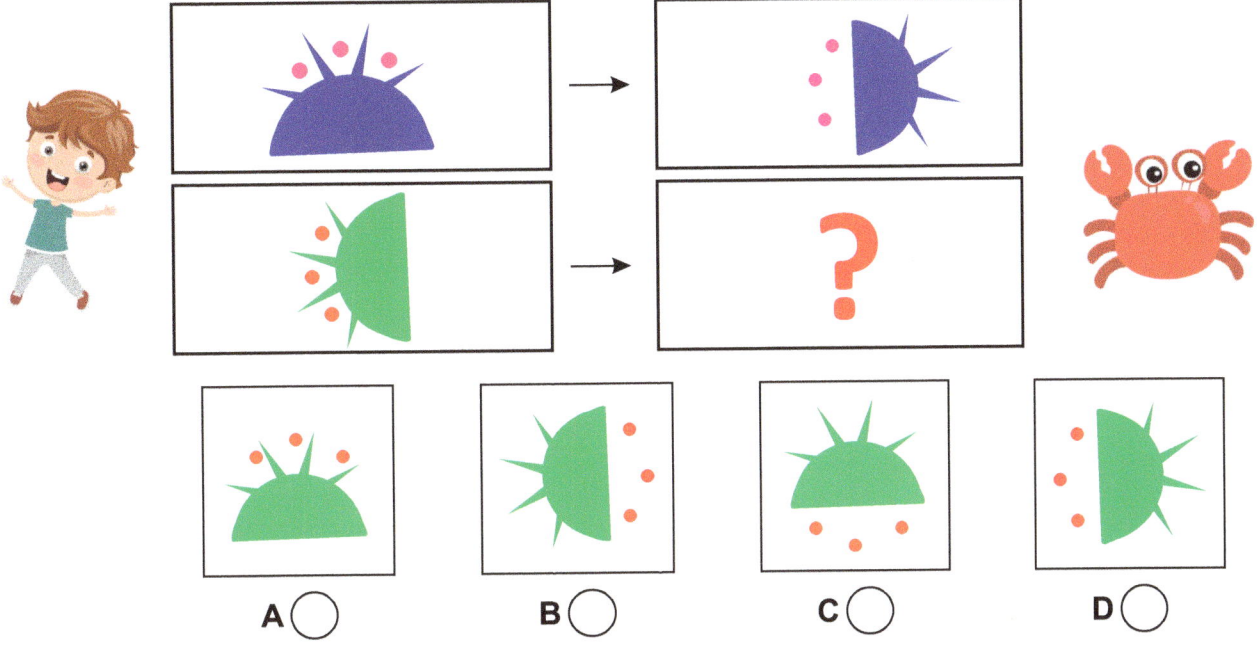

Q-18

Look at the question with the Blob Fish. The first row has some thing in common as the second row. Can you help Noah to identify what goes in the space of the question mark from the four given options A, B, C, and D. Choose the correct option.

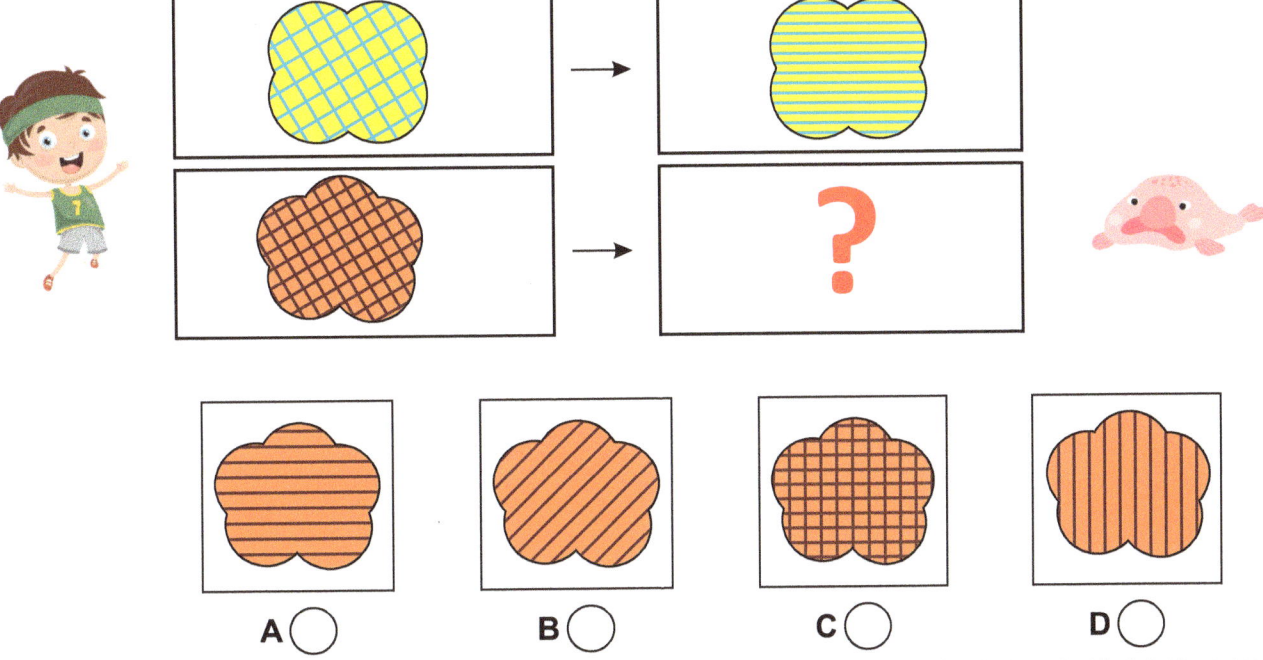

TEST - 1

NON VERBAL SECTION

PAPER FOLDING

Lets Start the Test...

Sample

Look at the question and put your finger on Bee. Amy folded the paper and made holes to it as shown. When the paper is unfolded how does it look? Help her bubble the right option.

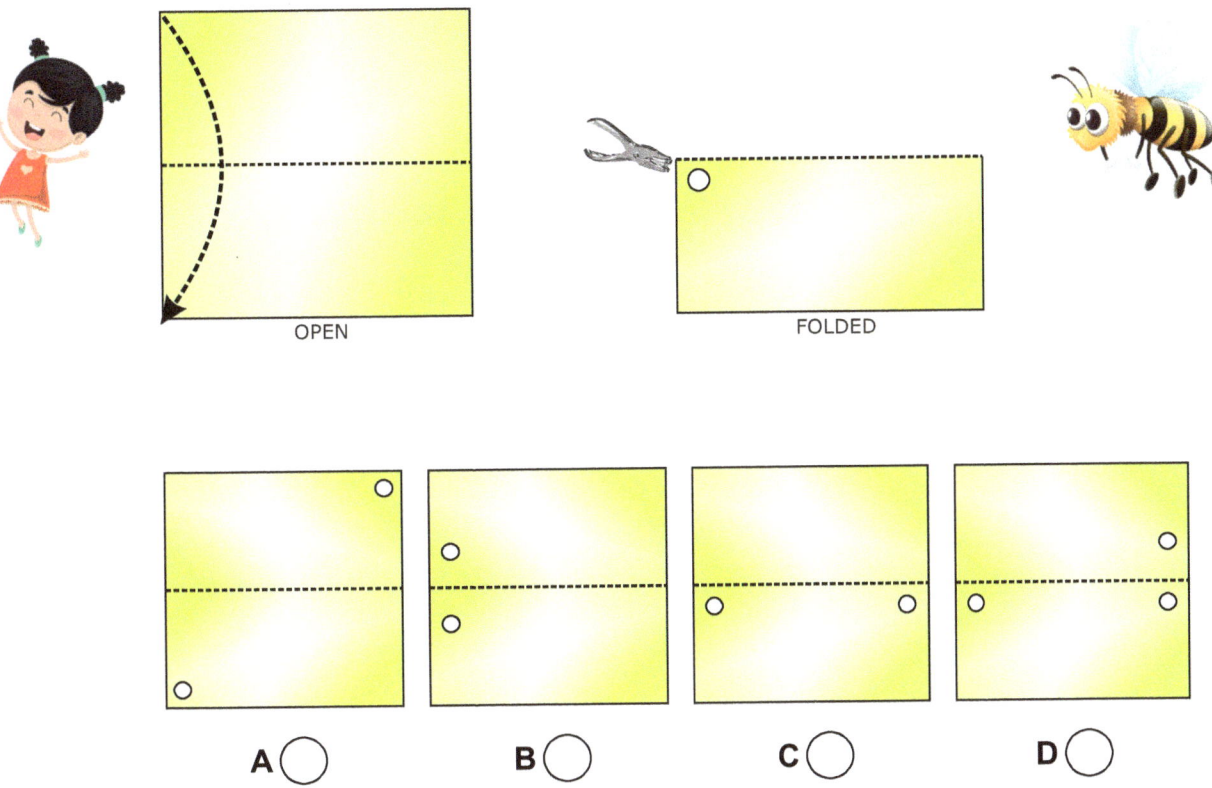

OPEN

FOLDED

A◯   B◯   C◯   D◯

Solution : B

A rectangle is folded once and hole is punched on top left corner. After

punching the figure is unfolded the holes are shown in the middle left corner as

shown in option B. Student choses the right option and fills the bubble completely.

Q-1

Look at the question and put your finger on Alligator. Brianna folded the paper and made hole to it as shown. When the paper is unfolded how does it look? Help her bubble the right option.

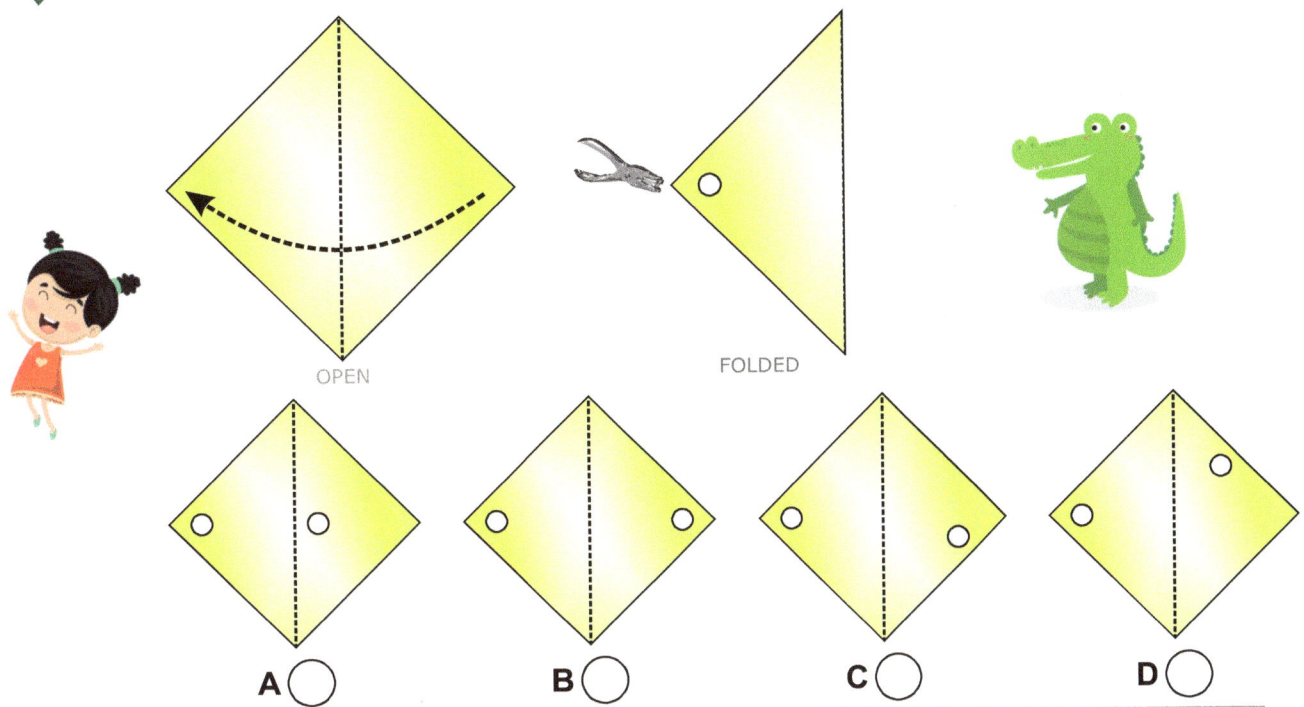

OPEN   FOLDED

A ◯   B ◯   C ◯   D ◯

Q-2

Look at the question and put your finger on Sparrow. Samuel folded the paper and made holes to it as shown. When the paper is unfolded how does it look? Help him bubble the right option.

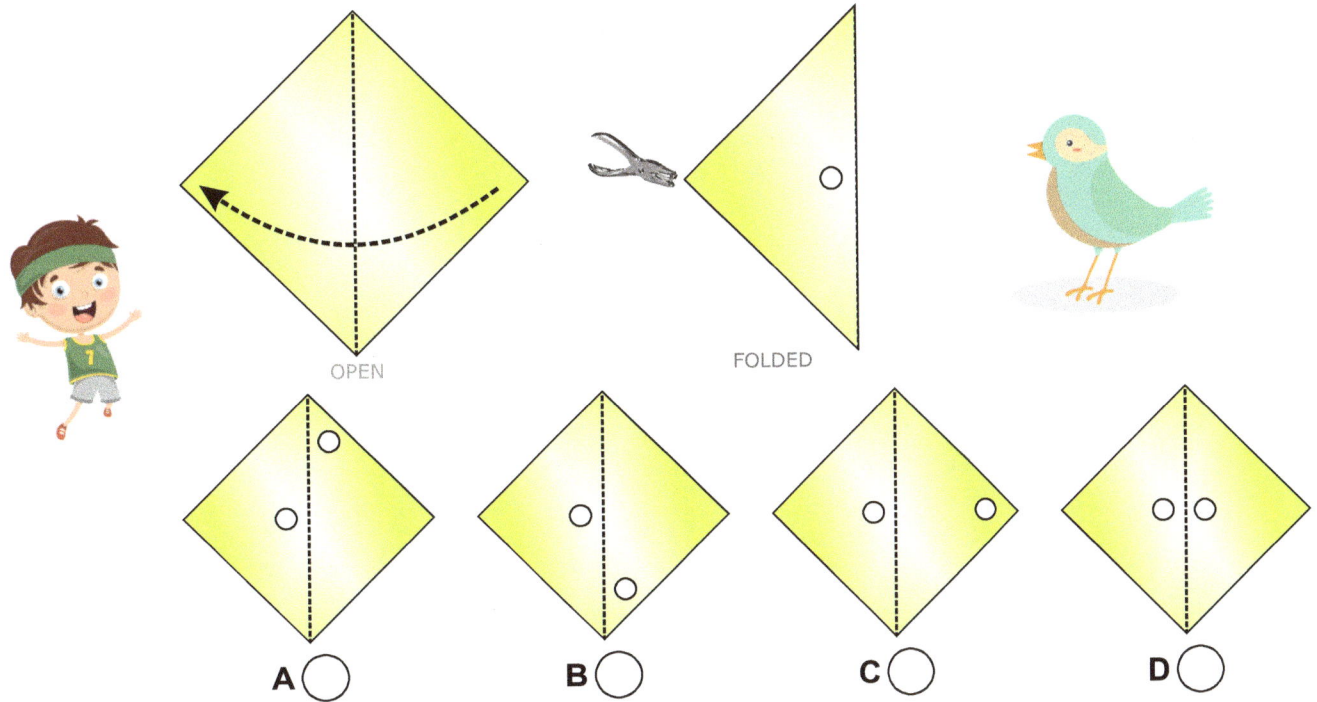

OPEN   FOLDED

A ◯   B ◯   C ◯   D ◯

Q-3

Look at the question and put your finger on Dolphin. Hailey folded the paper and made holes to it as shown. When the paper is unfolded how does it look? Help him bubble the right option.

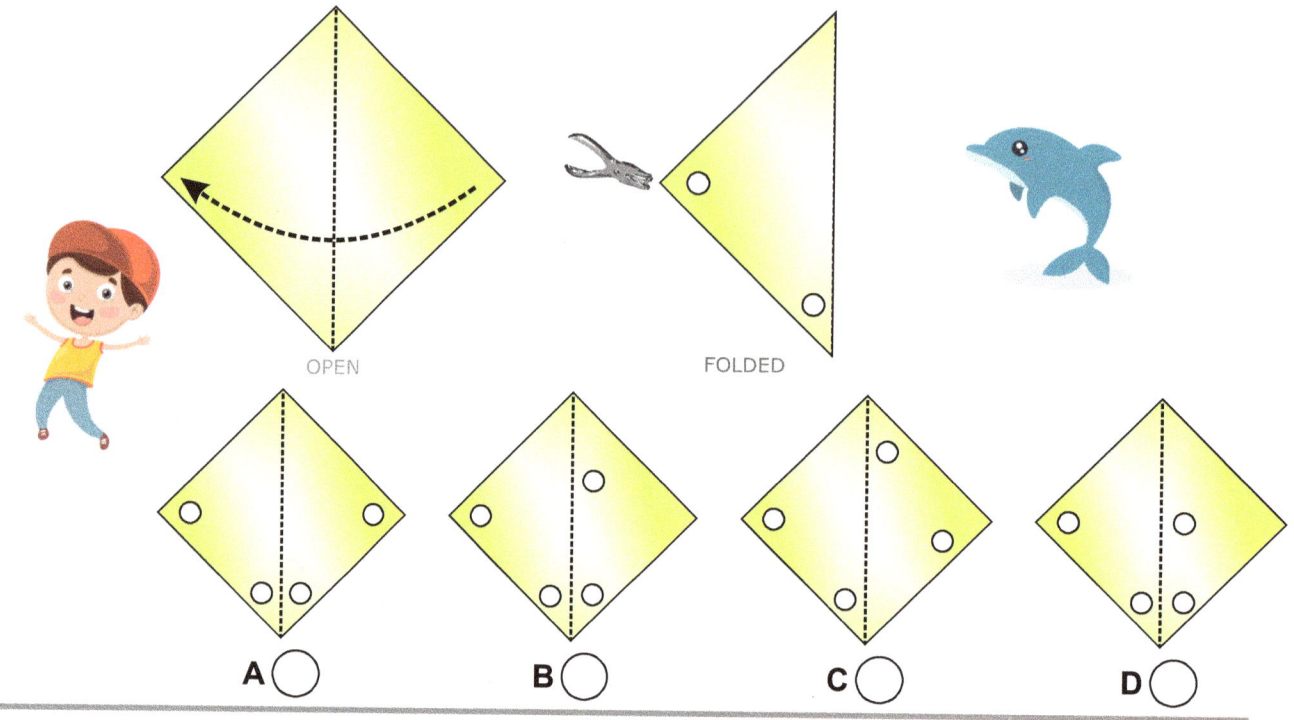

OPEN   FOLDED

A ◯   B ◯   C ◯   D ◯

Q-4

Look at the question and put your finger on JellyFish. Victoria folded the paper and made holes to it as shown. When the paper is unfolded how does it look? Help her bubble the right option.

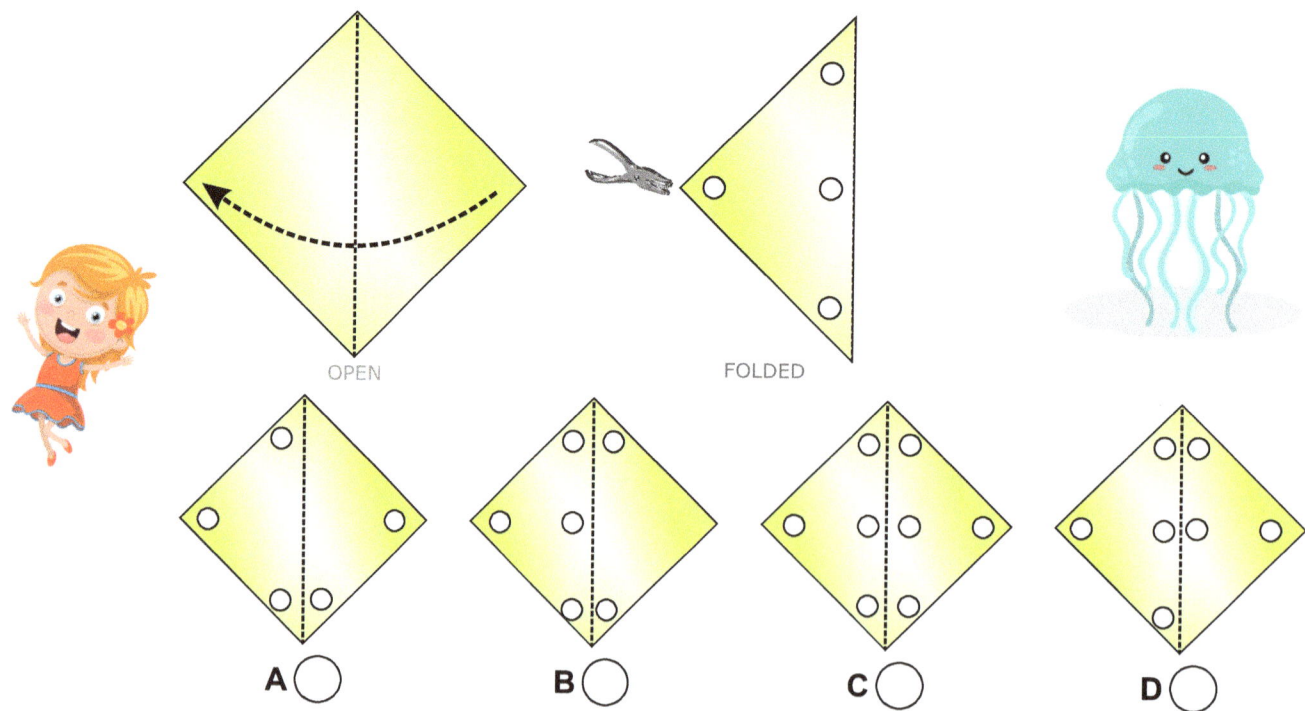

OPEN   FOLDED

A ◯   B ◯   C ◯   D ◯

www.math-knots.com

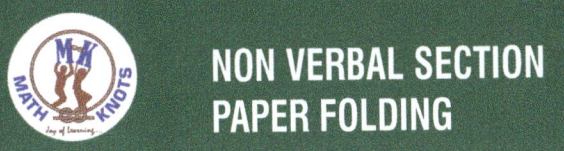

Q-5 Look at the question and put your finger on Fox. Noah folded the paper and made holes to it as shown. When the paper is unfolded how does it look? Help him bubble the right option.

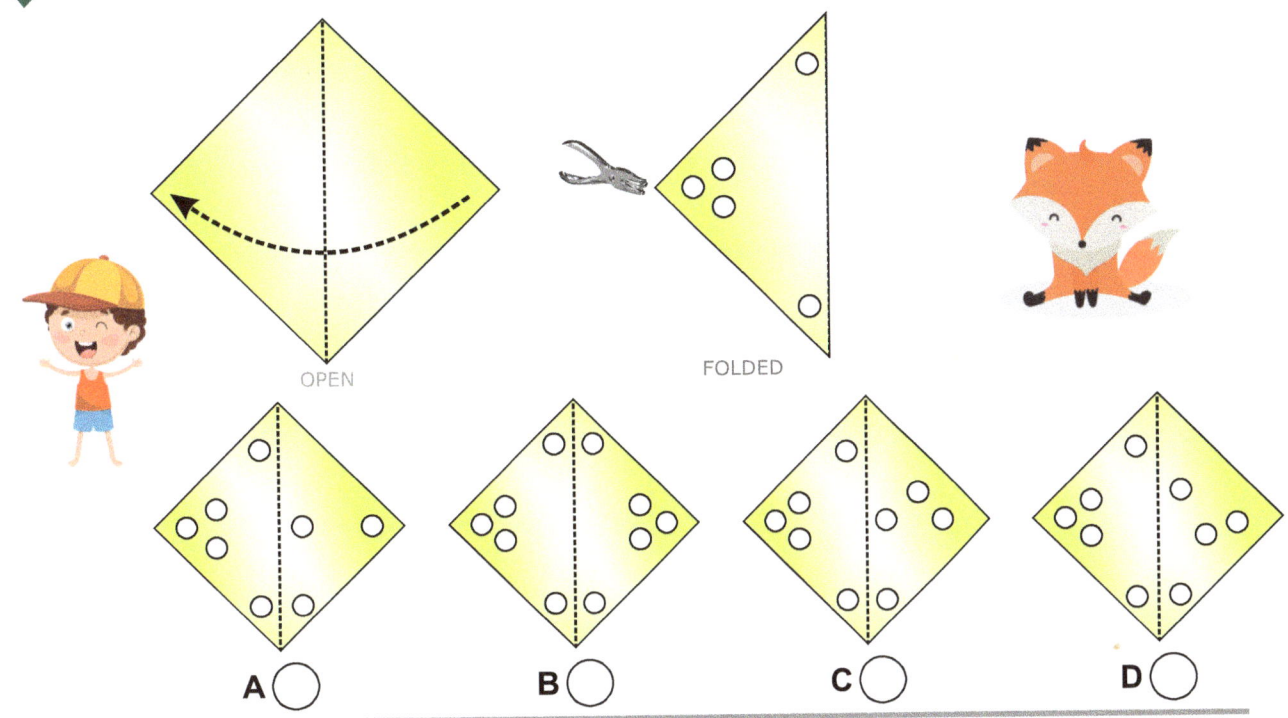

Q-6 Look at the question and put your finger on Giraffe. Zachary folded the paper and made holes to it as shown. When the paper is unfolded how does it look? Help him bubble the right option.

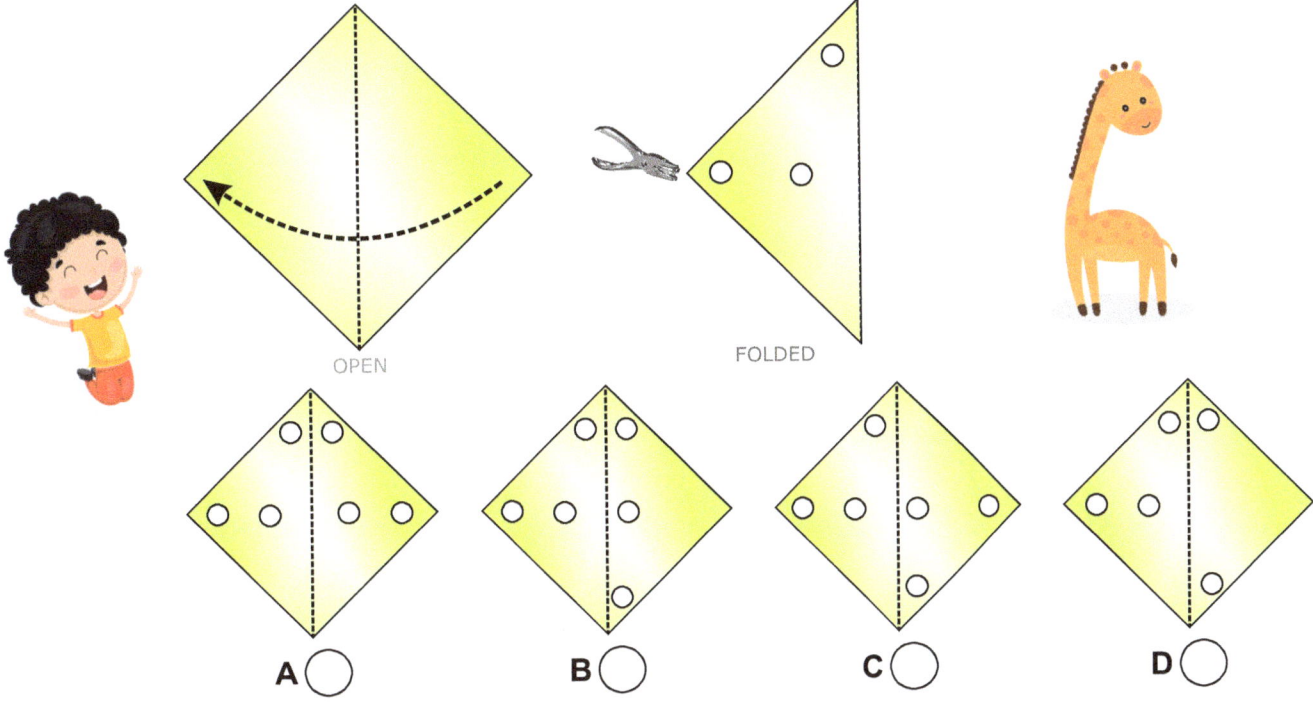

www.math-knots.com

Q-7

Look at the question and put your finger on Iguana. Rita folded the paper and made holes to it as shown. When the paper is unfolded how does it look? Help her bubble the right option.

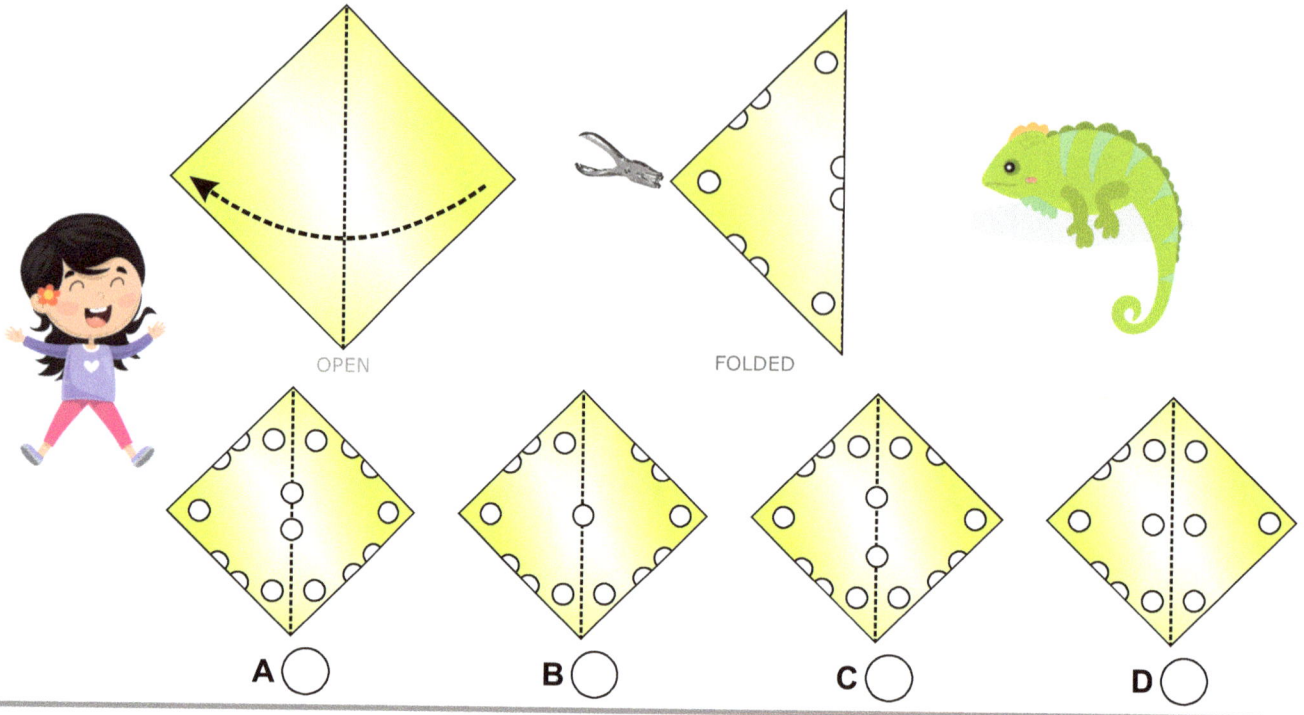

OPEN FOLDED

A ◯   B ◯   C ◯   D ◯

Q-8

Look at the question and put your finger on Monkey. Devin folded the paper and made holes to it as shown. When the paper is unfolded how does it look? Help him bubble the right option.

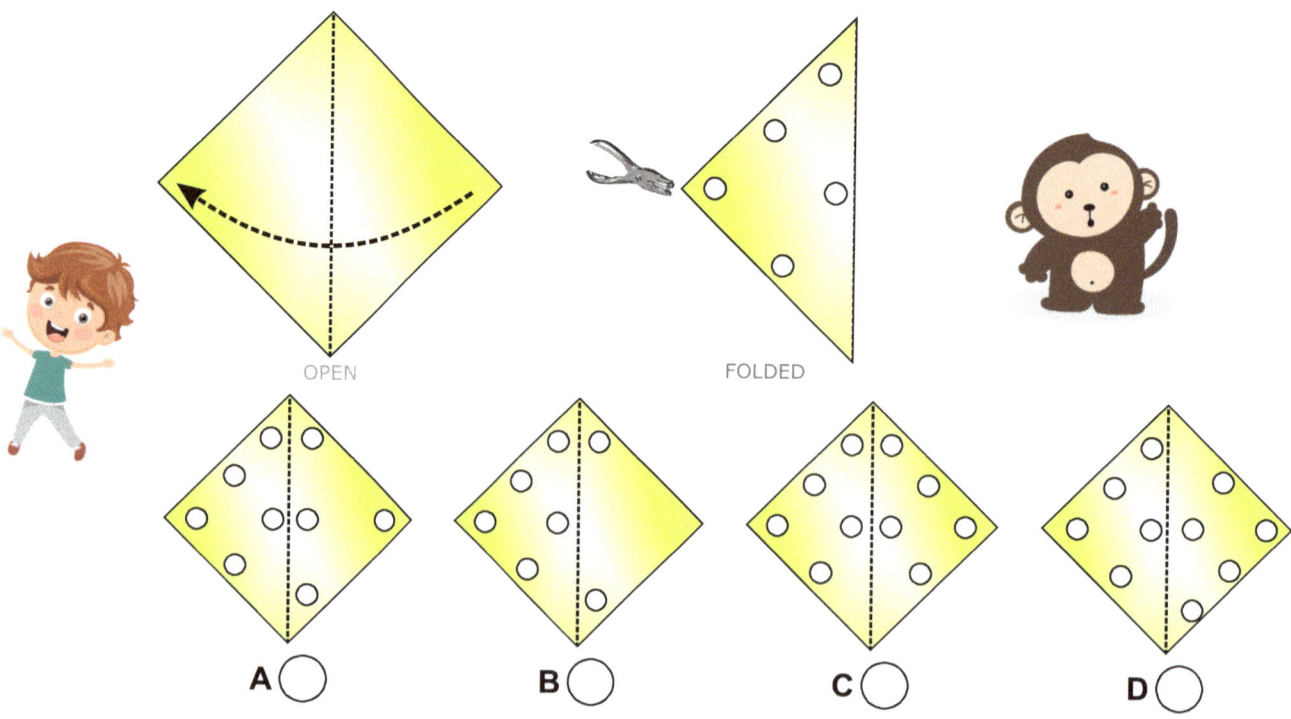

OPEN FOLDED

A ◯   B ◯   C ◯   D ◯

Q-9

Look at the question and put your finger on Koala Bear. Ashton folded the paper and made holes to it as shown. When the paper is unfolded how does it look? Help him bubble the right option.

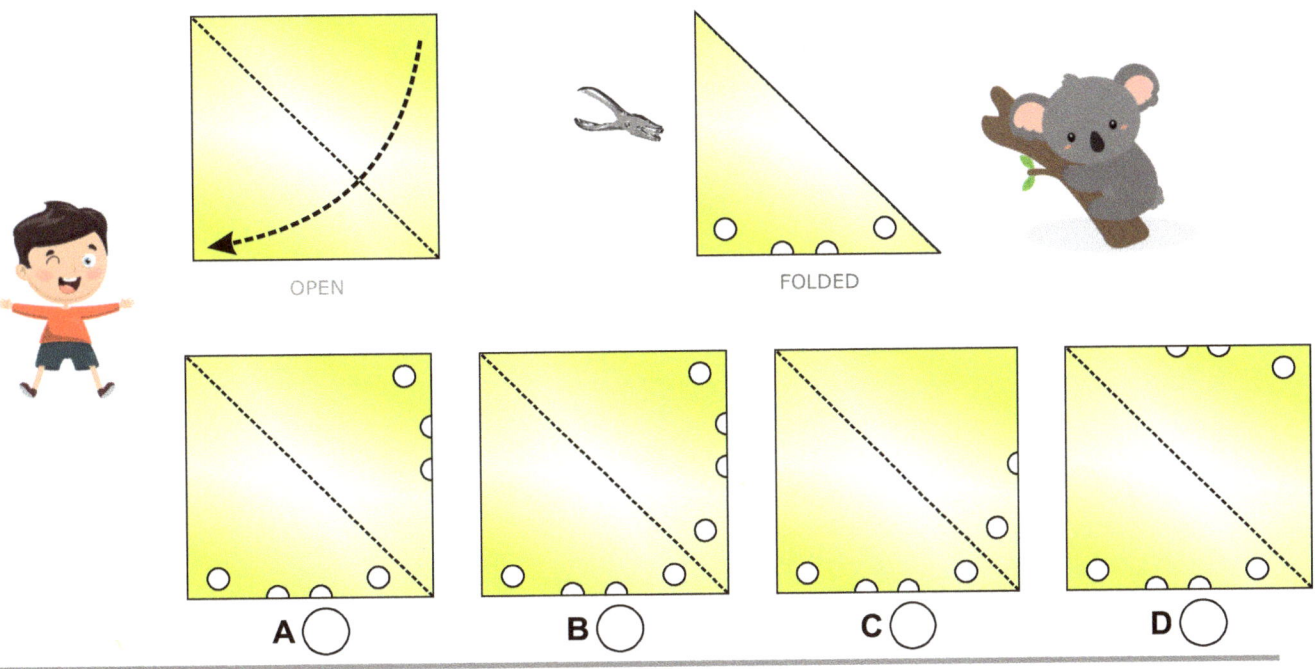

Q-10

Look at the question and put your finger on Pig. Sierra folded the paper and made holes to it as shown. When the paper is unfolded how does it look? Help her bubble the right option.

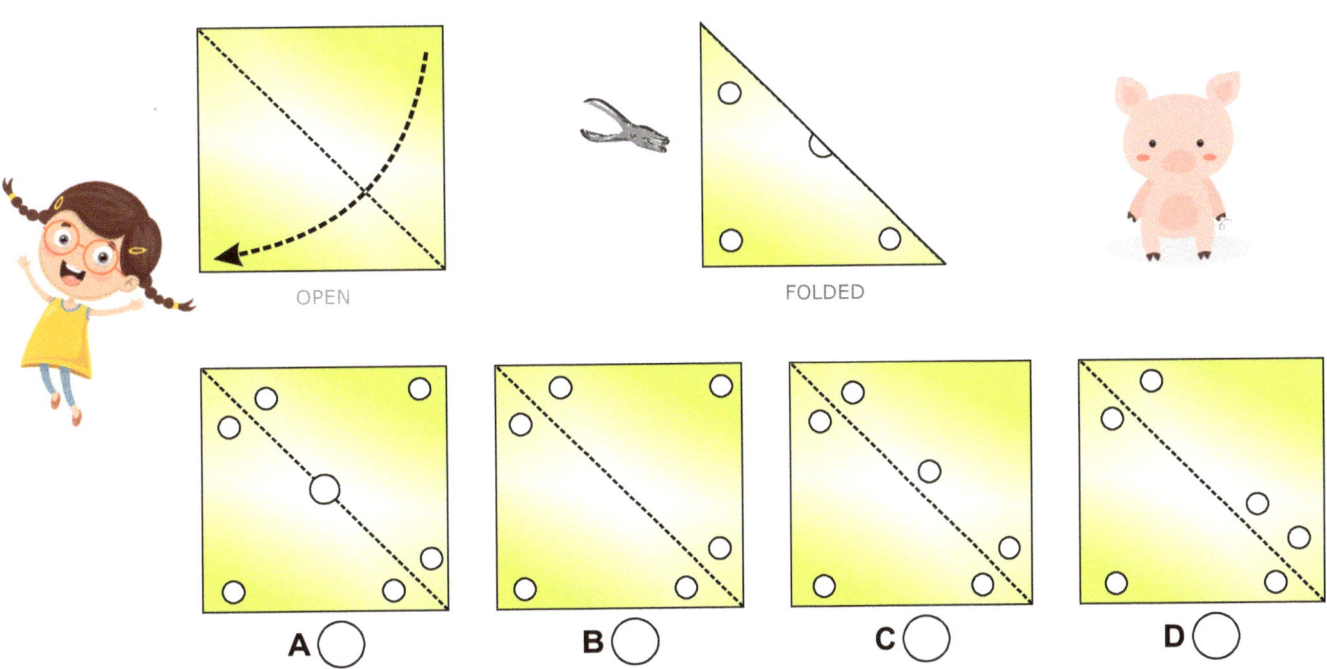

www.math-knots.com

Q-11

Look at the question and put your finger on Quail. Kathryn folded the paper and made holes to it as shown. When the paper is unfolded how does it look? Help her bubble the right option.

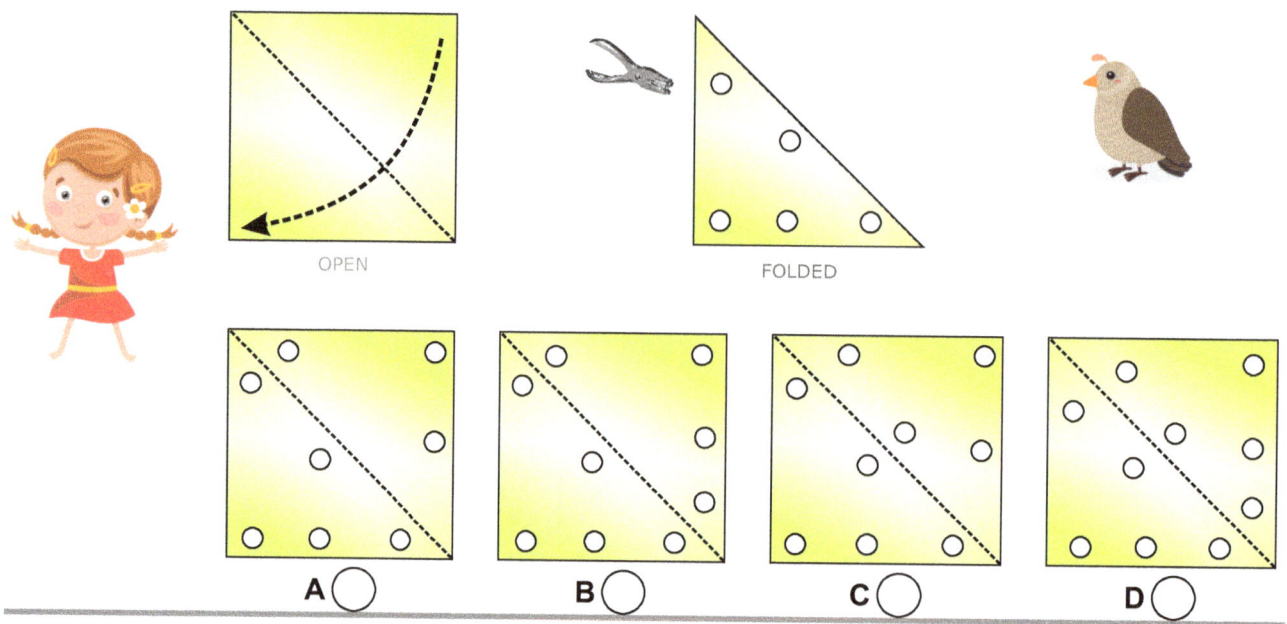

OPEN

FOLDED

A ◯   B ◯   C ◯   D ◯

Q-12

Look at the question and put your finger on Vampires Bat. Skylar folded the paper and made holes to it as shown. When the paper is unfolded how does it look? Help her bubble the right option.

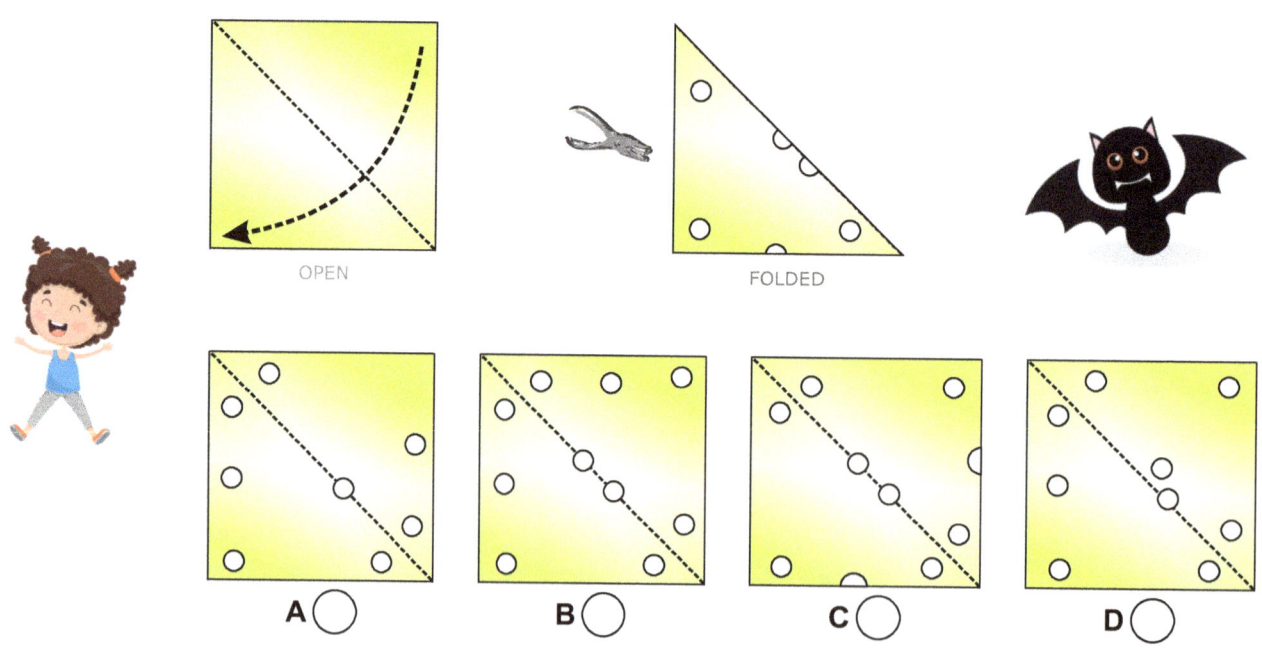

OPEN

FOLDED

A ◯   B ◯   C ◯   D ◯

www.math-knots.com

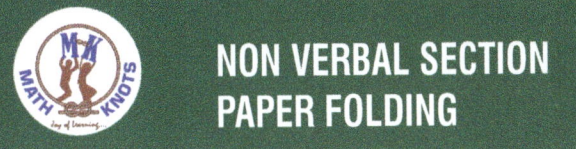

Q-13

Look at the question and put your finger on Lion. Rose folded the paper and made holes to it as shown. When the paper is unfolded how does it look? Help her bubble the right option.

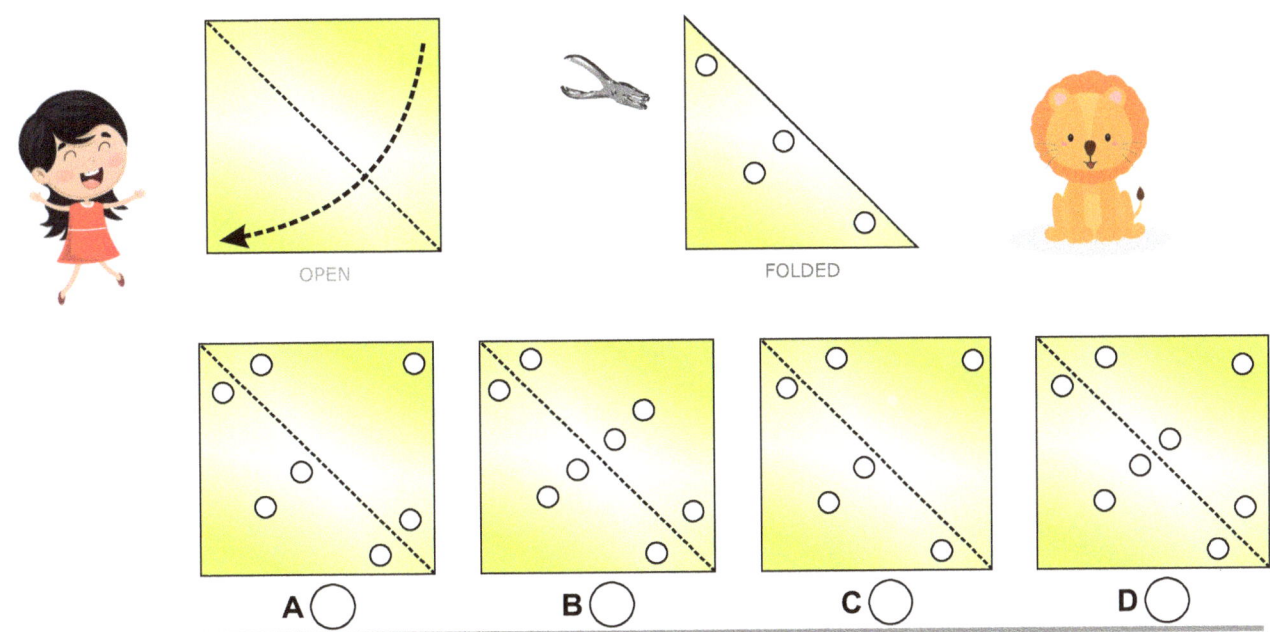

Q-14

Look at the question and put your finger on Raccoon. Matt folded the paper and made holes to it as shown. When the paper is unfolded how does it look? Help him bubble the right option.

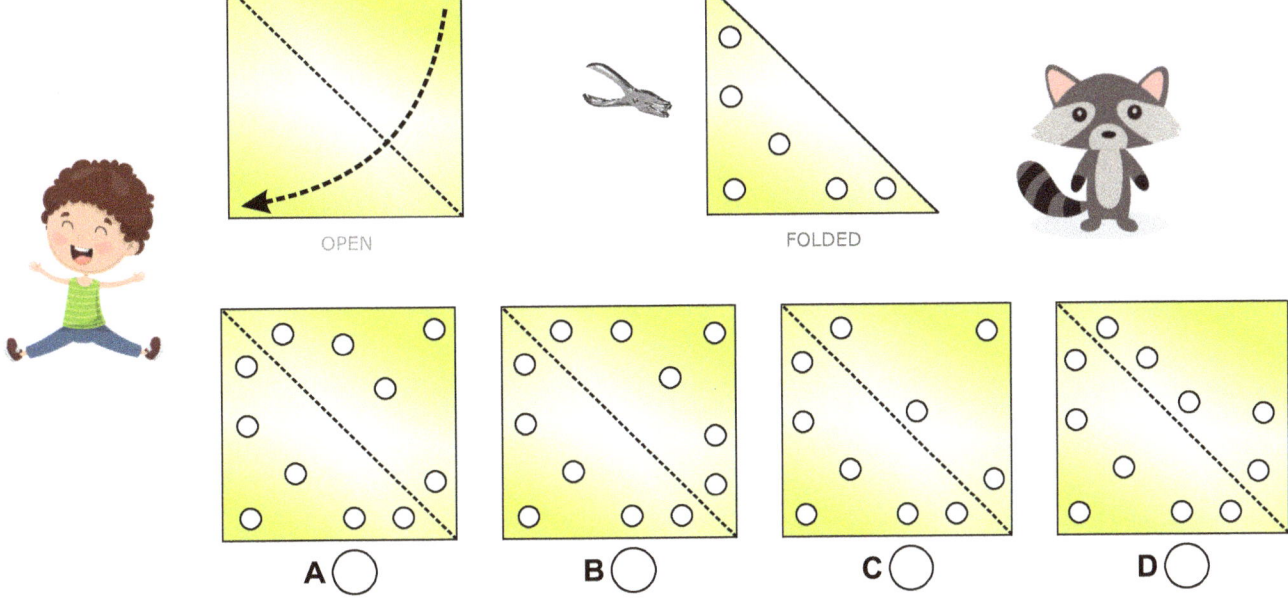

Q-15

Look at the question and put your finger on Octopus. Bryan folded the paper and made holes to it as shown. When the paper is unfolded how does it look? Help him bubble the right option.

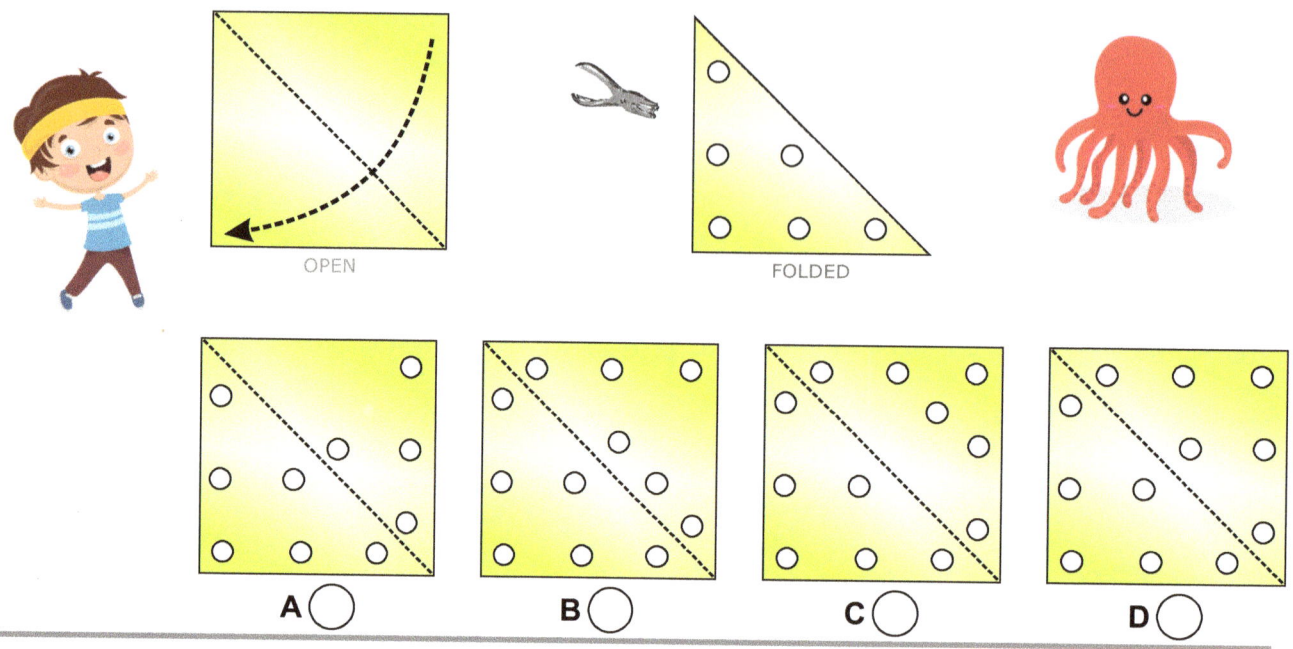

OPEN

FOLDED

A ◯   B ◯   C ◯   D ◯

Q-16

Look at the question and put your finger on Narwhal. Paige folded the paper and made holes to it as shown. When the paper is unfolded how does it look? Help her bubble the right option.

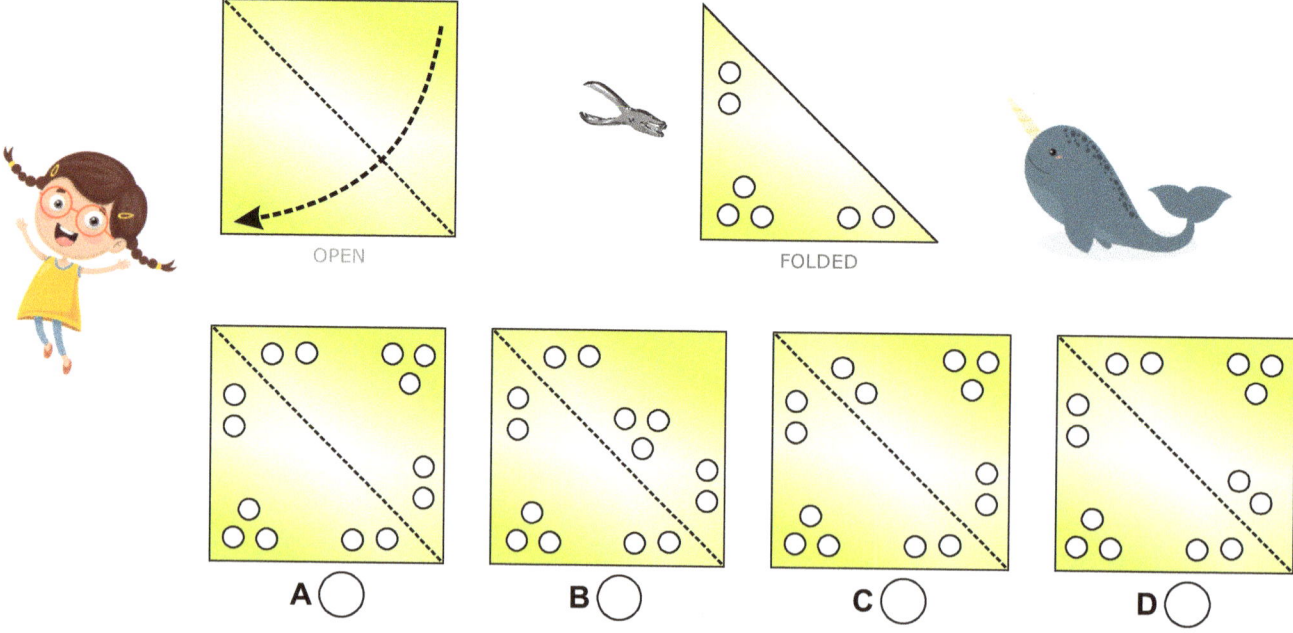

OPEN

FOLDED

A ◯   B ◯   C ◯   D ◯

MATH-KNOTS CHALLENGE

Q-17

Look at the question and put your finger on Turtle. Seth folded the paper and made holes to it as shown. When the paper is unfolded how does it look? Help him bubble the right option.

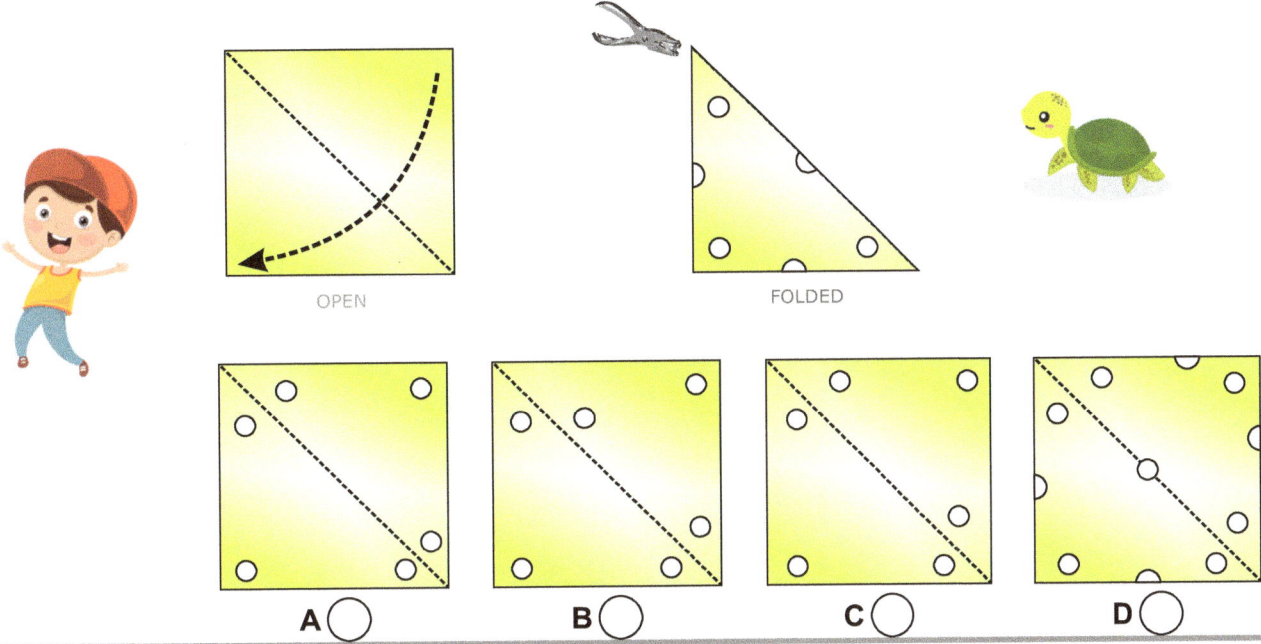

OPEN

FOLDED

A ◯ B ◯ C ◯ D ◯

MATH-KNOTS CHALLENGE

Q-18

Look at the question and put your finger on X-Ray Fish. Diana folded the paper and made holes to it as shown. When the paper is unfolded how does it look? Help her bubble the right option.

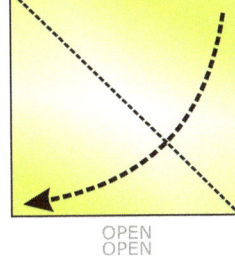

OPEN
OPEN

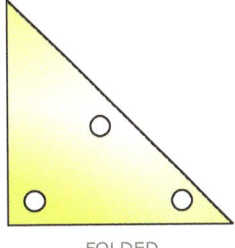

FOLDED

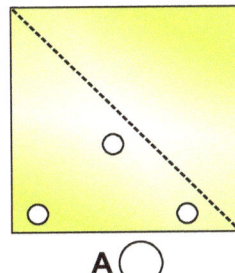

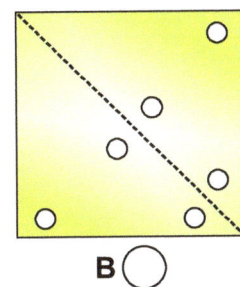

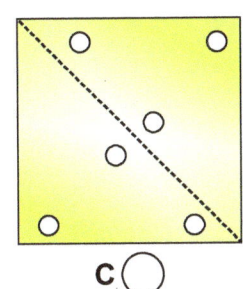

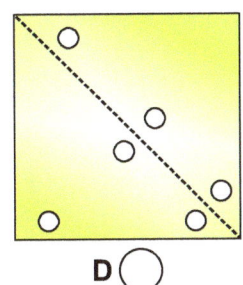

A ◯ B ◯ C ◯ D ◯

www.math-knots.com

MATH-KNOTS CHALLENGE

Q-19

Look at the question and put your finger on Yak. Maya folded the paper and made holes to it as shown. When the paper is unfolded how does it look? Help her bubble the right option.

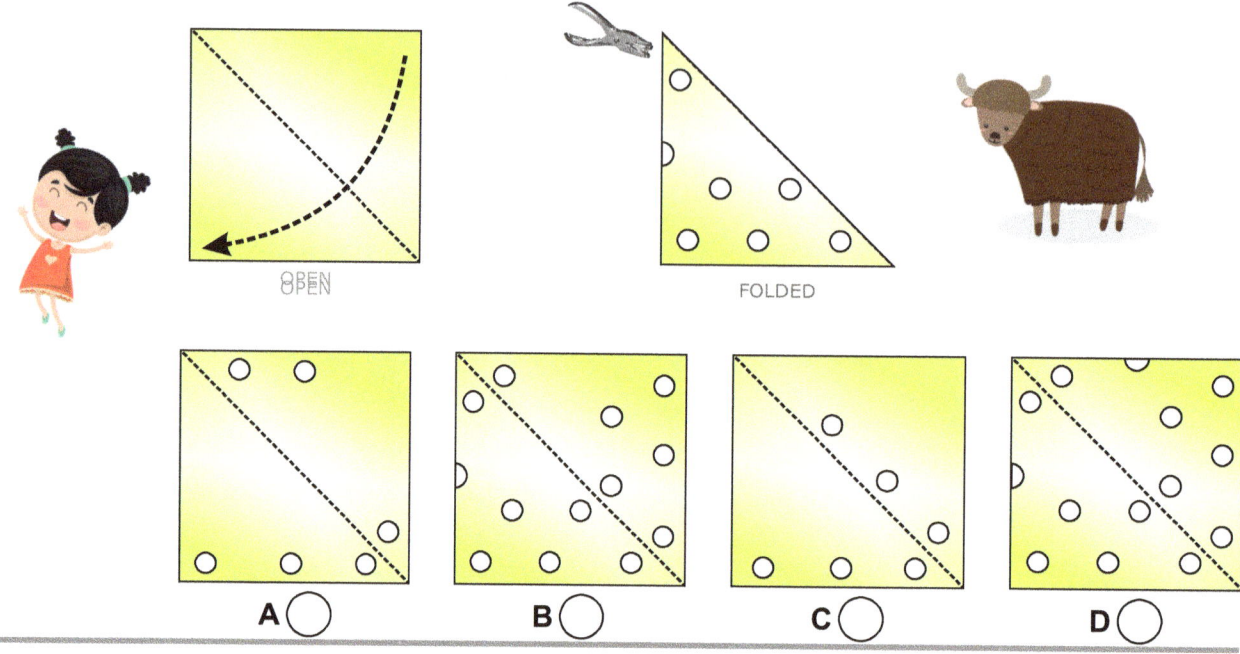

OPEN

FOLDED

A ○   B ○   C ○   D ○

MATH-KNOTS CHALLENGE

Q-20

Look at the question and put your finger on Walrus. Courtney folded the paper and made holes to it as shown. When the paper is unfolded how does it look? Help her bubble the right option.

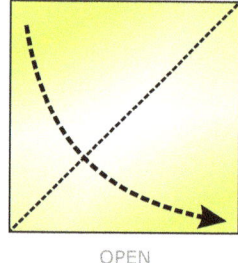
OPEN

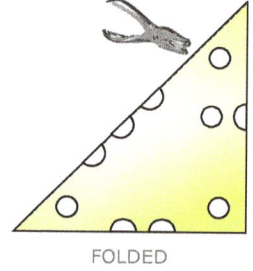
FOLDED

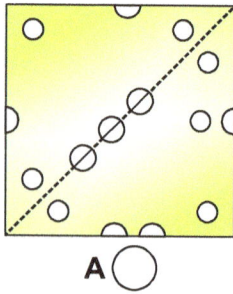
A ○

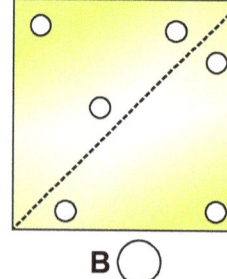
B ○

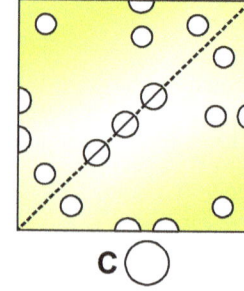
C ○

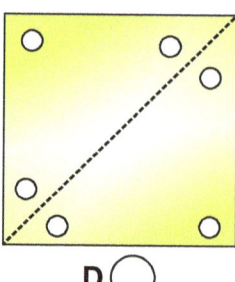
D ○

www.math-knots.com

TEST - 2

VERBAL SECTION

VERBAL CLASSIFICATION

Lets Start the Test...

www.math-knots.com

www.math-knots.com

Sample Three words are related in a certain way. Four options are given. Identify the choice that does not belong to the group ?

One	Two	Three	
Six	Eight	Five	Gate
A ◯	B ◯	C ◯	D ◯

Solution : D

Three words in the question belong to one group. One of the four choices doesn't belong to the same group. Identify and bubble the correct choice. In the given question all three in first row are words as well as numbers in words. Lets take a look at the answers. All choices are words but three are numbers in words and one other word gate, which is incorrect.

www.math-knots.com

All the questions in verbal classification test 2 are to be answered following the below question (instruction).

Three words are related in a certain way. Four options are given. Identify the choice that <u>does not belong</u> to the group ?

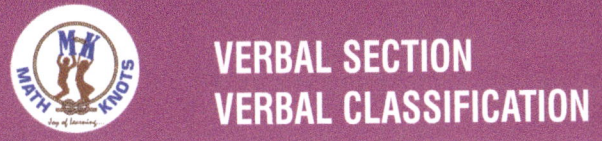
1. **Axe**   **Sickle**   **Spade**

    Farming   Rake   Shovel   Hoe

    A◯   B◯   C◯   D◯

2. **Lime**   **Mint**   **Neon**

    Emerald   Olive   Jade   Crimpson

    A◯   B◯   C◯   D◯

3. **Strength**   **Vigor**   **Courage**

    Muscle   Might   Cowardice   Firm

    A◯   B◯   C◯   D◯

4. **Book Case**   **Book Rack**   **Dresser**

    Coat Rack   Quilt   Chest   Ottoman

    A◯   B◯   C◯   D◯

5. **Mother**   **Father**   **Daughter**

    Son   Brother   Sister   Friend

    A◯   B◯   C◯   D◯

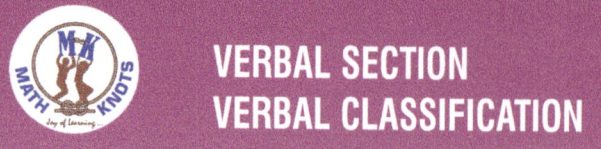
6. **Turtle**   **Snake**   **Chameleon**

    Rabbit   Crocodile   Dinosaur   Lizard

    A ◯   B ◯   C ◯   D ◯

7. **Screw Driver**   **Axe**   **Hammer**

    Lean   Scissors   Shovel   Chisel

    A ◯   B ◯   C ◯   D ◯

8. **Physics**   **Social**   **Math**

    English   Biology   Subjects   Chemistry

    A ◯   B ◯   C ◯   D ◯

9. **Lead**   **Chalk**   **Ink**

    Pencil   Crayon   Pen   Marble

    A ◯   B ◯   C ◯   D ◯

10. **Saw**   **Clamps**   **Spade**

    Dibber   Nail   Axe   Plough

    A ◯   B ◯   C ◯   D ◯

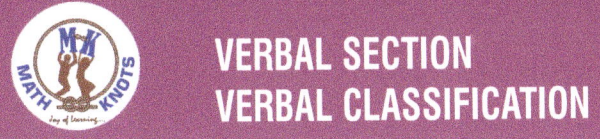
11. **Gallon**   **Pint**   **Cup**

Gram   Tablespoon   Ounce   Quart

A◯   B◯   C◯   D◯

12. **Dictionary**   **Novel**   **Magazine**

Newspaper   Stories   Comics   Thesis

A◯   B◯   C◯   D◯

13. **Ant**   **Caterpillar**   **Moth**

Insect   Spider   Scorpio   Wasp

A◯   B◯   C◯   D◯

14. **Crow**   **Pigeon**   **Sparrow**

Cuckoo   Parrot   Duck   Robin

A◯   B◯   C◯   D◯

15. **Mile**   **Foot**   **Yard**

Meter   Inch   Quart   Centimeter

A◯   B◯   C◯   D◯

16. **Mature**   **Grown**   **Ripen**

Complete   Young   Final   Ready

A ◯   B ◯   C ◯   D ◯

17. **Pistachio**   **Almond**   **Cashew**

Pecan   Macadamia   Walnuts   Beans

A ◯   B ◯   C ◯   D ◯

18. **Branch**   **Thorn**   **Leaves**

Tumor   Bud   Needles   Graft

A ◯   B ◯   C ◯   D ◯

www.math-knots.com

TEST - 2

VERBAL SECTION

SENTENCE COMPLETION

Lets Start the Test...

www.math-knots.com

Sample Look at the question with the Tennis Ball. Maya is trying to solve the below brain teaser. "Rik has more stamps then Ryan. Ryan has more stamps than Luke. Who has more stamps?" Bubble the correct option.

A ◯

B ◯

C ◯

D ◯

Solution : A

The Correct choice is A. The question doesn't compare with what Jack has.

Rik has the most stamps.

Rik > Ryan > Luke

www.math-knots.com

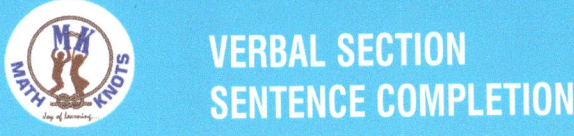
Q-1 Look at the question with the Writing Desk. Tom is learning his weekly vocabulary list from the school. He wants to know the meaning of the word trunk. Which of the below choices pictures the trunk? Help him to identify the correct picture and to bubble the right choice.

Q-2 Look at the question with the Coffee Cup. Beth went to the Zoo with her class today. She is looking to find which one of the below jumps but doesn't fly or climb from the given four choices as below. Identify the correct picture and help her to bubble the correct option.

www.math-knots.com

Q-3 Look at the question with the Clock. Nancy wants to bake a cake for her friend Cathy's surprise party. She is searching for something to start mixing the ingredients for baking. Identify the correct picture and help her to bubble the right choice.

Q-4 Look at the question with the Chair. Lisa is trying to solve the below brain teaser. Can you please help her in solving this? "The Parking lot in the mall has more silver cars than black cars. Red cars are less than black cars. Which color cars are the least in the parking lot? "Identify the correct solution and help her to bubble the right choice.

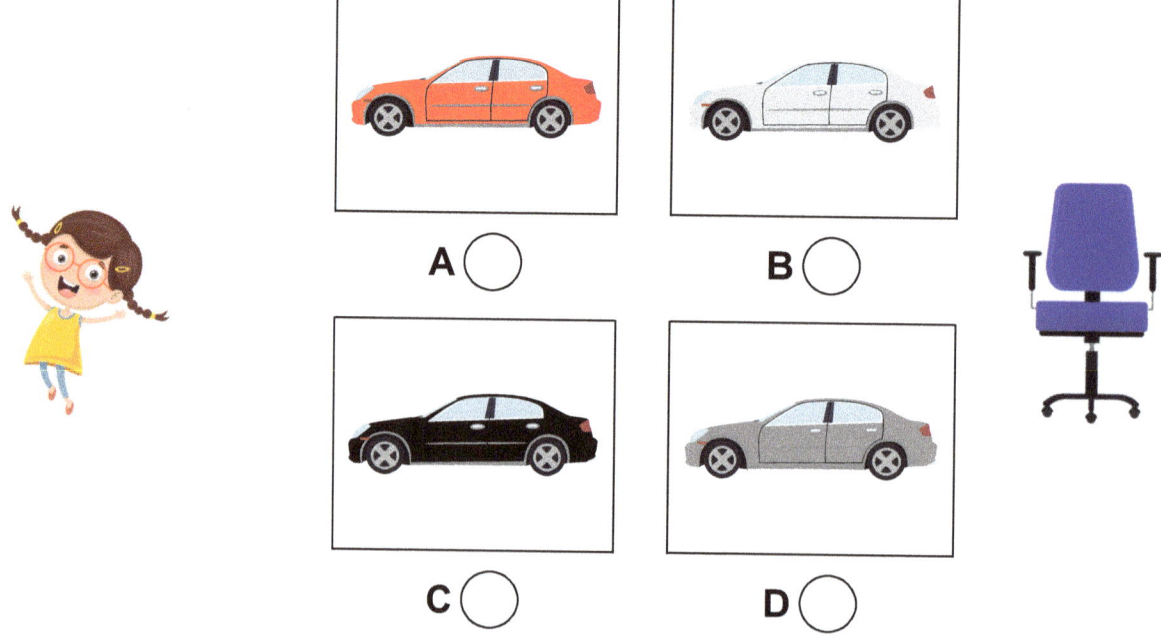

www.math-knots.com

Q-5 Look at the question with the Cellophane Tape. Matt is learning about sense organs in science class. Help him to find which of the below is not a sense organ. Identify the correct picture and help him to bubble the right choice.

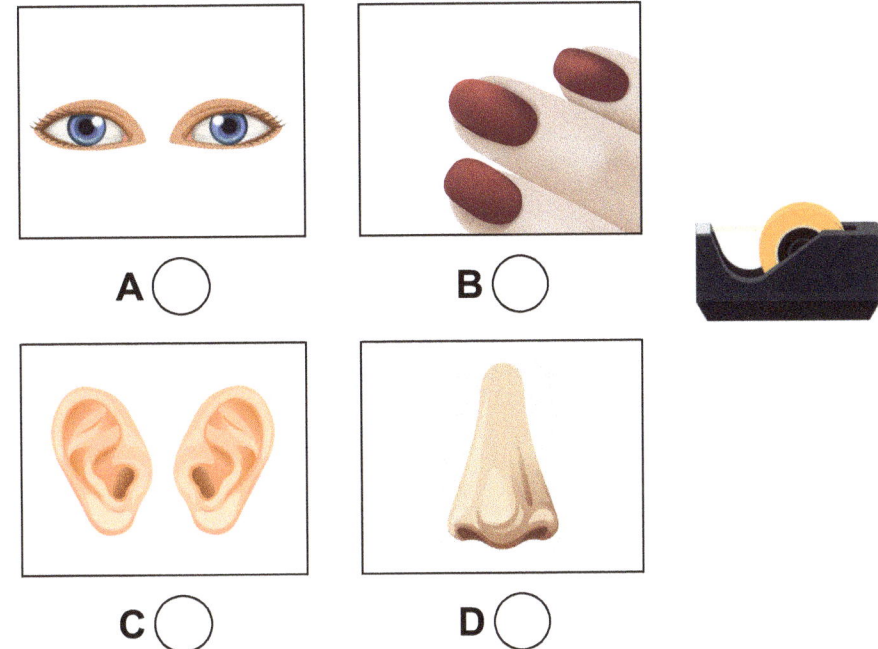

A ⃝   B ⃝

C ⃝   D ⃝

Q-6 Look at the question with the Stapler. Lara is learning about various holidays. Help her to find which of the below is not used for Halloween. Identify the correct picture and help her to bubble the right choice.

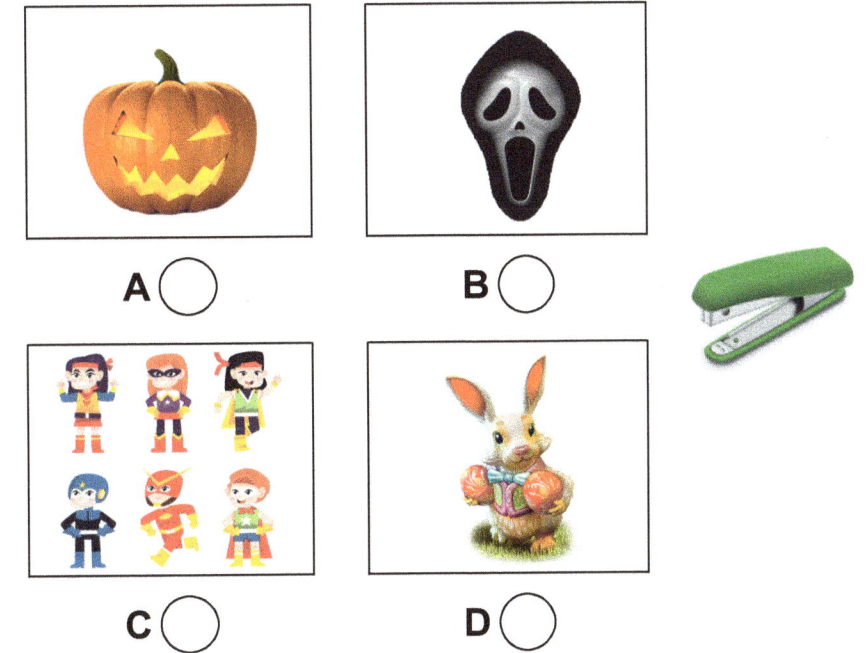

A ⃝   B ⃝

C ⃝   D ⃝

www.math-knots.com

Q-7 Look at the question with the Hole puncher. Gary wants to go to the park to play with his friends. Which of the below can he find in the park? Identify the correct picture and help him to bubble the right choice.

A ◯ B ◯

C ◯ D ◯

Q-8 Look at the question with the Pen Drive. Andrew is studying about various animals. He wonders which of the below has a pouch to hold its babies? Identify the correct picture and help him to bubble the right choice.

A ◯ B ◯

C ◯ D ◯

www.math-knots.com

Q-9

Look at the question with the Scissors. Laura collects various worms from the park and wants to examine them closely. Which of the below does she need for her research? Identify the correct picture and help her to bubble the right choice.

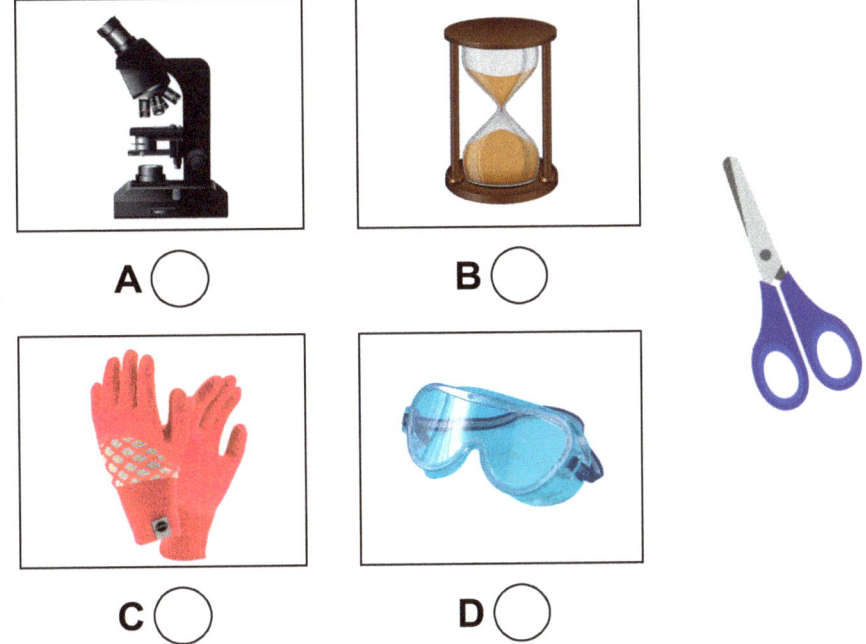

A ◯   B ◯

C ◯   D ◯

Q-10

Look at the question with the Push Pin. Tim manually shovels snow from drive ways during winter to earn his pocket money. Identify the correct picture and help him to bubble the right choice.

A ◯   B ◯

C ◯   D ◯

www.math-knots.com

Q-11

Look at the question with the Sun. Kate is getting ready for her skating class.Help her to get ready by choosing the correct option below. Identify the correct picture and help her to bubble the right choice.

A◯   B◯

C◯   D◯

Q-12

Look at the question with the Laptop. Nancy is trying to solve the below brain teaser. Can you please help her in solving this? Red house is wider than green house. Green house is wider than white house. Which house is the widest of all ? Identify the correct solution and help her to bubble the right choice. (Pictures not drawn to scale)

A◯   B◯

C◯   D◯

www.math-knots.com

Q-13

Look at the question with the Rain. Fire breaks in the yo-yo community. Rescue the community by choosing the correct option below. Identify the correct picture and help Alice to bubble the right choice.

A ◯ B ◯

C ◯ D ◯

Q-14

Look at the question with the Pen. Rosy is grouping her coins from her piggy bank. She wonders which coin has the highest value. Help her in identifying the right coin from the below. Identify the correct picture and help her to bubble the right choice.

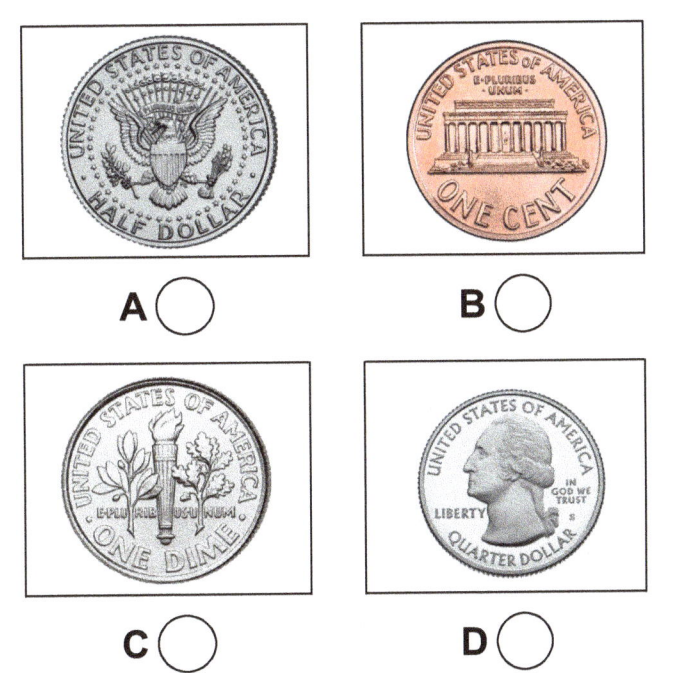

A ◯ B ◯

C ◯ D ◯

151   www.math-knots.com

Q-15

Look at the question with the Office Bag. Sophia wants to get a pet animal with lot of fur. Which of the below is her choice? Identify the correct picture and help her to bubble the right choice.

A ◯   B ◯

C ◯   D ◯

Q-16

Look at the question with the Pencil Holder. Thea wants to paint her room with blue color. She is missing few tools to paint her room. Can you please identify the missing from the below choices given? Help her to bubble the right choice.

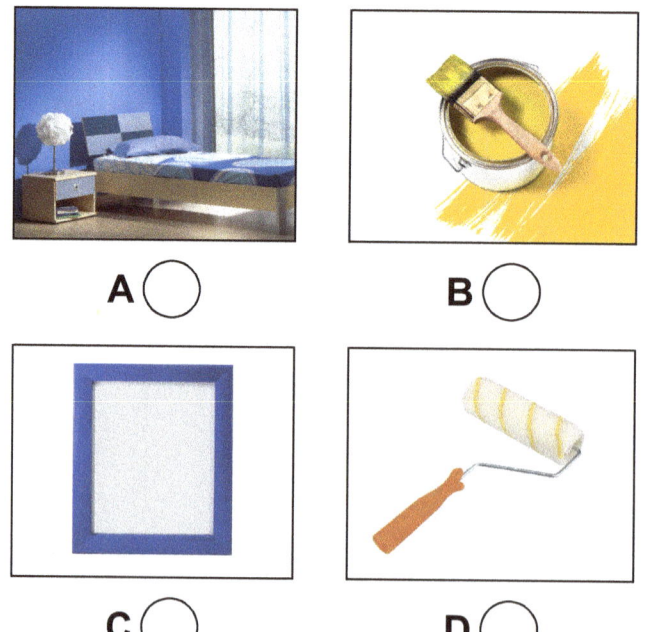

A ◯   B ◯

C ◯   D ◯

www.math-knots.com

Q-17

Look at the question with the Calculator. Ruby wants to toast bagel for her breakfast. Can you please help her in identifying the right choice from the below? Bubble the right choice.

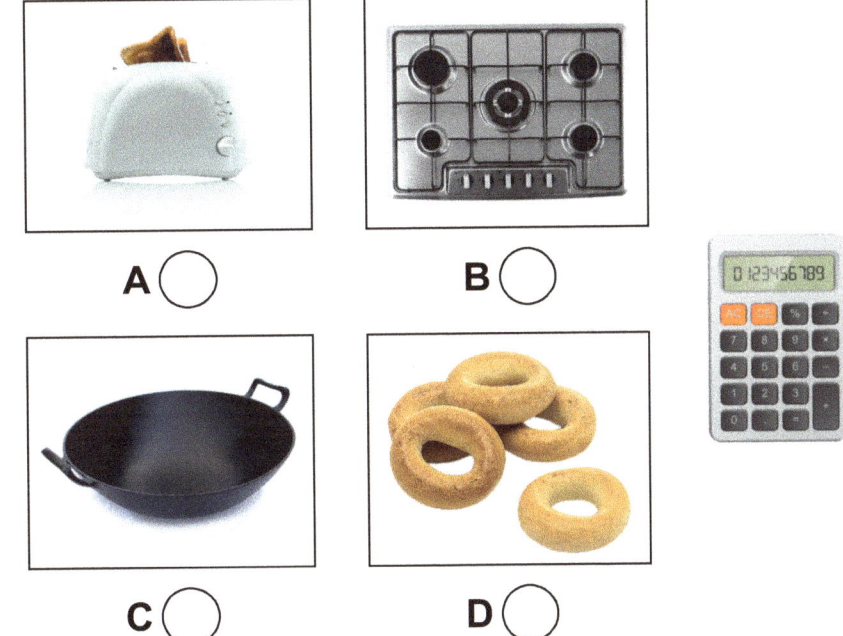

A ◯   B ◯

C ◯   D ◯

Q-18

Look at the question with the Table Light. Alan is getting ready for a beach trip. Which of the below does he need to pack? Identify the correct picture and help him to bubble the right choice.

A ◯   B ◯

C ◯   D ◯

www.math-knots.com

TEST - 2

VERBAL SECTION

VERBAL ANALOGIES

Lets Start the Test...

www.math-knots.com

www.math-knots.com

Sample The first two words are related in a certain way as the next two words. Identify the missing word.

Clouds : White :: Sky : ?

Bold   Blue   Silver   Yellow

A ◯   B ◯   C ◯   D ◯

Solution : B

First analogy is color of the clouds which is white. Color of sky is blue.

Right choice is B.

Student needs to think through how the first two are related and then relate it

to next analogy in the same way. Bubble the correct option.

All the questions in verbal analogies test 2 are to be answered following the below question (instruction).

The first two words are related in a certain way as the next two words. <u>Identify the missing word.</u>

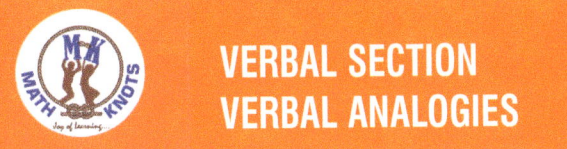
1.   Couple : Two :: Double :   ?

   Two   Triple   Quadruple   Octa

   A◯   B◯   C◯   D◯

2.   Mom : Mother :: Granny :   ?

   Pa   Maa   Grand Pa   Grand Mother

   A◯   B◯   C◯   D◯

3.   North : South :: East :   ?

   South   West   West North   East South

   A◯   B◯   C◯   D◯

4.   Car : Four Wheels :: Bicycle :   ?

   Two Wheels   Three Wheels   Eight Wheels   Six Wheels

   A◯   B◯   C◯   D◯

5.   Base Ball : Runs :: Tennis :   ?

   Score   Hits   Points   Runs

   A◯   B◯   C◯   D◯

6.   **Zoo : Elephant :: Nest :   ?**

Den   Bees   Dog   Bird

A◯   B◯   C◯   D◯

7.   **Monkey : Trees :: Hen :   ?**

Coop   Kennel   Bee Hive   Web

A◯   B◯   C◯   D◯

8.   **White : Peace :: Black :   ?**

Angry   Grumpy   Sad   Anxious

A◯   B◯   C◯   D◯

9.   **Feather : Light :: Mountain :   ?**

Feather   Flare   Glint   Heavy

A◯   B◯   C◯   D◯

10.   **Labor Day : September :: Christmas :   ?**

December   October   May   July

A◯   B◯   C◯   D◯

www.math-knots.com

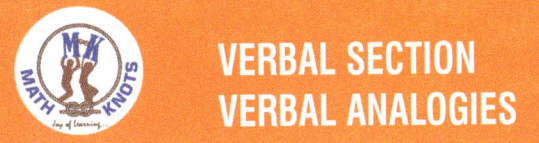

11.   Triangle : Three :: Hexagon :   ?

Four   Six   Eight   Five

A ◯   B ◯   C ◯   D ◯

12.   Apple : Trees :: Grapes :   ?

Bushes   Plants   Under Ground   Vines

A ◯   B ◯   C ◯   D ◯

13.   Basket Ball : Throw :: Soccer Ball :   ?

Push   Kick   Hit   Catch

A ◯   B ◯   C ◯   D ◯

14.   Lemon : Sour :: Chocolate :   ?

Spicy   Tangy   Sweet   Bland

A ◯   B ◯   C ◯   D ◯

15.   Duck : Duckling :: Hen :   ?

Cub   Chick   Calf   Herd

A ◯   B ◯   C ◯   D ◯

16.   **Head : Hat :: Ears :   ?**

Ear Plugs   Coat   Hat   Cotton

A◯   B◯   C◯   D◯

17.   **Helmets : Bicycles :: Seat Belts :   ?**

Train   Trycycle   Bike   Car

A◯   B◯   C◯   D◯

18.   **Thermometer : Temperature :: Anemometer :   ?**

Current   Wind Speed   Distance   Torque

A◯   B◯   C◯   D◯

www.math-knots.com

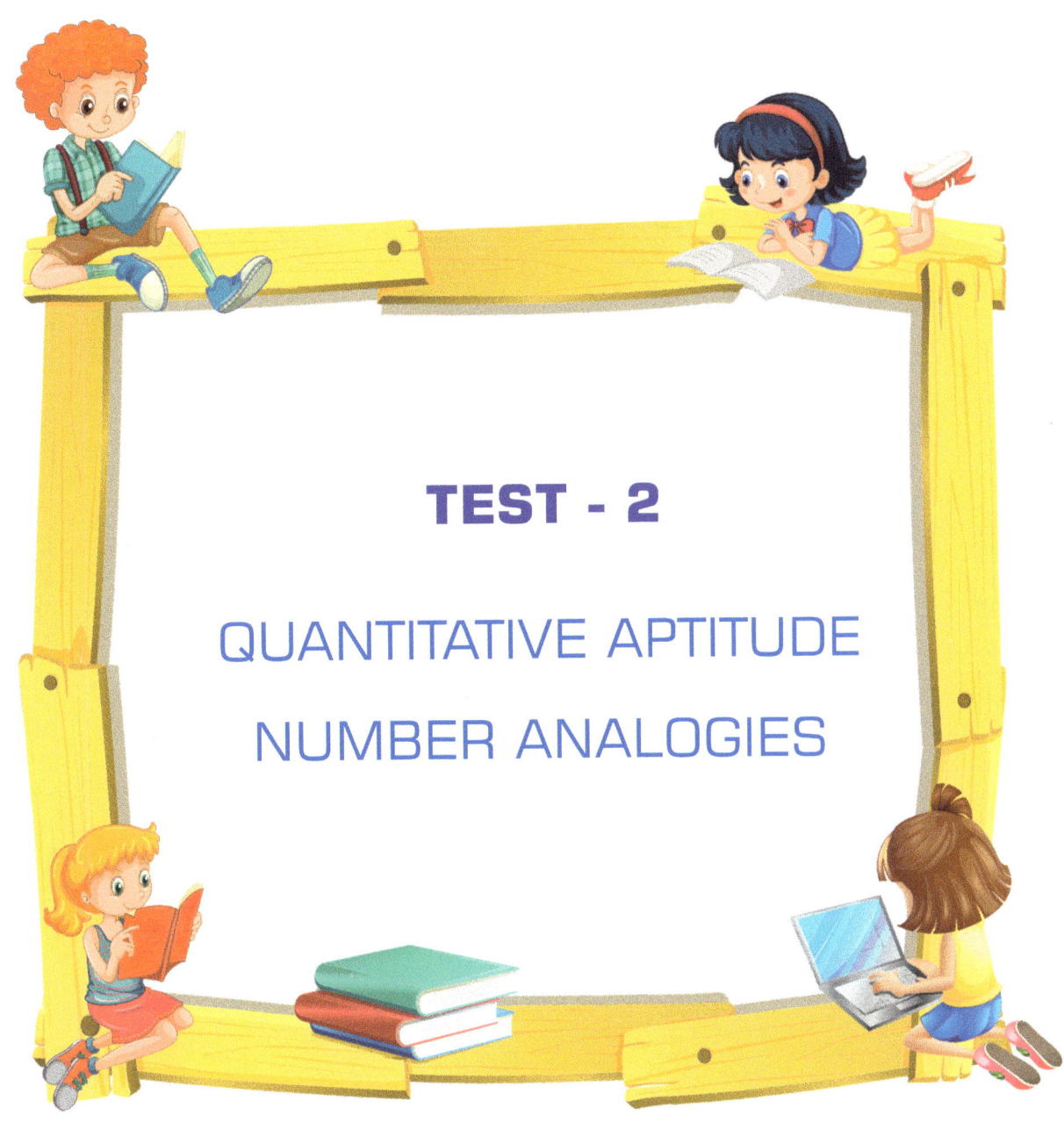

TEST - 2

QUANTITATIVE APTITUDE

NUMBER ANALOGIES

Lets Start the Test...

Sample Look at the question with the Parrot. Two boxes in the first row are related in a certain way which is similar to two boxes in the second row. Ken is trying to fill the bubble under the correct option. Help him to select from options A, B, C, and D.

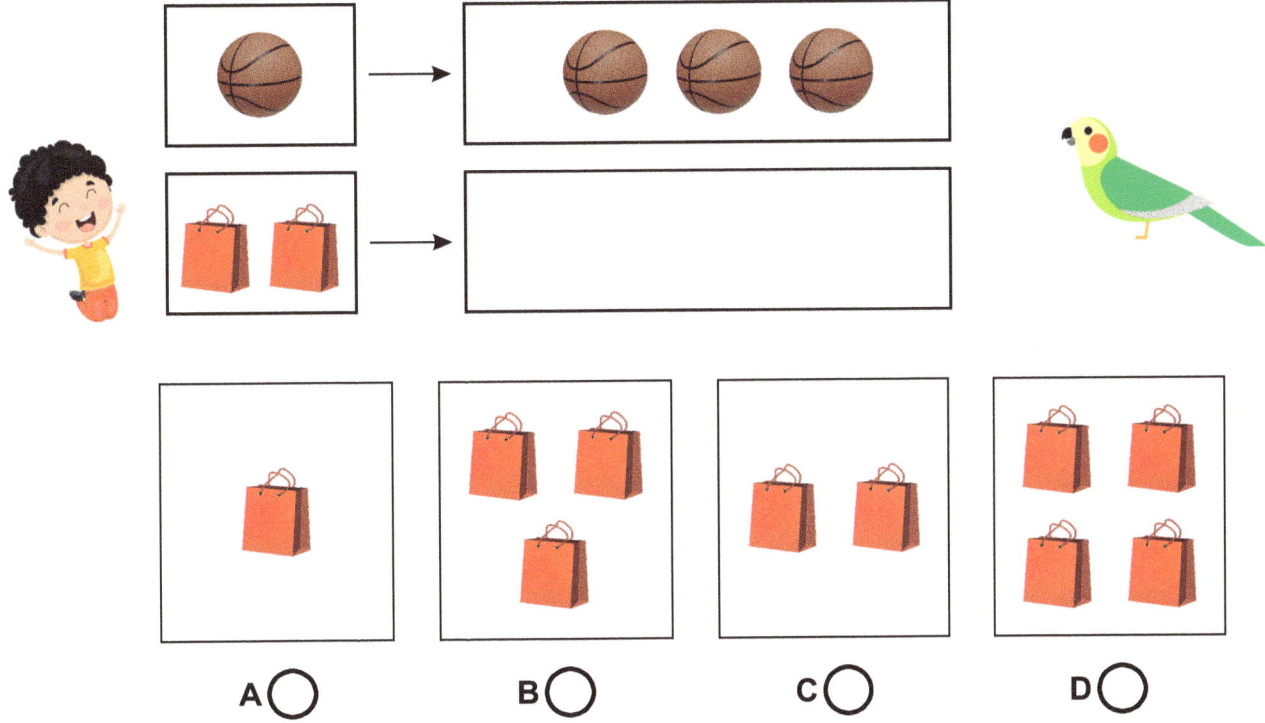

A ◯ B ◯ C ◯ D ◯

Solution : D

In first row one, ball to three balls [(1+2) adding two more]

In second row, two bags by adding two more will become four bags.

The analogies can be formed by adding or subtracting a certain number meaning increasing or decreasing by a certain quantity. Students needs to understand the right analogy and bubble the correct option.

Q-1 Look at the question with the Orange. Choose the picture that has the same number of shoes as in the first picture. Sam is trying to find the bubble under the correct option. Help him to select from options A, B, C, and D.

A ◯   B ◯   C ◯   D ◯

Q-2 Look at the question with the Lemon. Choose the picture that has which has the three times the amount of lipstick as shown in the first picture. Mary is trying to fill the bubble under the correct option. Help her to select from options A, B, C, and D.

A ◯   B ◯   C ◯   D ◯

www.math-knots.com

Q-3 Look at the question with the Pear. Choose the picture that has twice the number of Googles as shown in the first picture. Fred is trying to fill the bubble under the correct option. Help him to select from options A, B, C, and D.

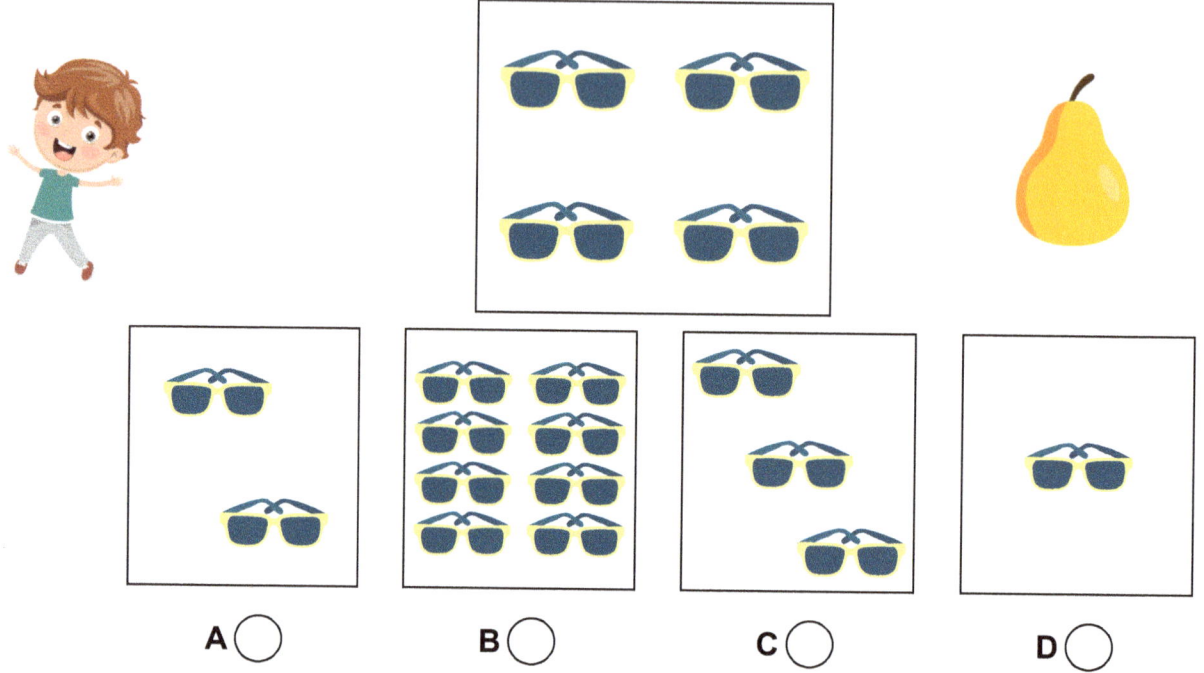

A ◯   B ◯   C ◯   D ◯

Q-4 Look at the question with the Banana. Count how many cars are in the first picture. Which one of the picture shows two fewer cars than the first picture? Robert is trying to fill the bubble under the correct option. Help him to select from options A, B, C, and D.

A ◯   B ◯   C ◯   D ◯

www.math-knots.com

Q-5 Look at the question with the Water Melon. Count how many cups are in the first picture. Which one of the picture shows one less than the first picture? Nora is trying to fill the bubble under the correct option. Help her to select from options A, B, C, and D.

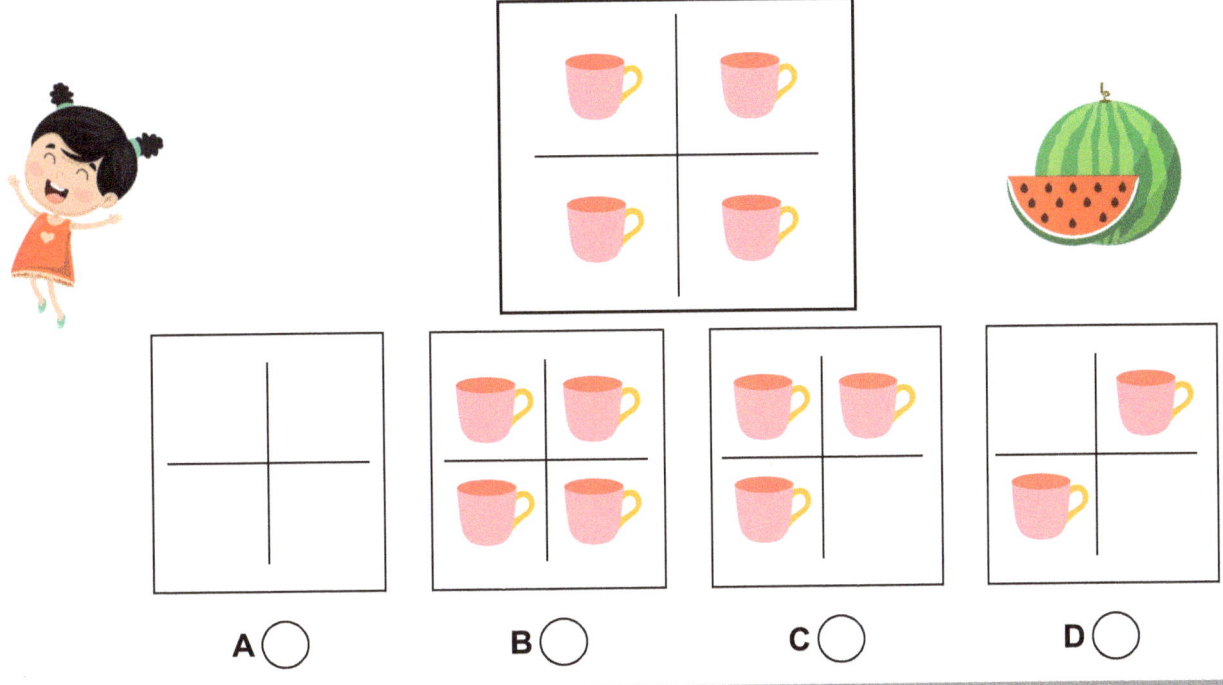

A◯ B◯ C◯ D◯

Q-6 Look at the question with the Apple. Count how many cups are in the first picture. Which one of the picture shows three fewer symbols than the first picture? Sofia is trying to fill the bubble under the correct option. Help her to select from options A, B, C, and D.

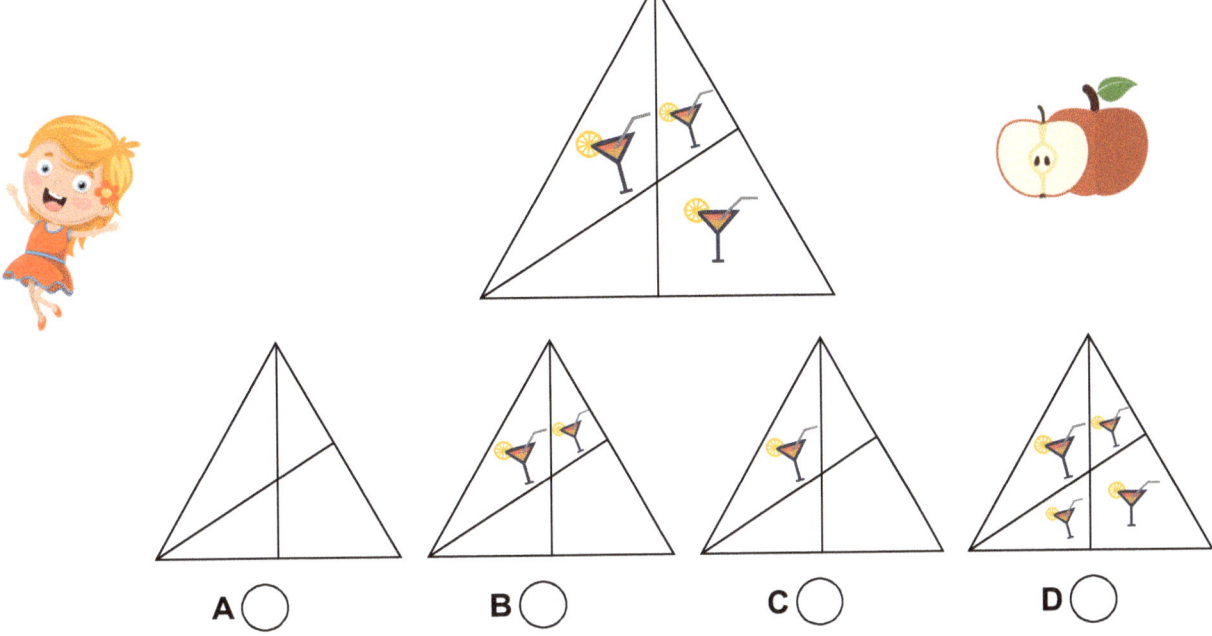

A◯ B◯ C◯ D◯

Q-7 Look at the question with the Grapes. Count how many laptops in first picture. Which one of the other picture shows one fewer laptop than the first picture? Ava is trying to fill the bubble under the correct option. Help her to select from options A, B, C, and D.

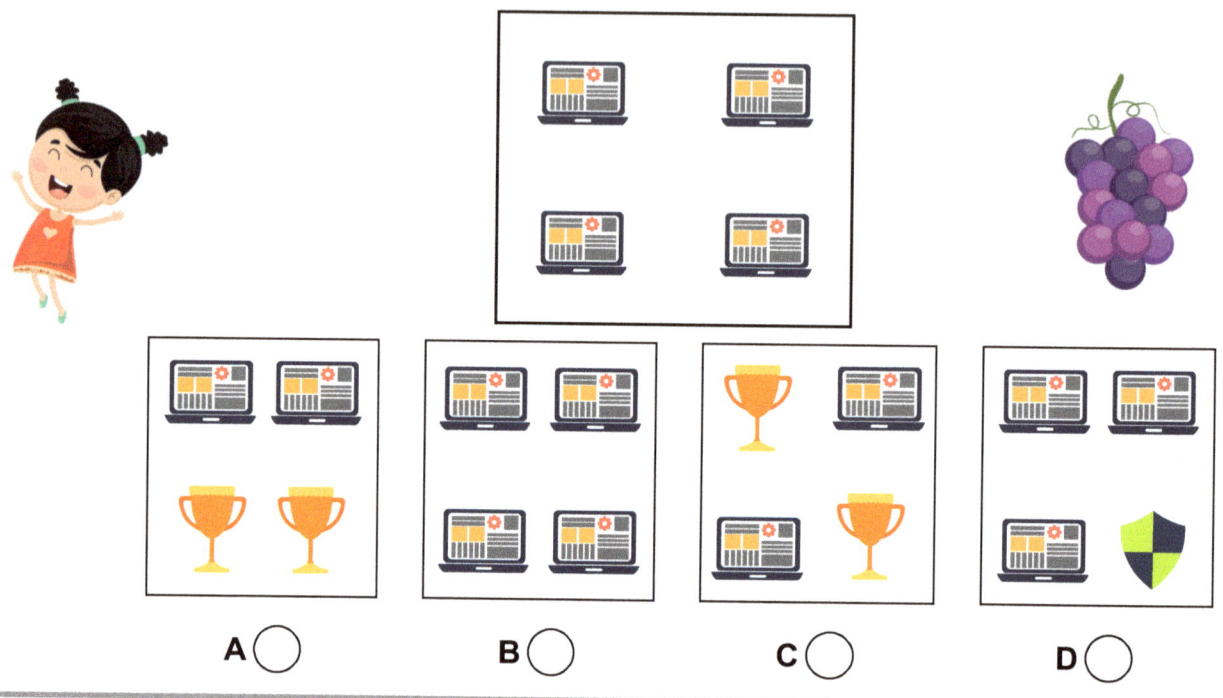

A ◯   B ◯   C ◯   D ◯

Q-8 Look at the question with the Mango. Count how many music systems in first picture. Which one of the other picture shows three fewer music systems? Johnson is trying to fill the bubble under the correct option. Help him to select from options A, B, C, and D.

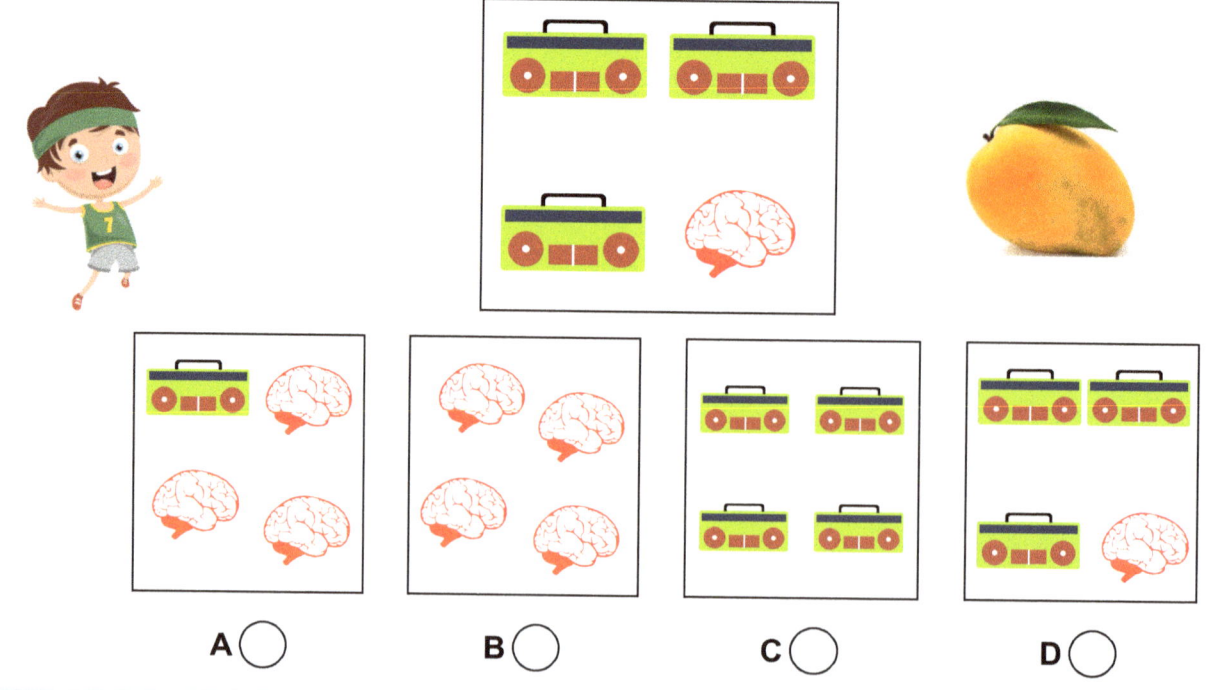

A ◯   B ◯   C ◯   D ◯

www.math-knots.com

Q-9

Look at the question with the Avacado. Count how many Cameras are in the first picture. Which one of the other picture shows one more Cameras than the first picture? Alexander is trying to fill the bubble under the correct option. Help him to select from options A, B, C, and D.

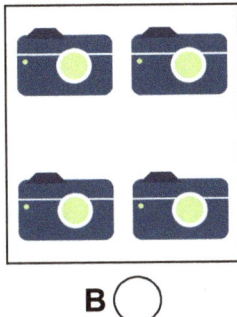

A ◯   B ◯   C ◯   D ◯

Q-10

Look at the question with the Carrot. Count how many leaves are in the first picture. Which picture shows two fewer leaves than the first picture? Lucas is trying to fill the bubble under the correct option. Help him to select from options A, B, C, and D.

A ◯   B ◯   C ◯   D ◯

www.math-knots.com

Q-11

Look at the question with the Pomangranate. Count how many houses are in the first picture. Which picture shows three fewer houses than the first picture? Ella is trying to fill the bubble under the correct option. Help her to select from options A, B, C, and D.

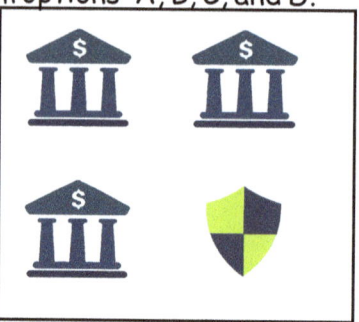

A ◯

B ◯

C ◯

D ◯

Q-12

Look at the question with the Cucumber. Count how many pendrives are in the first picture. Which one of the other picture shows two more pendrives than the first picture? Samuel is trying to fill the bubble under the correct option. Help him to select from options A, B, C, and D.

A ◯

B ◯

C ◯

D ◯

www.math-knots.com

Q-13

Look at the question with the Kiwi. Count all the objects in the first picture. Which one of the other objects show the same image? Anthony is trying to fill the bubble under the correct option. Help him to select from options A, B, C, and D.

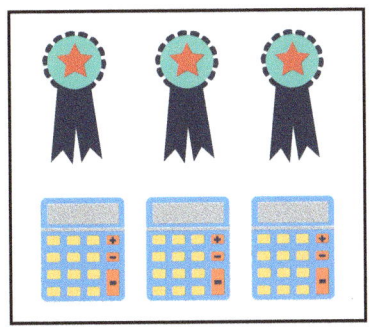

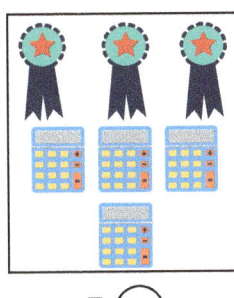

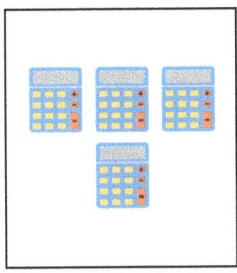

A ◯   **B** ◯   **C** ◯   **D** ◯

Q-14

Look at the question with the Coconut. Count the objects from first picture. Which one of the picture shows two more objects than first picture? Skylar is trying to fill the bubble under the correct option. Help her to select from options A, B, C, and D.

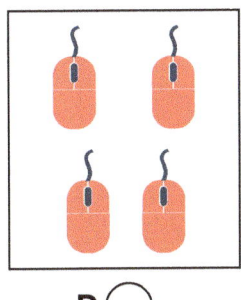

A ◯   **B** ◯   **C** ◯   **D** ◯

www.math-knots.com

Q-15

Look at the question with the Mango. Count the objects in the first picture. Which picture shows one more object than the first picture? Hannah is trying to fill the bubble under the correct option. Help her to select from options A, B, C, and D.

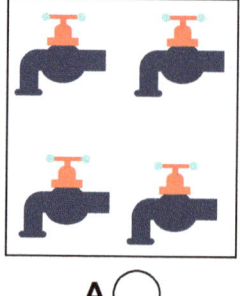

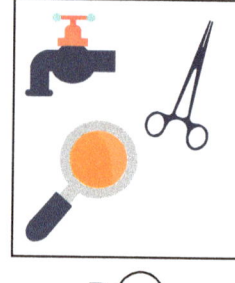

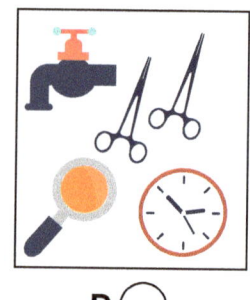

A◯   B◯   C◯   D◯

Q-16

Look at the question with the Cherry. Count the objects in the first picture. Which one of the other objects shows the same image? Mathew is trying to fill the bubble under the correct option. Help him to select from options A, B, C, and D.

A◯   B◯   C◯   D◯

www.math-knots.com

Q-17

Look at the question with the Water Melon. Count the objects in the first picture.   Which picture shows one more bulb than the first picture? Joseph is trying to fill the bubble under the correct option. Help him to select from options A, B, C, and D.

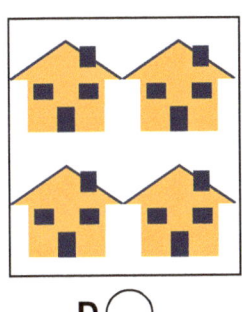

A ◯   B ◯   C ◯   D ◯

Q-18

Look at the question with the Strawberry. Count the objects in the first picture. Which picture shows the same image? Chloe is trying to fill the bubble under the correct option. Help her to select from options A, B, C, and D.

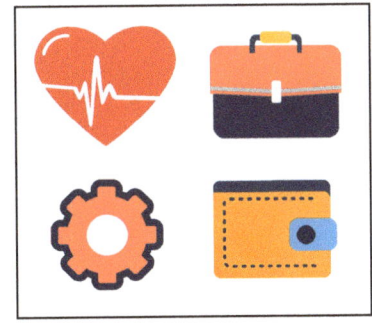

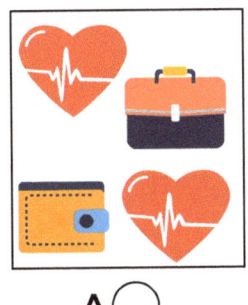

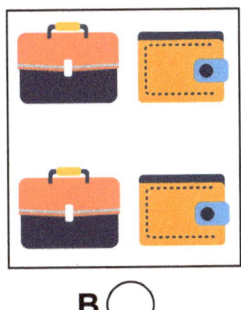

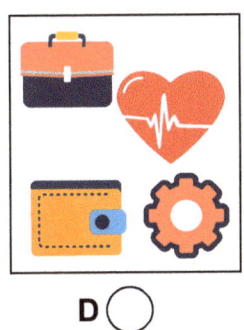

A ◯   B ◯   C ◯   D ◯

www.math-knots.com

TEST - 2

QUANTITATIVE APTITUDE

NUMBER SERIES

Lets Start the Test...

Sample Look at the question with the Triangle. Cathy is making a pattern with her hexagon shaped beads. Can you help her to identify what goes in the empty string from the given four options A, B, C, and D.

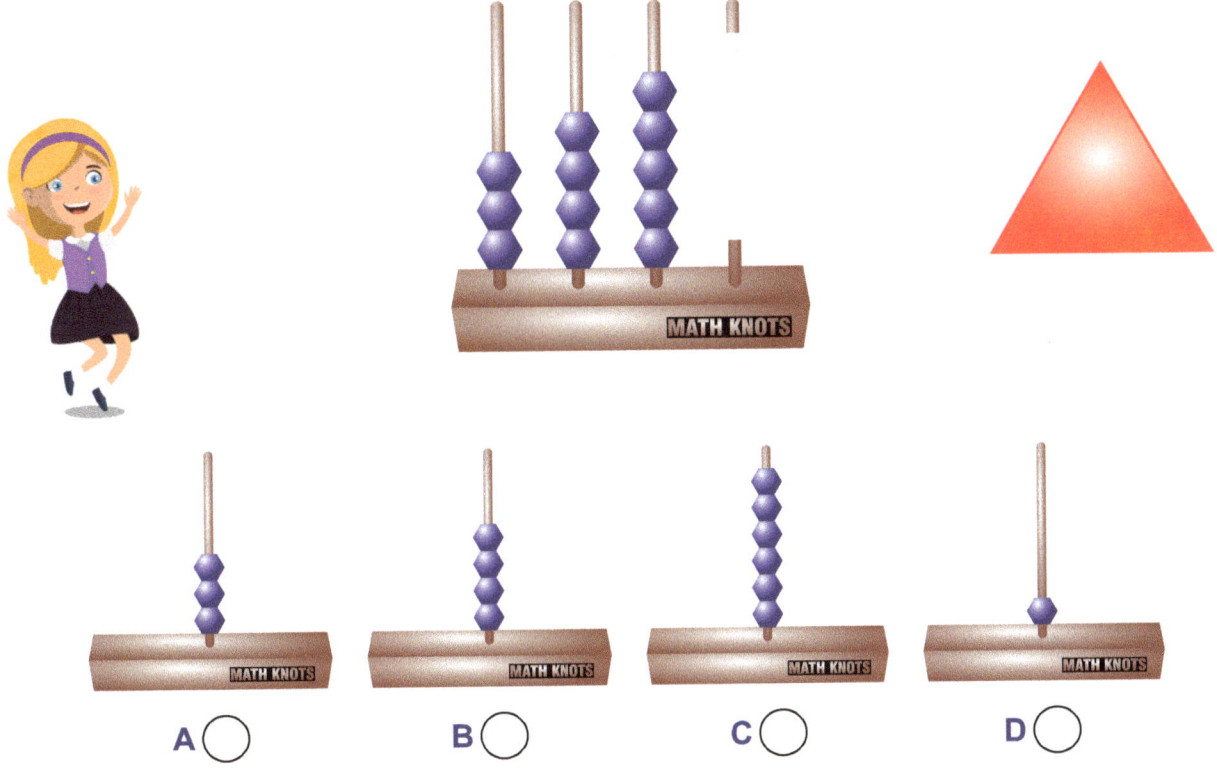

A◯ B◯ C◯ D◯

Solution : C

3,4,5.....

The beads are increasing by 1. So next string should have six beads.

Option C is the correct choice. The patterns can increase or decrease by a certain number of beads. Students are supposed to identify the correct pattern and answer the correct choice.

www.math-knots.com

Q-1 Look at the question with the Table. Camila is making a pattern with her hexagon shaped beads. Can you help her to identify what goes in the empty string from the given four options A, B, C, and D.

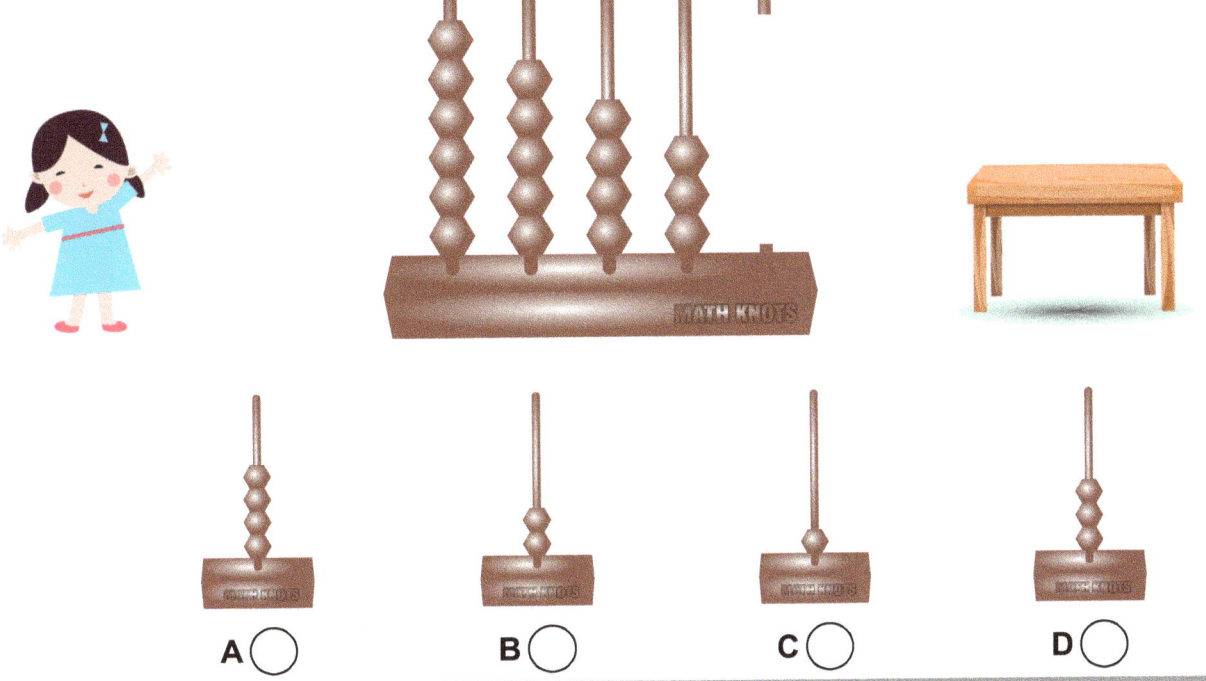

A ◯　　B ◯　　C ◯　　D ◯

Q-2 Look at the question with the Cot. Justin is making a pattern with his hexagon shaped beads. Can you help him to identify what goes in the empty string from the given four options A, B, C, and D.

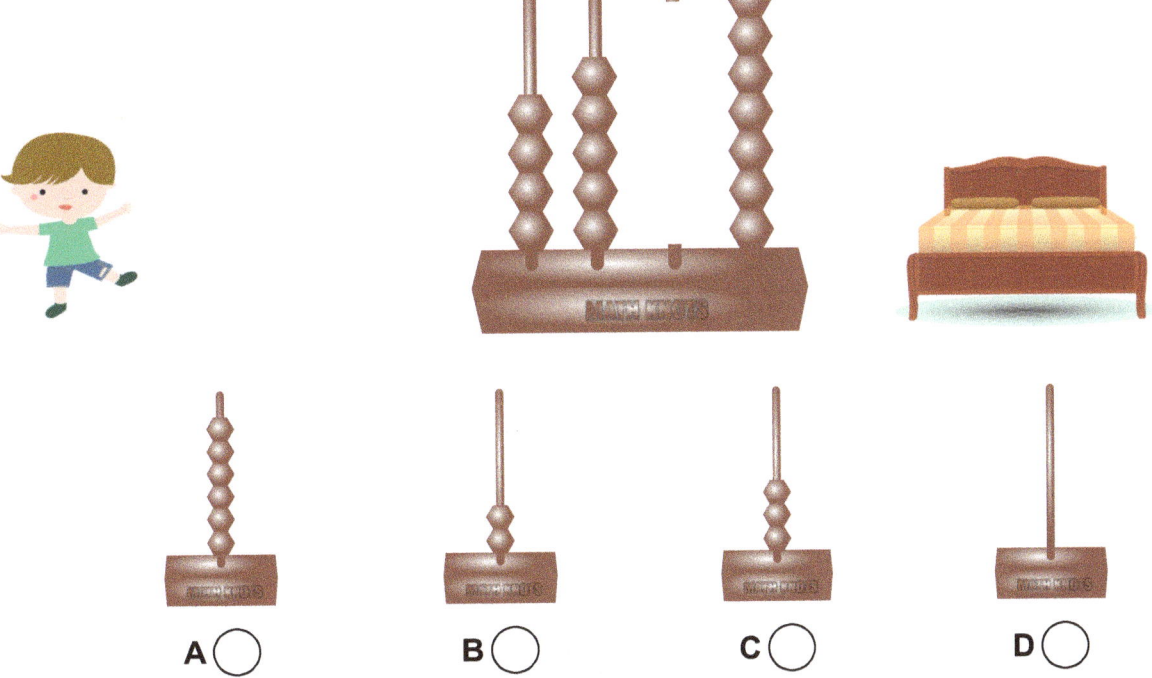

A ◯　　B ◯　　C ◯　　D ◯

www.math-knots.com

Q-3 Look at the question with the Clock. Wesley is making a pattern with his hexagon shaped beads. Can you help him to identify what goes in the empty string from the given four options A, B, C, and D.

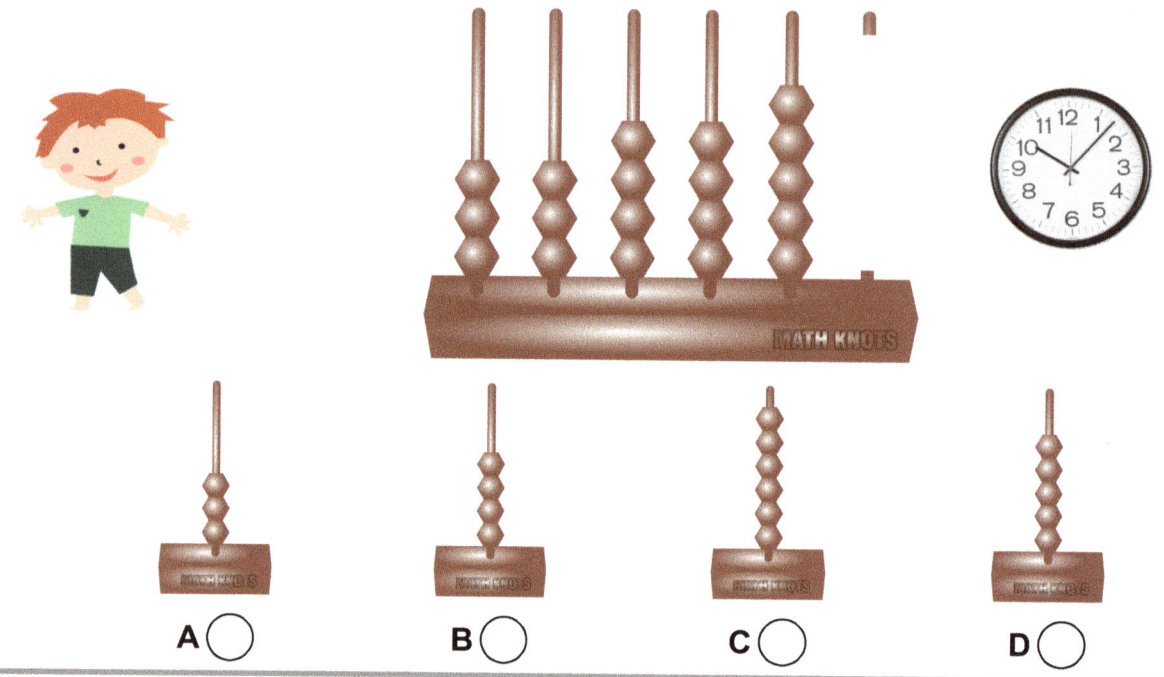

A ◯   B ◯   C ◯   D ◯

Q-4 Look at the question with the Camp Fire. Reva is making a pattern with her hexagon shaped beads. Can you help her to identify what goes in the empty string from the given four options A, B, C, and D.

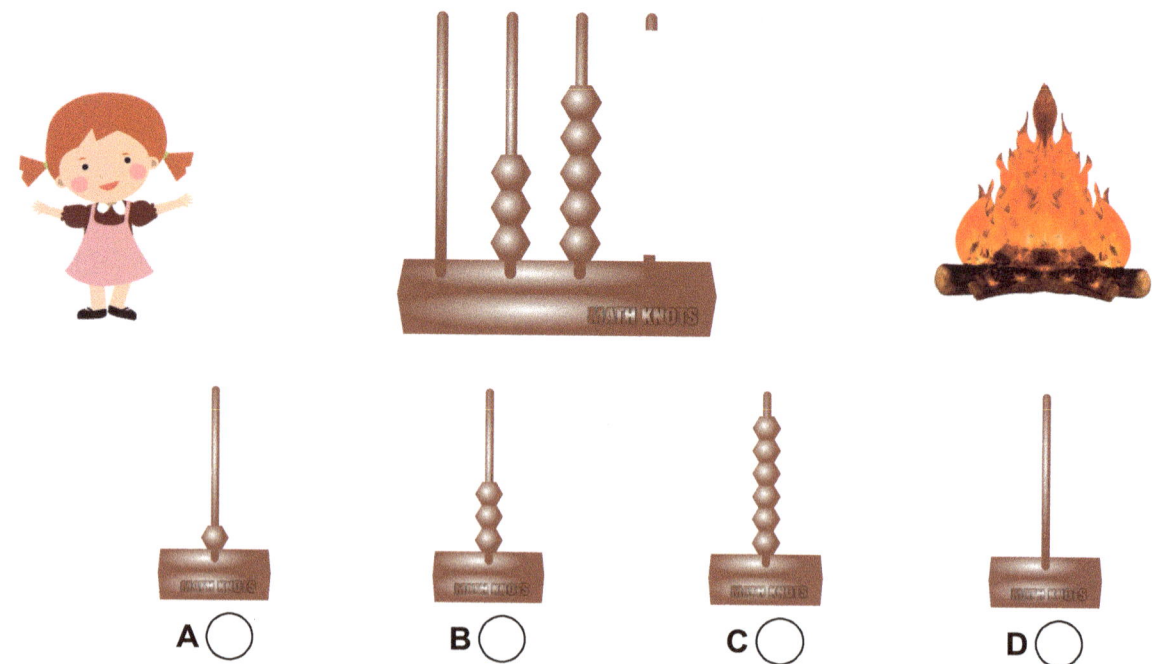

A ◯   B ◯   C ◯   D ◯

www.math-knots.com

Q-5 Look at the question with the Side Table. Morgan is making a pattern with her hexagon shaped beads. Can you help her to identify what goes in the empty string from the given four options A,B,C, and D.

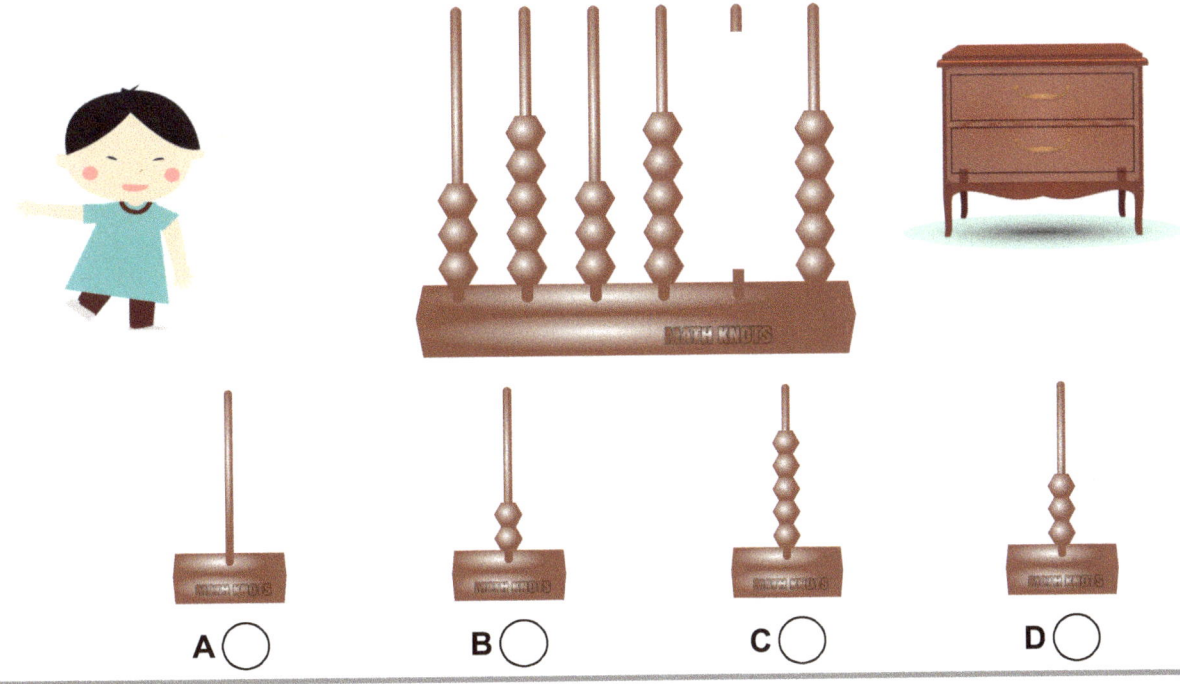

A ◯   B ◯   C ◯   D ◯

Q-6 Look at the question with the Chair. Lauren is making a pattern with her hexagon shaped beads. Can you help her to identify what goes in the empty string from the given four options A,B,C, and D.

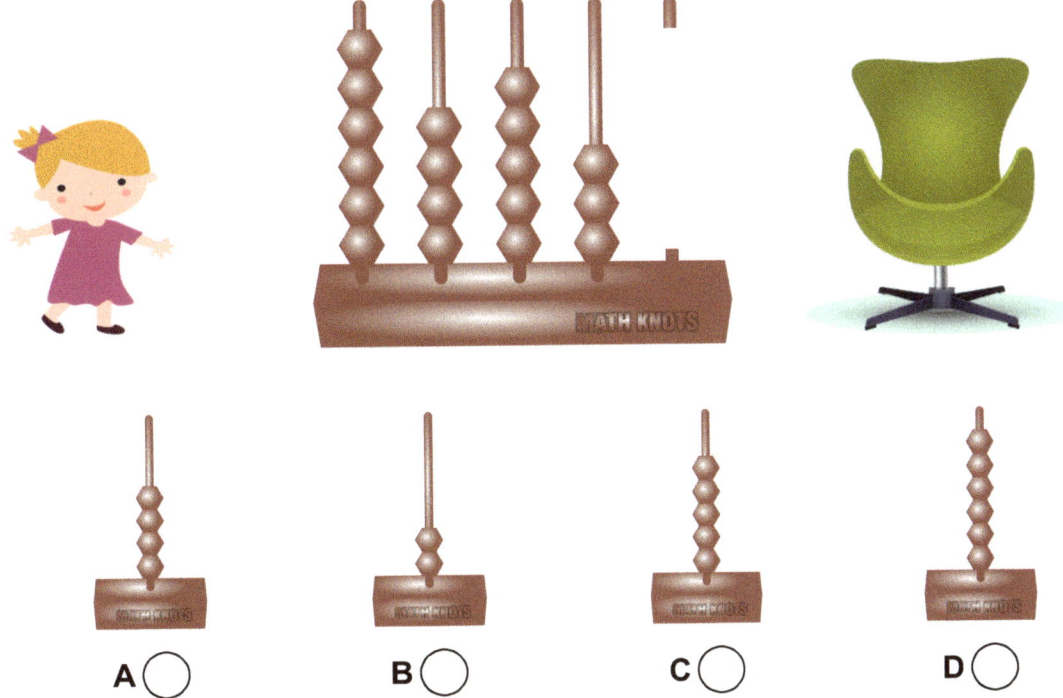

A ◯   B ◯   C ◯   D ◯

www.math-knots.com

Q-7 Look at the question with the Book Rack. Jace is making a pattern with his hexagon shaped beads. Can you help him to identify what goes in the empty string from the given four options A, B, C, and D.

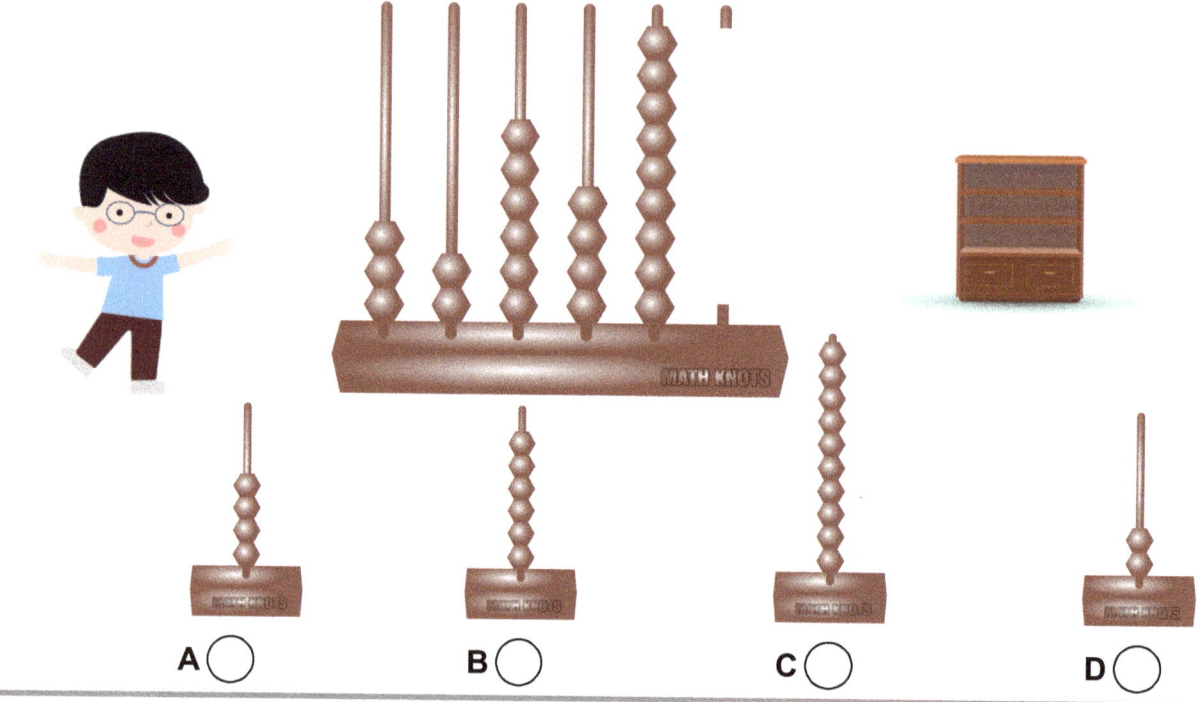

A ◯ **B** ◯ **C** ◯ **D** ◯

Q-8 Look at the question with the Tent. Eva is making a pattern with her hexagon shaped beads. Can you help her to identify what goes in the empty string from the given four options A, B, C, and D.

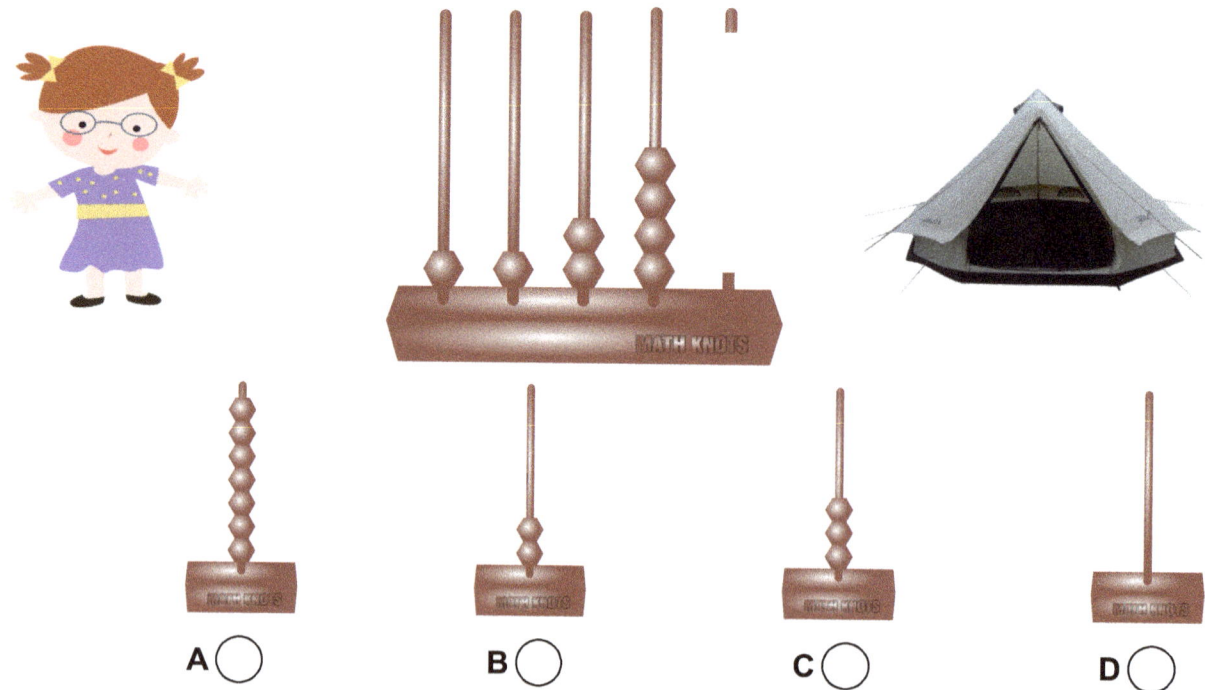

A ◯ **B** ◯ **C** ◯ **D** ◯

www.math-knots.com

Q-9

Look at the question with the Black Board. Ryder is making a pattern with his hexagon shaped beads. Can you help him to identify what goes in the empty string from the given four options A,B,C, and D.

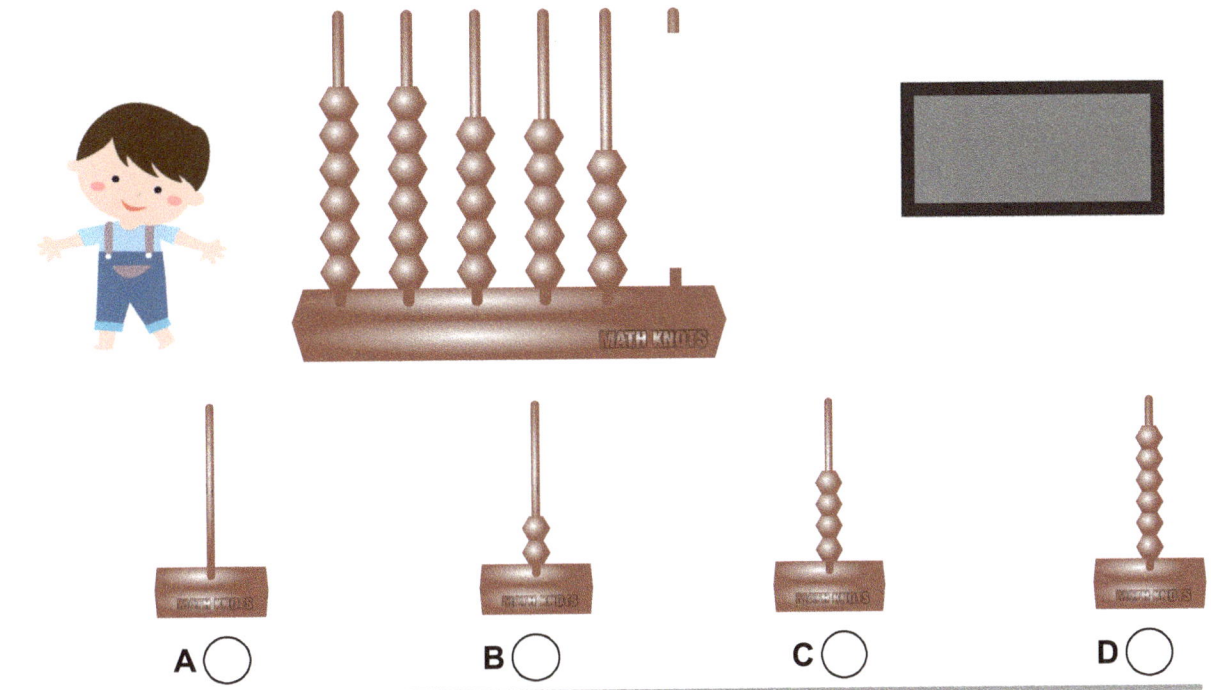

A ◯   B ◯   C ◯   D ◯

Q-10

Look at the question with the House. Elina is making a pattern with her hexagon shaped beads. Can you help her to identify what goes in the empty string from the given four options A,B,C, and D.

A ◯   B ◯   C ◯   D ◯

www.math-knots.com

Q-11 Look at the question with the Computer. Kayden is making a pattern with his hexagon shaped beads. Can you help him to identify what goes in the empty string from the given four options A, B, C, and D.

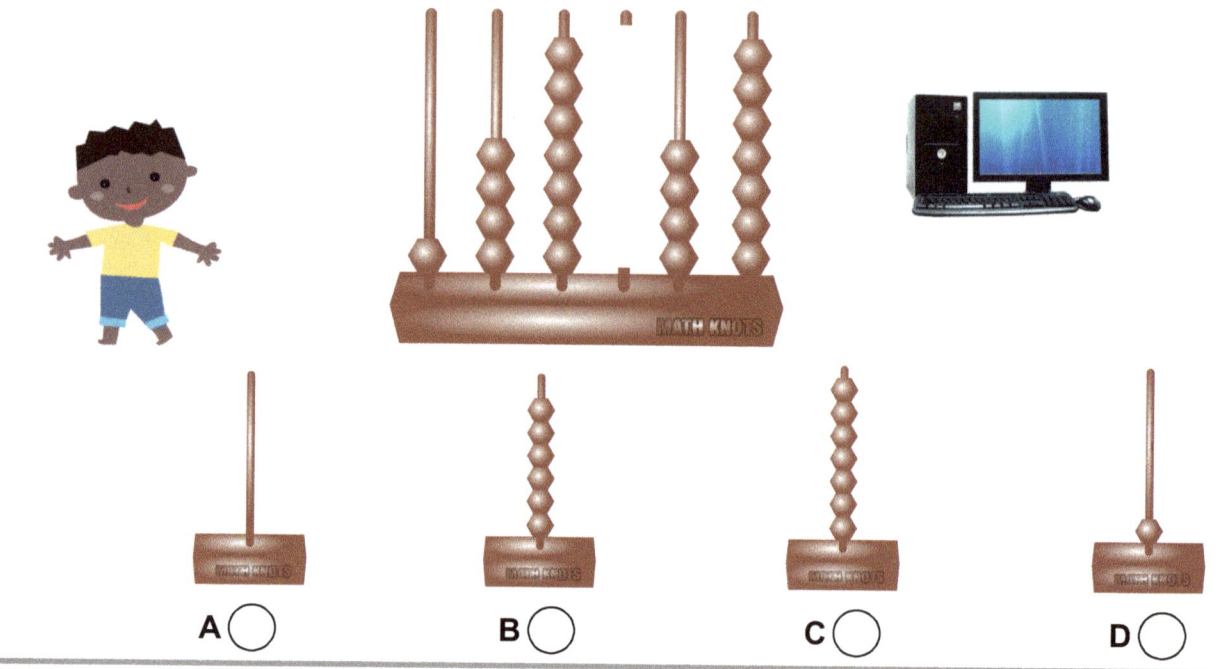

Q-12 Look at the question with the Mobile. Kinsley is making a pattern with her hexagon shaped beads. Can you help her to identify what goes in the empty string from the given four options A, B, C, and D.

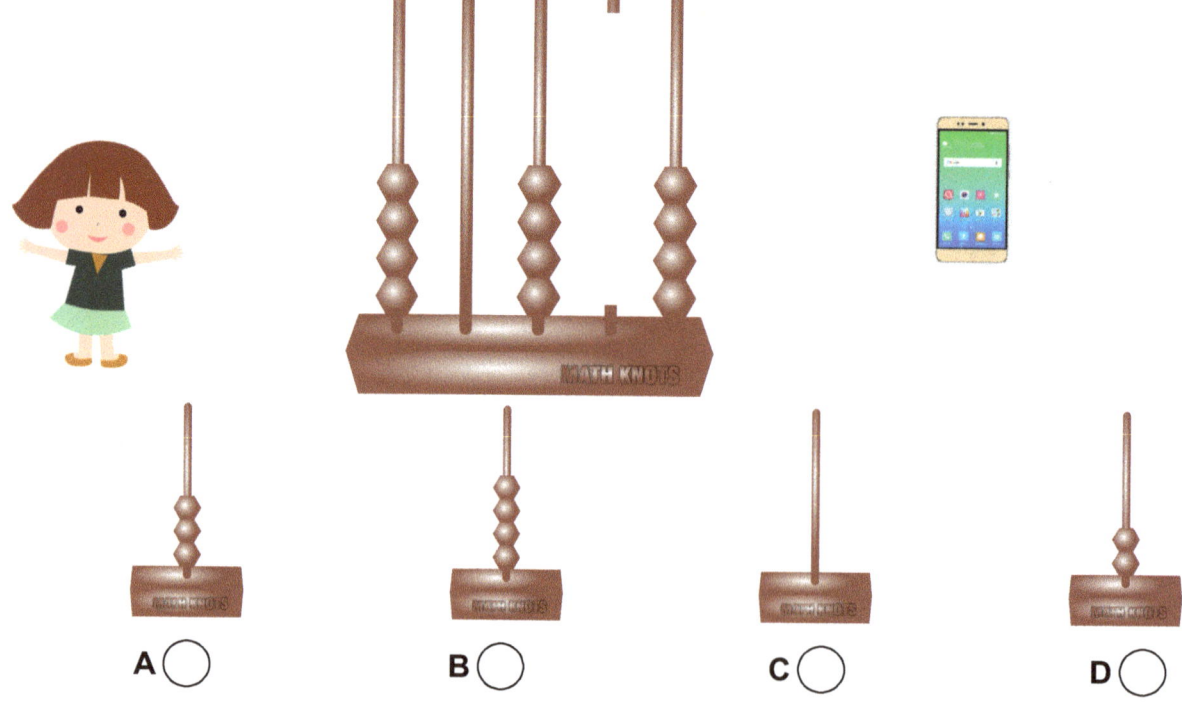

www.math-knots.com

Q-13 Look at the question with the Dressing Table. Ellie is making a pattern with her hexagon shaped beads. Can you help her to identify what goes in the empty string from the given four options A, B, C, and D.

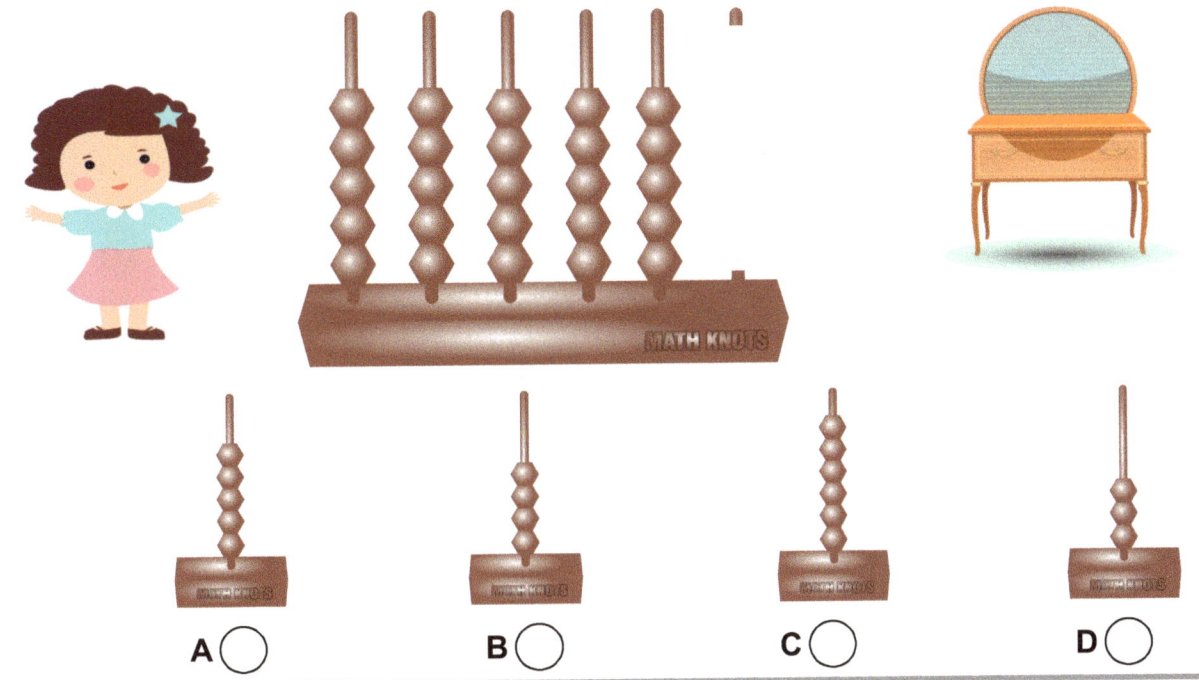

A ◯   B ◯   C ◯   D ◯

Q-14 Look at the question with the Writing Desk. Brandon is making a pattern with his hexagon shaped beads. Can you help him to identify what goes in the empty string from the given four options A, B, C, and D.

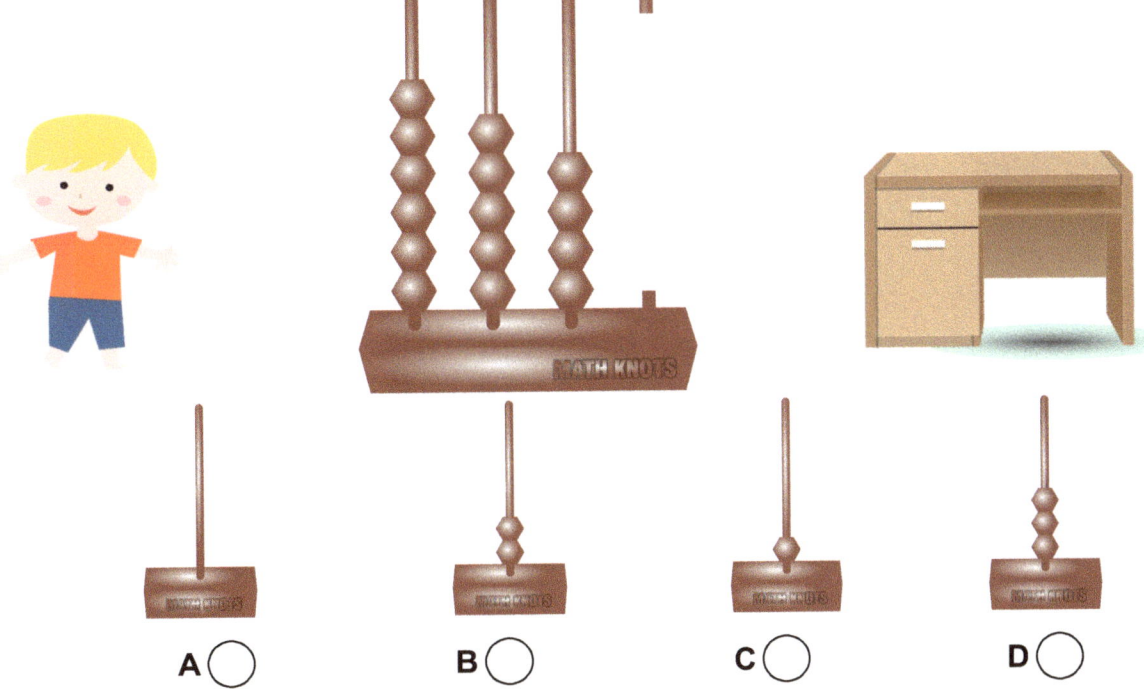

A ◯   B ◯   C ◯   D ◯

www.math-knots.com

Q-15

Look at the question with the Car. Keyden is making a pattern with his hexagon shaped beads. Can you help him to identify what goes in the empty string from the given four options A,B,C, and D.

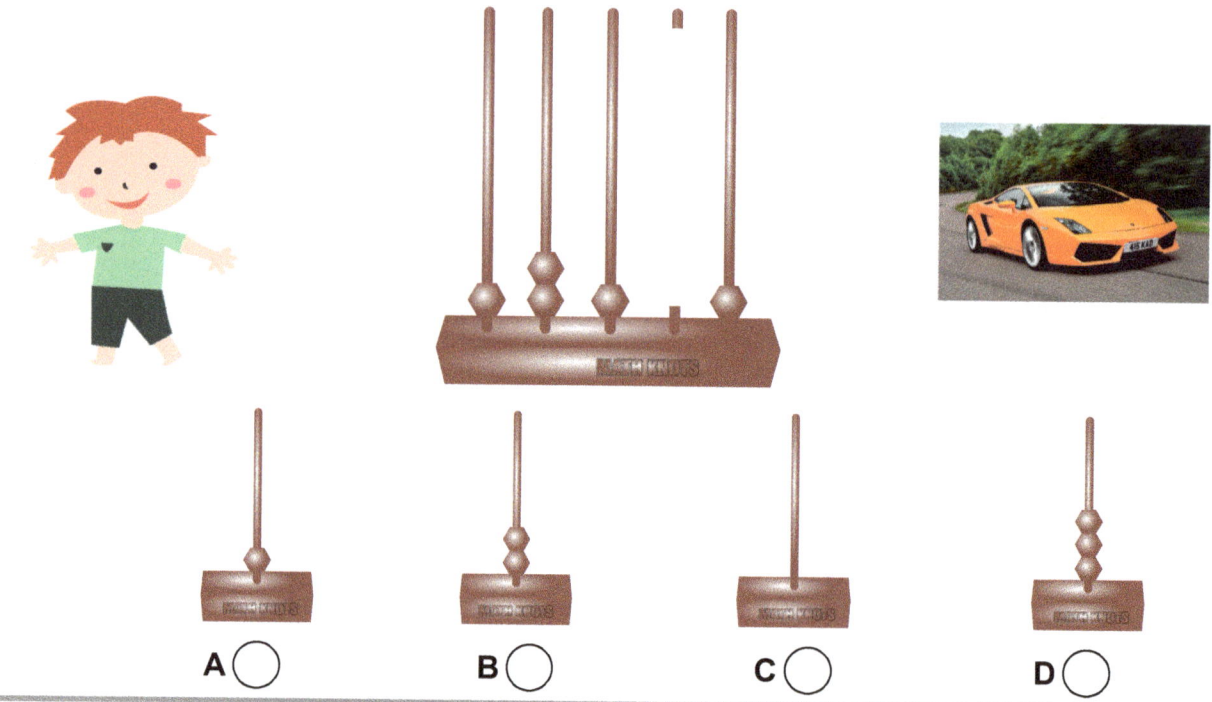

A ◯   B ◯   C ◯   D ◯

Q-16

Look at the question with the School Bus. Clara is making a pattern with her hexagon shaped beads. Can you help her to identify what goes in the empty string from the given four options A,B,C, and D.

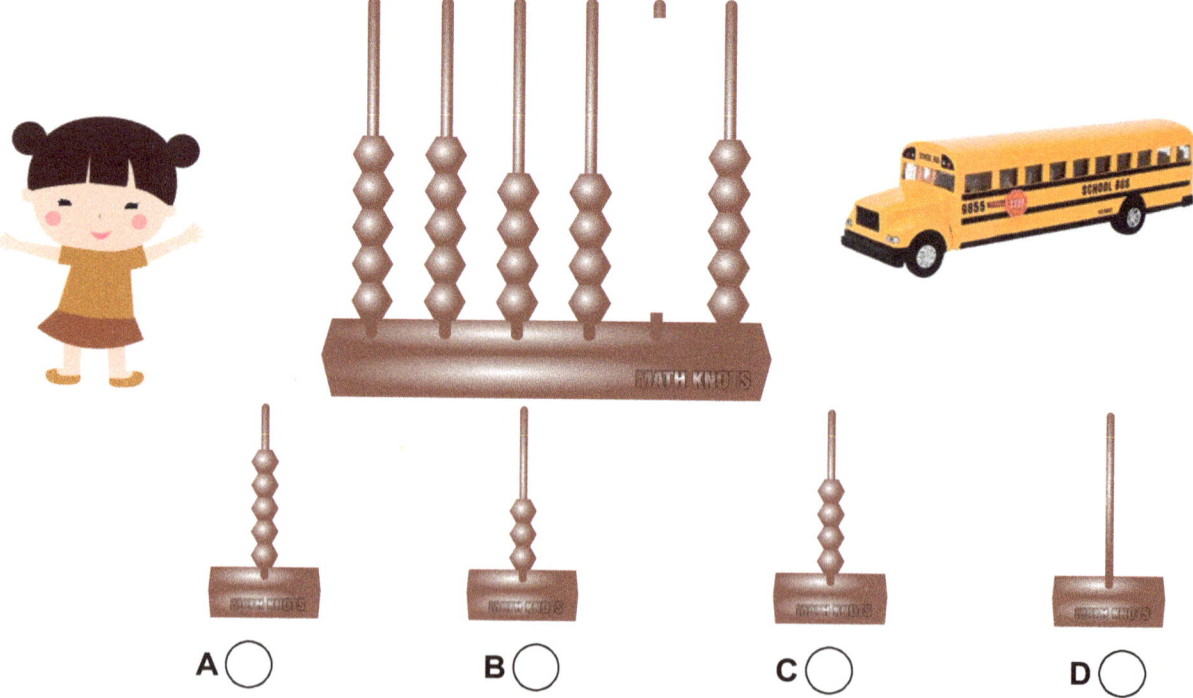

A ◯   B ◯   C ◯   D ◯

www.math-knots.com

Q-17 Look at the question with the Doll. Alyssa is making a pattern with her hexagon shaped beads. Can you help her to identify what goes in the empty string from the given four options A,B,C, and D.

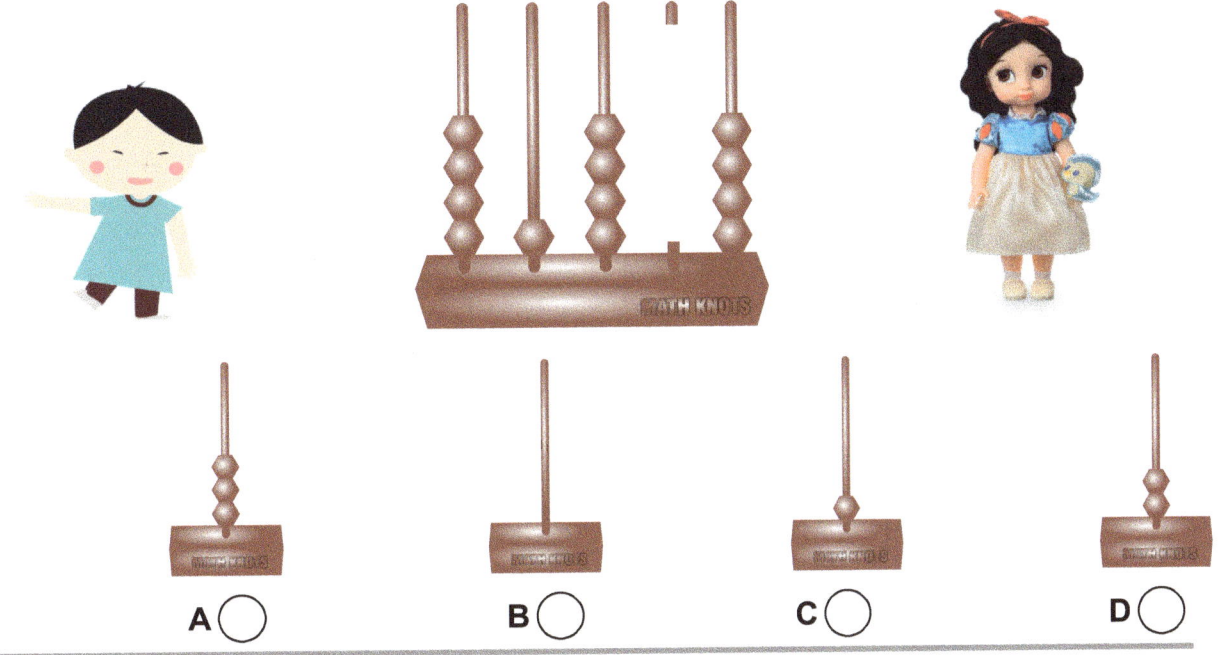

A ◯ B ◯ C ◯ D ◯

Q-18 Look at the question with the Printer. Julia is making a pattern with her hexagon shaped beads. Can you help her to identify what goes in the empty string from the given four options A,B,C, and D.

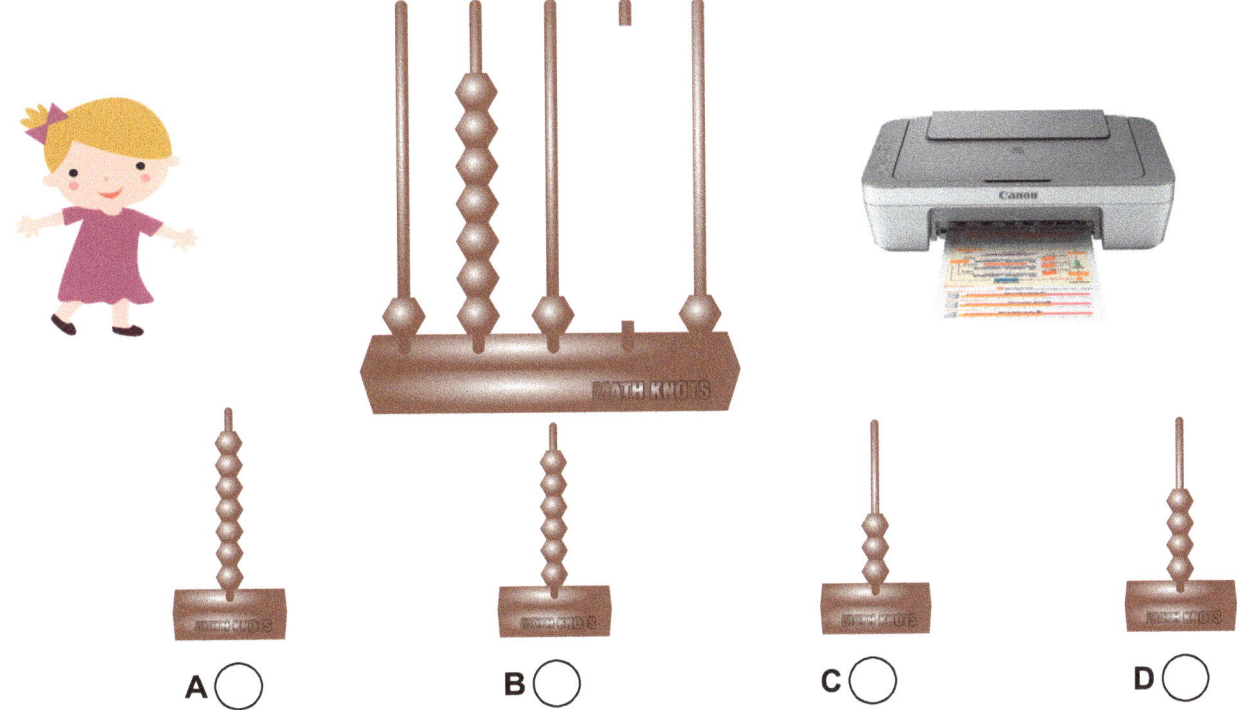

A ◯ B ◯ C ◯ D ◯

www.math-knots.com

TEST - 2

QUANTITATIVE APTITUDE

NUMBER PUZZLES

Lets Start the Test...

Sample Look at the question and put your finger on the Guitar. Ryan is wondering what is the missing number under the question mark ? Help him to find the missing number under the question mark and fill in the bubble.

 **2** + **?** = **3**

1	**0**	**5**	**2**
A○	B○	C○	D○

Solution : A

How much should be added to 2 to make it 3

3 - 2 = 1

Meaning if we add 1 to 2 we get a total of three.

www.math-knots.com

Q-1 Look at the question and put your finger on the Fox. Adan is wondering what is the missing number under the question mark ? Help him to find the missing number under the question mark and fill in the bubble.

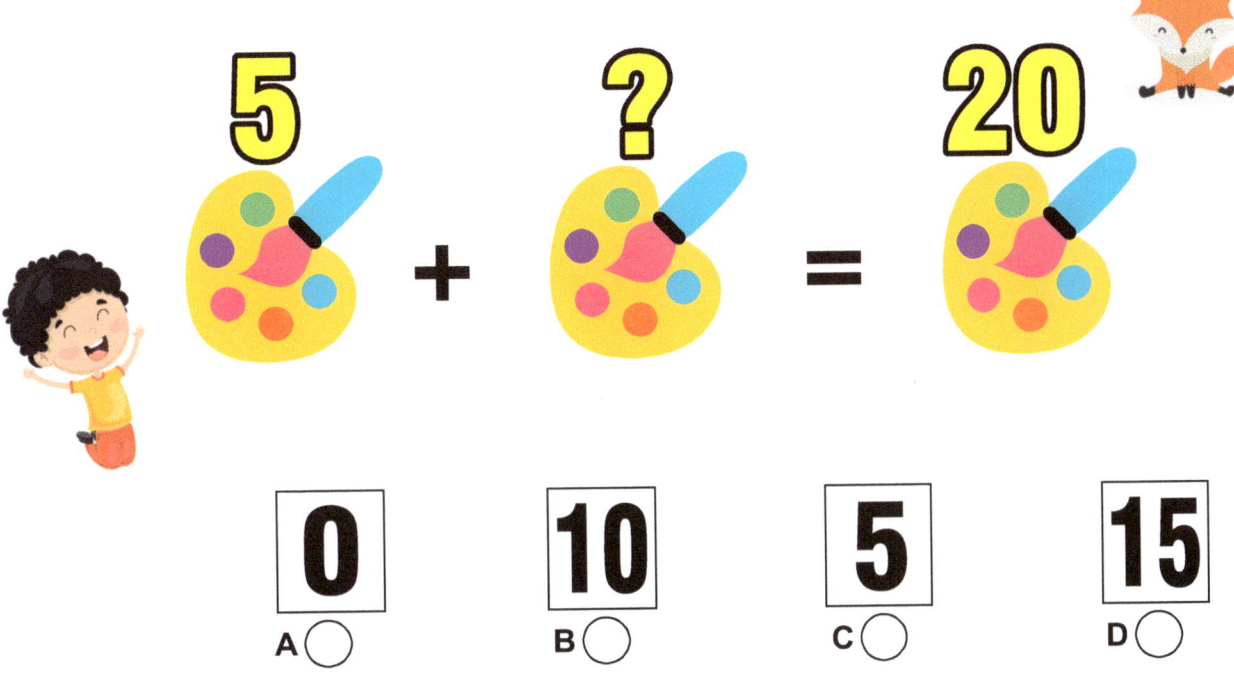

$$5 + ? = 20$$

0	10	5	15
A○	B○	C○	D○

Q-2 Look at the question and put your finger on the Giraffe. Tara is wondering what is the missing number is under the question mark ? Help her to find the missing number under the question mark and fill in the bubble.

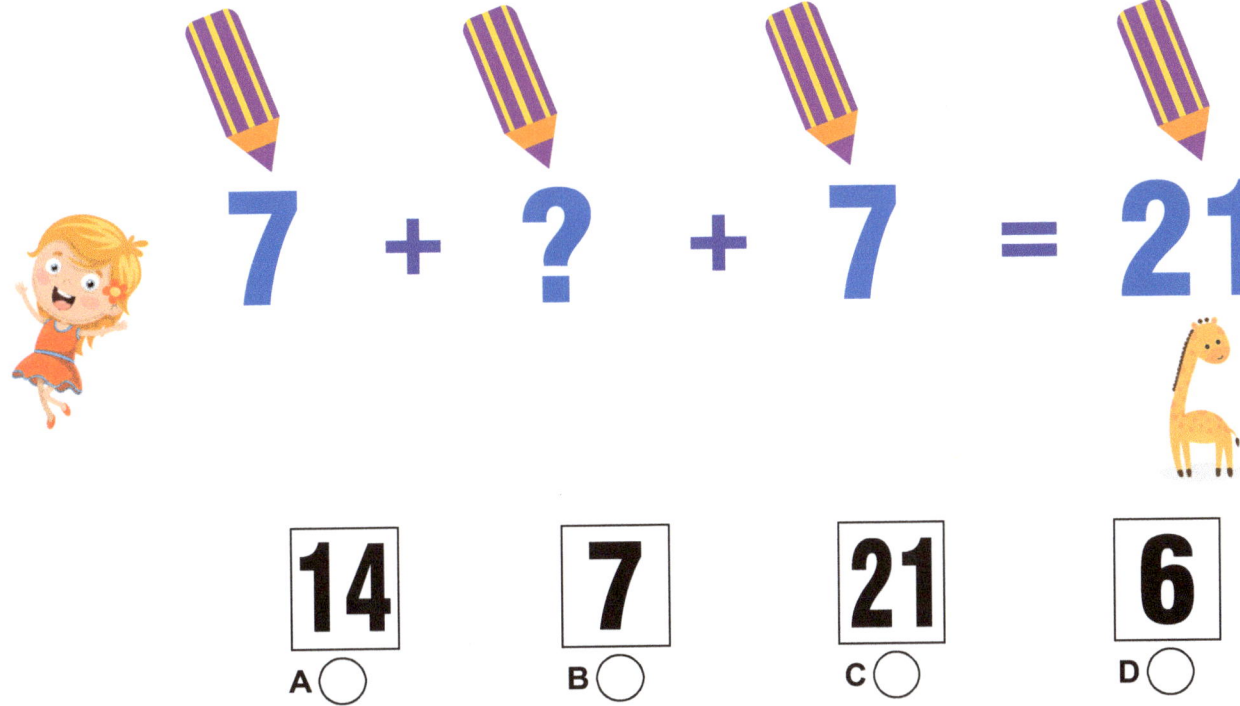

$$7 + ? + 7 = 21$$

14	7	21	6
A○	B○	C○	D○

www.math-knots.com

Q-3 Look at the question and put your finger on the Iguana. Jay is wondering what is the missing number under the question mark ? Help him to find the missing number under the question mark and fill in the bubble.

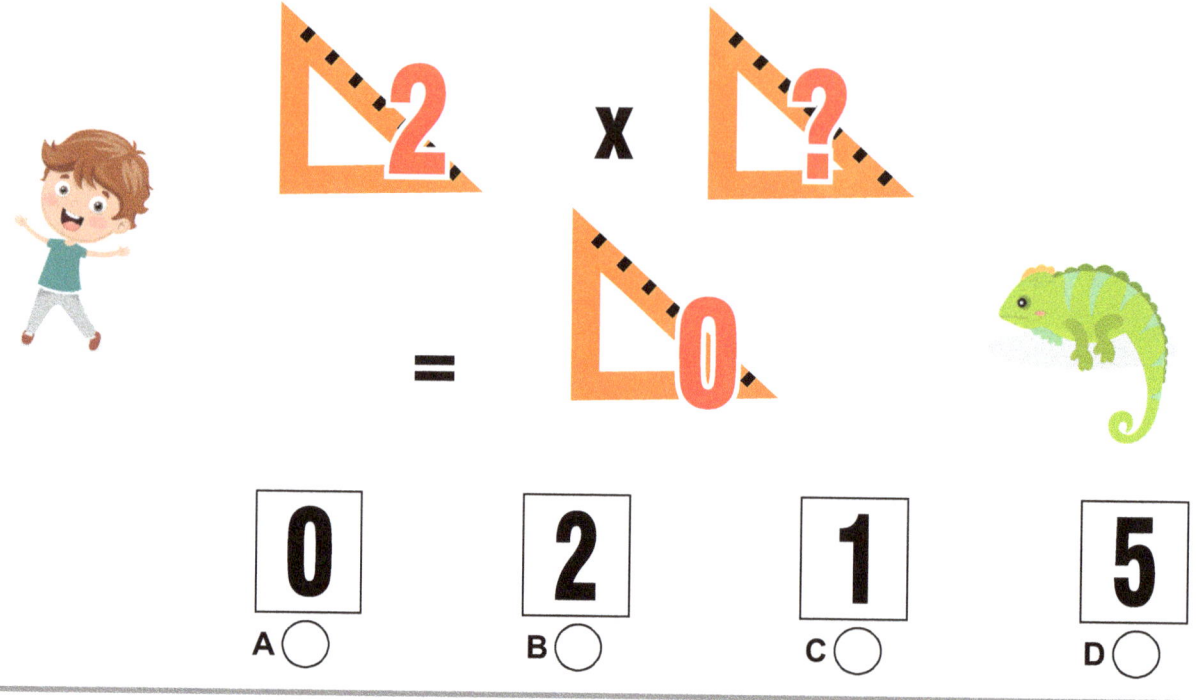

A ◯ 0	B ◯ 2	C ◯ 1	D ◯ 5

Q-4 Look at the question and put your finger on the Jelly Fish. Luke is wondering what is the missing number under the question mark ? Help him to find the missing number under the question mark and fill in the bubble.

A ◯ 5	B ◯ 0	C ◯ 1	D ◯ 2

www.math-knots.com

Q-5 Look at the question and put your finger on the Star Fish. Rak is wondering what is the missing number under the question mark ? Help her to find the missing number under the question mark and fill in the bubble.

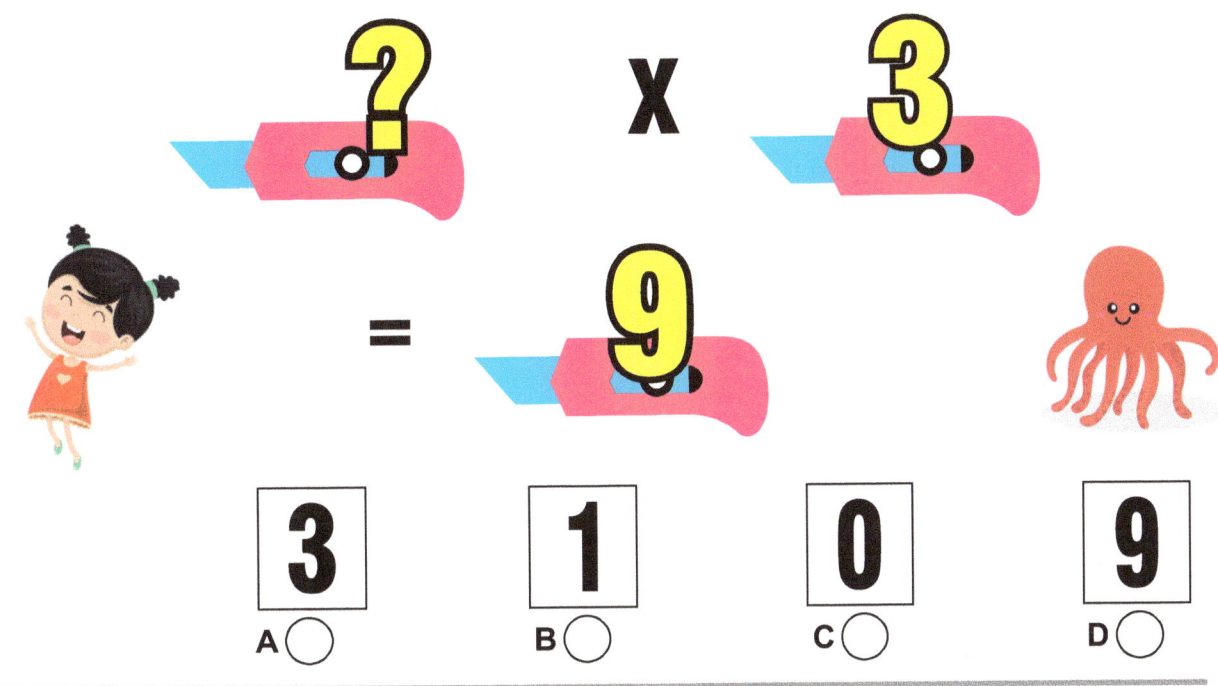

$$? \times 3 = 9$$

A ◯ 3   B ◯ 1   C ◯ 0   D ◯ 9

Q-6 Look at the question and put your finger on the Monkey. Helen is wondering what is the missing number under the question mark ? Help her to find the missing number under the question mark and fill in the bubble.

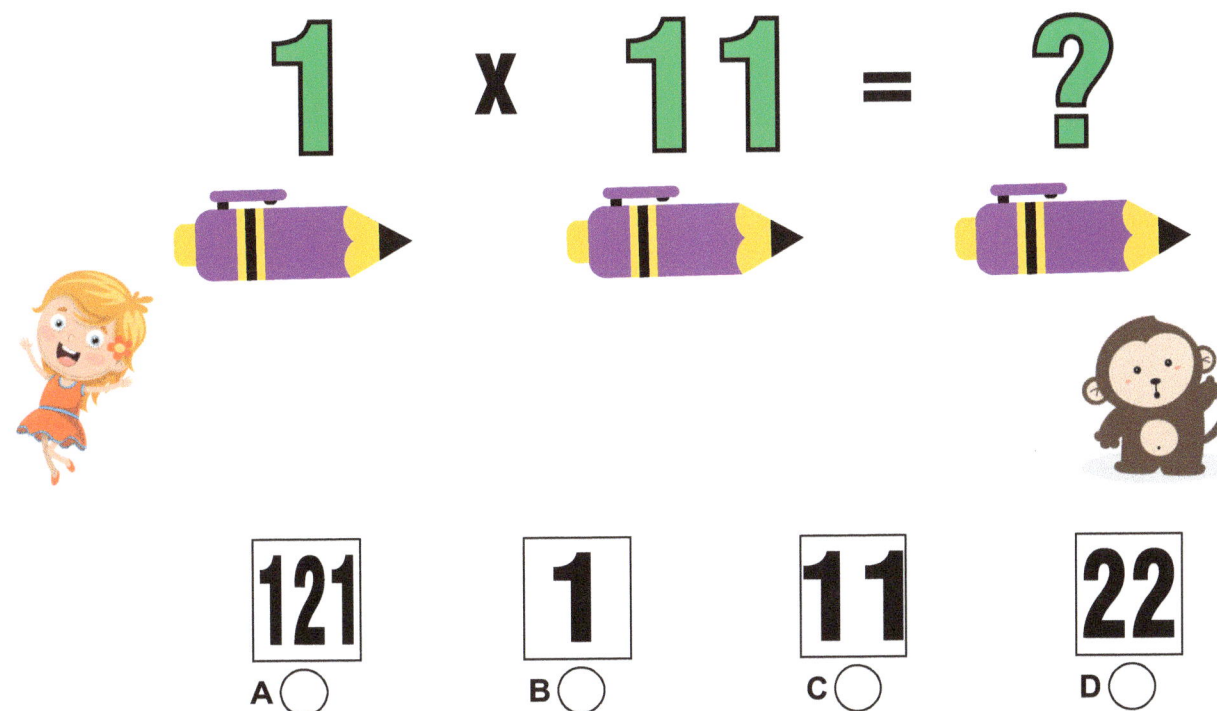

$$1 \times 11 = ?$$

A ◯ 121   B ◯ 1   C ◯ 11   D ◯ 22

 www.math-knots.com

Q-7 Look at the question and put your finger on the Lion. Monica is wondering what is the missing number under the question mark ? Help her to find the missing number under the question mark and fill in the bubble.

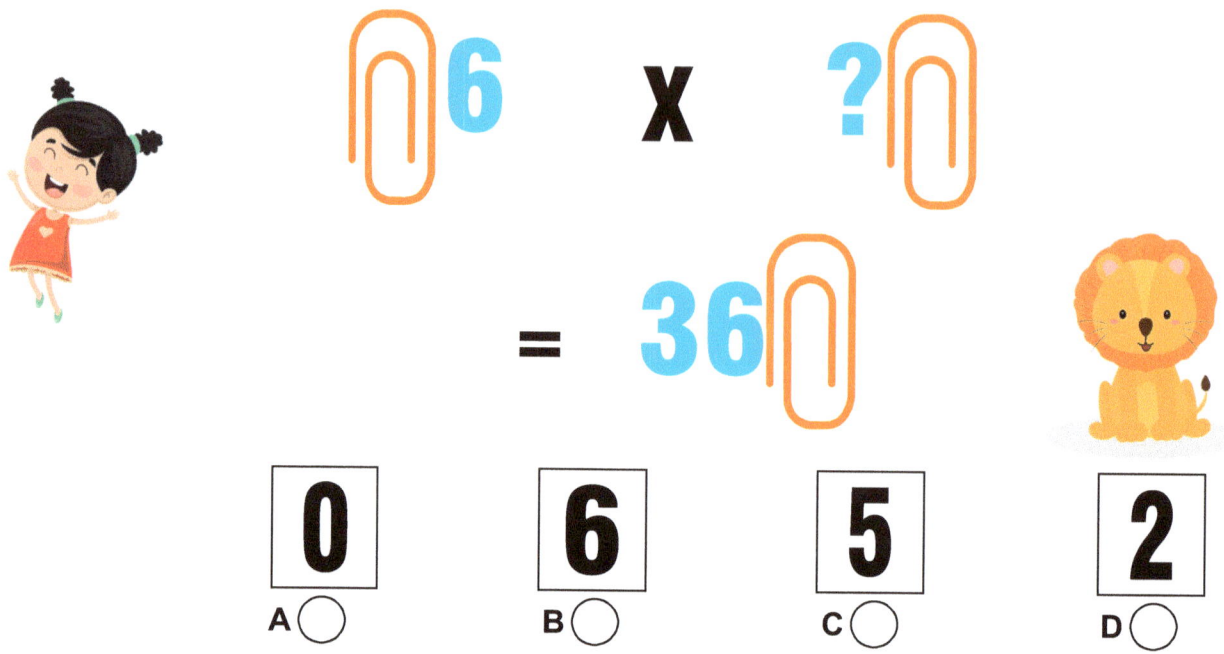

$$6 \times ? = 36$$

A	B	C	D
0	6	5	2

Q-8 Look at the question and put your finger on the Koala Bear. Isaac is wondering what is the missing number under the question mark ? Help him to find the missing number under the question mark and fill in the bubble.

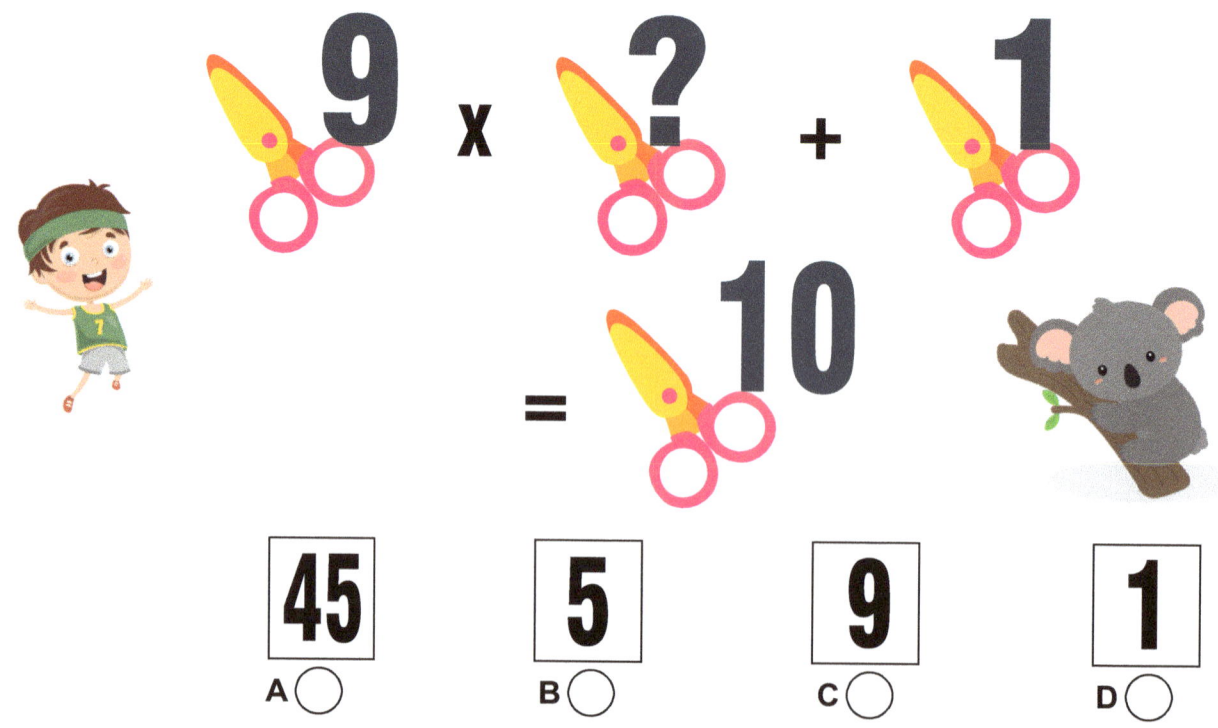

$$9 \times ? + 1 = 10$$

A	B	C	D
45	5	9	1

www.math-knots.com

Q-9 Look at the question and put your finger on the Narwhal. Joy is wondering what is the missing number under the question mark ? Help her to find the missing number under the question mark and fill in the bubble.

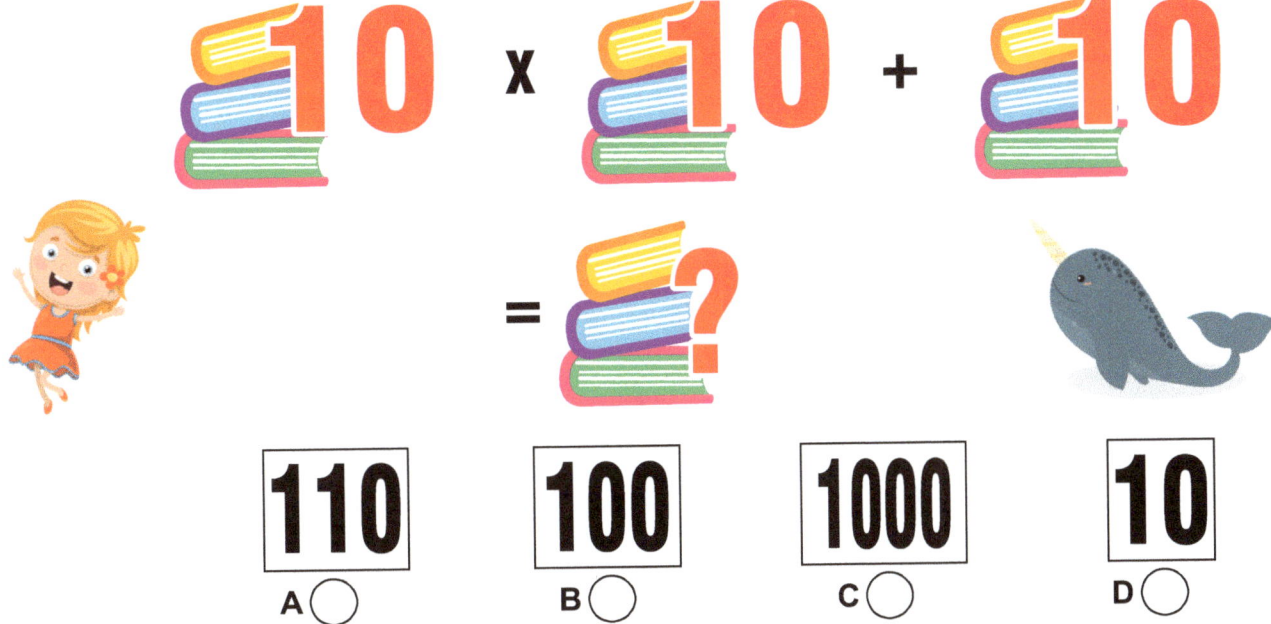

$$10 \times 10 + 10$$
$$= \ ?$$

110	**100**	**1000**	**10**
A◯	B◯	C◯	D◯

Q-10 Look at the question and put your finger on the Pig. Terry is wondering what is the missing number under the question mark ? Help him to find the missing number under the question mark and fill in the bubble.

$$0 + \ ? + 12$$
$$= 24$$

12	**4**	**20**	**10**
A◯	B◯	C◯	D◯

www.math-knots.com

Q-11 Look at the question and put your finger on the Hedgehog. Elsa is wondering what is the missing number under the question mark ? Help her to find the missing number under the question mark and fill in the bubble.

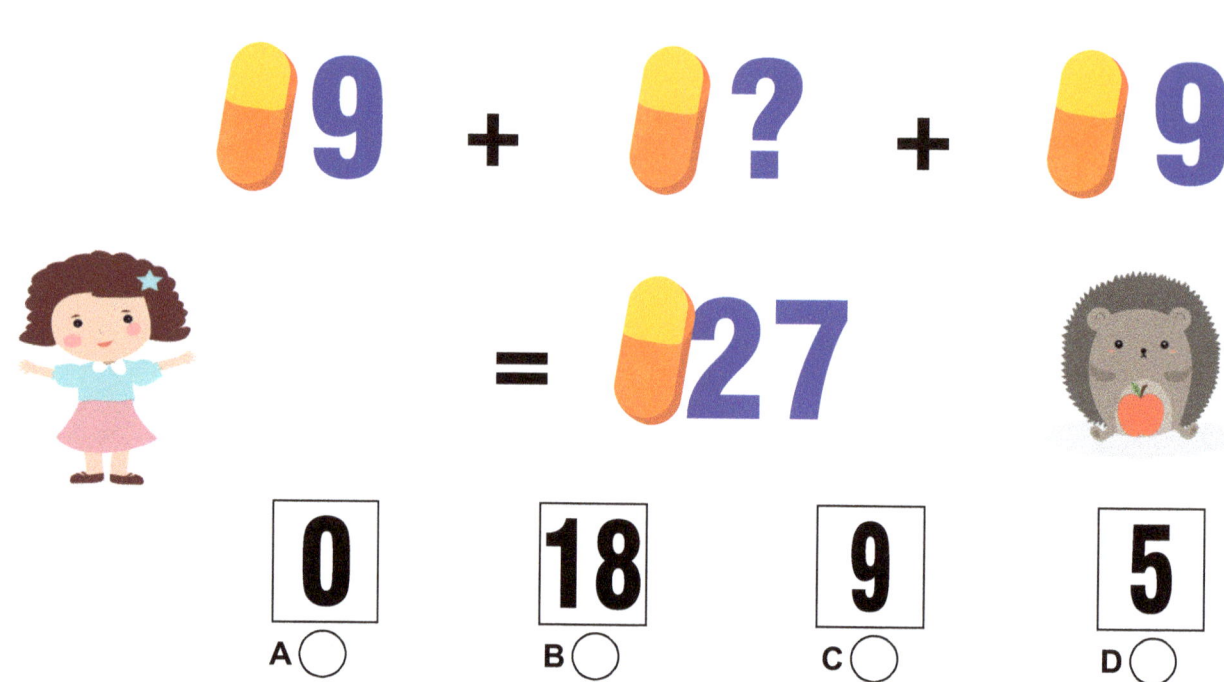

$$9 + ? + 9 = 27$$

A	B	C	D
0	18	9	5

Q-12 Look at the question and put your finger on the Quail. Tony is wondering what is the missing number under the question mark ? Help him to find the missing number under the question mark and fill in the bubble.

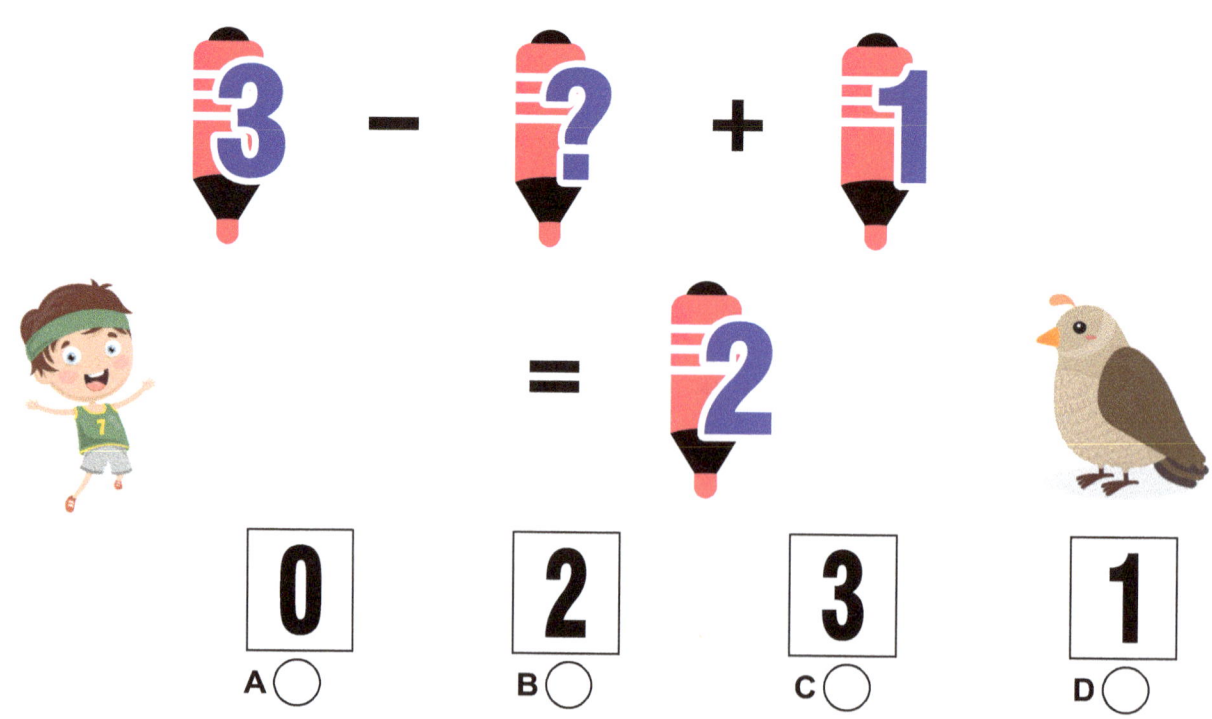

$$3 - ? + 1 = 2$$

A	B	C	D
0	2	3	1

www.math-knots.com

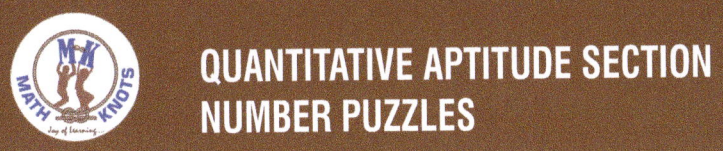
Q-13

Look at the question and put your finger on the Racoon. Nora is wondering what is the missing number under the question mark ? Help her to find the missing number under the question mark and fill in the bubble.

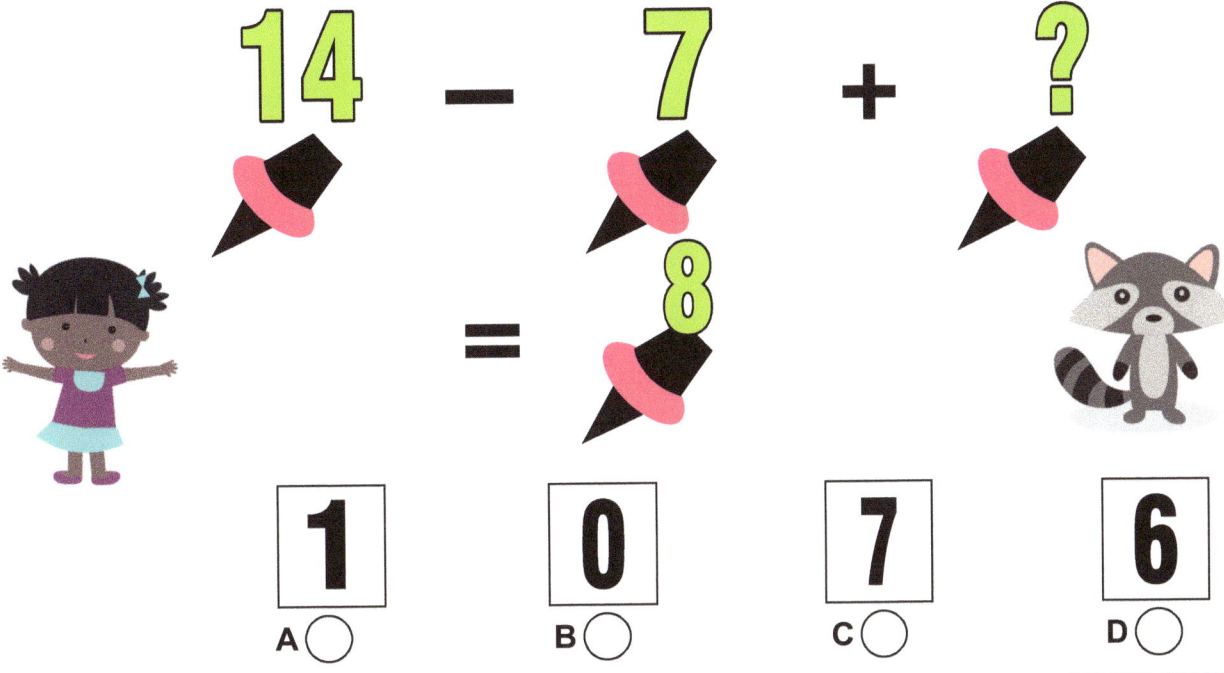

A ○	B ○	C ○	D ○
1	0	7	6

Q-14

Look at the question and put your finger on the Tortoise. Gloria is wondering what is the missing number under the question mark ? Help her to find the missing number under the question mark and fill in the bubble.

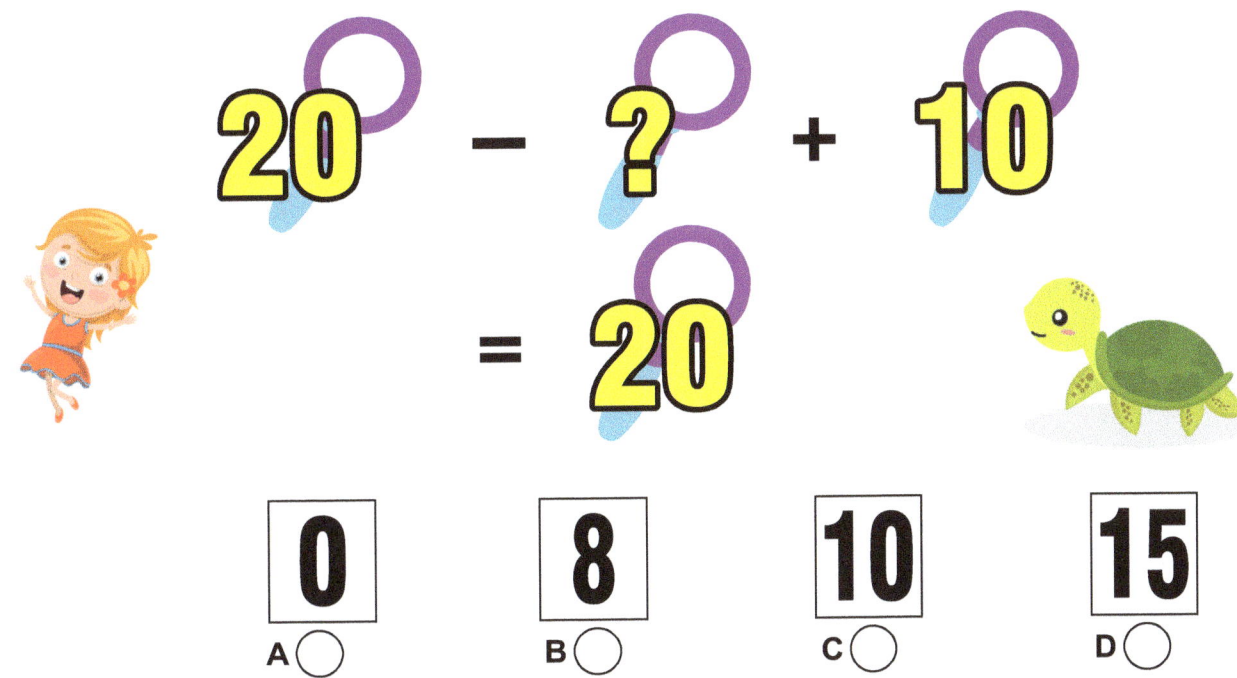

A ○	B ○	C ○	D ○
0	8	10	15

Q-15 Look at the question and put your finger on the Walrus. Kyra is wondering what is the missing number under the question mark ? Help her to find the missing number under the question mark and fill in the bubble.

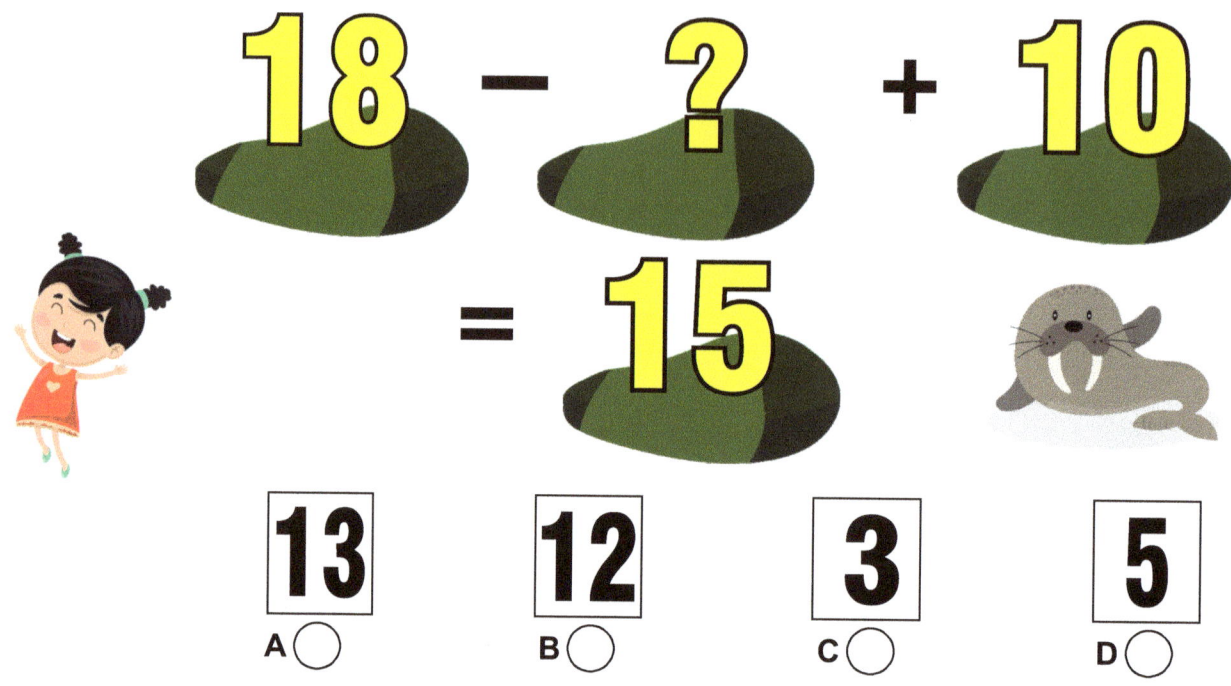

$$18 - ? + 10 = 15$$

13	12	3	5
A○	B○	C○	D○

Q-16 Look at the question and put your finger on the Vampires Bat. Julie is wondering what is the missing number under the question mark ? Help her to find the missing number under the question mark and fill in the bubble.

$$13 + 13 + ? = 39$$

10	13	19	3
A○	B○	C○	D○

www.math-knots.com

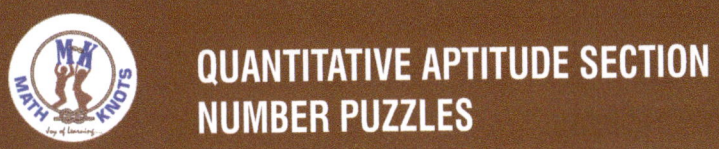
Q-17 Look at the question and put your finger on the Yak. Iris is wondering what is the missing number under the question mark ? Help her to find the missing number under the question mark and fill in the bubble.

 **81** -  **?** +  **20**

 = **100**

5	**2**	**1**	**10**
A ◯	B ◯	C ◯	D ◯

Q-18 Look at the question and put your finger on the Fish. Jane is wondering what is the missing number under the question mark ? Help her to find the missing number under the question mark and fill in the bubble.

 **33** +  **33** +  **?**

 =  **70**

4	**10**	**5**	**2**
A ◯	B ◯	C ◯	D ◯

www.math-knots.com

Q-19 Look at the question and put your finger on the Unicorn. Milo is wondering what is the missing number under the question mark ? Help him to find the missing number under the question mark and fill in the bubble.

 x  +

 =

10	30	0	4
A ◯	B ◯	C ◯	D ◯

Q-20 Look at the question and put your finger on the Parrot. Ruth is wondering what is the missing number under the question mark ? Help her to find the missing number under the question mark and fill in the bubble.

? x 25 + 25

= 25

25	0	15	35
A ◯	B ◯	C ◯	D ◯

www.math-knots.com

TEST - 2

NON VERBAL SECTION

FIGURE CLASSIFICATION

Lets Start the Test...

Sample Look at the question with the Tree. The first three pictures belong to one group in a common way. Help Bob to find out which of the below options belong to the same group. Identify the correct picture and help him to bubble the right choice.

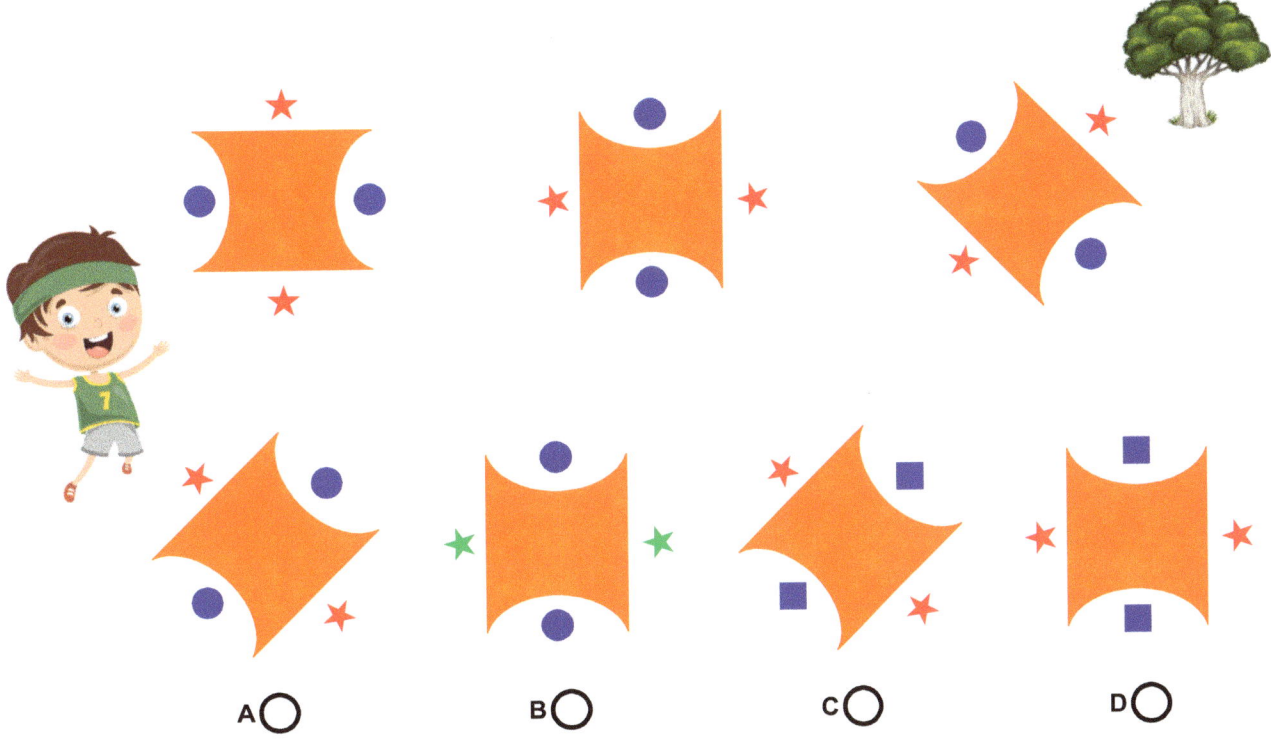

Solution : A

Option A is the only right choice. Option A matches the rest of the figure group in the same way. The other option vary in some way. Pay attention to all options before answering the right choice.

www.math-knots.com

Q-1 Look at the question with the Carrot. The first three pictures belong to one group in a common way. Help Jacob to find out which of the below options belong to the same group. Identify the correct picture and help him to bubble the right choice.

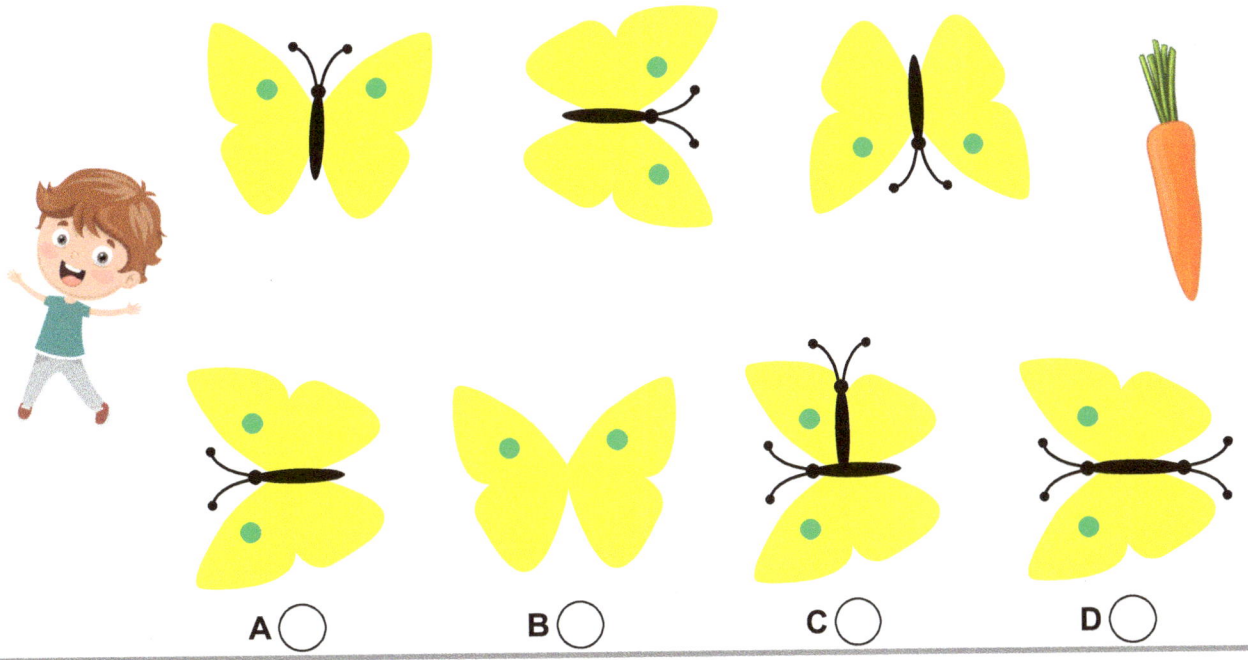

A◯   B◯   C◯   D◯

Q-2 Look at the question with the Spinach. The first three pictures belong to one group in a common way. Help Emma to find out which of the below options belong to the same group. Identify the correct picture and help her to bubble the right choice.

A◯   B◯   C◯   D◯

        www.math-knots.com

Q-3 Look at the question with the Green Chilli. The first three pictures belong to one group in a common way. Help Michael to find out which of the below options belong to the same group. Identify the correct picture and help him to bubble the right choice.

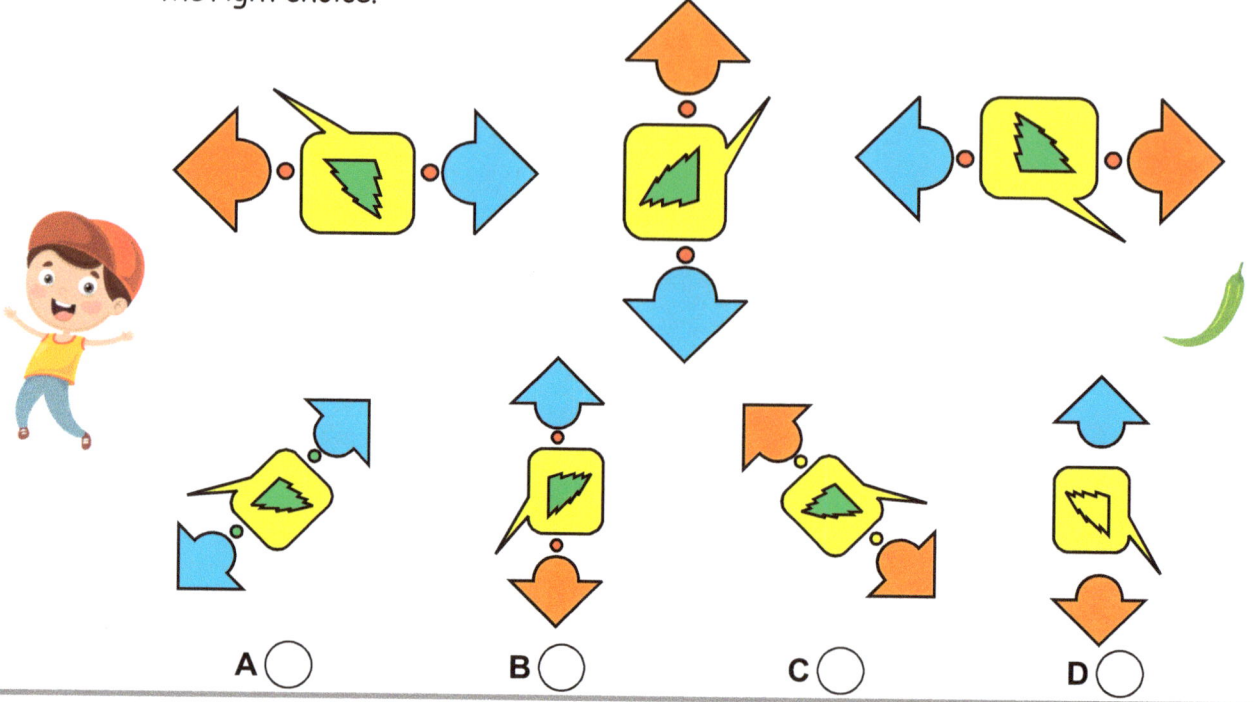

A ⃝   B ⃝   C ⃝   D ⃝

Q-4 Look at the question with the Pumpkin. The first three pictures belong to one group in a common way. Help Olivia to find out which of the below options belong to the same group. Identify the correct picture and help her to bubble the right choice.

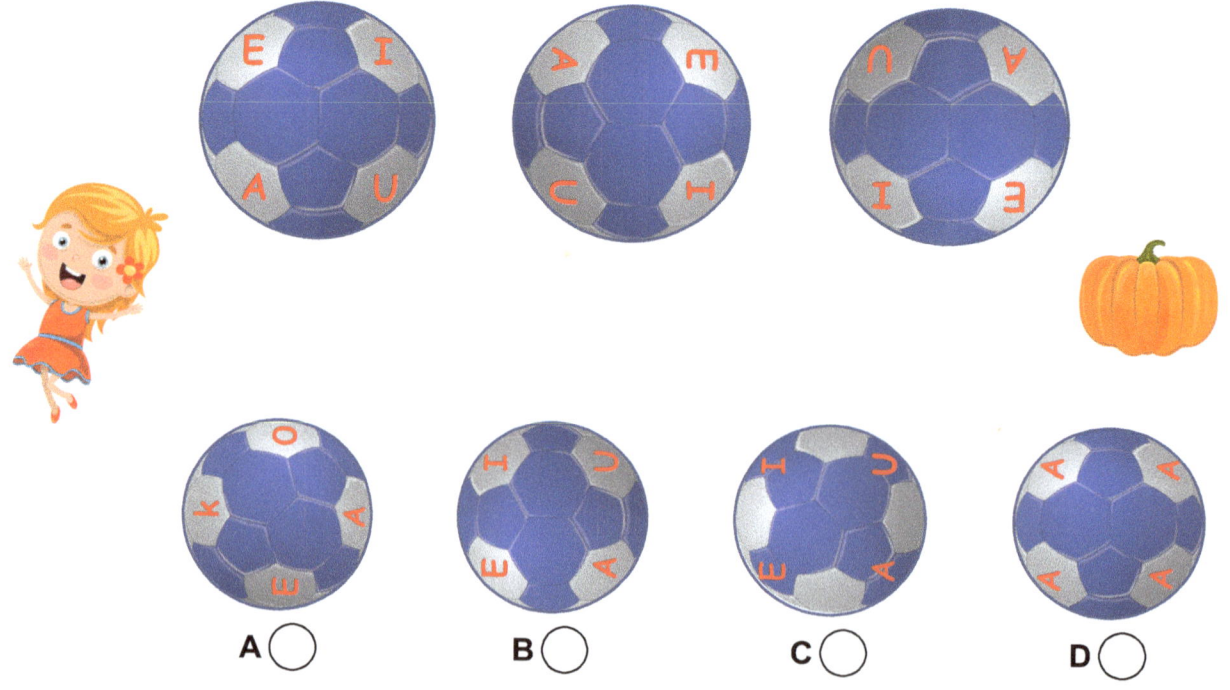

A ⃝   B ⃝   C ⃝   D ⃝

www.math-knots.com

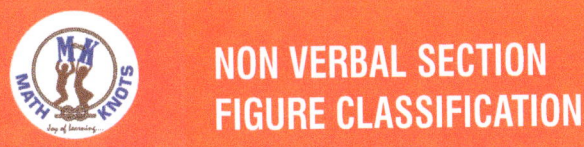
Q-5

Look at the question with the Broccoli. The first three pictures belong to one group in a common way. Help Matthew to find out which of the below options belong to the same group. Identify the correct picture and help him to bubble the right choice.

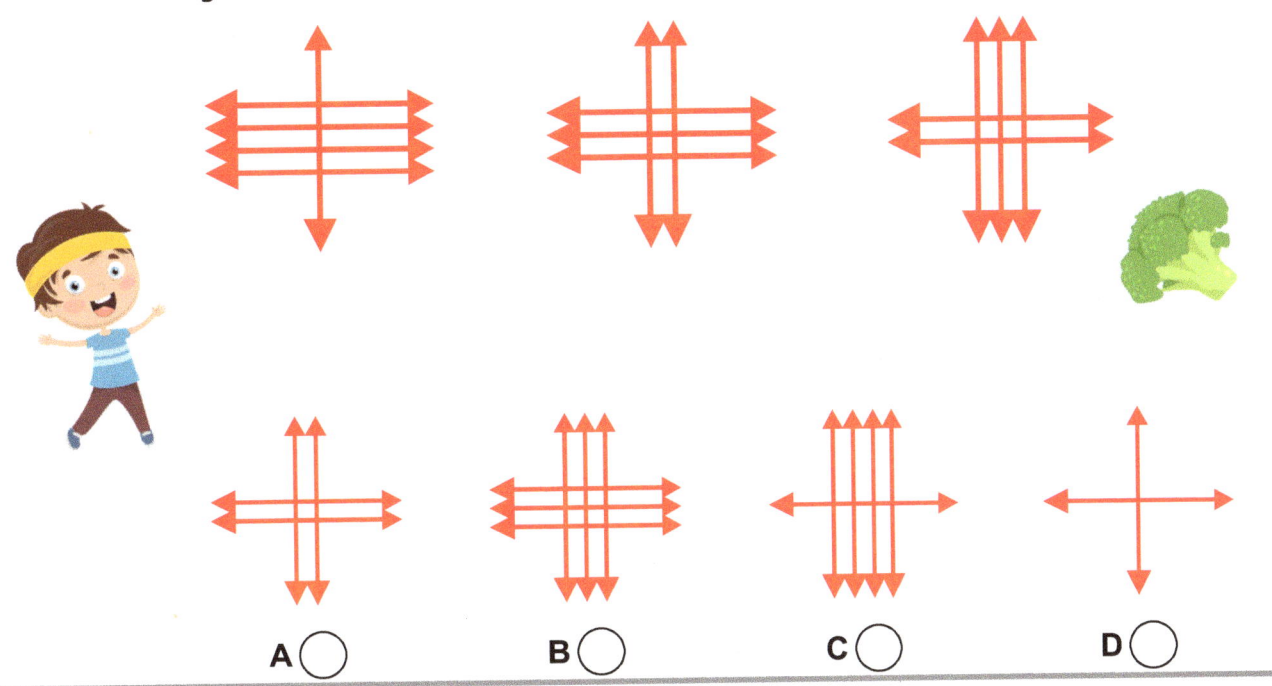

A ◯   B ◯   C ◯   D ◯

Q-6

Look at the question with the Eggplant. The first three pictures belong to one group in a common way. Help Sophia to find out which of the below options belong to the same group. Identify the correct picture and help her to bubble the right choice.

A ◯   B ◯   C ◯   D ◯

Q-7 Look at the question with the Corn. The first three pictures belong to one group in a common way. Help Ethan to find out which of the below options belong to the same group. Identify the correct picture and help him to bubble the right choice.

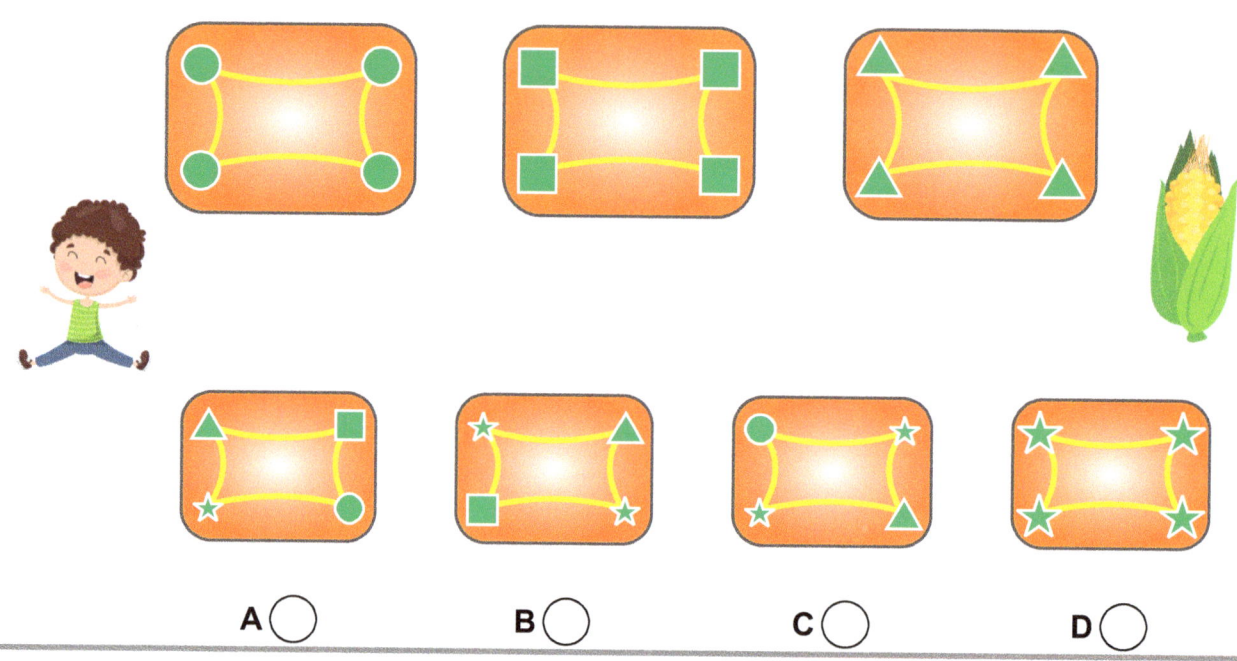

A ◯ B ◯ C ◯ D ◯

Q-8 Look at the question with the Cabbage. The first three pictures belong to one group in a common way. Help Elizabeth to find out which of the below options belong to the same group. Identify the correct picture and help her to bubble the right choice.

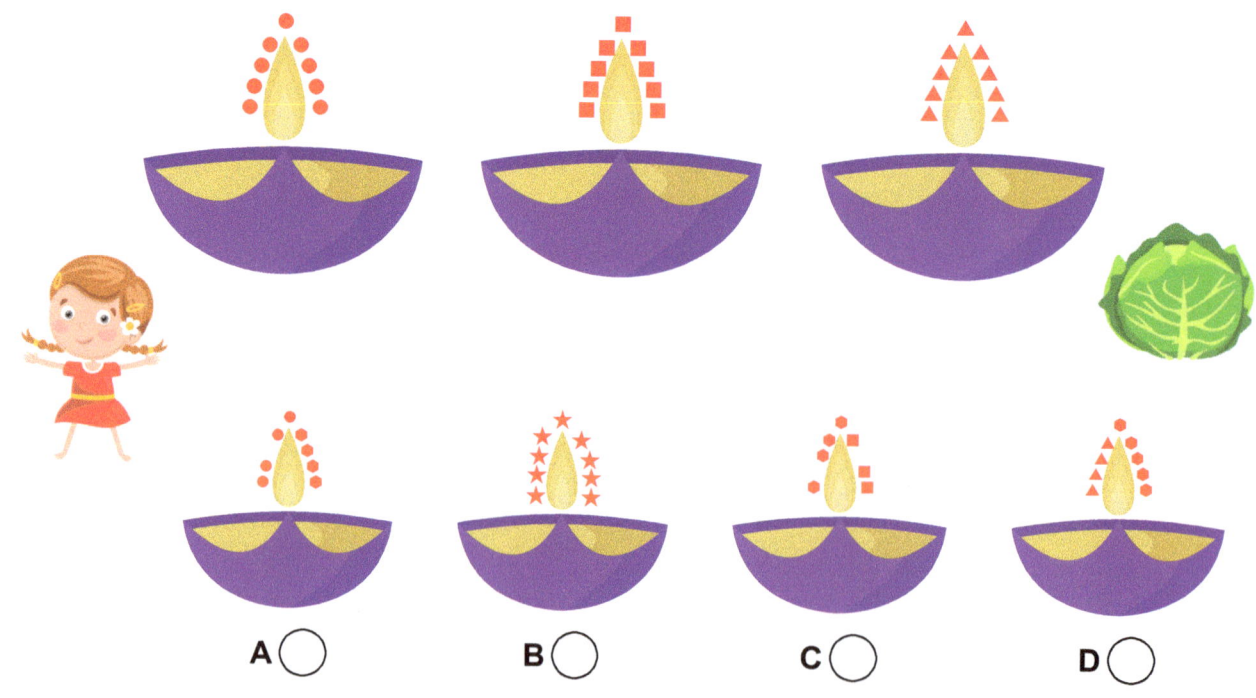

A ◯ B ◯ C ◯ D ◯

www.math-knots.com

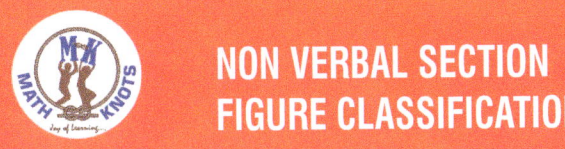

Q-9

Look at the question with the Olives. The first three pictures belong to one group in a common way. Help Andrew to find out which of the below options belong to the same group. Identify the correct picture and help him to bubble the right choice.

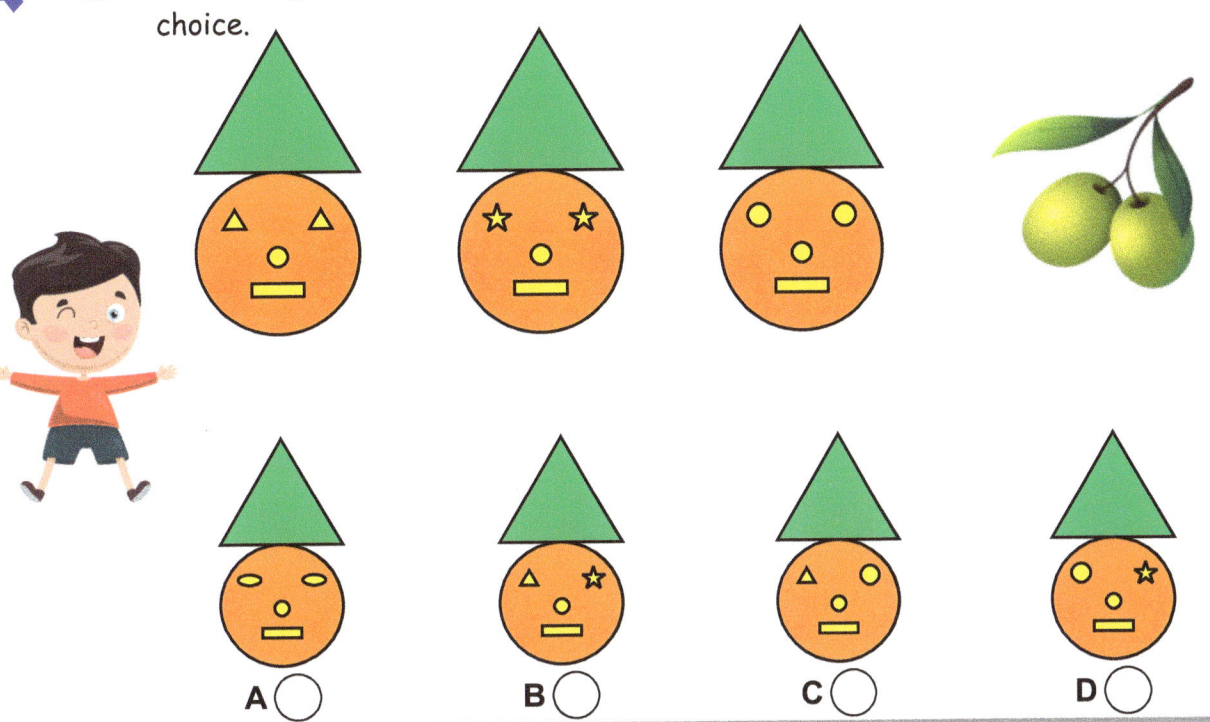

A ◯   B ◯   C ◯   D ◯

Q-10

Look at the question with the Ginger. The first three pictures belong to one group in a common way. Help Jessica to find out which of the below options belong to the same group. Identify the correct picture and help her to bubble the right choice.

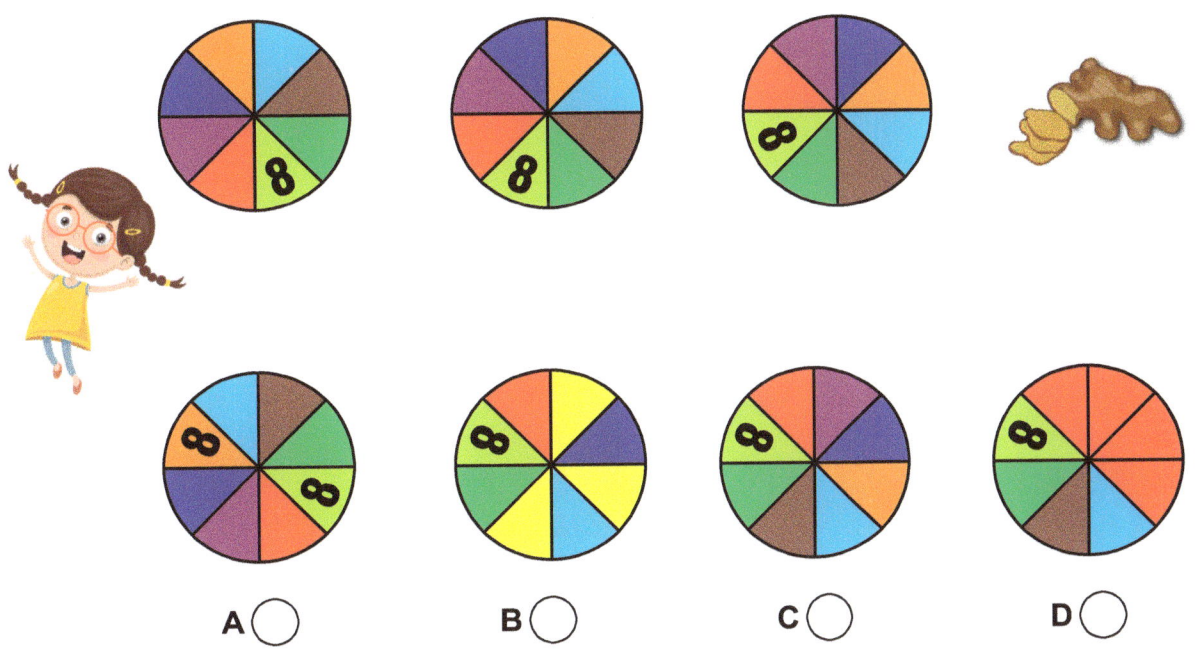

A ◯   B ◯   C ◯   D ◯

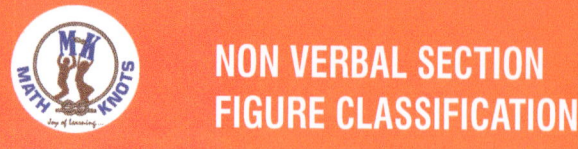
Q-11

Look at the question with the Tomato. The first three pictures belong to one group in a common way. Help Daniel to find out which of the below options belong to the same group. Identify the correct picture and help him to bubble the right choice.

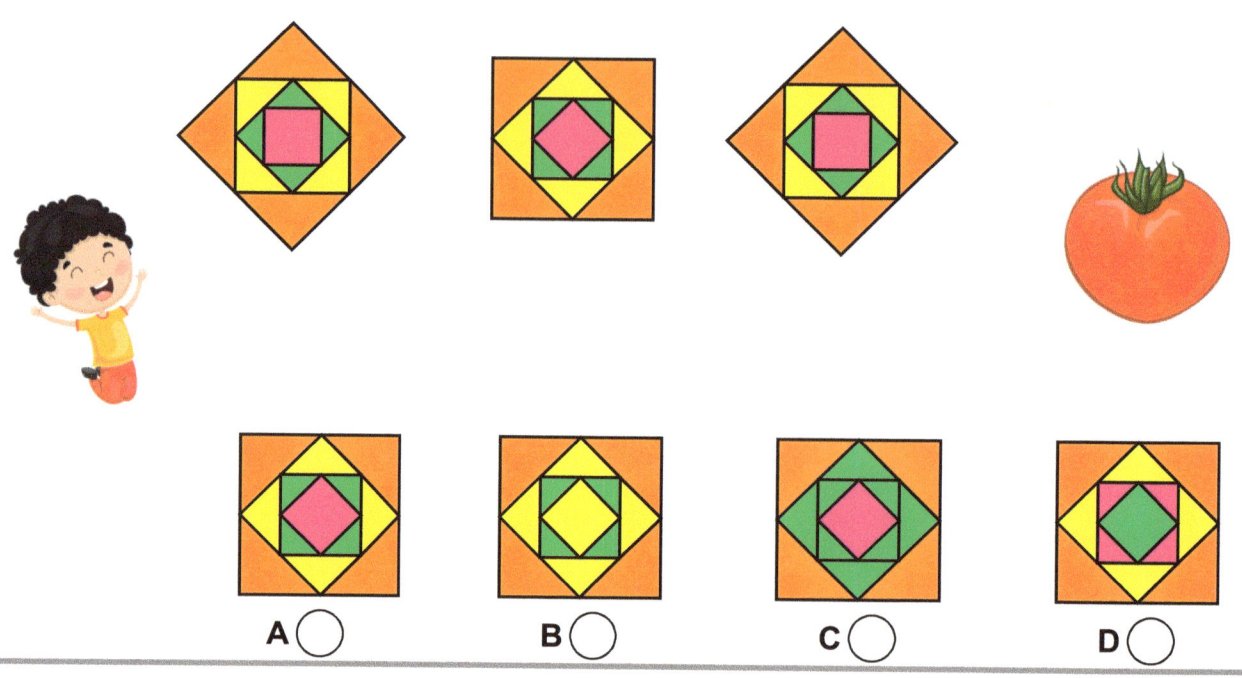

A ◯   B ◯   C ◯   D ◯

Q-12

Look at the question with the Onion. The first three pictures belong to one group in a common way. Help Julia to find out which of the below options belong to the same group. Identify the correct picture and help her to bubble the right choice.

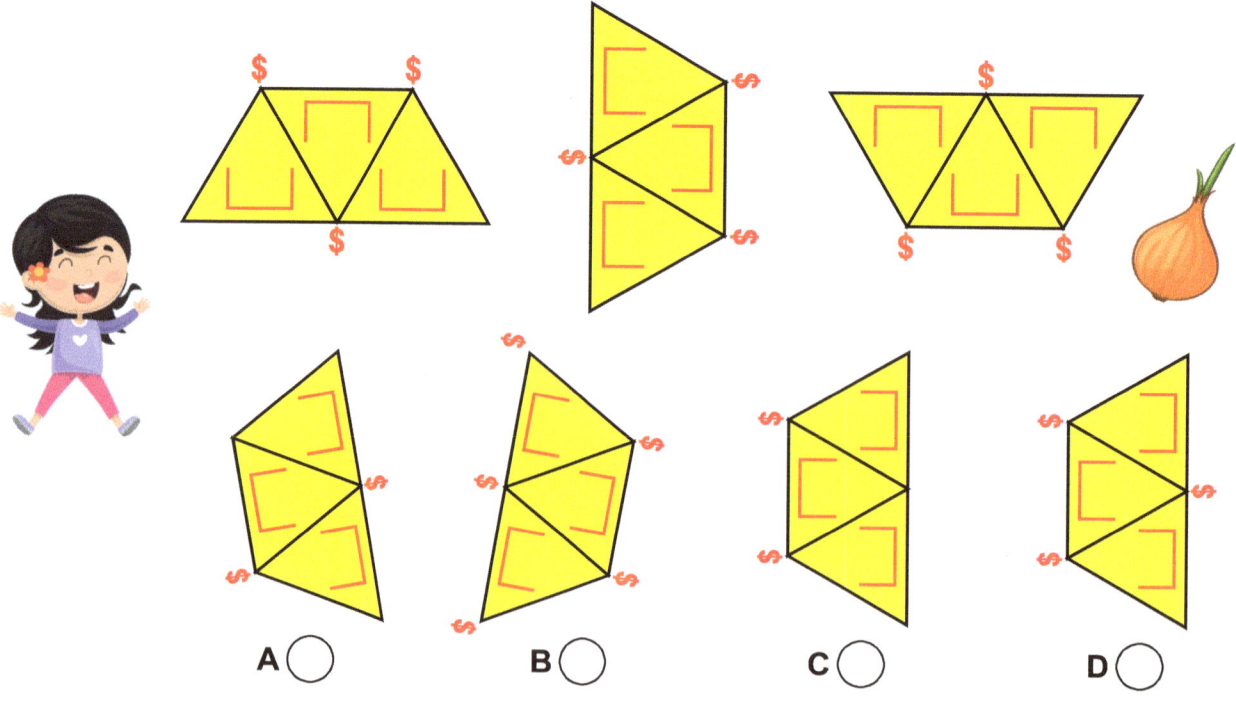

A ◯   B ◯   C ◯   D ◯

www.math-knots.com

Q-13

Look at the question with the Peas. The first three pictures belong to one group in a common way. Help Anthony to find out which of the below options belong to the same group. Identify the correct picture and help him to bubble the right choice.

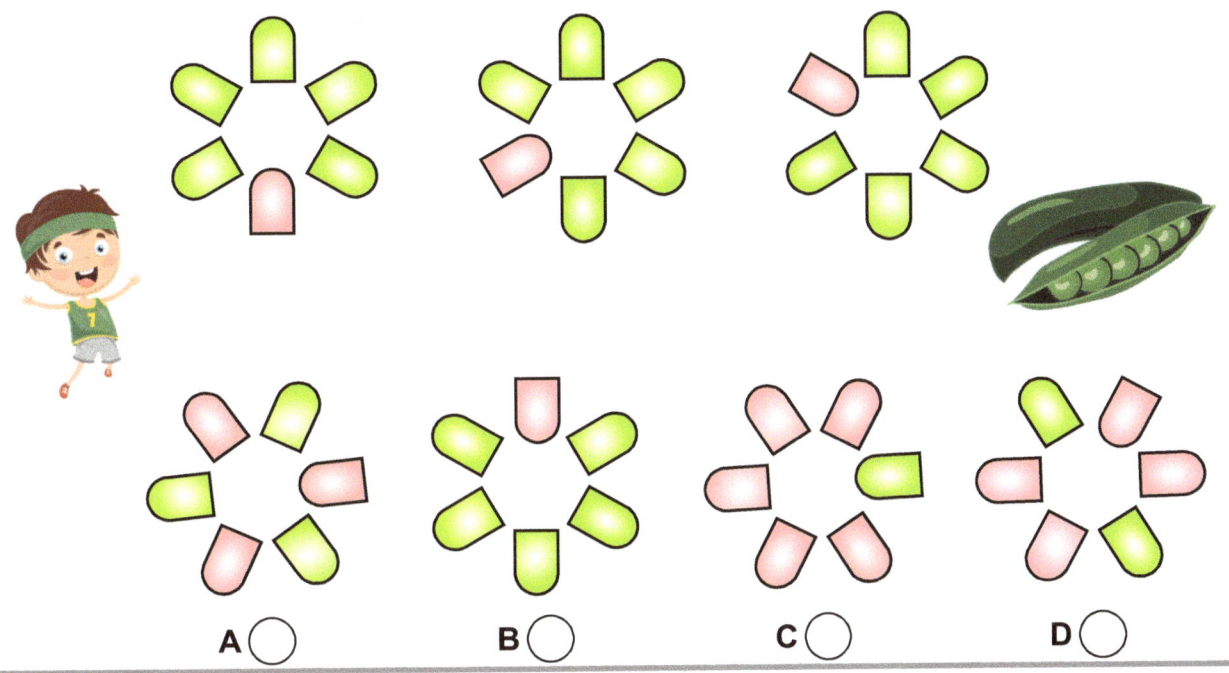

A ◯　　B ◯　　C ◯　　D ◯

Q-14

Look at the question with the Cucumber. The first three pictures belong to one group in a common way. Help Jenna to find out which of the below options belong to the same group. Identify the correct picture and help her to bubble the right choice.

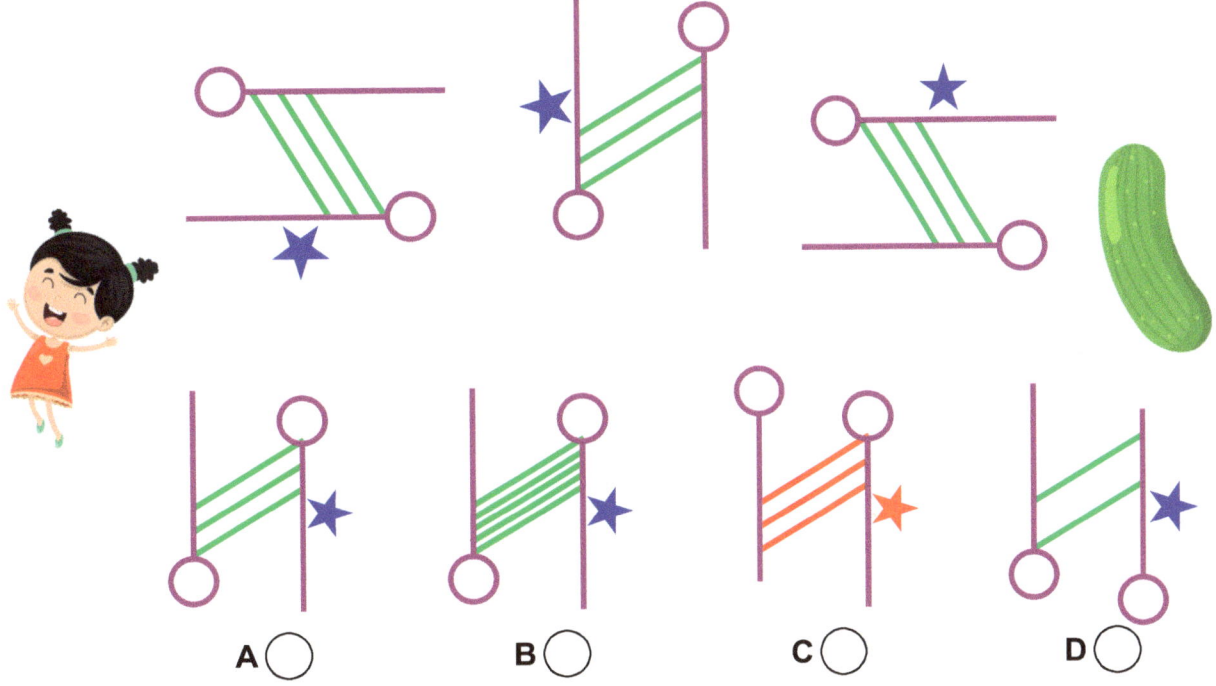

A ◯　　B ◯　　C ◯　　D ◯

www.math-knots.com

Q-15

Look at the question with the Radish. The first three pictures belong to one group in a common way. Help William to find out which of the below options belong to the same group. Identify the correct picture and help him to bubble the right choice.

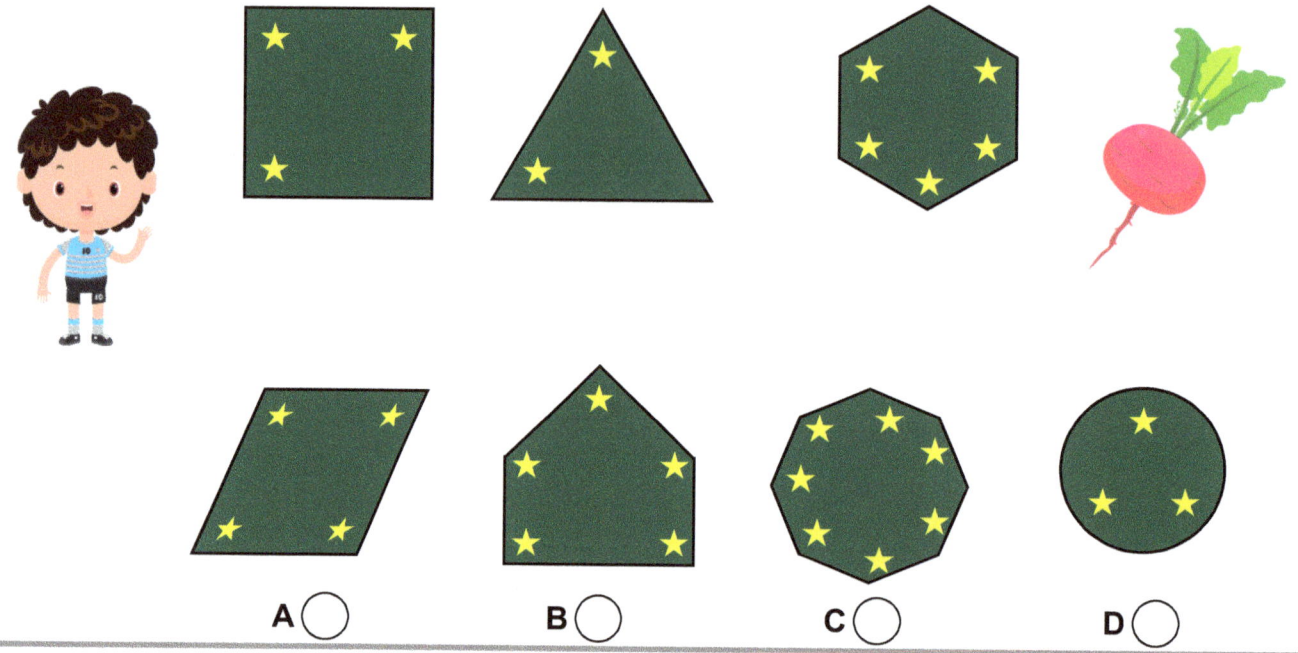

A◯   B◯   C◯   D◯

Q-16

Look at the question with the Potato. The first three pictures belong to one group in a common way. Help Mary to find out which of the below options belong to the same group. Identify the correct picture and help her to bubble the right choice.

A◯   B◯   C◯   D◯

www.math-knots.com

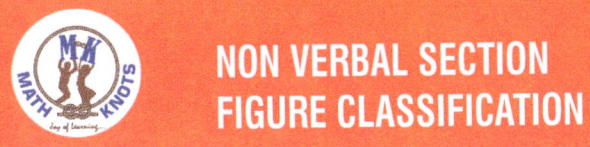

Q-17

Look at the question with the Garlics. The first three pictures belong to one group in a common way. Help Dan to find out which of the below options belong to the same group. Identify the correct picture and help him to bubble the right choice.

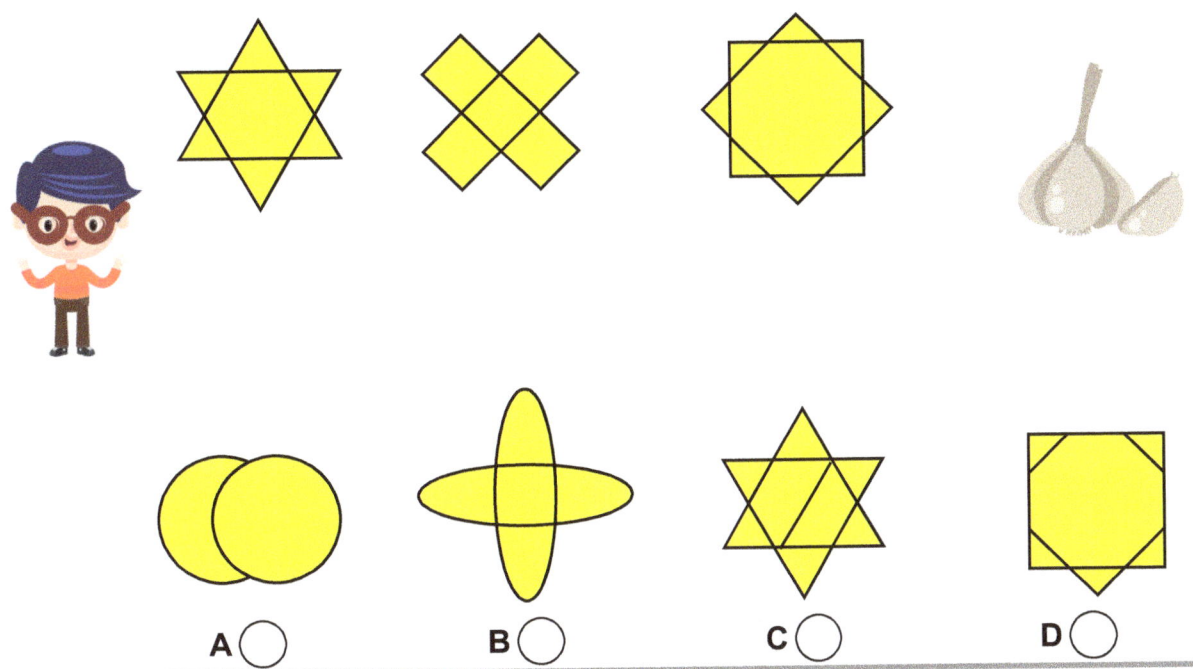

A ◯　　B ◯　　C ◯　　D ◯

Q-18

Look at the question with the Lettuce. The first three pictures belong to one group in a common way. Help Amy to find out which of the below options belong to the same group. Identify the correct picture and help her to bubble the right choice.

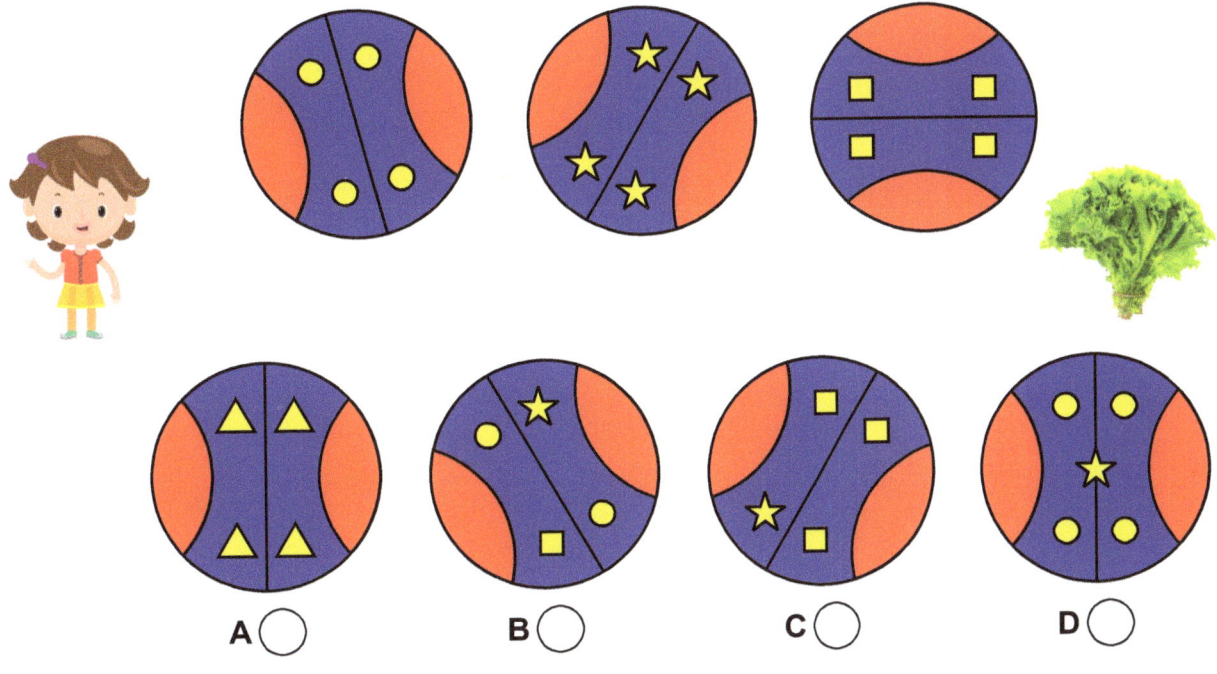

A ◯　　B ◯　　C ◯　　D ◯

www.math-knots.com

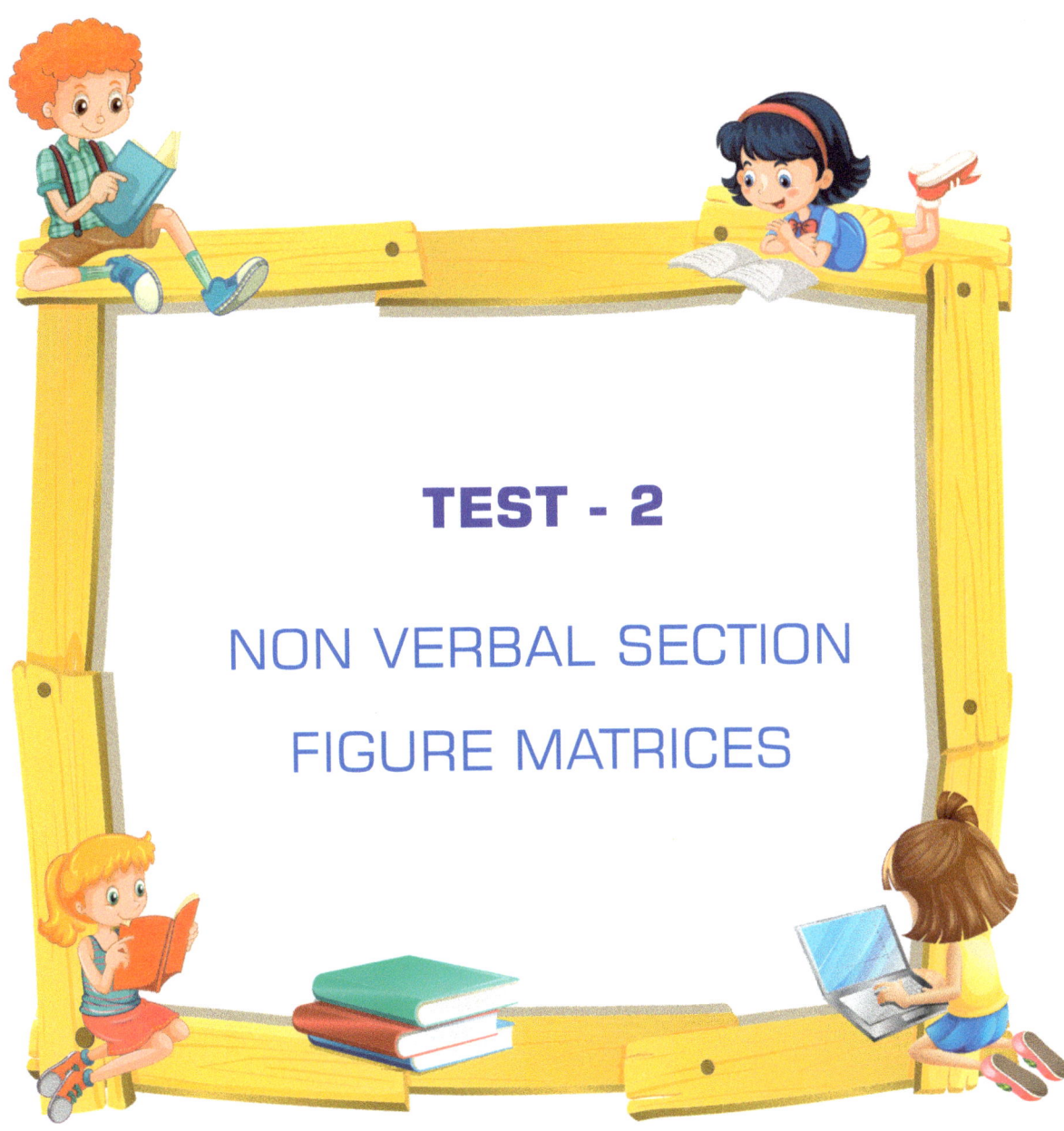

TEST - 2

NON VERBAL SECTION

FIGURE MATRICES

Lets Start the Test...

Sample

Look at the question with the Grapes. The first row has some thing in common as the second row. Can you help Mary to identify what goes in the space of the question mark from the four given options A, B, C, and D. Choose the correct option.

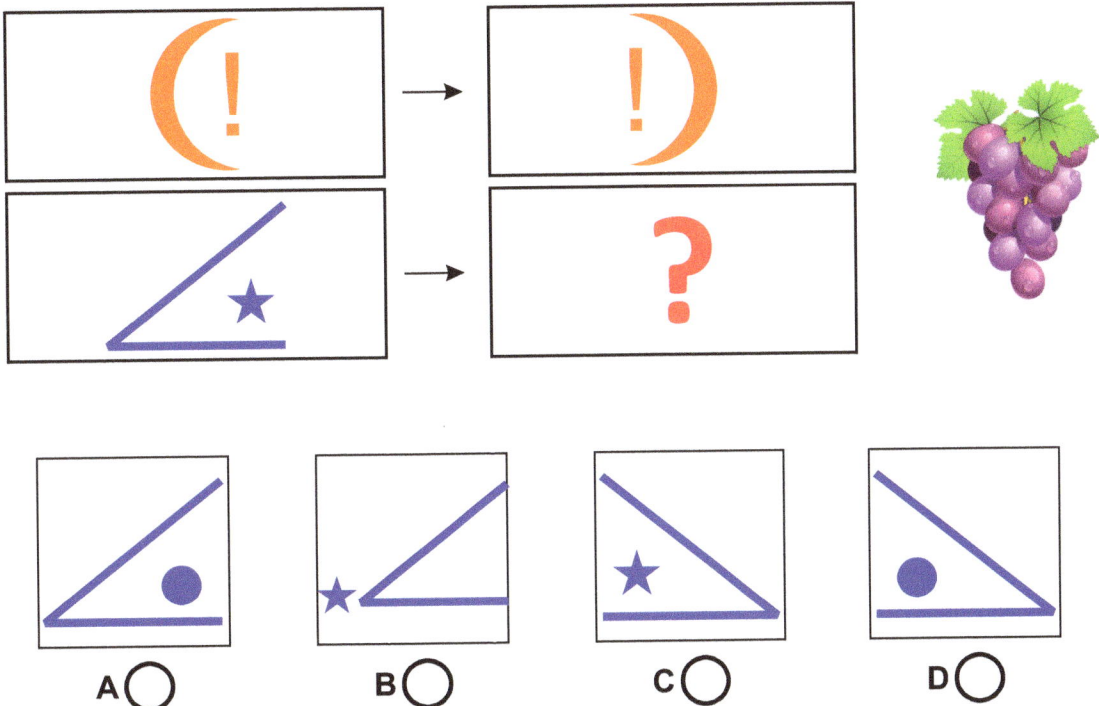

Solution : C

Option C is the right choice.

Two pictures in the first row are related in a certain way and the figures and flipped. When the picture in the second row is flipped it will be match to option C.

Students need to pay attention. Figures can be turning clock wise into anti clock wise and other possibilities.

Q-1

Look at the question with the Beetroot. The first row has some thing in common as the second row. Can you help Sophia to identify what goes in the space of the question mark from the four given options A, B, C, and D. Choose the correct option.

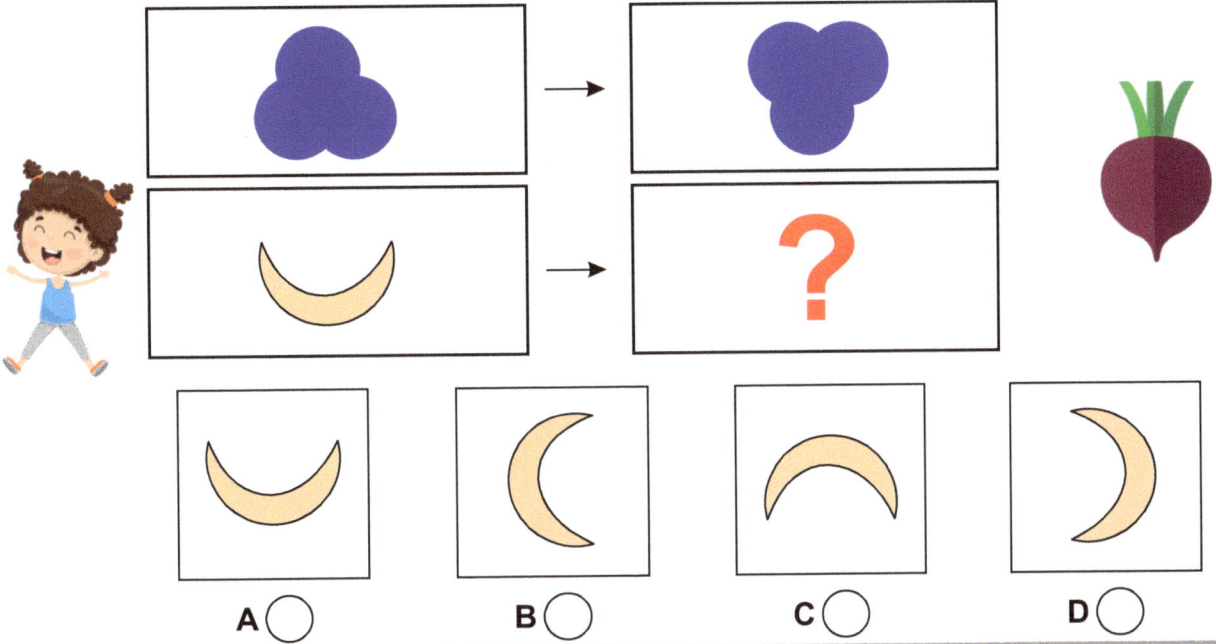

A ◯   B ◯   C ◯   D ◯

Q-2

Look at the question with the Tomato. The first row has some thing in common as the second row. Can you help Harry to identify what goes in the space of the question mark from the four given options A, B, C, and D. Choose the correct option.

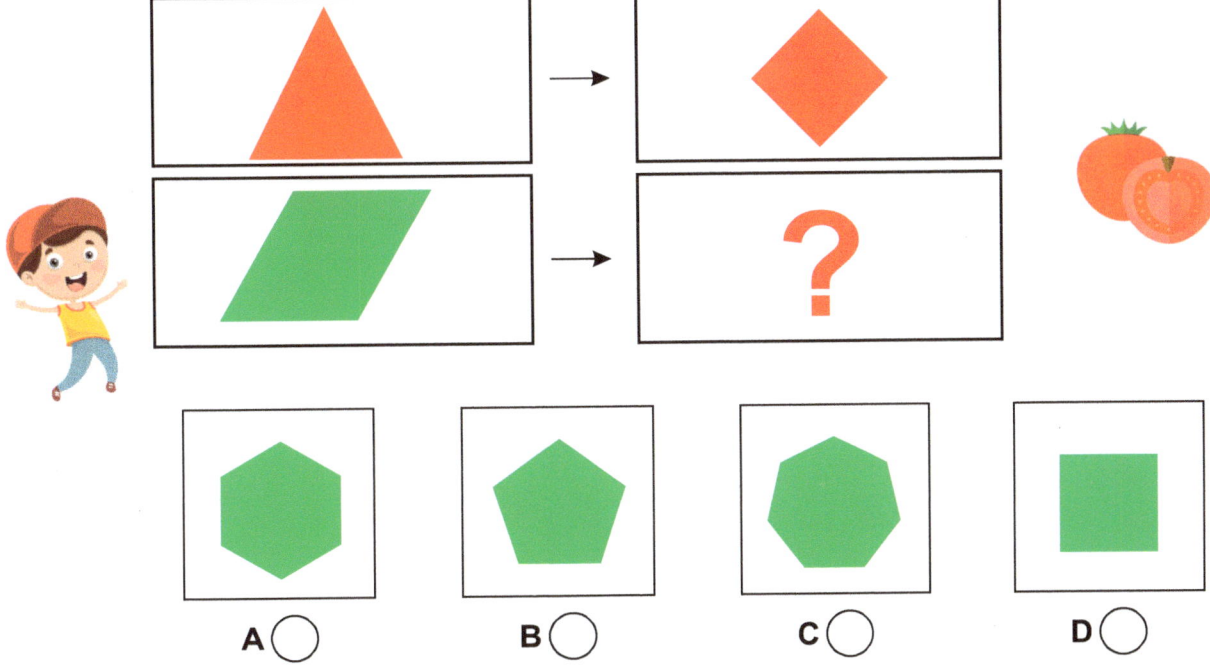

A ◯   B ◯   C ◯   D ◯

www.math-knots.com

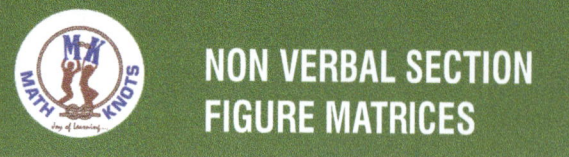
Q-3 Look at the question with the Cucumber. The first row has some thing in common as the second row. Can you help Amelia to identify what goes in the space of the question mark from the four given options A, B, C, and D. Choose the correct option.

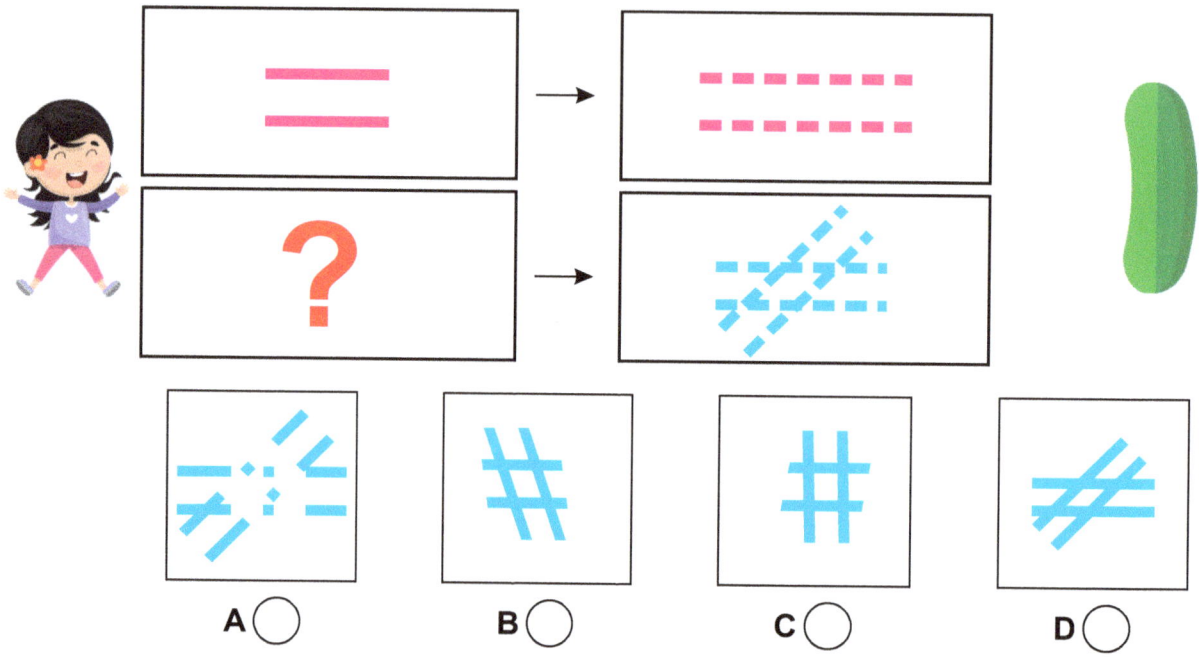

A◯ B◯ C◯ D◯

Q-4 Look at the question with the Cabbage. The first row has some thing in common as the second row. Can you help Jack to identify what goes in the space of the question mark from the four given options A, B, C, and D. Choose the correct option.

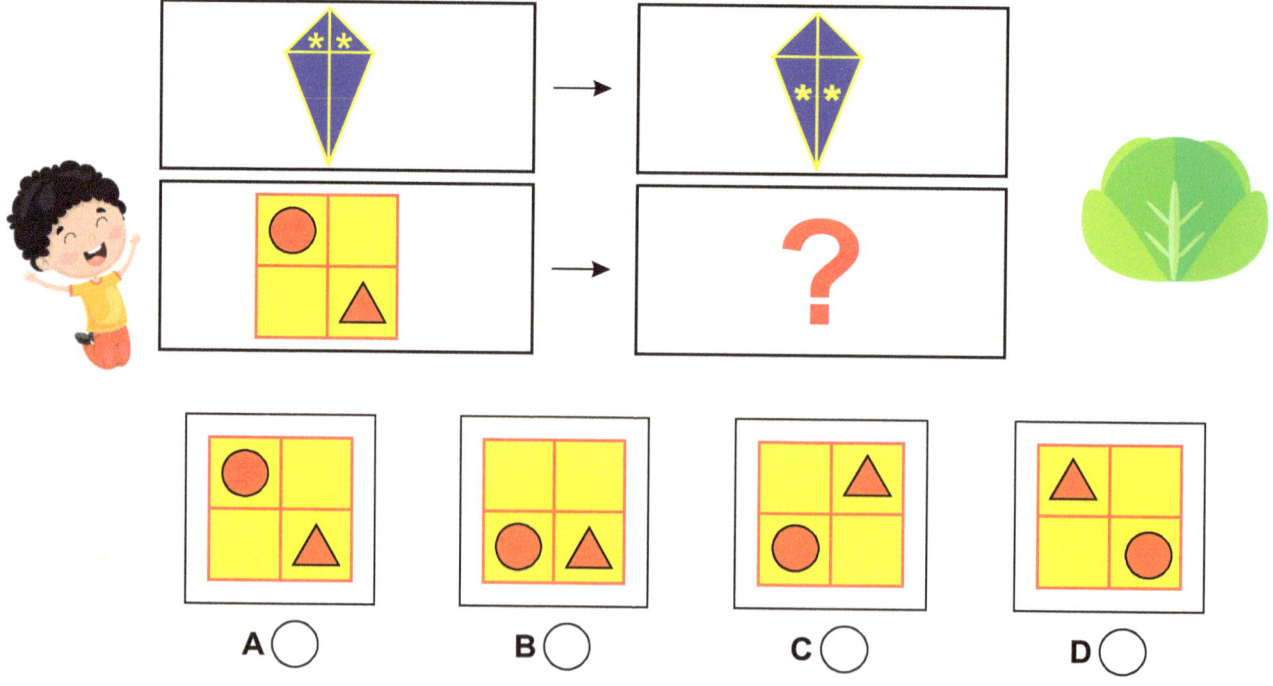

A◯ B◯ C◯ D◯

www.math-knots.com

Q-5

Look at the question with the Green Peas. The first row has some thing in common as the second row. Can you help Alexander to identify what goes in the space of the question mark from the four given options A, B, C, and D. Choose the correct option.

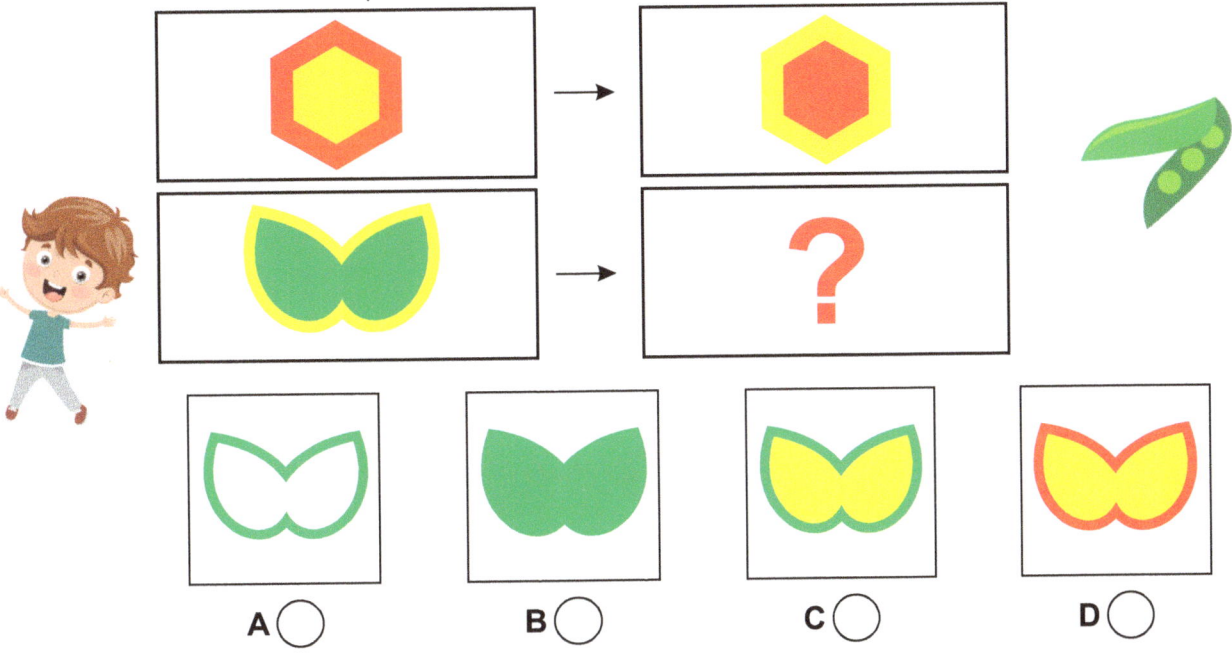

A ○   B ○   C ○   D ○

Q-6

Look at the question with the Chilly. The first row has some thing in common as the second row. Can you help Isabella to identify what goes in the space of the question mark from the four given options A, B, C, and D. Choose the correct option.

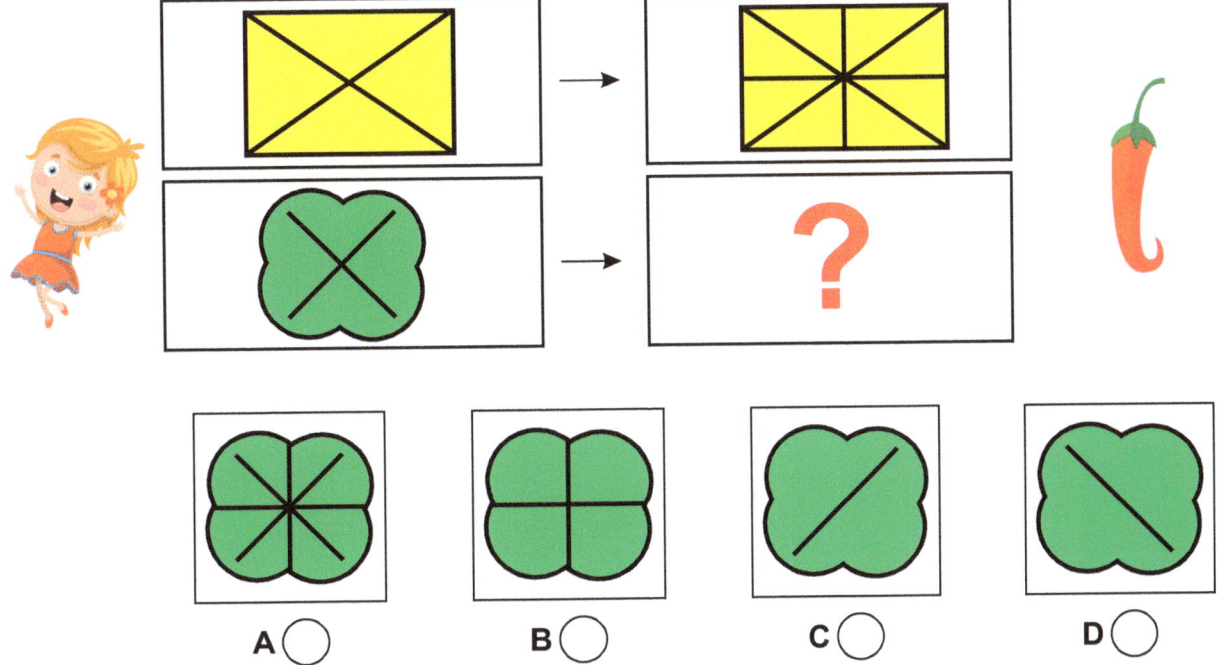

A ○   B ○   C ○   D ○

www.math-knots.com

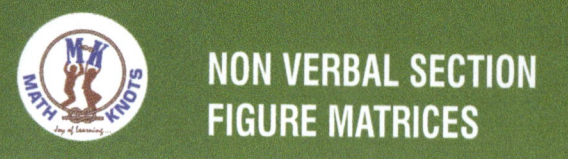

Q-7

Look at the question with the Potato. The first row has some thing in common as the second row. Can you help Max to identify what goes in the space of the question mark from the four given options A, B, C, and D. Choose the correct option.

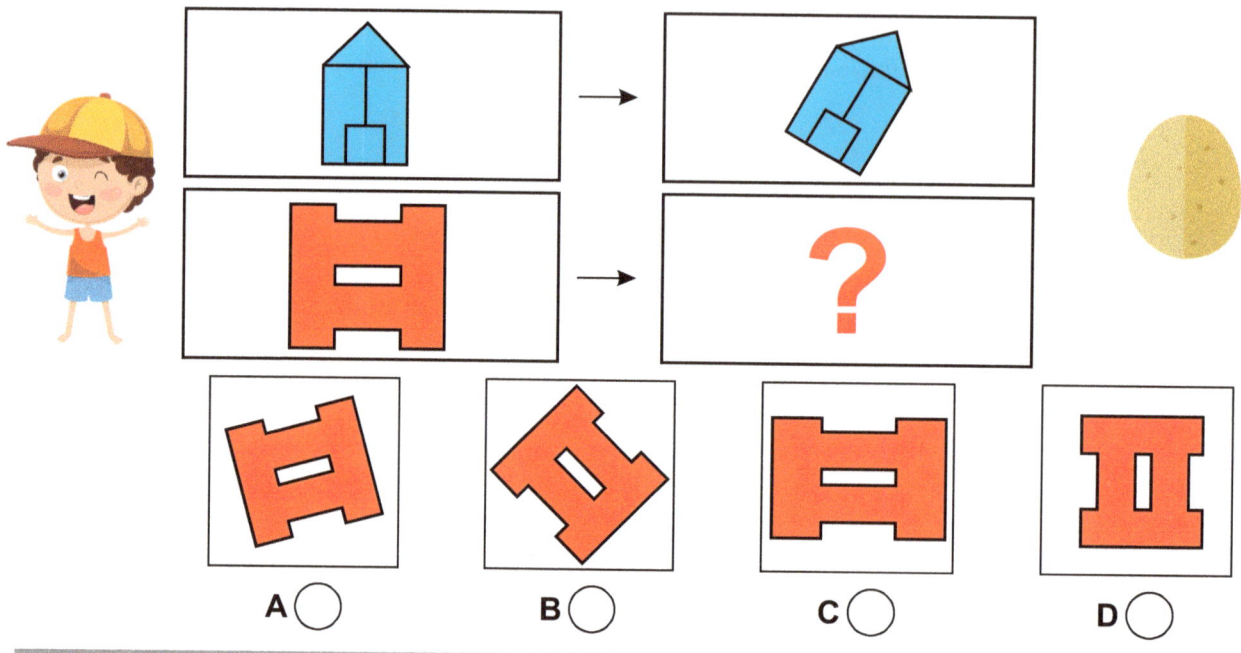

A◯   B◯   C◯   D◯

Q-8

Look at the question with the Brinjal. The first row has some thing in common as the second row. Can you help Lily to identify what goes in the space of the question mark from the four given options A, B, C, and D. Choose the correct option.

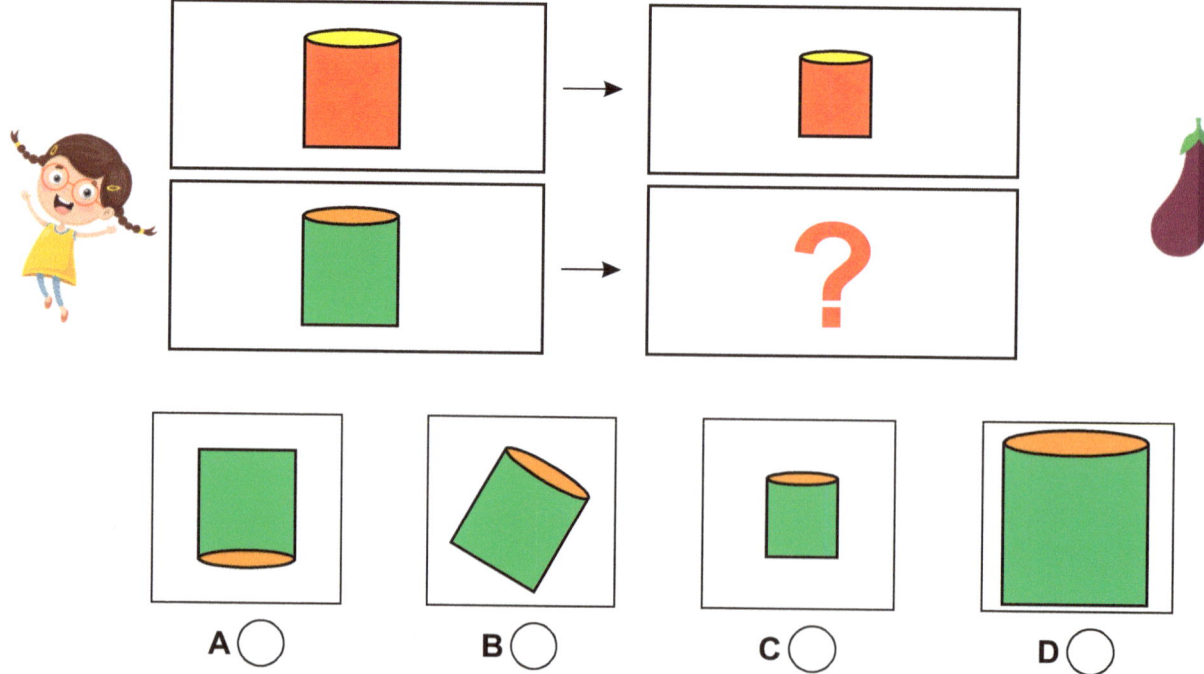

A◯   B◯   C◯   D◯

www.math-knots.com

Q-9

Look at the question with the Onion. The first row has some thing in common as the second row. Can you help Ethan to identify what goes in the space of the question mark from the four given options A, B, C, and D. Choose the correct option.

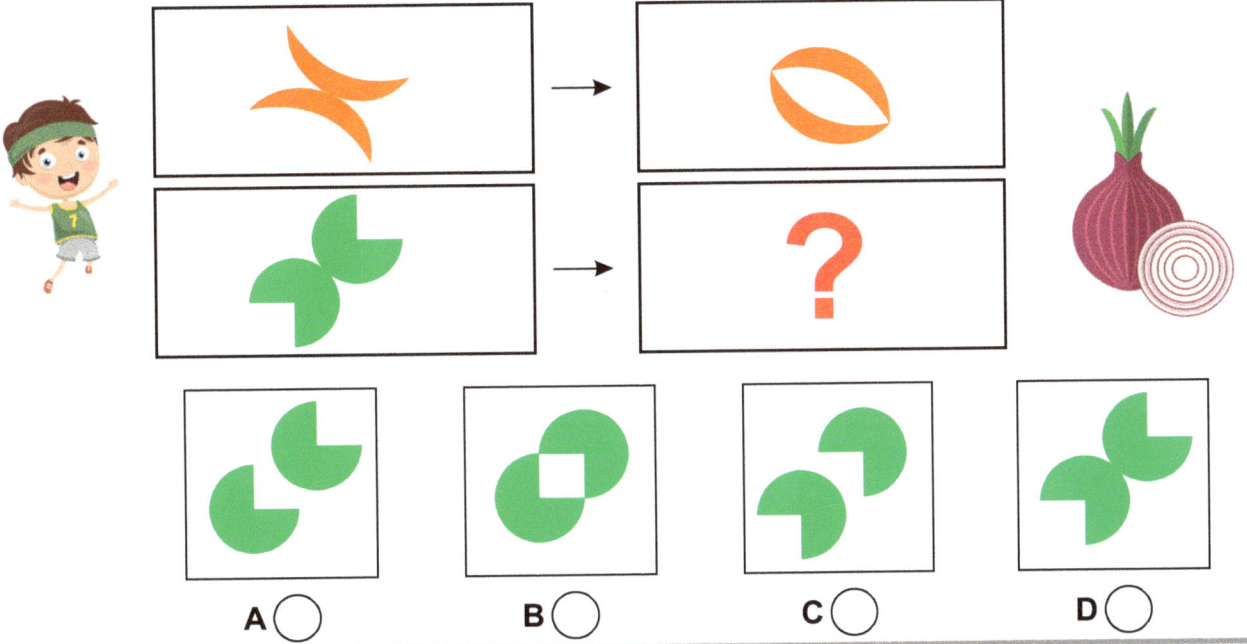

A ○   B ○   C ○   D ○

Q-10

Look at the question with the Garlic. The first row has some thing in common as the second row. Can you help Daniel to identify what goes in the space of the question mark from the four given options A, B, C, and D. Choose the correct option.

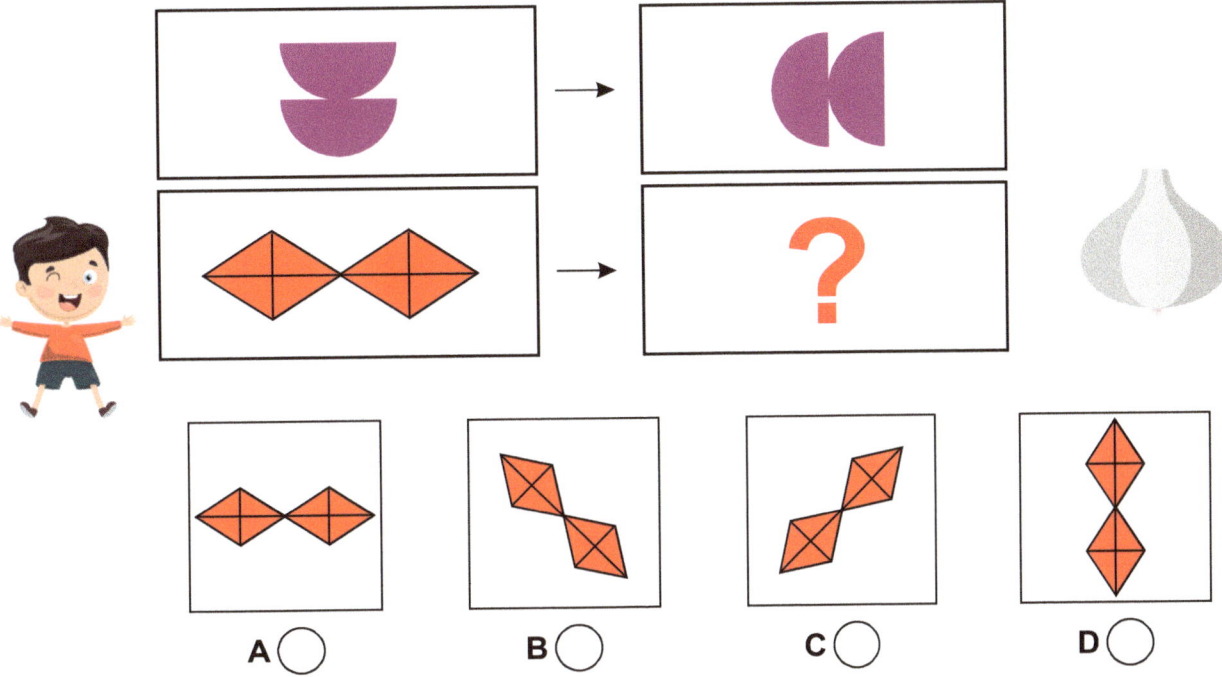

A ○   B ○   C ○   D ○

Q-11

Look at the question with the Corn. The first row has some thing in common as the second row. Can you help Logan to identify what goes in the space of the question mark from the four given options A, B, C, and D. Choose the correct option.

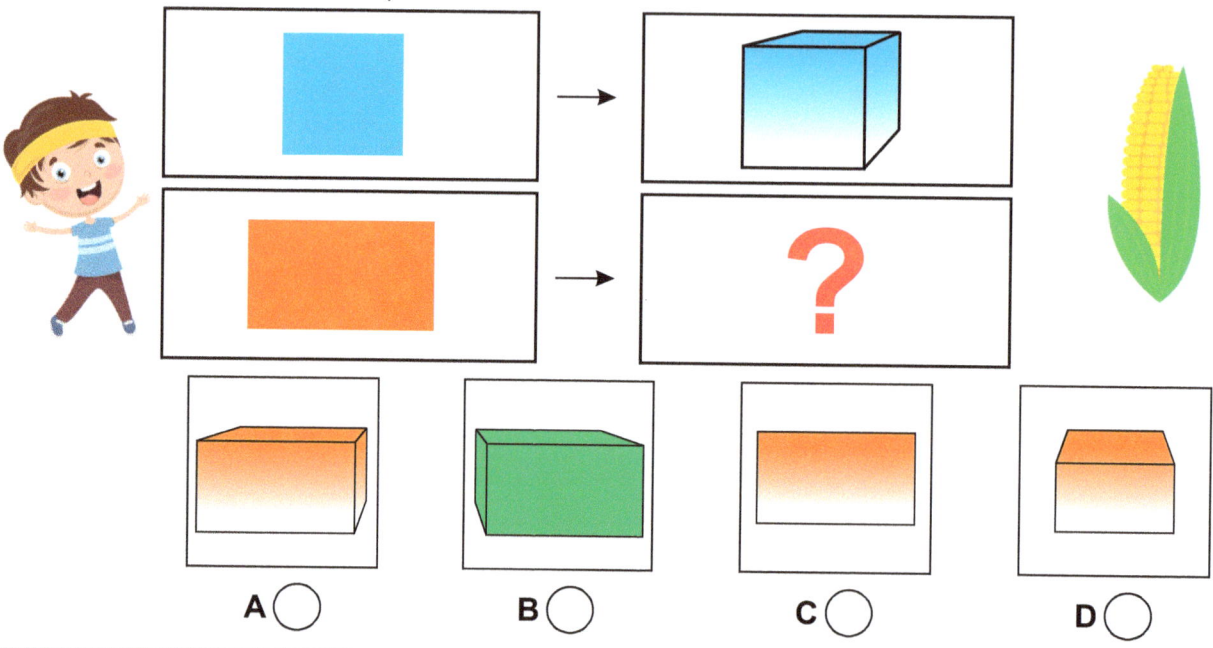

A ◯   B ◯   C ◯   D ◯

Q-12

Look at the question with the Carrot. The first row has some thing in common as the second row. Can you help Lucas to identify what goes in the space of the question mark from the four given options A, B, C, and D. Choose the correct option.

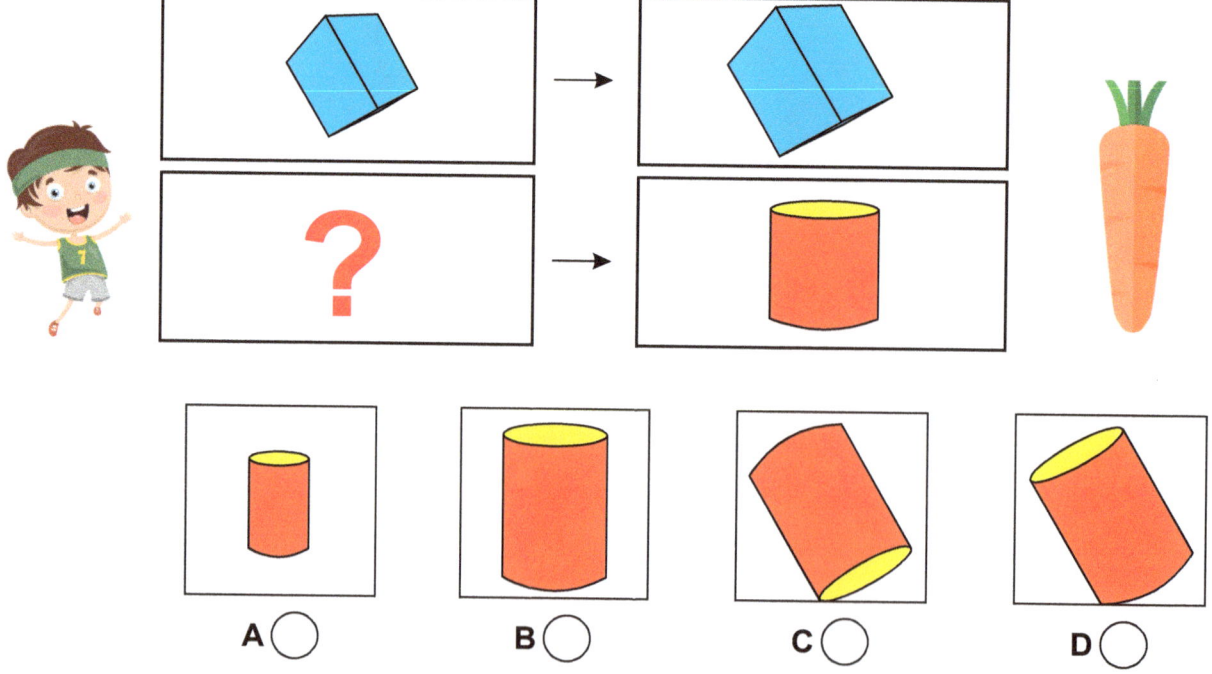

A ◯   B ◯   C ◯   D ◯

Q-13

Look at the question with the Pumpkin. The first row has some thing in common as the second row. Can you help Tracy to identify what goes in the space of the question mark from the four given options A, B, C, and D. Choose the correct option.

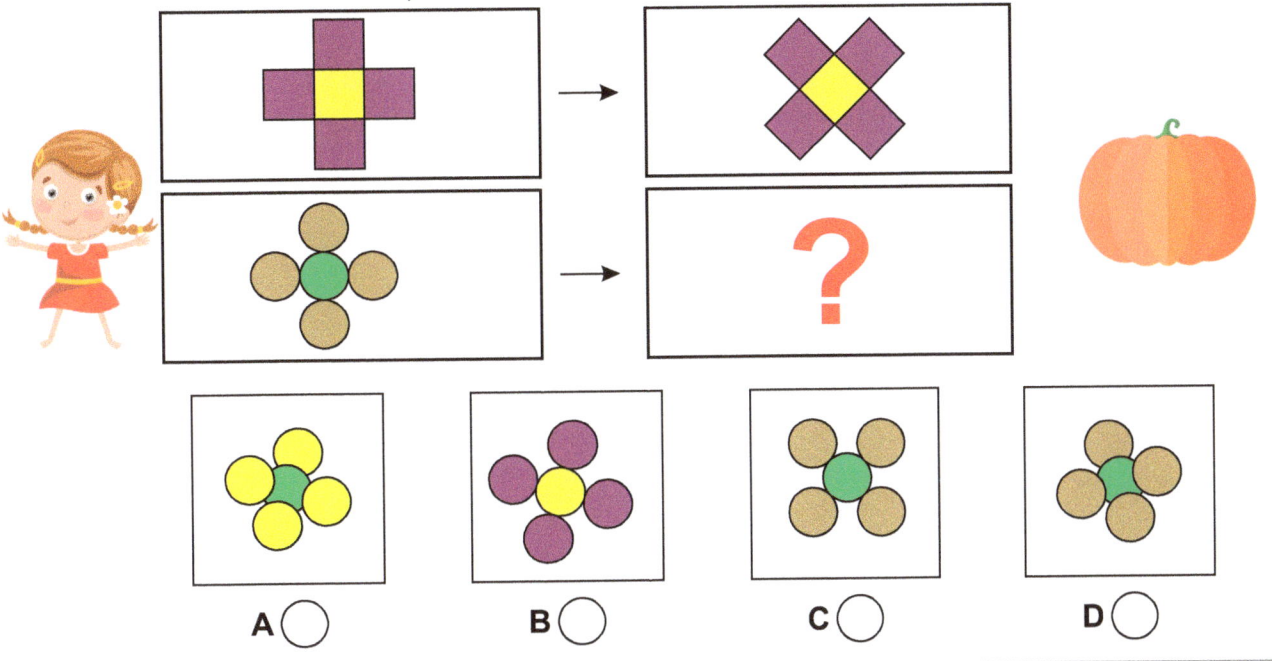

Q-14

Look at the question with the Celery. The first row has some thing in common as the second row. Can you help Ava to identify what goes in the space of the question mark from the four given options A, B, C, and D. Choose the correct option.

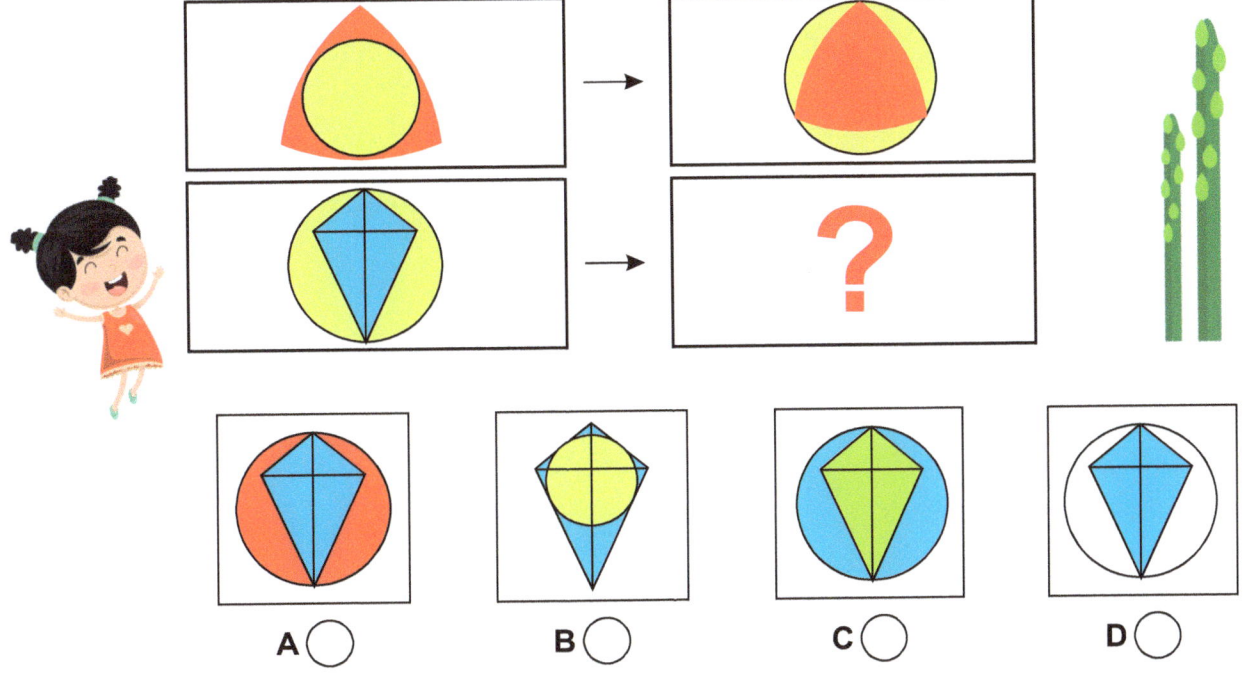

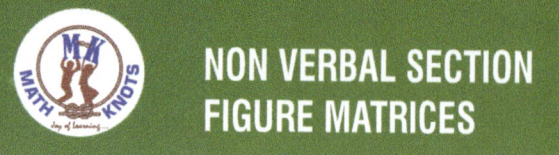

Q-15

Look at the question with the Capsicum. The first row has some thing in common as the second row. Can you help Amelia to identify what goes in the space of the question mark from the four given options A, B, C, and D. Choose the correct option.

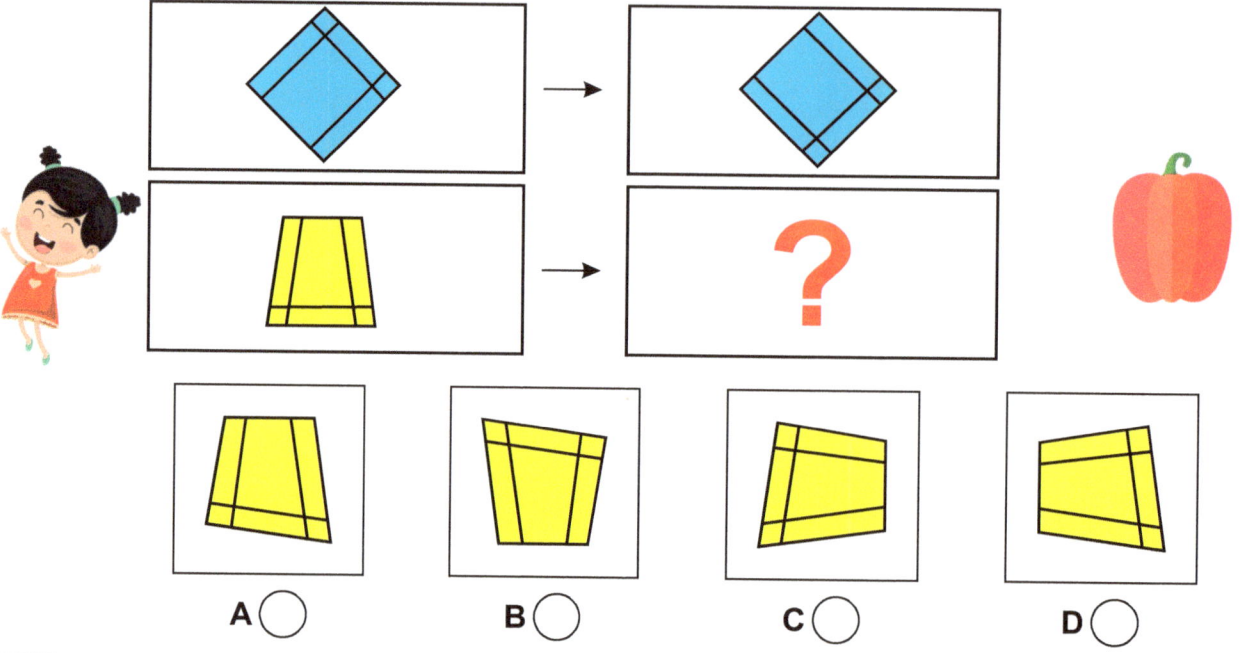

A ◯   B ◯   C ◯   D ◯

Q-16

Look at the question with the Mushroom. The first row has some thing in common as the second row. Can you help Samuel to identify what goes in the space of the question mark from the four given options A, B, C, and D. Choose the correct option.

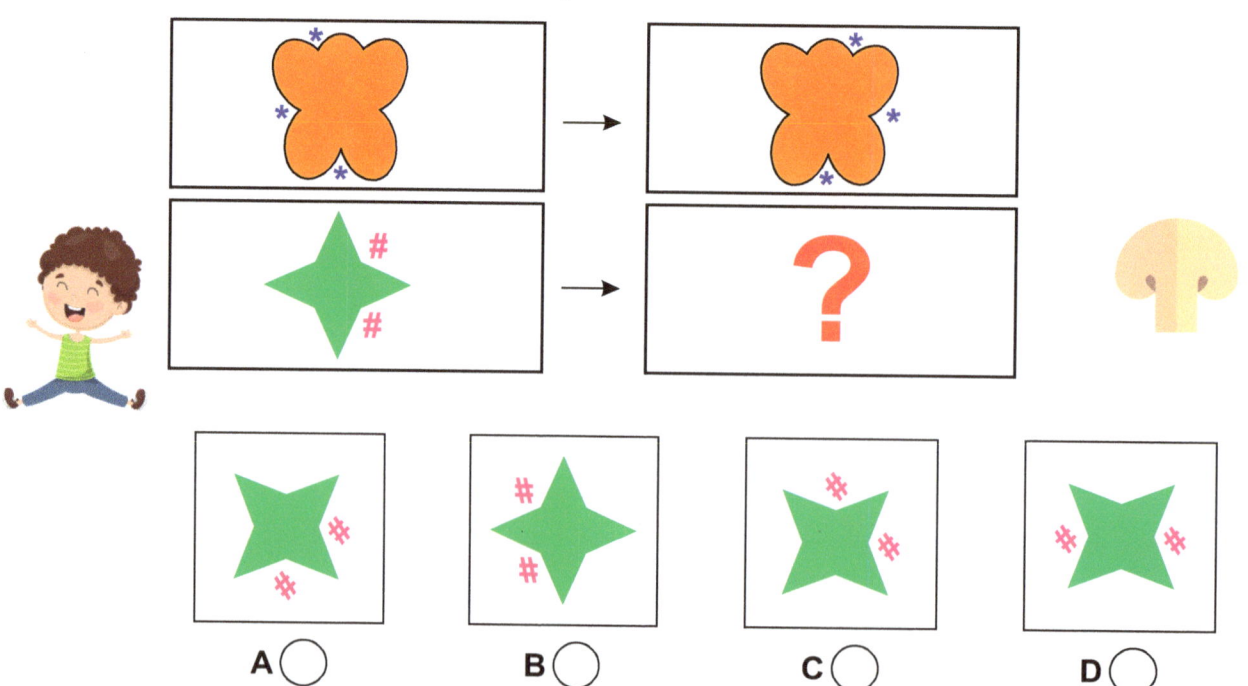

A ◯   B ◯   C ◯   D ◯

www.math-knots.com

Q-17

Look at the question with the Broccali. The first row has some thing in common as the second row. Can you help Ruby to identify what goes in the space of the question mark from the four given options A, B, C, and D. Choose the correct option.

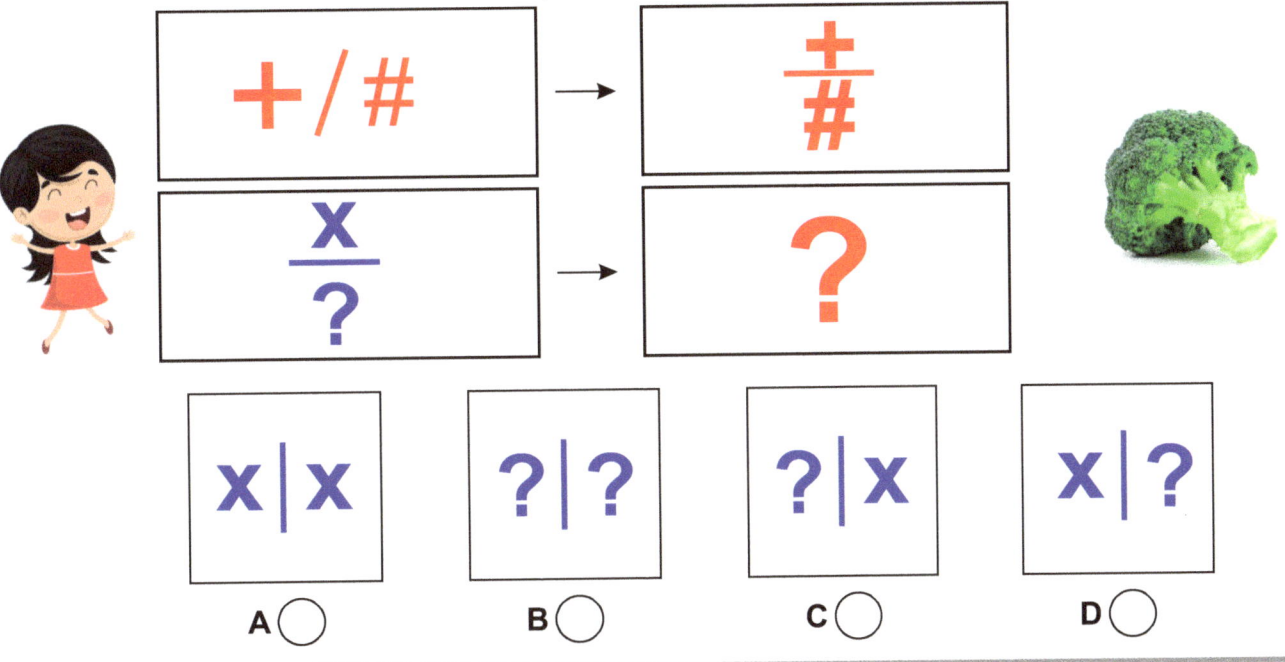

Q-18

Look at the question with the Lettuce. The first row has some thing in common as the second row. Can you help Mila to identify what goes in the space of the question mark from the four given options A, B, C, and D. Choose the correct option.

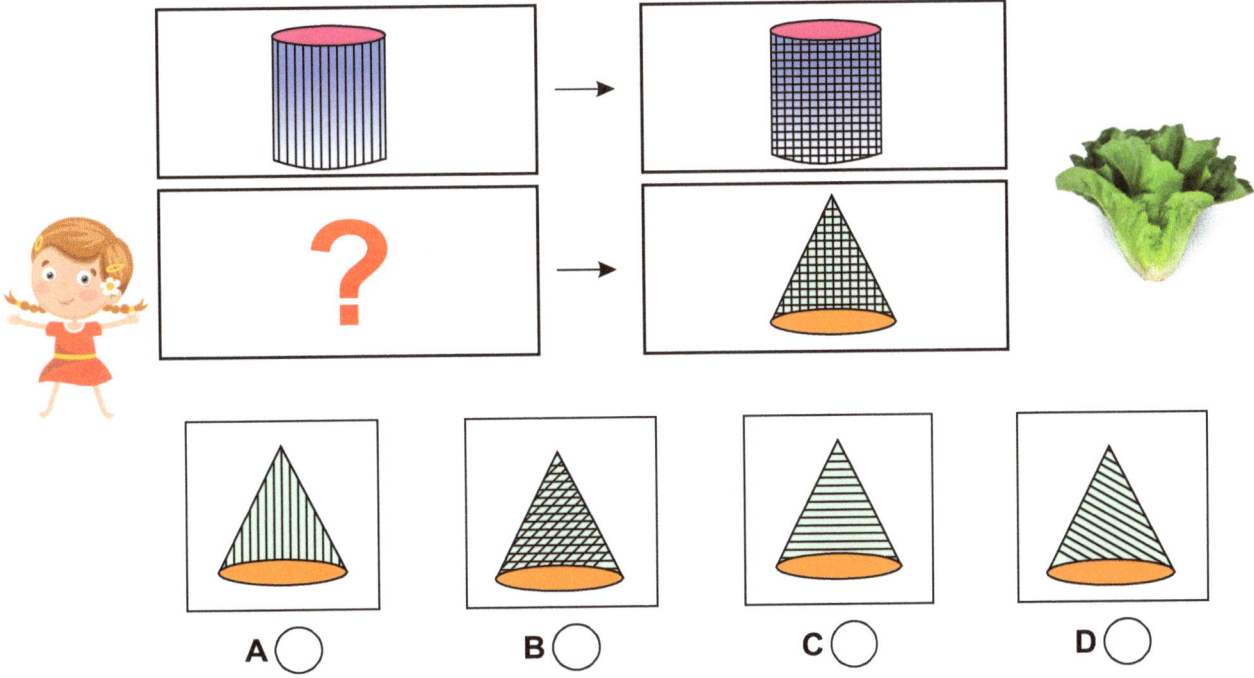

www.math-knots.com

www.math-knots.com

TEST - 2

NON VERBAL SECTION

PAPER FOLDING

Lets Start the Test...

www.math-knots.com

Sample

Look at the question and put your finger on Bee. Amy folded the paper and made holes to it as shown. When the paper is unfolded how does it look? Help her bubble the right option.

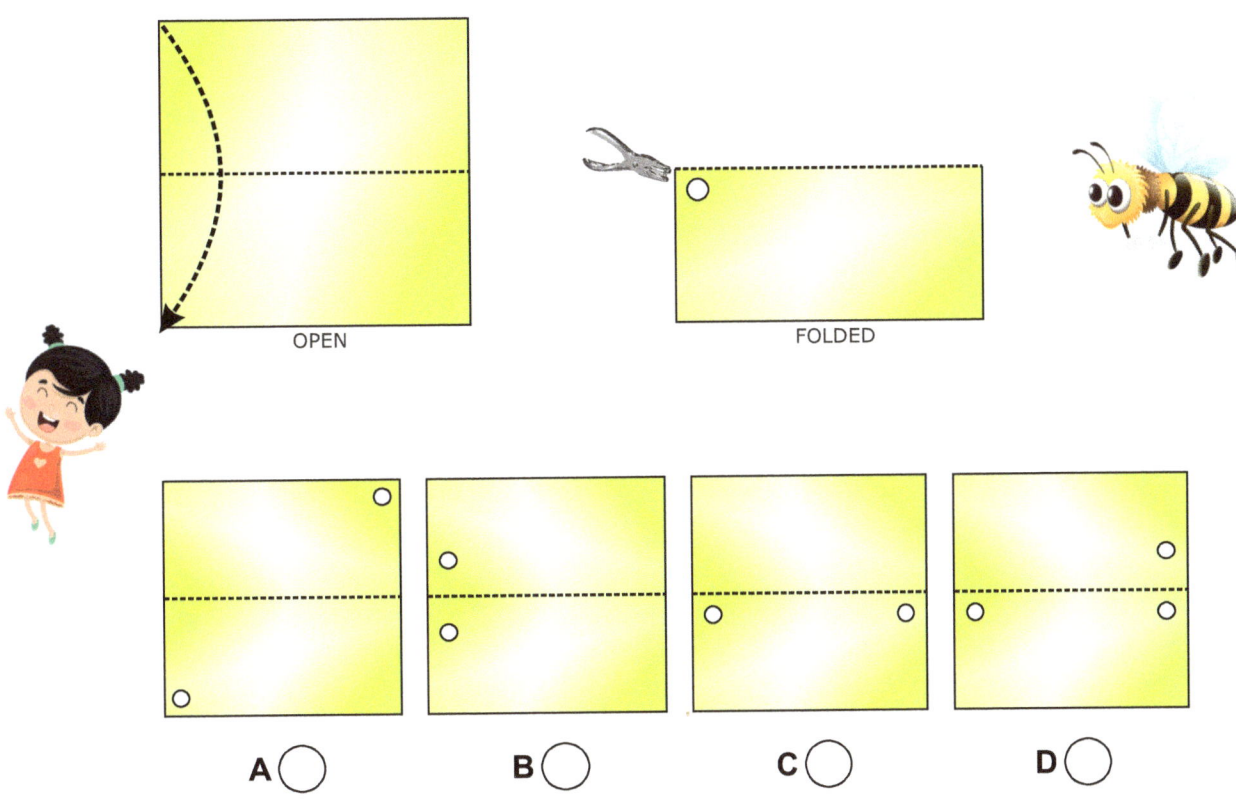

Solution : B

A rectangle is folded once and hole is punched on top left corner. After punching the figure is unfolded the holes are shown in the middle left corner as shown in option B. Student choses the right option and fills the bubble completely.

www.math-knots.com

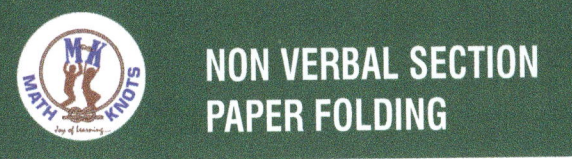
Q-1 Look at the question and put your finger on Paint mixing tray. Rebecca folded the paper and made hole to it as shown. When the paper is unfolded how does it look? Help her bubble the right option.

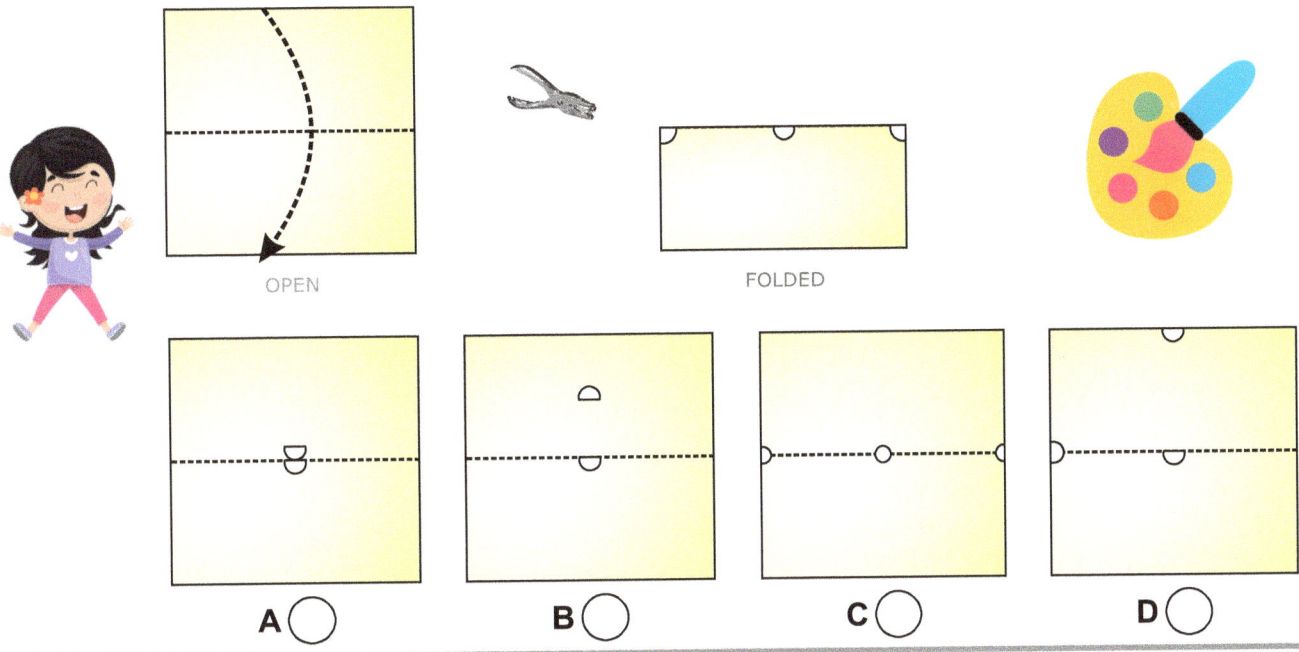

OPEN

FOLDED

A ○ B ○ C ○ D ○

Q-2 Look at the question and put your finger on Purple Pencil. Patrick folded the paper and made holes to it as shown. When the paper is unfolded how does it look? Help him bubble the right option.

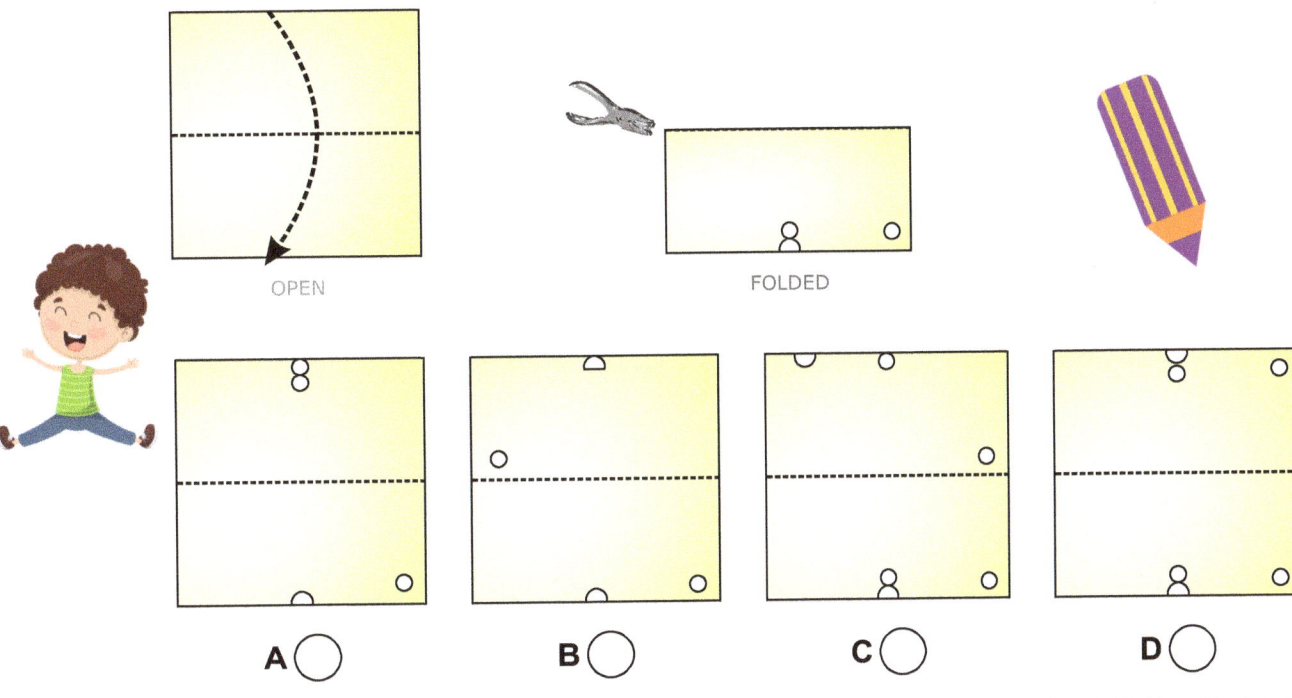

OPEN

FOLDED

A ○ B ○ C ○ D ○

www.math-knots.com

Q-3

Look at the question and put your finger on Ruler. Bryan folded the paper and made holes to it as shown. When the paper is unfolded how does it look? Help him bubble the right option.

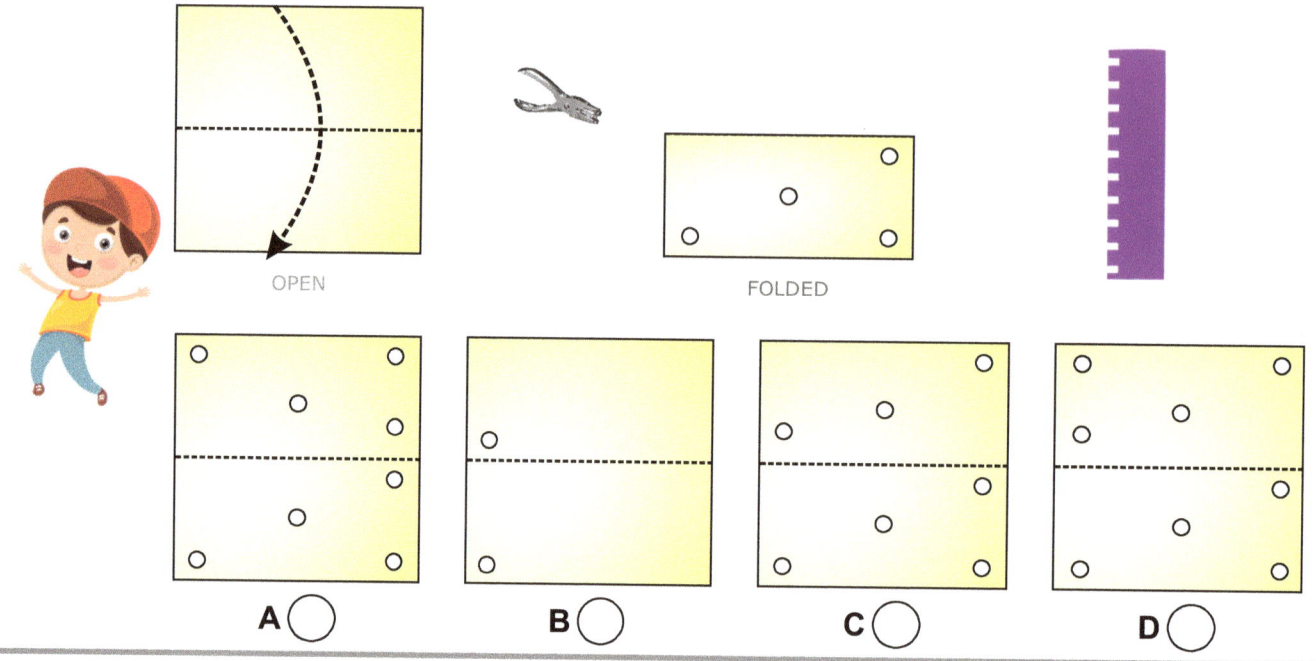

OPEN   FOLDED

A ○   B ○   C ○   D ○

Q-4

Look at the question and put your finger on Triangle. Jenna folded the paper and made holes to it as shown. When the paper is unfolded how does it look? Help her bubble the right option.

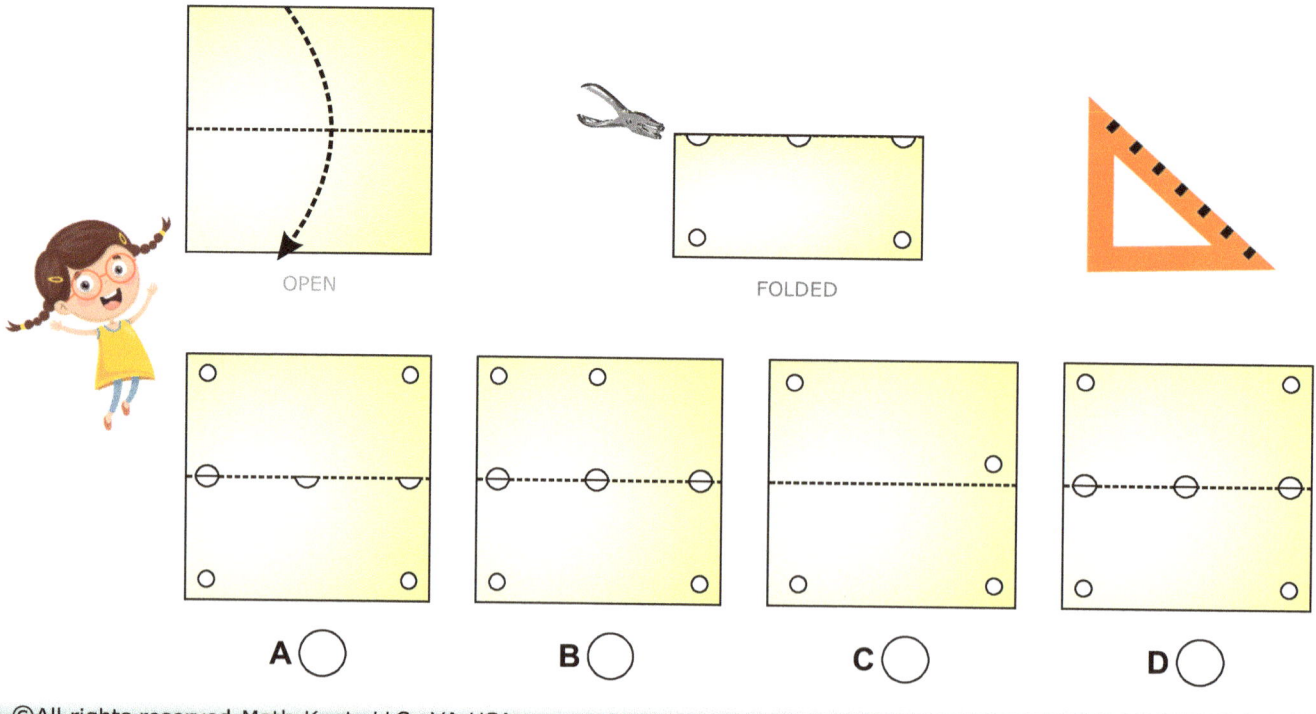

OPEN   FOLDED

A ○   B ○   C ○   D ○

www.math-knots.com

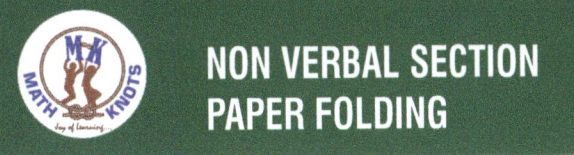

Q-5 Look at the question and put your finger on Calculator. Maya folded the paper and made hole to it as shown. When the paper is unfolded how does it look? Help her bubble the right option.

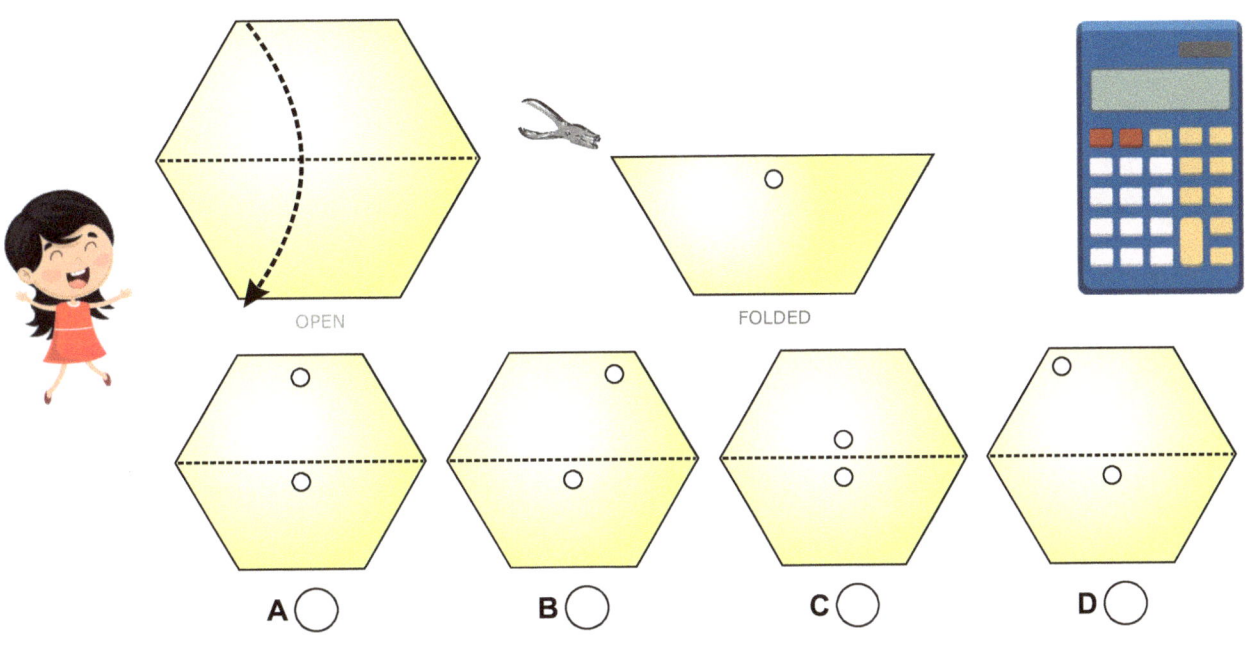

OPEN

FOLDED

A ◯   B ◯   C ◯   D ◯

Q-6 Look at the question and put your finger on Sharpner. Richard folded the paper and made holes to it as shown. When the paper is unfolded how does it look? Help him bubble the right option.

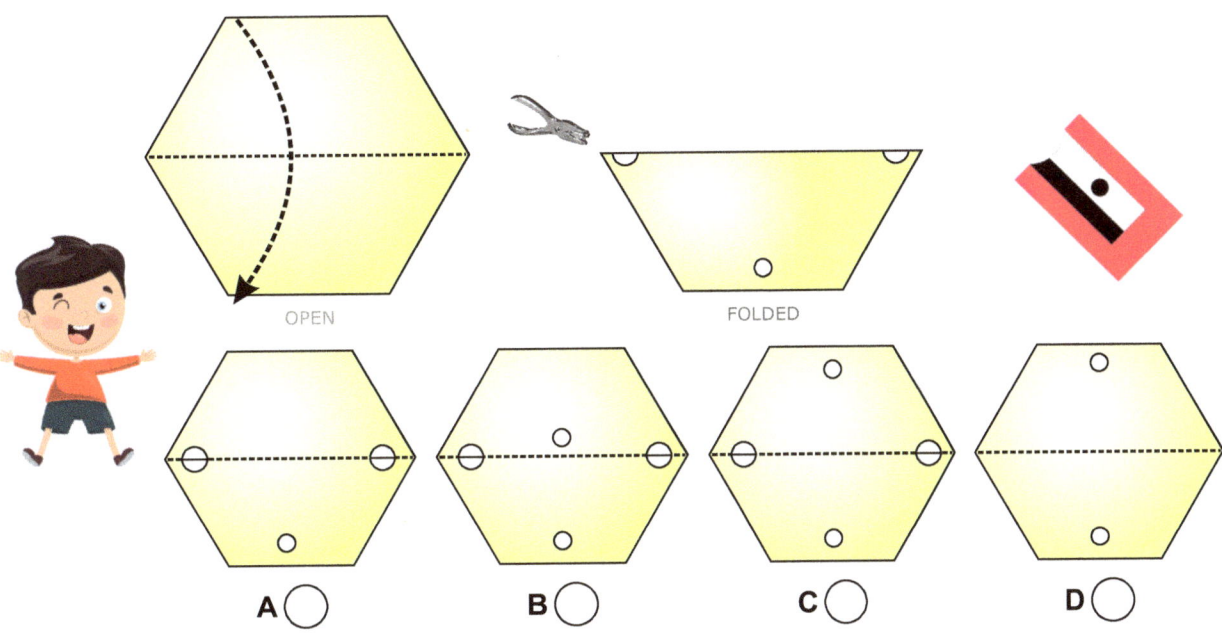

OPEN

FOLDED

A ◯   B ◯   C ◯   D ◯

www.math-knots.com

Q-7 Look at the question and put your finger on Magnifying Glass. Xavier folded the paper and made holes to it as shown. When the paper is unfolded how does it look? Help him bubble the right option.

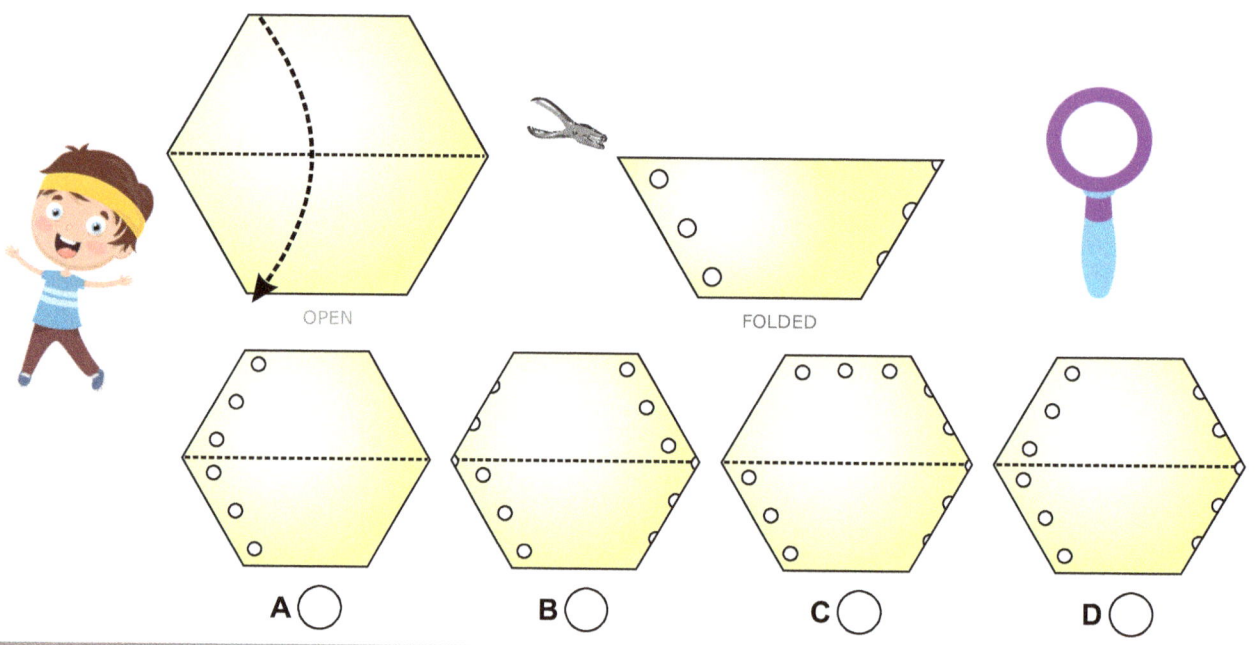

OPEN   FOLDED

A ◯   B ◯   C ◯   D ◯

Q-8 Look at the question and put your finger on Scissors. Grace folded the paper and made holes to it as shown. When the paper is unfolded how does it look? Help her bubble the right option.

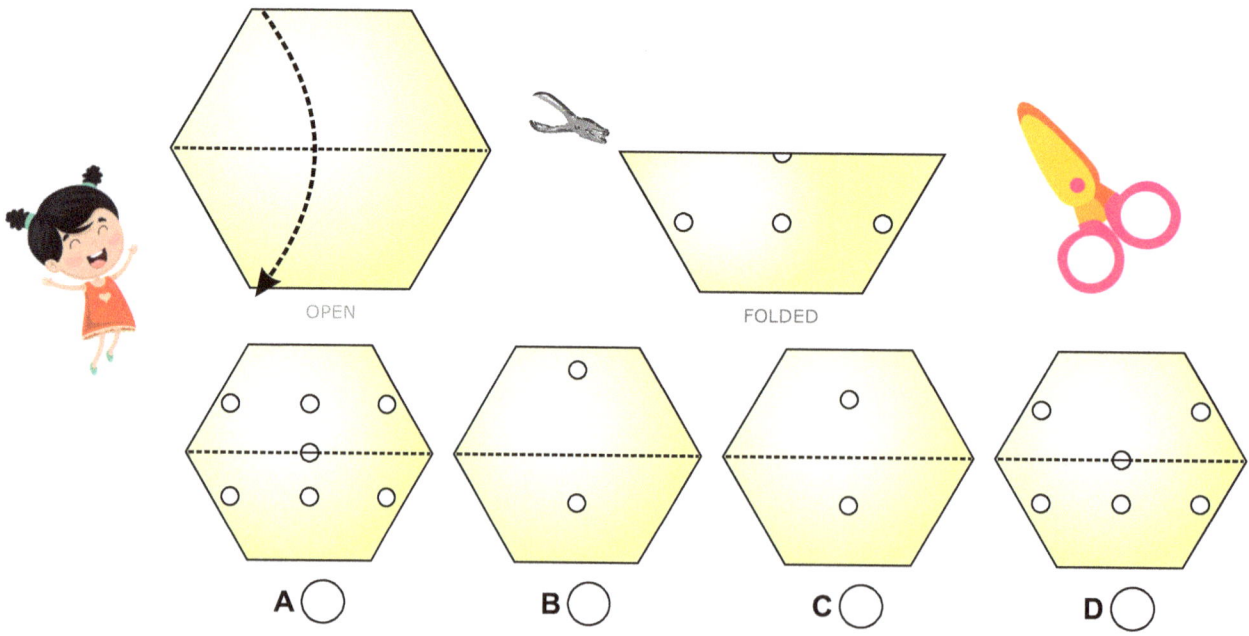

OPEN   FOLDED

A ◯   B ◯   C ◯   D ◯

www.math-knots.com

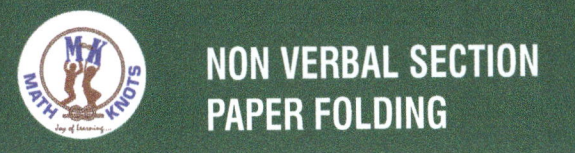

Q-9

Look at the question and put your finger on Blue Cryon. Angelina folded the paper and made holes to it as shown. When the paper is unfolded how does it look? Help her bubble the right option.

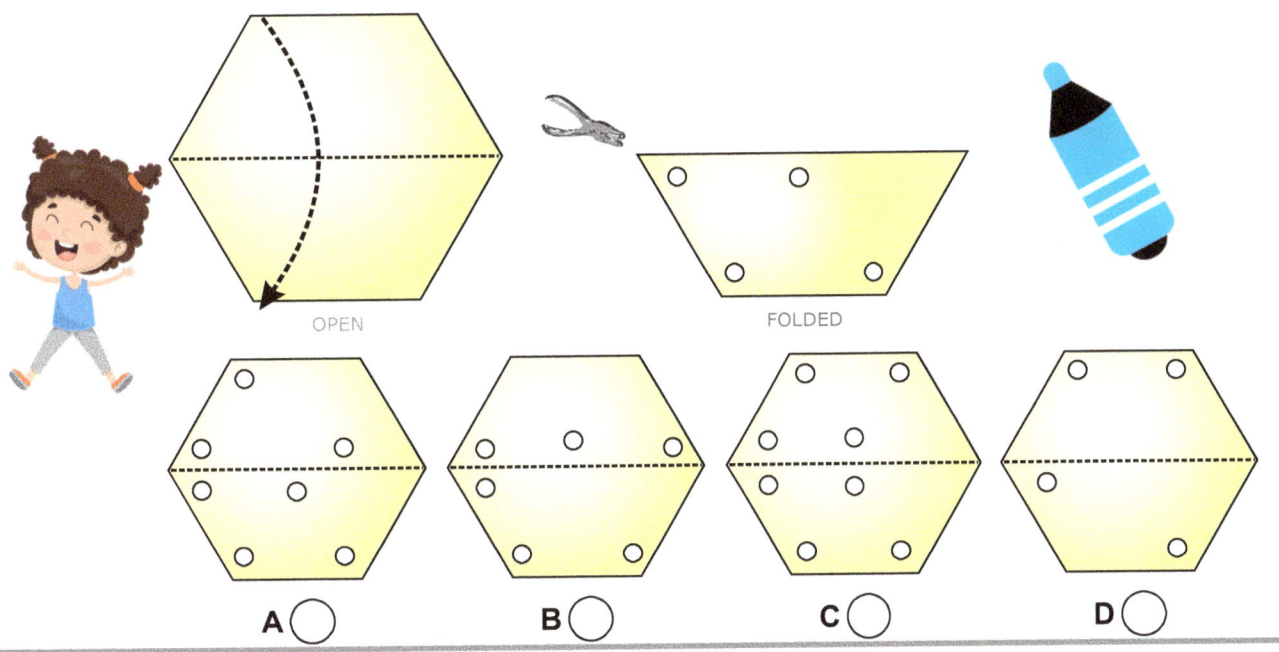

OPEN

FOLDED

A ◯ B ◯ C ◯ D ◯

Q-10

Look at the question and put your finger on Paper clip. Audrey folded the paper and made holes to it as shown. When the paper is unfolded how does it look? Help her bubble the right option.

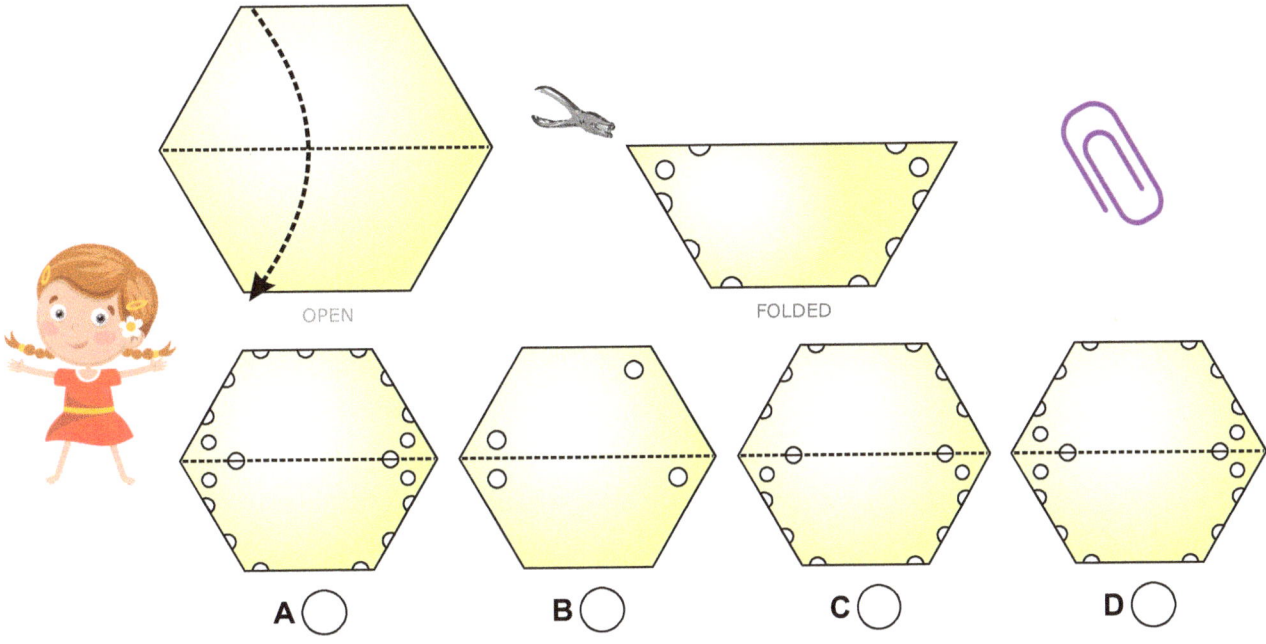

OPEN

FOLDED

A ◯ B ◯ C ◯ D ◯

www.math-knots.com

Q-11 Look at the question and put your finger on Books. Timothy folded the paper and made holes to it as shown. When the paper is unfolded how does it look? Help him bubble the right option.

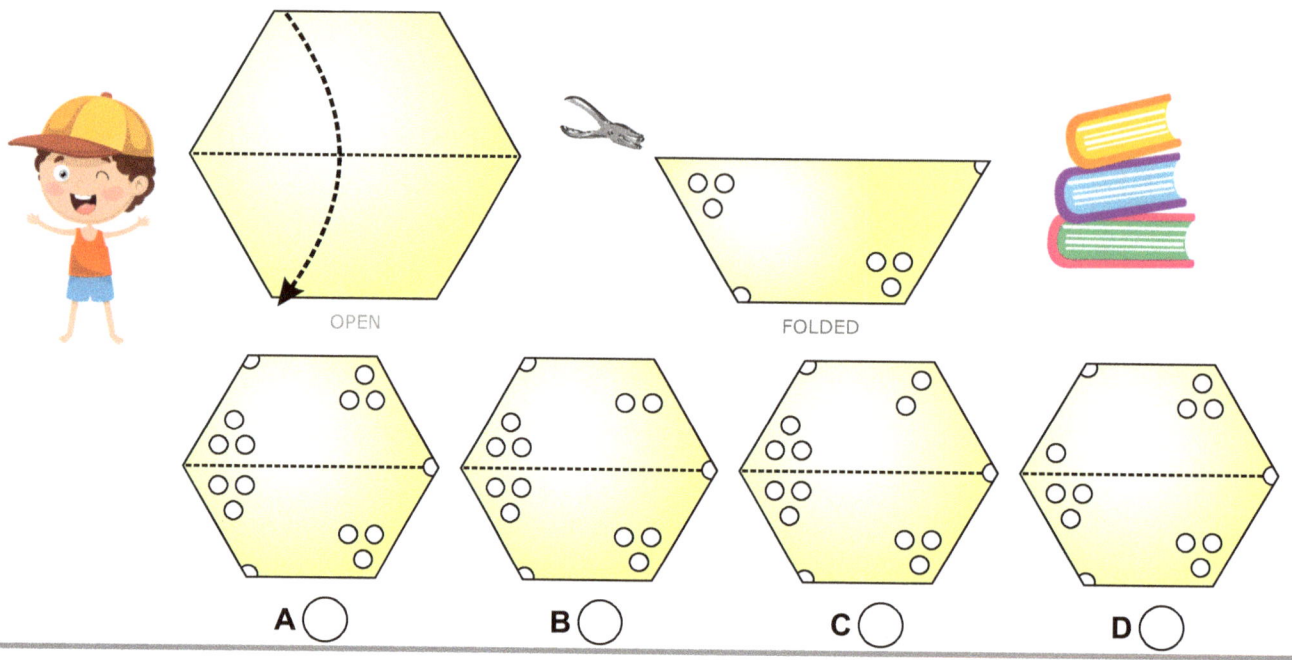

Q-12 Look at the question and put your finger on Stapler. Liam folded the paper and made holes to it as shown. When the paper is unfolded how does it look? Help him bubble the right option.

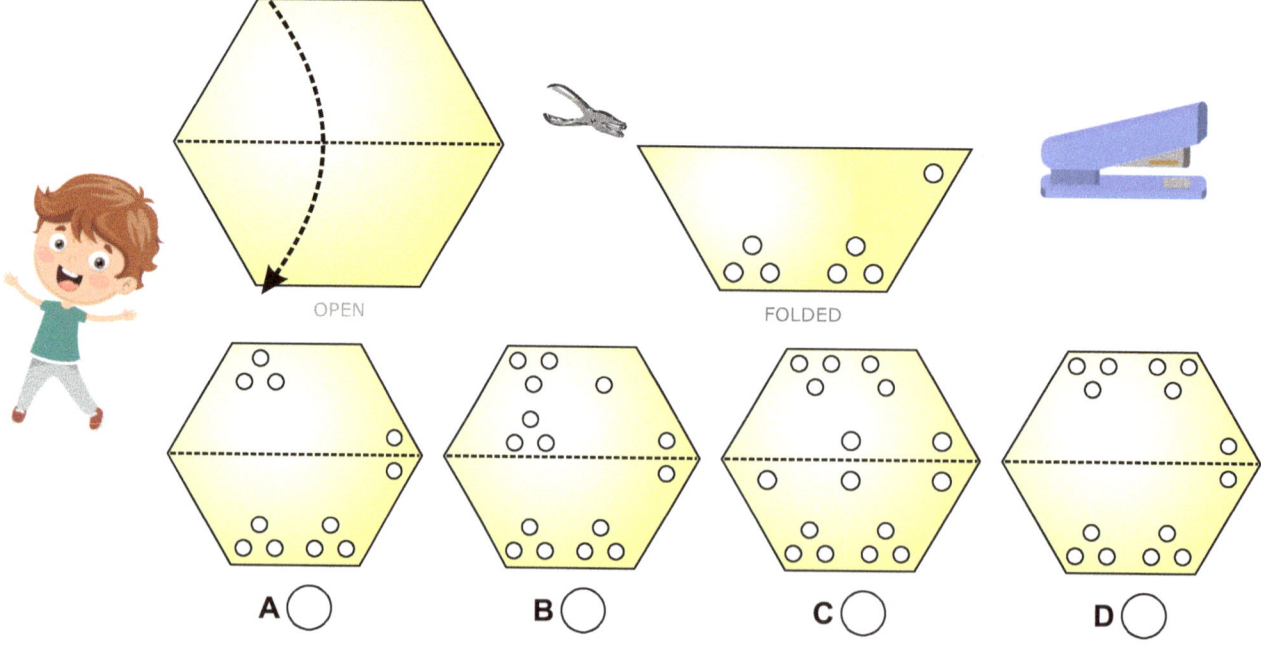

www.math-knots.com

Q-13

Look at the question and put your finger on Push Pin. Richard folded the paper and made holes to it as shown. When the paper is unfolded how does it look? Help him bubble the right option.

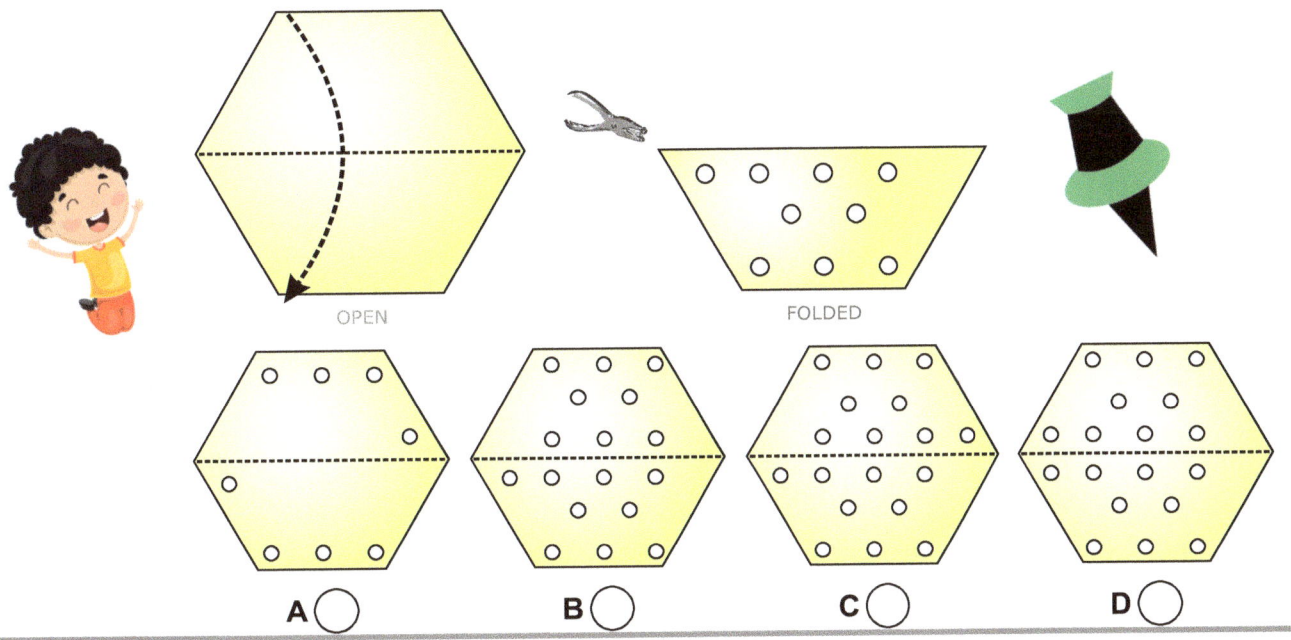

OPEN   FOLDED

A ◯   B ◯   C ◯   D ◯

Q-14

Look at the question and put your finger on Eraser. Erin folded the paper and made holes to it as shown. When the paper is unfolded how does it look? Help her bubble the right option.

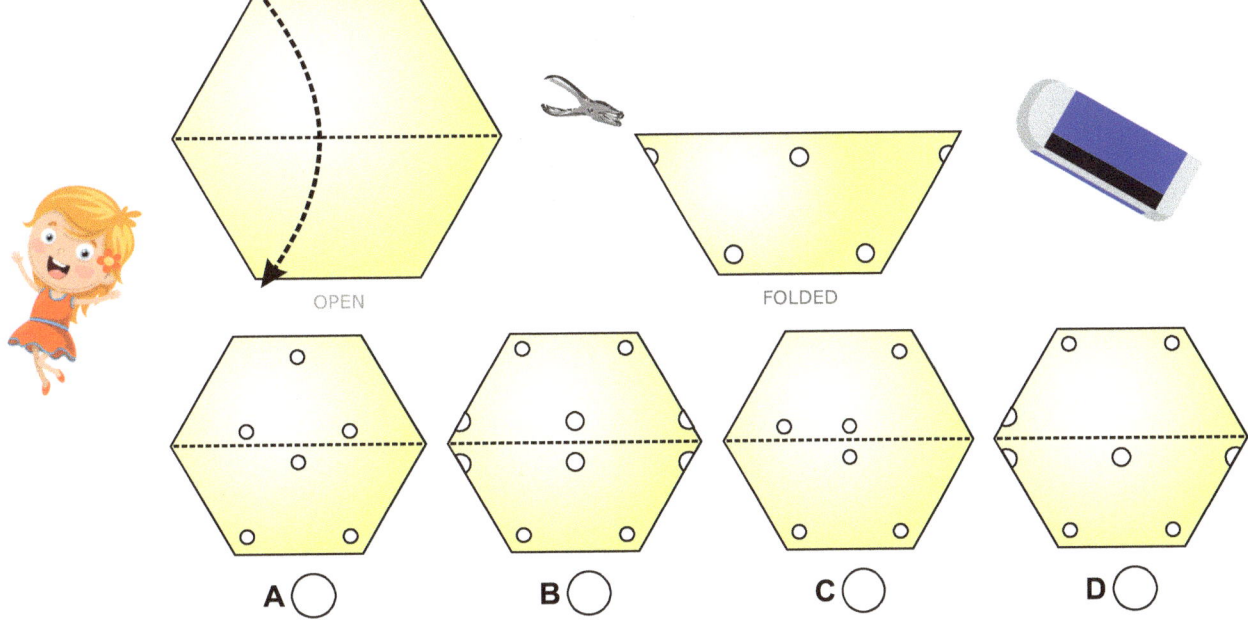

OPEN   FOLDED

A ◯   B ◯   C ◯   D ◯

Q-15

Look at the question and put your finger on Highlighter. Wyatt folded the paper and made holes to it as shown. When the paper is unfolded how does it look? Help him bubble the right option.

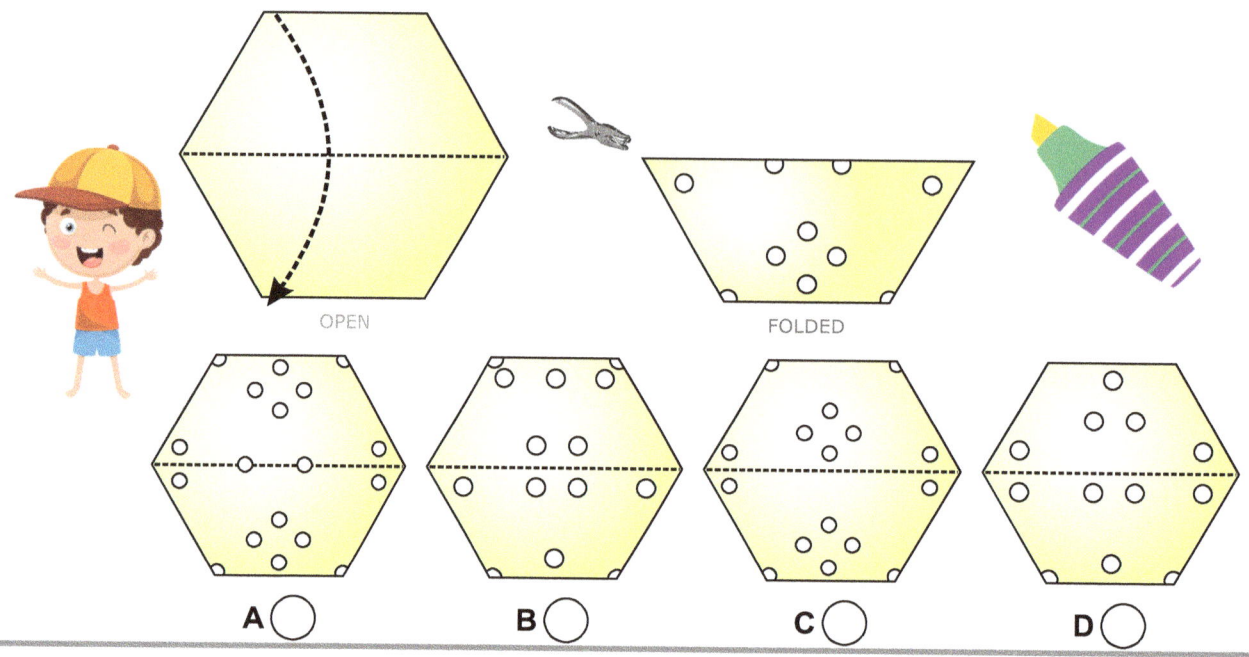

OPEN   FOLDED

A ◯   B ◯   C ◯   D ◯

Q-16

Look at the question and put your finger on Paint Box. Hayden folded the paper and made holes to it as shown. When the paper is unfolded how does it look? Help him bubble the right option.

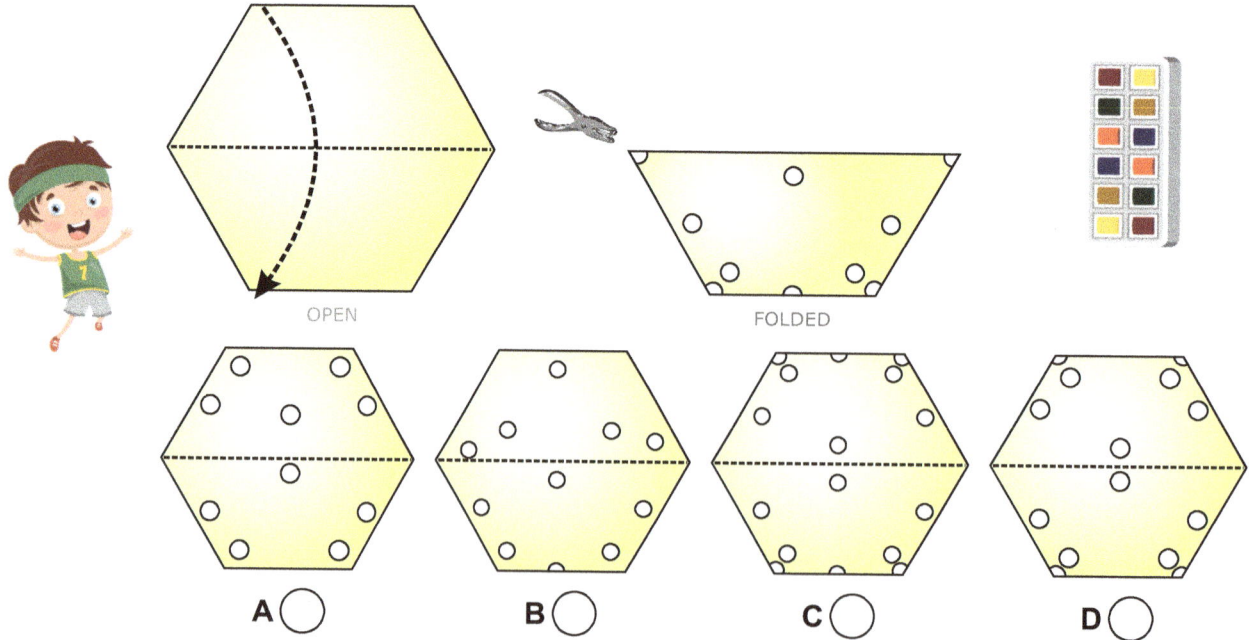

OPEN   FOLDED

A ◯   B ◯   C ◯   D ◯

www.math-knots.com

MATH-KNOTS CHALLENGE

Q-17

Look at the question and put your finger on Art Brush. Ariana folded the paper and made holes to it as shown. When the paper is unfolded how does it look? Help her bubble the right option.

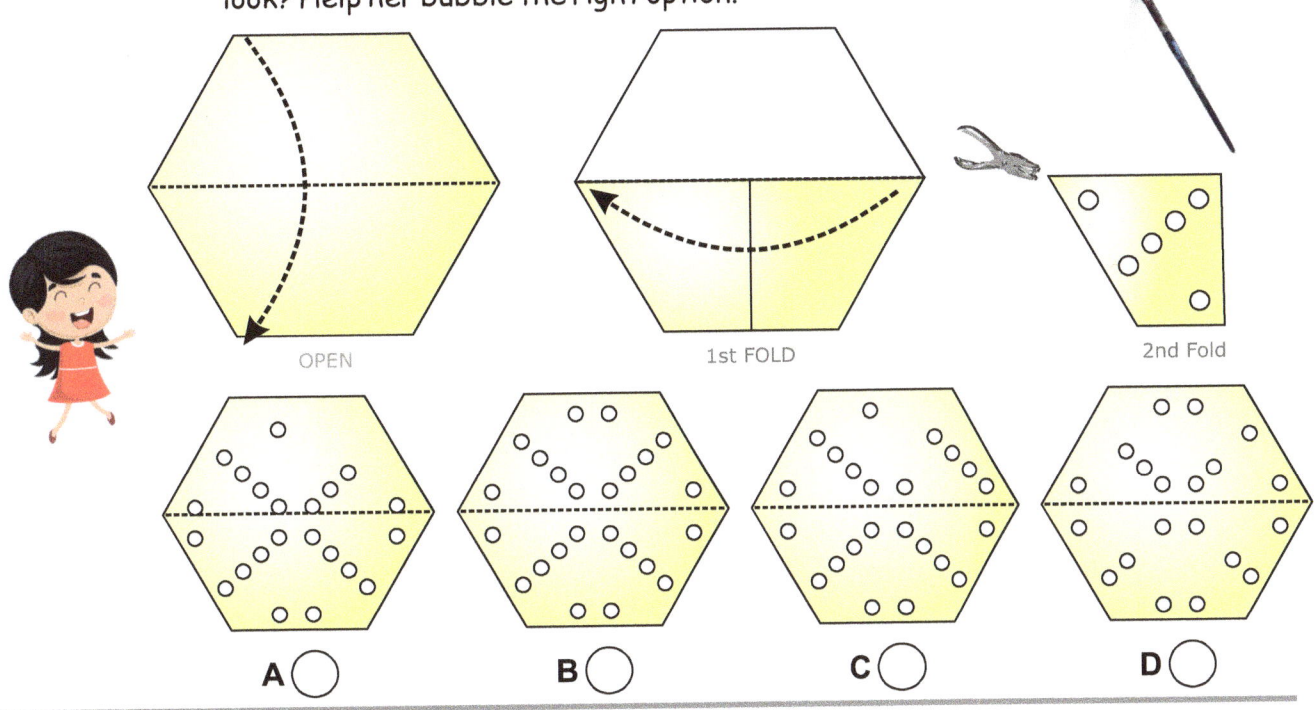

OPEN   1st FOLD   2nd Fold

A ◯   B ◯   C ◯   D ◯

MATH-KNOTS CHALLENGE

Q-18

Look at the question and put your finger on Pen. Jasmin folded the paper and made holes to it as shown. When the paper is unfolded how does it look? Help her bubble the right option.

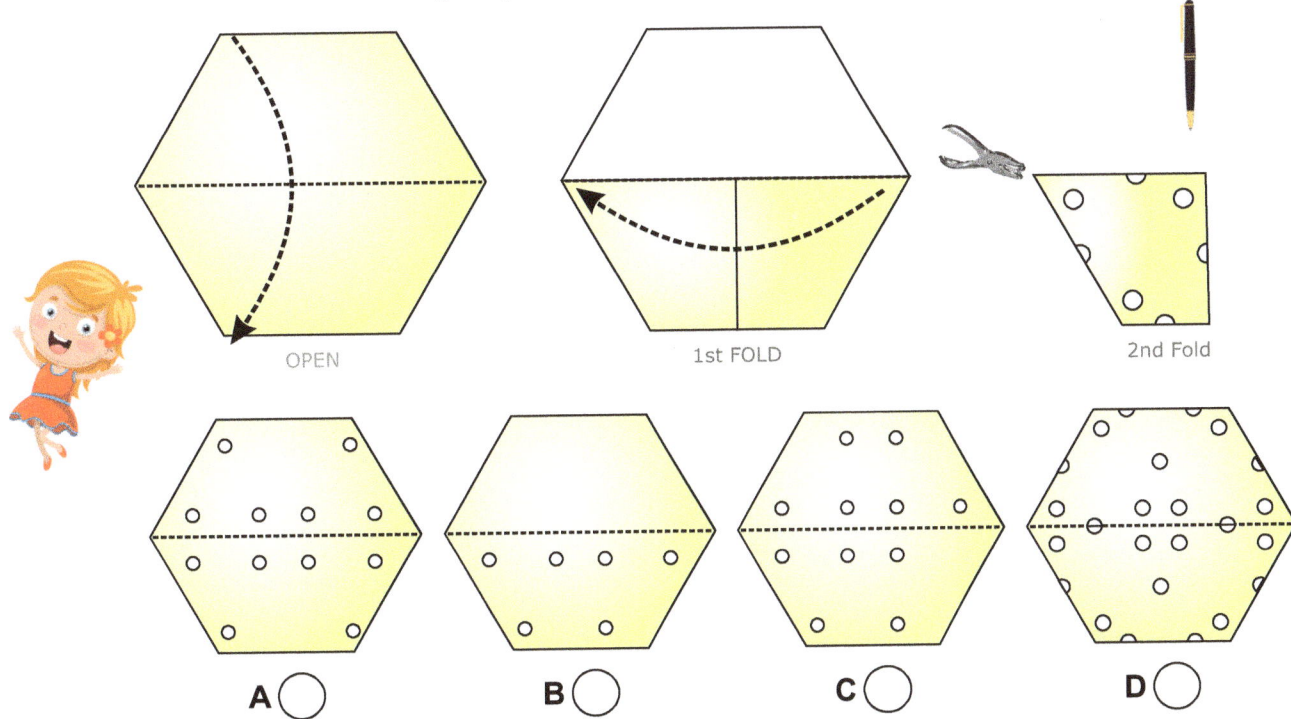

OPEN   1st FOLD   2nd Fold

A ◯   B ◯   C ◯   D ◯

MATH-KNOTS CHALLENGE

Q-19

Look at the question and put your finger on Back Pack. Patrick folded the paper and made holes to it as shown. When the paper is unfolded how does it look? Help him bubble the right option.

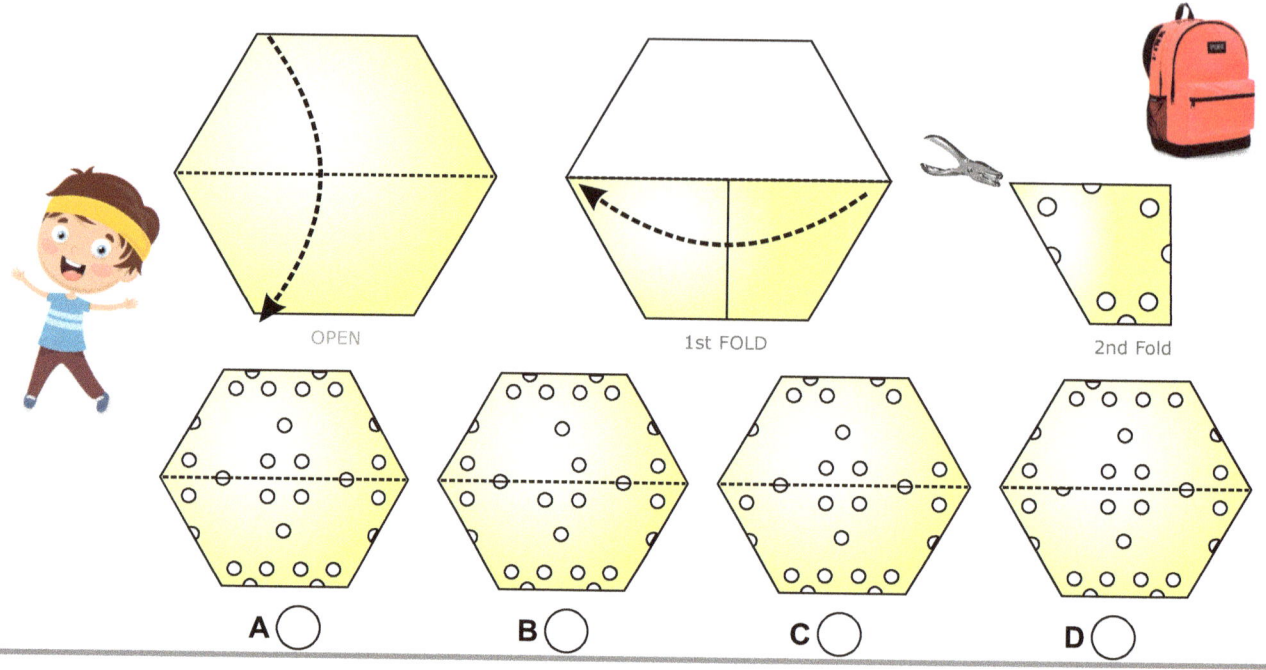

MATH-KNOTS CHALLENGE

Q-20

Look at the question and put your finger on Ruler. Evelyn folded the paper and made holes to it as shown. When the paper is unfolded how does it look? Help her bubble the right option.

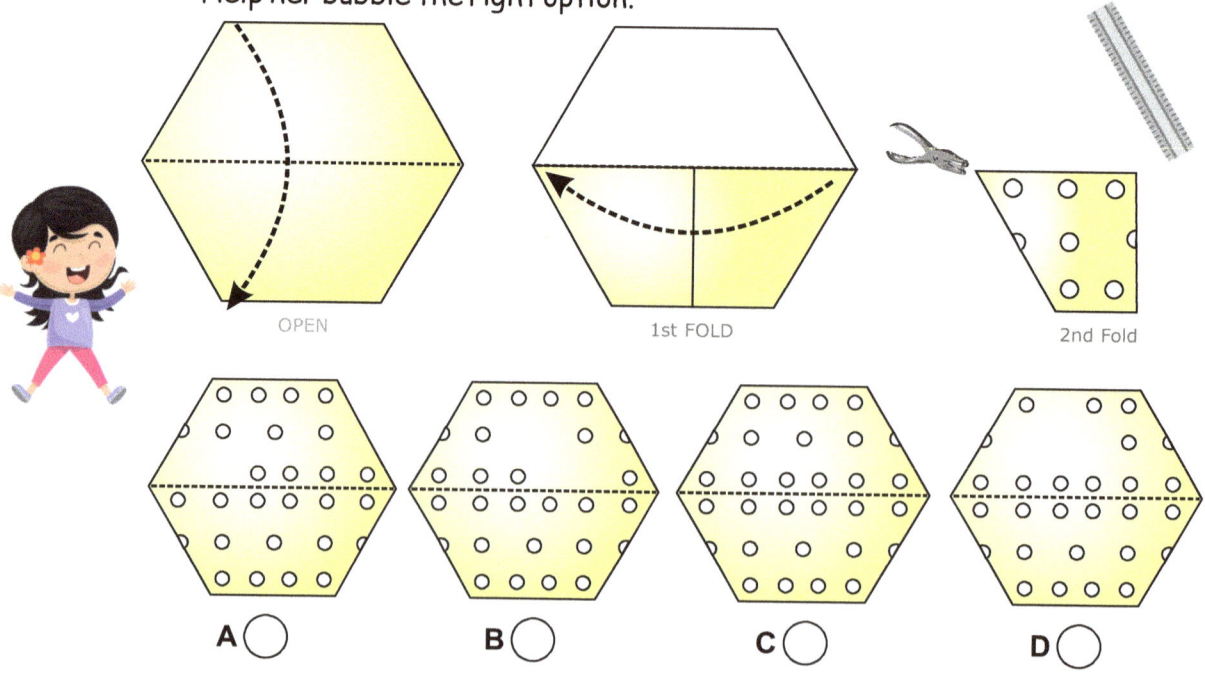

www.math-knots.com

ANSWER KEYS

TEST - 1 AND 2

Lets Start the Test...

www.math-knots.com

ANSWER KEY

1. B ;   Various continents

2. D ;   Types of houses

3. A ;   All are more than one in the human body

4. C ;   Branches of math

5. C ;   Various currencies

6. D ;   Same meaning

7. B ;   Shades of Yellow

8. A ;   Male animals

9. D ;   Solid figures

10. C ;   Types of looking; Wink is a momentary action

11. D ;   Various types of positive feelings

12. B ;   Things that girls wear on to their wrist / hand

13. D ;   Various performers in movies, plays, skits etc..

14. A ;   Milky way is a group of stars. All others are in sky as single entities

15. B ;   Various types of fruits

16. B ;   Various types of bugs not bug

17. C ;   Various types of tenses

18. D ;   Non-Metallic elements

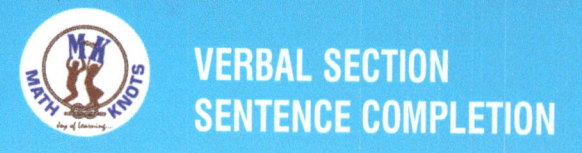
ANSWER KEY

1.   C

Cereal is a processed food. Others are vegetables

2.   D

Sam < Tom < Tim so Tim weighs the most

3.   A

Bumble Bee is the only one that flies among given choices

4.   C

Option A is the figure, Option B is thermostat and Option D is showing weather forecast. Option C shows the thermometer which measures our body temperature

5.   D

Tennis players use a bat with mesh to play the sport

6.   D

Mia facing west when she makes a right turn she is facing North again a right turn means she is facing west

7.   B

Potatoes and carrots are few vegetables that grow underground. From the given choices option B potato is the right choice

8.   A

Option A shows weighing scale for the cookies or any grocery items including fruits and vegetables. Option B to measure length, Option C to measure liquids and option D is the weighing scale mostly used for larger weights

9.   D

All options belong to school supplies. We write in books but can't write with books. Hence Option D is the right choice

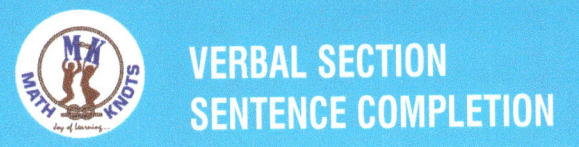
ANSWER KEY

10. A

Zebra has black and white stripes. Only option showing black and white is option A

11. C

A phone rings, Music plays, Drums make sound and finger rings doesn't ring. Right choice is Option C

12. B

No of sides of Octagon > No of sides of Pentagon> No of sides of Square Octagon has more sides than other two figures

13. D

Wind mill doesn't need electricity. It moves naturally in the direction of wind

14. C

Urmi needs to brush her teeth. She needs a tooth brush and tooth paste. From the given choices tooth brush is the right choice

15. A

To make a table we need to cut the wood. He needs a saw from the given choices

16. B

Air modulation will be done through mouth. Only instrument that is played is through mouth is mouth organ

17. D

Grapes doesn't belong to berries family

18. A

Green represents St. Patrick's Day. Option is the only choice of red color

www.math-knots.com

ANSWER KEY

1. A

2. C

3. D

4. B

5. A

6. C

7. D

8. A

9. D

10. B

11. A

12. C

13. D

14. A

15. D

16. B

17. A

18. C

www.math-knots.com

ANSWER KEY

1.   B

   1 Whole --> Half

   1 Whole --> Half

2.   C

   5 --> 6 (Add 1)

   7 --> 8 (Add 1)

3.   A

   4 --> 2 (Half)

   2 --> 1 (Half)

4.   D

   8 --> 10 (Add 2)

   6 --> 8 (Add 2)

5.   B

   Half --> Full

   Half --> Ful

6.   D

   Color extends to next section

7.   A

   2 --> 7 (Add 5)

   5 --> 10 (Add 5)

www.math-knots.com

ANSWER KEY

8. C

6 --> 4 (Subtract 2)

9 --> 7 (Subtract 2)

9. B

2 --> 9 (Add 7)

5 --> 12 (Subtract 7)

10. D

1 --> 8 (Add 7)

3 --> 10 (Add 7)

11. A

3 --> 2 (Subtract 1)

10 --> 9 (Subtract 1)

12. C

1 Pair --> 2 Pairs

3 Pairs --> 6 Pairs

13. B

4 --> 9 (Add 5)

1 --> 6 (Add 5)

14. C

6 --> 12 (Double)

3 --> 6 (Double)

www.math-knots.com

ANSWER KEY

15.   D

10 --> 2 (Subtract 8)

8 --> 0 (Subtract 8)

16.   B

One Grape --> Many Grapes

One Straw Berry --> Many Straw Berries

17.   A

7 --> 4 (Subtract 3)

5 --> 2 (Subtract 3)

18.   C

1 --> 3 (Add 2)

4 --> 6 (Add 2)

ANSWER KEY

1. **B**

2, 4, 2, 4, 2, 4; Numbers are increasing by 2

2. **D**

5, 0, 5, 0, 5; Number sequence 5 ,0 is repeating

3. **C**

1, 2, 3, 4; Each number is increasing by 1

4. **A**

3, 3, 1, 1, 3, 3, 1, 1; Each number is repeating twice and then decreasing by 2 ,repeating and then increasing by 2

5. **D**

4, 4, 6, 6, 8, 8; Each number is repeating twice and Numbers are increasing by 2 and then repeating again

6. **C**

9, 7, 5, 3; Numbers are decreasing by 2

7. **A**

5, 3, 1, 5, 3, 1, 5; Number sequence 5, 3, 1 is repeating.

8. **B**

1, 2, 4, 7; Numbers are increasing by 1, 2, 3 ..etc
Pattern is like 1, 1 + 1, 2 + 2, 4 + 3

9. **A**

1, 4, 7, 10; 1, 1 + 3, 4 + 3, 7 + 3; Starting with 1 Numbers are increasing by 3

www.math-knots.com

ANSWER KEY

10.   C

5, 4, 4, 5, 3, 6; First Alternate numbers are decreasing by 1 then next alternate numbers are increasing by 1

11.   B

3, 1, 5, 3, 1, 5, 3; Number sequence 3, 1, 5 is repeating

12.   C

2, 4, 2, 4, 2, 4; Number sequence 2, 4 is repeating

13.   D

4, 4, 4, 3, 3, 3, 2; Numbers are repeating three times and then decreasing by 1 ,repeat three times and so on

14.   B

10, 7, 4, 3, 0; Starting with number 10 and decreasing by 3

15.   A

5, 7, 7, 5, 7, 7, 5; Repeating sequence of 5, 7 and 7

16.   C

9, 8, 10, 9, 11 ; First Alternate numbers are increasing by 1 then next alternate numbers are increasing by 1

17.   D

6, 6, 5, 5, 6, 6, 5 ; Numbers are repeating twice and then decreasing by 1, repeating twice, then increasing by 1 and repeating. In other words 6, 6, 5, 5 is a repeating pattern

18.   A

4, 3, 2, 4, 3, 2; Repeating sequence of 4, 3 and 2

259   www.math-knots.com

ANSWER KEY

1.   A

$4 + 4 = 8$

2.   D

$16 + 6 = 22$

3.   B

$7 + 12 = 19$

4.   C

$3 + 8 = 11$

5.   D

$15 + 15 = 30$

6.   B

$9 + 0 = 9$

7.   A

$11 + 10 = 21$

8.   C

$3 + 6 + 9 = 18$

9.   A

$12 + 2 + 1 = 15$

10.   B

$1 + 2 + 6 = 9$

ANSWER KEY

11.   B

$$12 + 12 + 12 = 36$$

12.   C

$$13 + 14 + 15 = 42$$

13.   A

$$25 + 0 + 25 = 50$$

14.   C

$$9 + 16 + 10 = 35$$

15.   D

$$18 + 1 + 18 = 37$$

16.   B

$$30 + 35 + 5 = 70$$

17.   D

$$40 + 41 + 7 = 88$$

18.   C

$$19 + 19 + 4 = 38 + 4 = 42$$

19.   D

$$11 + 7 + 7 = 25$$

20.   B

$$25 + 50 + 75 = 75 + 75 = 150$$

ANSWER KEY

1.   D   Crescent shape moon with yellow color more and blue color less

2.   B   Fly with six antennas with same colors

3.   B   Mango with a steam and two leaves

4.   A   Star with # ,$ and @ next to each other in the same order

5.   D   Triangle with two little square shapes attached to one side. Match the figure with same colors, shapes and sizes

6.   C   Plant steam with 5 leaves in total

7.   A   Rectangle with four little pictures in each corner, with two small curves on the side and a big curve in between

8.   B   Leaf with a small stem and six lines inside of the same shade color

9.   D   Figure with straight lines either horizontal, vertical or angular but not checks. They should have two different lines in each figure. So, A, B, and C are not right answers

10. C   Pencil divided into red ,blue and yellow colors in order with yellow color as tip

ANSWER KEY

11.	A	Pot shaped picture with a yellow figure enclosed by a curve with three orange circles. Pay attention to options
12.	D	Circle with straight lines enclosed by a diamond shape. Outside diamond are 4 different figures and colors as well
13.	A	Figure with 6 diamonds, alternate yellow and red
14.	A	Each figure is divided into 4 equal areas or figures of same kind
15.	B	A line with Blue and orange squares on one side. Green and red squares on the other side
16.	D	A square divided into four sections .Each section has lines : 1,2,3 and 4 in order
17.	C	Different shapes of figures ,across the tear drop. Pay attention to colors and figure positions
18.	A	Circle enclosing a small circle(yellow) and a T shaped figure towards inside. Adjacent to T two green arrows originating from a point, pointing outwards

www.math-knots.com

ANSWER KEY

1.   D

Turning 90° to right side

2.   A

6 sides figure to 7 sides figure

7 sides figure to 8 sides figure

3.   B

Turning into an angle

4.   D

Broken lines are connected

5.   C

Reducing size and switch the sides of outer figures
(moving to the other sides)

6.   D

4 items --> 6 items

7.   B

1 item to 2 items; 2 items to 4 items by turning 90
degrees.

8.   A

Adding the same figure above the line in same direction
in the bottom as well

9.   C

Turning to right side slightly

10.   B

Half to full

www.math-knots.com

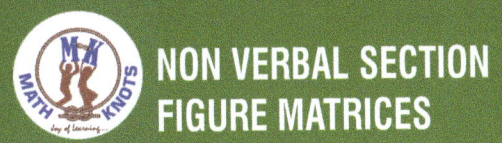

ANSWER KEY

11.   B

Two pictures forming into a complete full picture.

One figure remains same, other one flips and joins.

12.   D

Big figure is flipped and inside object is outside.

13.   C

Flipping the figure top to bottom or right to left

14.   D

Outer border is filled

15.   B

One broken figure is enclosed by a closed figure of the same and also includes the same figure inside

16.   C

Signs inside the figure are moving down.

outside figures are moving in clock wise direction.

17.   C

Turning the figure to right side (Clock wise) and circles are moving to the flat side of figure.

18.   A

Checks are reduced to horizontal lines

(Vertical lines are deleted)

ANSWER KEY

1. B ;

2. D ;

3. A ;

4. C ;

5. B ;

6. A ;

7. A ;

8. C ;

9. B ;

10. A ;

11. D ;

12. C ;

13. B ;

14. B ;

15. D ;

16. A ;

BONUS CHALLENGE QUESTIONS

17. D ;

18. B ;

19. D ;

20. C ;

www.math-knots.com

ANSWER KEY

1.   A ;   Various types of farming tools

2.   D ;   Shades of green. Crimpson is a shade of red

3.   C ;   Same meaning

4.   B ;   House furnishings

5.   D ;   Members of family blood relation

6.   A ;   Types of reptiles

7.   A ;   Various types of tools

8.   C ;   Names of various subjects

9.   D ;   Various tools to write

10.   B ;   Farming tools

11.   A ;   Various types of liquid measurements

12.   D ;   Various types of books to read

13.   A ;   Various insects

14.   C ;   Birds that can fly not swim

15.   C ;   Various types of distance measurements

16.   B ;   Last stage of any activity or process

17.   D ;   Various types of nuts

18.   A ;   Various types of branches of tree

ANSWER KEY

1.   A

Trunk means the main woody stem of a tree as distinct from its branches and roots

2.   C

Frog is the only one which jumps

3.   D

Nancy is baking a cake not the baking cake. She doesn't need tea kettle or coffee maker. She needs measuring spoon from the given choices

4.   A

Silver Cars > Black Cars > Red Cars ; Red cars are less in parking lot

5.   B

Nails do not belong to Sense organs

6.   D

Bunnies are used for Easter

7.   D

Teeter Totters are found in parks

8.   B

Kangaroos have a pouch to hold their baby

9.   A

To magnify and examine small things, we use microscope

www.math-knots.com

ANSWER KEY

10.   C

Given choices that don't belong are grass cutter, coat and gloves. Snow shovel is used to remove snow

11.   A

Skating shoes are needed for skating class

12.   C

Red house is the widest of all. Pictures are not drawn to scale

13.   B

We need fire truck to rescue from fire

14.   A

Half Dollar has highest value in the given four choices

15.   B

Dogs have lot of fur. Out of given four choices dog is the only pet animal

16.   D

Room is getting painted with blue color so it's not room with blue color. Paint Roller is needed to paint the room

17.   A

Ruby needs a toaster to toast her bagel

18.   C

Jacket, warm shoes and gloves are used in winter. Alan needs shorts for beach trip

www.math-knots.com

ANSWER KEY

1.   A

2.   D

3.   B

4.   B

5.   C

6.   D

7.   B

8.   C

9.   D

10.   A

11.   B

12.   D

13.   B

14.   C

15.   B

16.   A

17.   D

18.   B

www.math-knots.com

ANSWER KEY

1.   C

   $5 = 5$

2.   A

   $3 \times 5 = 15$

3.   B

   $2 \times 4 = 8$

4.   A

   $3 - 2 = 1$

5.   C

   $4 - 1 = 3$

6.   A

   $3 - 3 = 0$

7.   D

   $4 - 1 = 3$

8.   B

   $3 - 3 = 0$

9.   A

   $1 + 1 = 2$

10.   C

   $3 - 2 = 1$

www.math-knots.com

ANSWER KEY

11.   D

$$3 - 3 = 0$$

12.   A

$$3 + 2 = 5$$

13.   A

$$6 = 6$$

14.   C

$$3 + 2 = 5$$

15.   D

$$4 + 1 = 5$$

16.   C

$$4 = 4$$

17.   A

$$2 + 1 = 3$$

18.   D

$$4 = 4$$

ANSWER KEY

1.   B

6, 5, 4, 3, 2; Starting with six ,numbers are decreasing by 1

2.   A

4, 5, 6, 7; Starting with four ,numbers are increasing by 1

3.   D

3, 3, 4, 4, 5, 5; Each number is repeating twice and then increasing by 1, repeating and then increasing by 1

4.   C

0, 3, 5, 6; Starting with zero numbers are increasing in the pattern of 3, 2, 1.
Pattern is like this : 0, 0 + 3, 3 + 2, 5+1

5.   D

3, 5, 3, 5, 3, 5; Number sequence 3, 5 is repeating

6.   A

6, 4, 5, 3, 4; First Alternate numbers are decreasing by 1 then next alternate numbers are decreasing by 1

7.   B

3, 2, 6, 4, 9, 6; First Alternate numbers are increasing by 3 then next alternate numbers are increasing by 2

8.   A

1, 1, 2, 4, 7; Numbers are increasing by 0, 1, 2, 3 ..etc
Pattern is like 1, 1 + 0, 1 + 1, 2 + 2 , 4 + 3

ANSWER KEY

9.   C

6, 6, 5, 5, 4, 4; Starting with 6 Each number is repeating twice and then decreasing by 1, repeating and then decreasing by 1

10.   A

0, 3, 6, 9; each number is three more than previous number

11.   D

1, 4, 7, 1, 4, 7; Number sequence 1, 4, 7 is repeating

12.   C

4, 0, 4, 0, 4; Number sequence 4, 0 is repeating

13.   A

5, 5, 5, 5, 5; Numbers are repeating the same

14.   D

6, 5, 4, 3; Starting with six numbers are decreasing by 1

15.   B

1, 2, 1, 2, 1; Repeating sequence of 1 and 2

16.   A

5, 5, 4, 4, 5, 5; Repeating sequence of 5, 5, 4 and 4

17.   C

4, 1, 4, 1, 4; Repeating sequence of 4 and 1

18.   A

1, 7, 1, 7, 1; Repeating sequence of 1 and 7

www.math-knots.com

ANSWER KEY

1. D

$5 + 15 = 20$

2. B

$7 + 7 + 7 = 21$

3. A

$2 \times 0 = 0$ (ZERO Multiplied by any number equals to Zero)

4. D

$2 \times 5 = 10$
($2 + 2 + 2 + 2 + 2 = 10$, Multiplication is a repeated addition)

5. A

$3 \times 3 = 9$
($3 + 3 + 3 = 9$, Multiplication is a repeated addition)

6. C

$1 \times 11 = 11$
(Multiplication is a repeated addition)

7. B

$6 \times 6 = 36$
($6 + 6 + 6 + 6 + 6 + 6 = 36$, Multiplication is a repeated addition)

8. D

$9 \times 1 + 1 = 9 + 1 = 10$
(Multiplication is a repeated addition)

9. A

$10 \times 10 + 10 = 110$
$(10 + 10 + 10 + 10 + 10 + 10 + 10 + 10 + 10 + 10 +$

ANSWER KEY

10. A

0 + 12 + 12 = 12 + 12 = 24

11. C

9 + 9 + 9 = 18 + 9 = 27

12. B

3 – 2 + 1 = 1 + 1 = 2

13. A

14 – 7 + 1 = 7 + 1 = 8

14. C

20 – 10 + 10 = 10 + 10 = 20

15. A

18 – 13 + 10 = 5 + 10 = 15

16. B

13 + 13 + 13 = 26 + 13 = 39

17. C

81 – 1 + 20 = 80 + 20 = 100

18. A

33 + 33 + 4 = 66 + 4 = 70

19. D

6 X 6 + 4 = 36 + 4 = 40

20. B

0 X 25 + 25 = 0 + 25 = 25

www.math-knots.com

ANSWER KEY

1.	A	Yellow butterflies, with two antennas
2.	D	Two objects
3.	B	Multiple figures joined together. Different directions
4.	B	Soccer ball with A, E ,I and U letters in grey area
5.	C	Total 5 arrows in each figure
6.	A	Symmetric figures
7.	D	Rectangle enclosing 4 small figures of the same kind. The smaller figures are joined by a curve
8.	B	A lamp with 9 similar figures across the flame
9.	A	Eyes are of same shape. Nose is a circle and mouth is like rectangle
10.	C	Multi color wheel with 8 in green triangle only

 www.math-knots.com

ANSWER KEY

11.	A	Orange, Yellow, Green and Pink colors in an order
12.	D	Three similar triangles joined together. U shape pointing to the tip of triangle. A $ sign is being placed where two triangles are joined (in corners)
13.	B	Five green shapes pointing out and one pink shape pointing towards center
14.	A	Same figure with colors, shape and sizes
15.	C	Stars are one less than the sides of the figure enclosing them
16.	D	Four figures(any) in a straight line inside the square
17.	B	Two similar figures one on top of other
18.	A	Four similar figures enclosed in the circle

www.math-knots.com

ANSWER KEY

1.   C

Flipping upside down

2.   B

3 sides figure to 4 sides figure

4 sides figure to 5 sides figure

3.   D

Solid lines to broken lines

4.   C

Inside objects are moving to other empty spaces (up and down)

5.   C

Same figure, colors or interchanging

6.   A

4 parts --> 8 items

7.   B

Straight figure to angular figure

8.   C

Big figure to small figure

9.   B

Objects are turning to opposite side making a closed figure

10.   D

Turning clock wise direction.

www.math-knots.com

ANSWER KEY

11.   A

2-D picture to 3-D picture.

12.   A

2-D picture to 3-D picture.

13.   C

Turning to right side.

14.   B

Outer figure becomes inner figure.

15.   C

Turning clock wise direction (1 turn).

16.   B

External objects are flipping to other side.

17.   C

Turning the figure.

18.   A

Checks are reduced to horizontal lines(Vertical lines
 are deleted)

www.math-knots.com

ANSWER KEY

1.   C ;

2.   D ;

3.   A ;

4.   D ;

5.   C ;

6.   C ;

7.   D ;

8.   A ;

9.   C ;

10.   D ;

11.   A ;

12.   D ;

13.   D ;

14.   B ;

15.   A ;

16.   C ;

BONUS CHALLENGE QUESTIONS

17.   B ;

18.   D ;

19.   A ;

20.   C ;

- We have provided 16 paper folded and punched final figures.

- These pages can be tored, pictures can be cut. Student can fold the pictures along the line and understand the concept.

- This will help them in understanding their visualization of the figures.

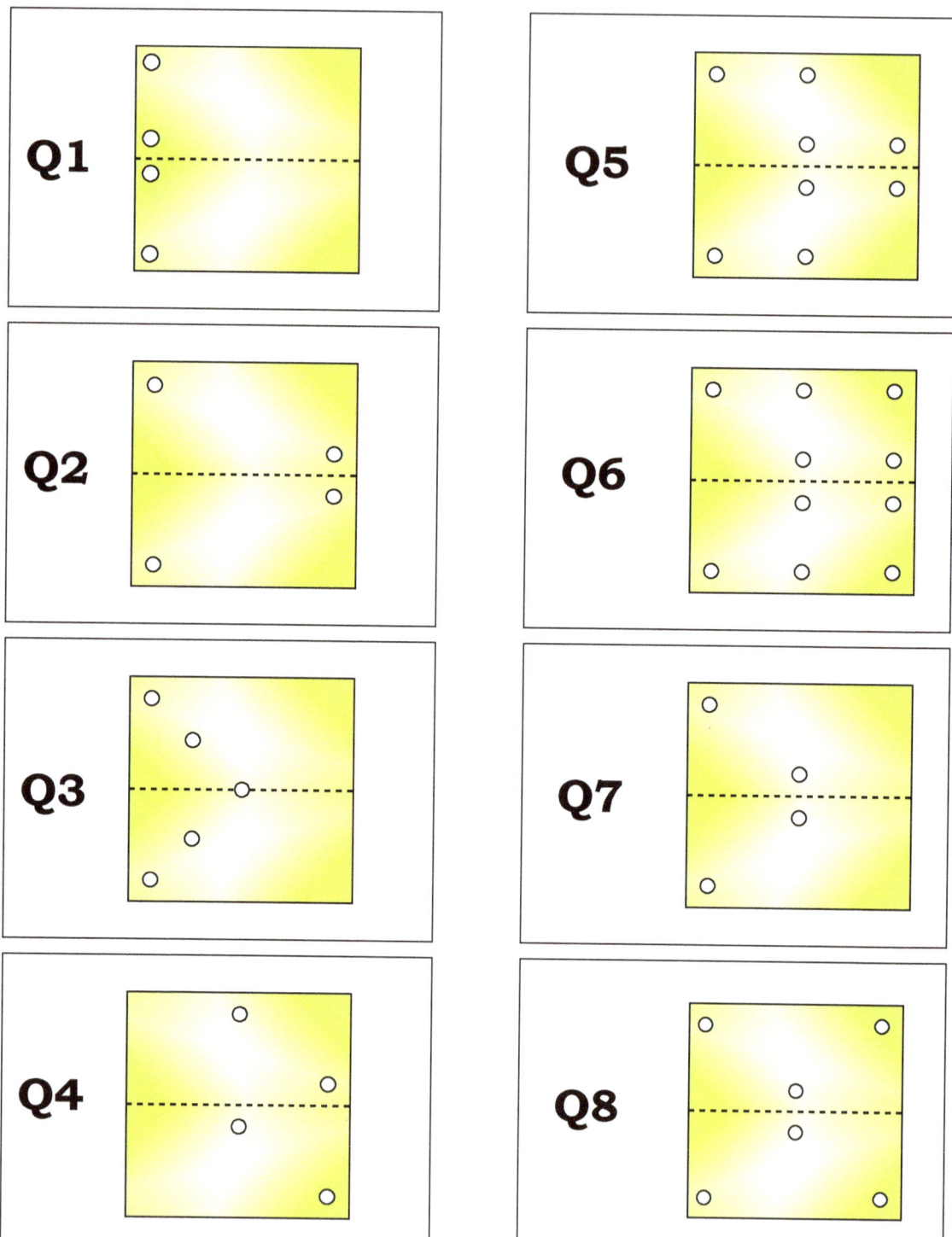

Q9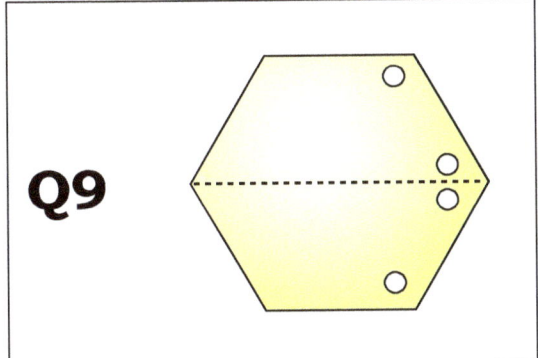

Q13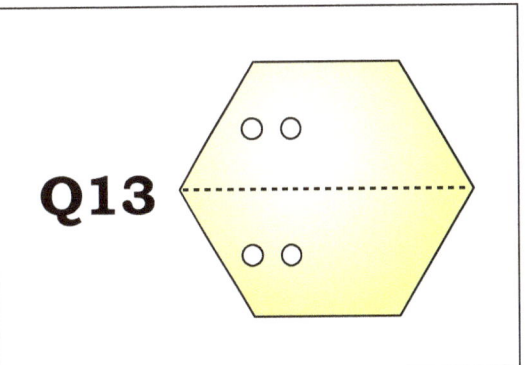

Q10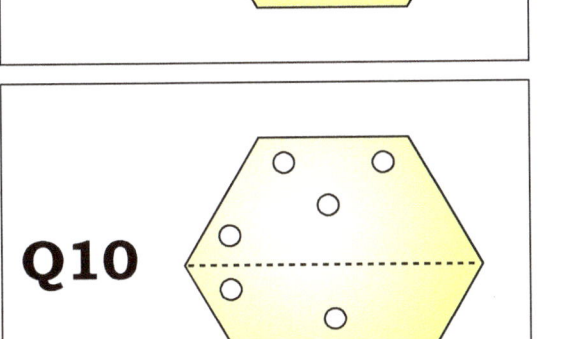

Q14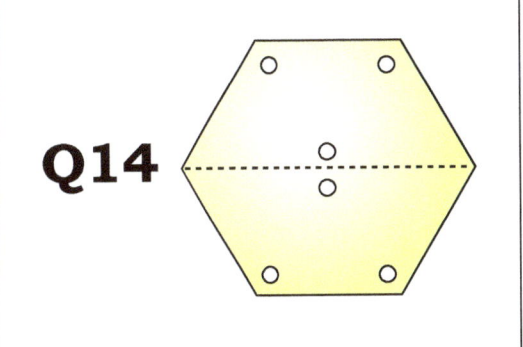

Q11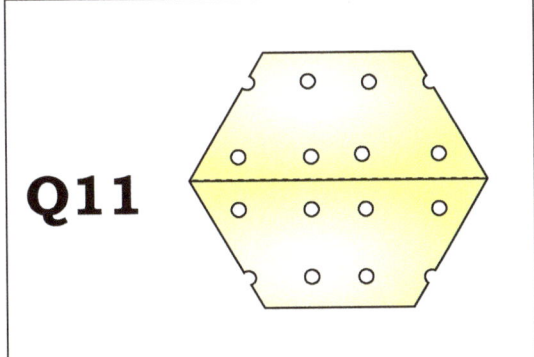

Q15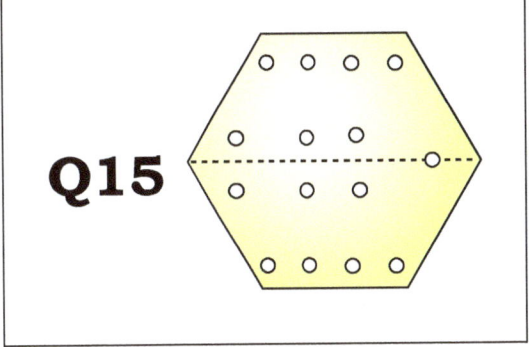

Q12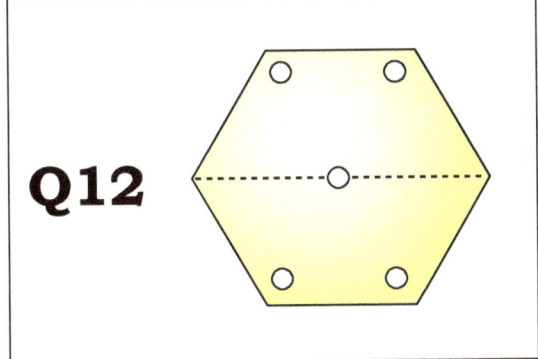

Q16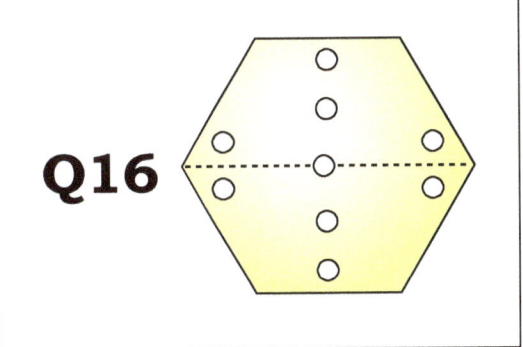

www.math-knots.com

	A	B	C	D
Q1.	○	○	○	○
Q2.	○	○	○	○
Q3.	○	○	○	○
Q4.	○	○	○	○
Q5.	○	○	○	○
Q6.	○	○	○	○
Q7.	○	○	○	○
Q8.	○	○	○	○
Q9.	○	○	○	○
Q10.	○	○	○	○
Q11.	○	○	○	○
Q12.	○	○	○	○
Q13.	○	○	○	○
Q14.	○	○	○	○
Q15.	○	○	○	○
Q16.	○	○	○	○
Q17.	○	○	○	○
Q 18.	○	○	○	○
Q 19.	○	○	○	○
Q 20.	○	○	○	○

www.math-knots.com